5/17/14

Your voice matters.
Continue to do
wonderful things.
Blessings
Liz Lugo

populace, ending in the tragic fragmentation of individuals, families, and communities from the American way of life that has espoused to cherish life, liberty and equality.

—Dr. Glenn L. Starks, Adjunct Professor,
Northcentral University

As meticulously documented as *How Do Hurricane Katrina's Winds Blow?* is, it conveys the author's passion for justice. Beginning with the broad historical sweep of the Trans-Atlantic Slave Trade, it comes to focus on one dramatic instance of post-Katrina racially motivated legislation before grounding the evil of racism in the more basic problem of dehumanization. Lugo demonstrates the power of law to reinforce the process of dehumanization, but equally the need for law to restrain it.

—Antonio R. Flores, President and CEO,
Hispanic Association of Colleges and Universities

How Do Hurricane Katrina's Winds Blow?

Recent Titles in
Racism in American Institutions

The Color of Politics: Racism in the American Political Arena Today
Chris Danielson

Out of Bounds: Racism and the Black Athlete
Lori Latrice Martin, Editor

How Do Hurricane Katrina's Winds Blow?

Racism in 21st-Century New Orleans

LIZA LUGO, JD

Racism in American Institutions
Brian D. Behnken, Series Editor

PRAEGER

AN IMPRINT OF ABC-CLIO, LLC
Santa Barbara, California • Denver, Colorado • Oxford, England

Library of Congress Cataloging-in-Publication Data

Lugo, Liza.
How do Hurricane Katrina's winds blow? : racism in 21st-century New Orleans/Liza Lugo, JD.
pages cm. — (Racism in American institutions)
Includes bibliographical references and index.
ISBN 978-1-4408-2888-1 (hardback) — ISBN 978-1-4408-2889-8 (ebook) 1. Racism—Louisiana—New Orleans. 2. African Americans—Louisiana—New Orleans—Social conditions—21st century. 3. Zoning, Exclusionary—Law and legislation—Louisiana—New Orleans. 4. Hurricane Katrina, 2005—Social aspects. 5. Social stratification—United States. 6. United States—Race relations. I. Title.
F379.N59N44436 2014
305.8009763′35—dc23 2013046462

ISBN: 978-1-4408-2888-1
EISBN: 978-1-4408-2889-8

18 17 16 15 14 1 2 3 4 5

This book is also available on the World Wide Web as an eBook.
Visit www.abc-clio.com for details.

Praeger
An Imprint of ABC-CLIO, LLC

ABC-CLIO, LLC
130 Cremona Drive, P.O. Box 1911
Santa Barbara, California 93116-1911

This book is printed on acid-free paper ∞

Manufactured in the United States of America

Contents

Series Foreword

How Do Hurricane Katrina's Winds Blow? is the second book to be published in Praeger Publisher's new series, Racism in American Institutions (RAI). The RAI series examines the ways in which racism has become, and remains, a part of the fabric of many American institutions. For example, while the United States may have done away with overtly racist acts such as extralegal lynching, racism still affects many of America's established institutions from public schools to corporate offices. Schools may not be legally segregated; and, yet, many districts are not integrated. Prisons are another example, when one considers the racist policies within the legal and penal systems that account for so many people of color behind bars. This open-ended series of one-volume works examines the problem of racism in established American institutions. Each book in the RAI Series traces the prevalence of racism within a particular institution throughout the history of the United States and explores the problem in that institution today, looking at ways in which the institution has attempted to rectify racism, but also the ways in which it has not.

Liza Lugo's book on Hurricane Katrina is perfectly suited for the RAI Series. As many Americans came to realize, Katrina not only destroyed levees, flooded neighborhoods, and took many lives, the storm revealed seemingly hidden—although upon close scrutiny easily identifiable—contemporary discriminatory patterns and practices. Lugo details the impact that Katrina had on New Orleans by exploring the historical racist systems that facilitated the storm's devastating impact on the city and its citizens. Thus, the storm ripped away a veneer of civility and progress in New Orleans and left in its wake the poverty, racism, and inequality that was present just beneath the surface. Lugo clearly shows that many of the circumstances that led to the storm's most debilitating impacts had a very long history, one that could be summed up in one of the city's most famous nicknames: New Orleans, the City That Care Forgot. That nickname originated in the 1930s, but it could as easily have been written in the 1870s or

1880s, or more recently in the 1980s, 1990s, or early 21st century. As such, racism in the city's urban politics, government, employment, and housing, as well as its relationship to the state of Louisiana, the Gulf South, and the United States as a whole, became institutionalized in the late 19th and throughout the 20th century.

Liza Lugo is perfectly suited to write this book. An attorney by training, she has studied American racism and African American history for the past decade. Her education gives *How Do Hurricane Katrina's Winds Blow?* an authoritatively legalistic perspective, but Lugo's story goes well beyond the law. Her book is a social, legal, and historical study of not just New Orleans, not just Katrina, but of the African-American lived perspective throughout U.S. history.

Brian D. Behnken
Iowa State University
Ames, Iowa

Preface

One of these days the people of Louisiana are going to get good government and they aren't going to like it.

—Huey Long, Louisiana governor from 1928 to 1932

In the months following Hurricane Katrina, the most destructive hurricane ever to hit the United States, Louisiana's St. Bernard Parish Council passed several ordinances restricting residential homeowners from renting their properties. The most controversial of these ordinances restricted rentals of single-family homes to blood relatives. Local outcry charged the parish with racial discrimination and essentially perpetuating the history of racial segregation. Inevitably, a lawsuit against the council ensued. The scope of the devastation caused by the hurricane resulted in a critical housing shortage; and it became immediately clear that minority populations, particularly African Americans, were disproportionately affected. Those in opposition to the ordinance were concerned the law would further frustrate the efforts of minorities to access one of the most basic rights and needs of humanity, housing.

This book addresses the question of whether the ordinances passed by St. Bernard Parish, which later removed the "non–blood relative" language, were in violation of the Equal Protection Clause of the U.S. Constitution and the Fair Housing Act along with the remedies available for such violation. In a broader context, the book describes the history of the subjugation and dehumanization of African Americans, the effects of second-class citizenship, and the road to healing using the basic principles of good government to create and maintain policy free of dehumanization.

Chapter 1 documents the history of institutional subjugation based on race in Louisiana and the New Orleans area. This chapter covers the timeline from slavery until the decision in *Plessy v. Ferguson* (1896), a Louisiana case that sanctioned the separate but equal doctrine. The history of the Isleños, individuals from the Canary Islands, is significant because they are not considered minorities in the context of race relations but are classified with white Europeans and held political power. The early settlements of St. Bernard Parish, comprised of Isleños, established sugar cane plantations upon the land granted to them during the periods of French and Spanish colonization. Therefore, the history of Louisiana is different from that of most of the United States. This chapter details the black codes (rooted in the French and Spanish Code Noir, which governed every area of the life of slaves and free blacks in Louisiana). The effects of the Emancipation Proclamation, the Civil War, and reconstruction assisted Louisiana in perpetuating slavery, black codes, and segregation. Louisiana's segregation policy has a 400-year history, from the time of its settlement until today. What is significant during this era is the creation of a permanent underclass of people, namely African Americans, established by the federal government and the laws of the colonies, which later became states of the Union.

Chapter 2 documents the legal history of Louisiana from the time of Jim Crow through the end of the 20th century, including the decision of the Supreme Court of the United States in *Brown v. Board of Education* (1954), which overturned *Plessy,* and the Civil Rights Movement. It is during this period that institutional segregation gained a stronghold. Lack of space during the heyday of slavery and plantation ownership created unique residential patterns in New Orleans because whites distrusted and wanted to keep an eye on the activities of African Americans. This resulted in African Americans living in the "backyard" and was later reinforced by segregationist policy. The chapter also details massive resistance by the state, particularly the New Orleans area, to the *Brown* decision where desegregation efforts sparked violence against African Americans and white flight, a social imposition of segregation rather than one created in law. The desegregation of American schools began in Louisiana. The mass exodus of whites, eased with the expansion of freeways and employment in suburbs such as St. Bernard Parish, left New Orleans with one of the largest African-American populations in the country. That white exodus effectively shut African Americans out of employment and residential growth in the New Orleans area—particularly in St. Bernard Parish. Because Louisiana did not exist in a vacuum, the race relations throughout the United States during this era are also documented.

Chapter 3 documents the climatic conditions of New Orleans in the 21st century and the city's societal ills, including high crime, failing school systems, poverty, and the infestation of drugs. When Hurricane Katrina pummeled the area in 2005, a mere five years into the new century, it was a natural disaster that uncovered the *national disaster* of the 400-year subjugation of African Americans. The pervasive history of second-class citizenship was devastating to the African-American population of the New Orleans area, particularly in the face of a natural disaster. The disproportionate effect on African Americans was not created because of Hurricane Katrina; rather, it was created by law and societal construct from the birth of the nation. The chapter also documents the racist attitudes of St. Bernard Parish Council members, particularly the parish president, which established the baseline for attitudes that were relevant to the decision-making process in passing the restrictive ordinances. Furthermore, society's overall antiblack sentiment is evidenced in this chapter and throughout the text.

Chapter 4 describes the evolution of the non–blood relative ordinance, including the motivations and local sentiment as well as the lawsuit filed by the Greater New Orleans Fair Housing Action Center (GNOFHAC). The chapter aligns the recent policy to that of segregationist policy and statutes of the state of Louisiana and the history of defiance of federal law, constitutional principles, and court mandates. Furthermore, the chapter evidences the climate of U.S. politics and society, which have perpetuated segregationist values into the 21st century as well as provide evidence of legislative intent and an analysis of the totality of the circumstances.

Chapter 5 describes the unconstitutionality and illegality of the St. Bernard Parish ordinances despite the fact that the parties settled out of court. Herein begins the legal analysis of the equal protection clause of the U.S. Constitution, including what constitutes state action, the level of scrutiny to be applied by the courts, and the parish's violation of the Civil Rights Act and the Fair Housing Act.

Chapter 6 describes the lawsuits by GNOFHAC and the Department of Justice, the positions of the parties, and the cost of the tug-of-war initiated by St. Bernard Parish as a result of its repeated failure to comply with court orders. The chapter also includes the terms of the settlement of the case and the parish's failure to admit liability.

Chapter 7 documents the current state of affairs in the New Orleans area and, on a broader scale, the nation. Based on the extensive history of discrimination and residential segregation, the discriminatory intent of the St. Bernard Parish Council, and the disparate impact on African Americans and the community at large, there is a serious fracture in government and society that needs repair. This book acknowledges that the problems in government and society stem from the disease of dehumanization, the methods of transmission, and the symptomology as evidenced by domestic violence, genocide, and mental illness. This chapter suggests remedies based on the basic principles of good government and eliminating dehumanization.

The documents and tables provided in the appendices include acts of Congress, presidential Executive Orders, state and local statutes, and other laws that perpetuated a system of dehumanization in the United States. Additionally, there are lists regarding the composition of Congress, including the list of African-American representation in Congress; African-American firsts; and American civil rights leaders and activists. Statistical information is provided on violent crimes in the United States and the history of hurricanes in Louisiana. Finally, to assist readers, this book provides a recommended reading list and resource list.

The terms "blacks," "Negro," and "whites" (whether in lowercase or capitalized) are both societal and legal terms used to describe and define "race" and are used in this book to reflect history. Capitalization of the terms is determined by context. Please note that for a significant period of time, courts and law did not capitalize terms used to identify race, particularly with regard to African Americans, because this segment of the population was not deemed to be "a person." While many may consider these terms racist or offensive, please know the terms are not used with such intention.

This book does not include an exhaustive list of the numerous organizations and individuals who fought and indeed laid down their lives in resistance of slavery, segregation, and oppression, but their deeds are not to be devalued, dismissed, or remain unnoticed. This book presents the case that government- and society-sanctioned dehumanization via white supremacy in the United States, particularly in Louisiana, is undisputed and is historically significant. This book contains many violent and offensive descriptions as well as racial epithets that are historically accurate. Discretion is advised.

Acknowledgments

First and foremost, I thank the Creator for breathing life into me and surrounding me with an incredible support system—any gifts or talents I have, I owe to Him and His Grace. I can do whatever I need to do through Christ who strengthens me. It is Him who makes all things possible.

My sincerest appreciation and sympathy to the diaspora of Hurricane Katrina: your strength and the candor with which you told your story to media outlets served as an inspiration and a wake-up call to the world. May God bless all of you in your hours of need and every day of your life. Know that you are not forgotten. To the team at ABC-CLIO, this project would not have been possible without your tremendous support and efforts, and I will forever be grateful. Thank you to Vanessa Naranjo and your promotional team for all of your hard work and support of this project. Kim Kennedy-White, thank you for recognizing the value of this work from my proposal and for your continued encouragement. You have changed my life. Brian D. Behnken, it is an honor for me that you found this book worthy of inclusion in the Racism in American Institutions (RAI) series. Thank you for your support and encouragement in the editor's foreword. To the copyeditor and the team at Premedia Global, thank you for your patience with me during the editing process. You all did an incredible job.

I am grateful to all of the civil rights leaders and activists of the past and present who inspired me and countless others to carry on their values, work, and dreams, including John Quincy Adams, James Madison, Thomas Jefferson, Frederick Douglass, W. E. B. Du Bois, Alice Paul, A. P. Tureaud, Albert Einstein, Ruby Bridges, Martin Luther King Jr., Thurgood Marshall, Gloria Steinem, Malcolm X, and President Barack H. Obama. There are too many to list. Those who have passed on have left an incredible legacy for all Americans for generations to come. Know that your dreams live on long after your departure from this world.

Special thanks to my photographer on this project, M. J. Clark, for making the trip with me to New Orleans, St. Bernard Parish, and the Lower Ninth Ward and for his work on this special assignment. I am forever grateful for Mr. Clark's photographic talents, which he so generously donated to the development of this book. This would not be the same without his photographs demonstrating the magnitude of the reality (eight years following Katrina) in the aforementioned affected areas; after all, a picture is worth a thousand words. His willingness to undertake and enthusiasm for conducting impromptu interviews with the locals was truly remarkable. Thank you so much.

My humble gratitude goes out to all of my law professors at the University of Florida Levin College of Law (2005–2008). It was a privilege to study under your tutelage, especially my criminal law professor Michael L. Seigel, JD, Associate Dean International Studies, Sam T. Dell Term Professor of Law, and Director of the Criminal Justice Center and Criminal Clinic; my property law professor Danaya C. Wright, JD, PhD, Clarence J. Te Selle Professor of Law; and my constitutional law professor Charles Collier, JD, Professor of Law, Affiliate Professor of Philosophy. Your encouragement and guidance were critical to any success I may have as a legal scholar. I am also grateful for the brilliance of Berta Esperanza Hernandez-Truyol, JD, LLM, Levin Mabie & Levin Professor of Law at the University of Florida Levin College of Law, who cemented my love and respect for international human rights and for providing me with the opportunity to work as a research assistant on the issue of the right to health in Latin American countries—researching the case law of the Inter-American Court was an enlightening experience. I am most grateful to Michelle S. Jacobs, JD, Professor of Law and Assistant Director of the Criminal Justice Center at the University of Florida Levin College of Law—who is a gift to each of her students. Professor Jacobs worked tirelessly in guiding me on the issues of Critical Race Theory. It is because of her immeasurable contributions of encouragement and direction regarding the research and writing of my original paper on the subject of Hurricane Katrina's aftermath that this particular endeavor, this book, is even possible. We were in it from the very beginning. Thank you for emphasizing the importance of this issue and your advice: "Don't file this away somewhere!" And, please, don't ever stop teaching Critical Race Theory, especially at this critical time in America's history. The time is ripe.

Also, I was fortunate to have many excellent professors during my undergraduate pursuits at the University of Tampa (2003–2005), and it is because of them that I have an understanding and appreciation for government and the law: Robert Kerstein, Dana Professor, Government and World Affairs; Thomas Hickey, now Professor of Social Sciences at SUNY Cobleskill, New York; and Professor James Harf. I am greatly indebted to James A. Beckman, now Chair and Associate Professor of Legal Studies at the University of Central Florida, for being an incredible teacher of race and the law and, even better my mentor. Professor Beckman provided me with some of my first professional undertakings as a researcher and writer while under his tutelage at the University of Tampa—my first ever research assistant opportunity for his book *Affirmative Action Now: A Guide for Students, Families, and Counselors* (2006) and, more recently, the gift of writing a chapter for his anthology *Affirmative Action: Contemporary Perspectives* (2014). Professor Beckman's support, faith, and encouragement continue to be a great source of inspiration for me. Special thanks to my mentors and professors at Pasco-Hernando Community College (2000–2003), including Bob Bade, Connie LaMarca-Frankel, Carmine Bell, and Michael Sadusky. You all gave me a great educational foundation, which extended far beyond the classroom. I am forever grateful.

To my legal internship mentors within the Offices of Inspector General in Washington, DC, who encouraged me during the challenges of law school and provided unparalleled learning opportunities: Frank La Rocca, Counsel to the Inspector General, National Aeronautics and Space Administration (NASA) and Peggy Fischer, former Assistant Inspector General of Investigations of the National Science Foundation (NSF). It has been a blessing to know both of you.

I am also grateful for the wonderful friends that are always there to cheer me on during the "slumps" and the achievements, specifically my law school colleagues who never fail to remind me that they are proud of me, Kelly Ann L. May, Esq., and Gerrard Grant, Esq. You two are the best. And my personal "dream team" of encouragers: Leslie "Les" Fudge, Deborah Cotton, Cheryl Robinson-Ridley, Heather "Birdie" Sattler, Alyssa and Aaron Garner, and Trudy Buchanan—I thank God for your friendships. To Adam "Smarty-Pants" Powell, thank you for all of the exciting debates on U.S. race relations, Supreme Court opinions, and affirmative action—it's always a blast. And to his beautiful wife, Cailin Powell, thank you for your love and unwavering support these past three years—God gave me an angel. I love you guys. Thank you Alexis Leighanna Treadwell for welcoming me into your family. I love you. Great things are coming your way, Sweetie.

I am blessed to have parents who love me: my father, Juan A. Lugo; my mother, Ruth Celina Ocasio-Pessin; and my stepfather, Robert E. Pessin, "Dad-a-roni." My grandmothers were a living example of what it is to be a strong woman. Rest in peace, mi abuela Maria Filomena Santiago-Rodriguez (1916–2013). "Bendiciones a Granny," my amazing 95-year-old grandmother Josefina Ocasio, whose famous phrase "case closed" became a mantra of sorts for me. And I so appreciate the beautiful and generous hearts of my brother John Paul and my sister Wendy. I am so proud of you both. Thank you to my godparents, "Titi" Cary and "Padrino" Cesar, for always being there for me from day one. I love you both. To all of my cousins, my uncles, and my aunts—I love that I can always be myself with you.

My children have always been a source of pride for me and the greatest motivation in my life to model positivity, hard work, and love. Thank you, Michael Joseph, Anthony John, and Liza-Marie for always being true to yourselves and me. It is a privilege to be your mother and a gift to watch you grow into adults. My deepest gratitude and love goes to SFC Darryl C. Treadwell, who has remained by my side with unconditional love, endless encouragement, and a fantastic dose of laughter, all of which inspire me every day to become a better person. I am blessed to have you in my life—"Te adoro."

Introduction

The enumeration in the Constitution, of certain rights, shall not be construed to deny or disparage others retained by the people.

—The Ninth Amendment of the U.S. Constitution,
One of the greatest statements of law

New Orleans, a humid subtropical region in the southern United States, is known for being the birthplace of jazz; for its mixtures of Spanish, French, African, and Creole culture; and for some of the best restaurants and food in the country. The images of the city burned into our memories include lacy cast iron balconies; lively festivals; Mardi Gras with its parades of grand costumes, intricate Krewe floats, and the tossing of thousands of beads; and, of course, eclectic shopping districts. The hustle and bustle of the French Quarter is dotted with everything from historic hotels to voodoo priestesses and strip clubs to streetcars that still operate today. New Orleans is a blend of historic eras and the modern world. Riverboats, ferries, shipping barges, and soaring pelicans all share the winding Mississippi, a diamond-studded waterway courtesy of the sun's reflection.

New Orleans was originally named La Nouvelle-Orléans on May 7, 1718, by Jean-Baptiste Le Moyne de Bienville and the French Mississippi Company and was named for Phillipe d'Orléans.[1] In 1763, France lost control of the new colony to Spain with the Treaty of Paris. Spain controlled the region until 1801 and then transferred it back to France. President Thomas Jefferson is credited with expanding the territory of the United States by acquired New Orleans and the surrounding area from Napoléon via the Louisiana Purchase. The city, in addition to being a major role player in the slave trade, was a critical port for importing international goods and exporting food[2] and cotton sources for the rest of the nation up through the Mississippi River.

The steamboat *Natchez* is the only authentic steamboat that runs on the Mississippi River. It is located at the end of Toulouse Street at the Mississippi River. This photo was taken at dawn. (Liza Lugo, JD, May 2013)

According to the *Journal of American History*:

> A natural levee was selected as the site for New Orleans. A large labor force was necessary to make that piece of land habitable since it was subject to regular flooding and endemic waterborne disease. In 1719, the French colonial Compagnie des Indes imported one thousand European criminals and contract laborers to fortify New Orleans's natural levees. They soon died of disease and starvation; and the company immediately began to import African captives. Though mortality rates were high for the slaves, those who survived built levees, dug drainage ditches, cleared forests, and prepared timber for building boats and houses. Without the benefit of the institution of slavery, New Orleans would not exist.[3]

Located on the Mississippi River in southeastern Louisiana, New Orleans is also bordered on the north by the immense Lake Pontchartrain, a shore within the city's limits and by Lake Borgne on the east side.[4] Surrounded by miles of water on three sides, a peninsular area, it is also known as the Crescent City in honor of the sashaying curve of the Mississippi. Louisiana is the only one of the 50 states to divide its political subdivisions

The Cathedral-Basilica of Saint Louis, King of France, also known as St. Louis Cathedral, is the oldest cathedral in the United States. The parish was established in 1720. A fire destroyed the original building in 1788. After more renovations and expansions, by 1854, it became the building that remains to this date. Hurricane Katrina was responsible for some roof damage, which damaged its massive organ. The organ was repaired and reinstalled in 2008. (Liza Lugo, JD, May 2013)

into parishes with local governments equal to counties in other states; likewise, its political uniqueness is found in its roots of French and Spanish civil codes (also known as Napoleonic Code) rather than English common law. Where English common law is based upon court precedent, Napoleonic Code is rooted in civilian law, which uses scholarly research and the courts' interpretation of the intent of the legislature.[5] Just as it is the only state to have parishes, it is the only civil law state in America. New Orleans occupies the entirety of Orleans Parish while the metropolitan area of New Orleans extends into other parishes, including in the west, St. Charles, St. John, and St. James; in the south, Jefferson, Plaquemines, and St. Bernard; and in the north, St. Tammany.

The majority of Louisiana's land is uniquely created by the runoff of the Mississippi River, resulting in fascinating landscapes of deltas, marshes, and swamps where alligators and poisonous snakes slither their way through the murky waters. However, the marshes have also been home to many fur-bearing animals. In fact, prior to World War II, St. Bernard Parish in particular was nationally known for its abundance of mink.[6] The landscape of southeastern Louisiana is so famous that it is inextricably connected to images of the tranquil waters of the bayous lined with weeping willows and the branches of grand live oaks bending beneath the weight of Spanish moss. New Orleans is also known as the most haunted city in the United States. From the ghosts of the infamous slave torturer Madame Delphine LaLaurie to that of the voodoo queen Marie Laveau, the souls of Confederate soldiers and other spirits of the dead are said to create a plethora of paranormal activity in the city.

According to the Census Bureau, the City of New Orleans maintained steady increases in its population for a full 200 years (1769 through the 1960s), with the greatest increase occurring between 1830 and 1840, when the population increased by 121 percent due to the domestic slave trade and the influx of Haitians following the Haitian Revolution. At that time, New Orleans was the wealthiest city in America, and the majority of its population was of African ancestry. After the Civil War, freed slaves from neighboring plantations moved into the city, thus doubling the "black" population. The total population of the city peaked in 1960 when there were 627,525 residents. But something happened in the 1950s and 1960s —desegregation, forced integration, and the civil rights movement made a great impact on the makeup of New Orleans. From 1970 on into the 21st century, there was a steady decrease in the city's population, resulting mainly from the self-imposed segregation of whites who moved to neighboring parishes in opposition to integration.[7] But the greatest decrease in population was from 2000 to 2010, when New Orleans lost more than 29 percent of its population. And smack in the middle of that decade was Hurricane Katrina. By 2010, the city's population had dropped to levels not seen since 1910.[8]

Census records from 2010 indicate that 32 percent of the population in Louisiana is "black," but African Americans represent just 13 percent of the entire population of the United States.[9] The highest concentrations of "blacks" are in the southern states: Alabama;[10] Washington, D.C.;[11] Georgia;[12] Maryland;[13] Mississippi;[14] South Carolina;[15] and, of course, Louisiana. According to the 2000 Census, there were 36,419,434 "black or African-Americans alone or in combination" with another ethnicity representing 12.9 percent of the entire U.S. population. By 2010, there was a slight increase to 42,020,743 representing 13.6 percent of the population.[16]

But 60 percent of the population in the city of New Orleans was African American, according to the 2010 census.

Unfortunately, the African-American population has not been well represented in government either at the state or federal level in policy and via proxy. In all of U.S. history, there have been only four black state governors: P. B. S. Pinchback (D-LA), who served 13 months;[17] Douglas Wilder (D-VA), who served four years during the 1990s;[18] and Deval Patrick (D-MA) and David Patterson (D-NY), both elected in 2007 and currently in office.[19] Only three African Americans ever served as Louisiana lieutenant governors, but *none* since Reconstruction following the Civil War.[20]

African Americans also have a history of limited representation in the U.S. Congress. In the entire history of the House of Representatives, just 131 African Americans have been elected to office. Incredibly, approximately 43 percent of them were elected *following Katrina*. Just four African Americans have ever represented Louisiana in the House: one in the 19th century who served for two years;[21] two in the 20th century beginning in the 1990s;[22] and two, thus far, in the 21st century.[23] Not one African American represented Louisiana in the House from 1877 until 1991, a full 115 years, until William Jefferson Jennings was elected. Jennings served several terms during the 1990s and 2000s. Cedric Richmond, the second African American representing Louisiana since the 19th century, was elected to the House of Representatives in 2011 and is still serving.

A mere eight African Americans in total were ever elected to the U.S. Senate (three from the South) beginning with Hiram Rhodes Revels (R-MS) (1869–1871), a freeman his whole life,[24] but *not one* African American representing Louisiana has *ever* been elected to serve in the U.S. Senate. Moreover, just *one African American at a time* was a member of the U.S. Senate, until 2013, this past election. Two are currently serving, making this a historic moment in the nation's history.[25] After 232 years of U.S. government, for the first time, the nation elected a man with African blood to hold America's highest office: President Barack Hussein Obama.[26] All other presidents were white males. No female has ever received a major party nomination for the presidency, never mind election as president. And exclusively, white males have served as vice president. The unadulterated truth is that if one combines the current representation in Congress (the Senate and the House) with the seat of the presidency, 48 African Americans represent over 42 million African Americans on the federal level.[27] No, we are not "there" yet.

None of this is a coincidence, but neither is it a conspiracy, at least for the most part. Conspiracy, according to the *Encyclopædia Britannica*, is defined as an "agreement between two or more persons to commit an *unlawful* act or to accomplish a lawful end by unlawful means . . . Individual conspirators need not even know of the existence or the identity of all other conspirators."[28] What happened in the United States was *all legal*, predating its birth until the last third of the 20th century. Those with African roots were "merchandise" and therefore deemed not human until the mid-1860s. Therefore, if they were "not persons," there were no personal rights, liberties, or allowances for political participation.[29] Still, even after the abolishment of slavery, the granting of citizenship and voting rights, and the right to equal protection under law from their respective states, African Americans were relegated to second-class citizenship *by law* until the early 1960s. So, any possible charges of conspiracy were incurred from the 1960s to the present. Once all civil rights were granted to African Americans by law, "any agreement between two or more persons" to deny those rights would be "an unlawful act."[30]

While the legislative and social history of Louisiana was based on white supremacy, to a great extent, the state's geographic vulnerability to the wrath of Mother Nature also played an important role in prolonging the injustice. From the time of its colonial founding through the present, no less than 109 hurricanes, floods, and fires ravaged its land, and its people suffered greatly. Indeed, according to the National Oceanic Atmospheric Administration (NOAA), out of the top 10 worst hurricanes in U.S. history, four directly hit Louisiana and more specifically, New Orleans and the surrounding parishes: Last Island Hurricane in Terrebonne Parish on August 9, 1856; Cheniere Caminada, Louisiana, in Jefferson Parish on October 2, 1893[31]; the New Orleans Hurricane of 1915; and Hurricane Katrina on August 29, 2005.[32] Over time, between the hurricanes of Cheniere Caminada in 1893 until Hurricane Katrina in 2005, hurricanes claimed the lives of over 5,200 persons in New Orleans and the surrounding areas.[33]

New Orleans has many nicknames in addition to the Crescent City. The Big Easy, has roots in two possible references: the ease with which jazz musicians were able to find work in New Orleans and the great number of speakeasies in operation in the city during the Prohibition years. The City That Care Forgot dates back to the late 1930s and alludes to the carefree attitudes of its citizens—yet this is actually an *illusion,* at least for many African Americans in the city. From the time of Jim Crow to after Hurricane Katrina, it was the City That Forgot to Care.

New Orleans is world renowned not only for its food and culture, but for the beautiful lace-like wrought iron balconies that grace its buildings, particularly in the French Quarter. This photo captures the view from a balcony room at the Hotel St. Marie facing Toulouse Street. (Liza Lugo, JD, May 2013)

Hurricane Katrina's winds undoubtedly blew the roofs off of not only the homes in New Orleans, but those of the entire nation. Below the façade of the peaceful nature of the bayous and behind the elaborate Mardi Gras masks, there was something more unnerving than the ghosts of the city from centuries past: the continuance of segregation and racial hatred rooted in the dehumanization of generations of African Americans in southeastern Louisiana (and the United States as a whole). Katrina would prove to be more than a natural disaster; it would expose a national disaster. The storm exposed the effects of centuries of racial hatred; and, along with the storm surge, it brought with it more segregationist policy.

St. Bernard Parish passed a series of ordinances in an effort to *deny* housing in the aftermath of Katrina. And finally, it fixated itself on getting what it really wanted—housing would be based on the ancestry of its residents:

> Considering the great social and economic need to encourage single family residence owners to return, rebuild, and resume living in the parish and to reoccupy their homes *in already long established neighborhoods*; Considering the public purpose, benefit and *need to maintain the integrity and stability of established neighborhoods as centers of family values and activities*; considering the public benefits to be obtained from *securing for the community the blessings of quiet enjoyment of their pre-existing neighborhoods*; and Considering the necessity to foster and encourage a community and family atmosphere in the neighborhood . . . [and, therefore:]
>
> No person or entity shall *rent, lease, loan, or otherwise allow occupancy or use of any* single family residence . . . *by any person or groups of persons, other than a family member(s) related by blood* within the first second, or third direct ascending or descending generation(s) without first obtaining a Permissive Use Permit from the . . . Council.[34]

My personal aim is that this book will inform the general citizenry of the United States that there is a pathology of dehumanization of Americans, what the methods of transmitting dehumanization are, and the symptoms of it from which we suffer. It is the story the continuous struggle to be treated with human dignity and the opportunities we have to heal. Citizens will have the opportunity to see beyond the rhetoric of racism, discrimination, reparations, and affirmative action.

Attorneys, the soldiers in the war of civil liberty, should find this text useful in presenting effective arguments to the courts regarding discriminatory practices based on any human quality by referencing the historical significance of instituting dehumanization into our legal structure, the battles to remove it, and the failure of businesses, organizations, government agencies, and individuals to comply with the law. This is the root of the many disproportionate effects assigned to the African-American population in particular despite their enormous contributions, on every level, to the growth and status of the United States of America.

My greatest hope is for Americans to *know who they are* and to inspire them to take responsibility for the gift of freedom, which is in their hands. Holding this responsibility, citizens become involved in the political arena or processes and develop and protect human rights from whatever station they may hold in this life. Your voice matters. I implore government officials to use a back-to-basics, multidisciplinary approach to develop "a more perfect Union"[35] that will live up to our principles of the "inalienable rights"[36] of humankind and to enforce the law. In this manner, the United

States can become the greatest example of democratic principle the world has ever known.

The following is not merely an account of Hurricane Katrina, nor is it the story of New Orleans or Louisiana. It is not a fairytale. The following is not just an account of African-American history. This, at its essence, is the chronicle of the American citizen.

This book is dedicated to the diaspora of Africa and New Orleans.

Definitions

Remember, words have meaning.

Black: Pronunciation: blăk

1. Destitute of light, or incapable of reflecting it; of the color of soot or coal; of the darkest or a very dark color, the opposite of white; characterized by such a color as black cloth; black hair or eyes.
2. In a less literal sense: Enveloped or shrouded in darkness; very dark or gloomy; as, a black night; the heavens black with clouds.
3. Fig.: Dismal, gloomy, or forbidding, like darkness; destitute of moral light or goodness; atrociously wicked; cruel; mournful; calamitous; horrible.
4. Expressing menace or discontent; threatening; sullen; foreboding; as, to regard one with black looks.
5. Black act the English statute 9 George I [1714–1727], which makes it a felony to appear armed in any park, warren, and so on or to hunt or steal deer or other such animals with the face blackened or disguised. Subsequent acts inflicting heavy penalties for malicious injuries to cattle and machinery have been called black acts.

Dehumanization: *n.* listed as a related term for dehumanize but is not defined in the dictionary

Dehumanize *tr.v.* de·hu·man·ized, de·hu·man·iz·ing, de·hu·man·iz·es

1. To deprive of human qualities such as individuality, compassion, or civility: *slaves who had been dehumanized by their abysmal condition.*
2. To render mechanical and routine.

Negro: Ne´gro Pronunciation: nē´grô

1. (n) A black man; especially, one of a race of black or a very dark persons who inhabit the greater part of tropical Africa and are distinguished by crisped or curly hair, flat noses, and thick protruding lips; also any black person of unmixed African blood, wherever found.

2. A person of dark skin color descended at least in part from African Negroes; in the United States, an African American.
3. (a) Of or pertaining to Negroes; black

Nigger: nig′ger

1. *usually offensive; see usage paragraph below* : a black person
2. *usually offensive; see usage paragraph below* : a member of any dark-skinned race
3. a member of a socially disadvantaged class of persons

Usage Discussion of NIGGER

Nigger in senses 1 and 2 can be found in the works of such writers of the past as Joseph Conrad, Mark Twain, and Charles Dickens, but it now ranks as perhaps the most offensive and inflammatory racial slur in English. Its use by and among blacks is not always intended or taken as offensive, but, except in sense 3, it is otherwise a word expressive of racial hatred and bigotry.

Race: n.

1. a breeding stock of animals
2. (a) a family, tribe, people, or nation belonging to the same stock
   (b) a class or kind of people unified by shared interests, habits, or characteristics
3. (a) an actually or potentially interbreeding group within a species; also a taxonomic category (as a subspecies) representing such a group
   (b) BREED
   (c) a category of humankind that shares certain distinctive physical traits.

Racism:

1. a belief that race is the primary determinant of human traits and capacities and that racial differences produce an inherent superiority of a particular race
2. racial prejudice or discrimination

Refugee: Ref"u"gee′

1. (n) One who flees to a shelter or place of safety.
2. Especially, one who, in times of persecution or political commotion, flees to a foreign power or country for safety; as, the French refugees who left France after the revocation of the edict of Nantes.

White: Pronunciation: hwīt

1. Reflecting to the eye all the rays of the spectrum combined; not tinted with any of the proper colors or their mixtures; having the color of pure snow; snowy; the opposite of black or dark; as, white paper; a white skin
2. Destitute of color, as in the cheeks, or of the tinge of blood color; pale; pallid; as white with fear.
3. Having the color of purity; free from spot or blemish, or from guilt or pollution; innocent; pure.
4. Gray, as from age; having silvery hair; hoary.
5. Characterized by freedom from that which disturbs and the like; fortunate; happy; favorable.
6. Regarded with special favor; favorite; darling.

Chapter 1

From Slavery to Jim Crow

What, to the American slave, is your 4th of July?
I answer; a day that reveals to him, more than all other days in the year,
the gross injustice and cruelty to which he is the constant victim.
To him, your celebration is a sham; your boasted liberty, an unholy license;
your national greatness, swelling vanity;
your sounds of rejoicing are empty and heartless;
your denunciation of tyrants, brass fronted impudence;
your shouts of liberty and equality, hollow mockery;
your prayers and hymns, your sermons and thanksgivings,
with all your religious parade and solemnity, are, to Him,
mere bombast, fraud, deception, impiety, and hypocrisy
a thin veil to cover up crimes which would disgrace a nation of savages.[1]

"The Meaning of July Fourth for the Negro"

By Frederick Douglass

On July 5, 1852

Speech at an event commemorating the signing of the Declaration of Independence

Rochester's Corinthian Hall
Rochester, New York

Since its initial settlement to the present date, Louisiana subjugated African Americans and nonwhites and sought to separate the races through law, custom, and societal structure beginning with slavery. Additionally, the state has a history of ignoring federal law and mandates in areas related to race relations. The subjugation and institutional discrimination stem from the greatest evil—dehumanization. For African Americans in Louisiana, the South, and in fact, all of the United States, the history of dehumanization extends back hundreds of years. Remedies began on a federal level but it is well known that Louisiana and other states circumvented the provisions by establishing state laws that created a social and racial caste system based on white supremacy. In all fairness, Louisiana is not an anomaly. Rather, the creation of a permanent underclass of black people can be traced back some 600 years beginning with the Transatlantic Slave Trade, the continuous perpetration of the domestic slave trade, and apartheid[2] in the centuries that followed. Thirteen migrations have either formed or transformed "African America."[3] However, two were involuntary: the Transatlantic Slave Trade (the greatest forced migration in history) and the domestic slave trade. It is imperative to gain an understanding of the past to have an awareness of the present so that we may effect change in the future.

It is undeniable that throughout human history slavery has existed. In fact, it was common practice. Most historians have described the issue as a political one rather than a moral one. It is difficult to find a more heinous holocaust than the one committed against the African, which began in the 16th century and continues into the present day. Slavery in the United States began with the Transatlantic Slave Trade (from 16th century through the 19th century) and despite all claims that it is past history, the dehumanization of those with African blood continues to persist—from the American Civil War to the recent civil wars among African nations; from Jim Crow[4] in the United States to the Nuremburg laws of Germany and apartheid in South Africa; from human trafficking as we now know it to "recruitment" of child soldiers on the African continent. Nearly the entire world participated in this dehumanization and is accountable. The entirety of dehumanization and the resulting slavery was created and sanctioned by government officials and law.[5]

The Transatlantic Slave Trade

The Transatlantic Slave Trade, which continued through the mid-1800s, was the largest forced migration of people in human history, involving more than 12 million Africans in more than 35,000 voyages over a period of 350 years. No transportation of human beings could ever rival the experience of the African. Kidnapped, they were forced by traders to walk wearing shackles in "slave caravans" to forts on the coastline; and some of these walks were as long as 1,000 miles. Accordingly, "shackled and underfed, only half the people survived these death marches. Those too sick or weary to keep up were often killed or left to die."[6] Those who did survive the death marches were then placed in dungeons, also known as "barracoons,"[7] for a period of up to one year while waiting to be transferred to the slave ships.[8] For 350 years,[9] against their own will, men, women, and children were brought to places like Goree Island, where the transport across the Atlantic Ocean would begin. It is no coincidence that the threshold of Goree Island was termed "the door of no return." These human beings were viewed as chattel or merchandise not worthy of human treatment. Rape of the women was a common occurrence as they were used and abused for breeding purposes.

In his eyewitness account of the Transatlantic Slave Trade, Alexander Falconbridge, a surgeon for several slave ships, wrote about the slave traders who held the Africans captives during the late 1700s:

> The traders frequently beat those Negroes which are objected to by the captains and use them with great severity. It matters not whether they are refused on account of age, illness, deformity, or for any other reason. At New Calabar, in particular, the traders have frequently been known to put them to death. Instances have happened at that place, when Negroes have been objected to, that the traders have dropped their canoes under the stern of the vessel and instantly beheaded them in sight of the captain.[10]

During the voyages across the ocean, the Africans were packed like cargo shelved on boards eight or nine feet wide. "[T]he sexes were separated, kept naked, packed close together."[11] They were on their backs with their heads often between the legs of another; they were chained in pairs "wrist-to-wrist" or "ankle-to-ankle" to decks so narrow in space there was no room to stand or breathe; and they were forced to endure laying in each other's urine, feces, vomitus, and blood.[12] On average, the travel period lasted just over two months; and the "filthy conditions ensured endemic gastrointestinal diseases, and a range of epidemic pathogens that, together with periodic breakouts of violent resistance, meant that between twelve and thirteen percent, respectively, of those embarked" died brutal and inhumane deaths from disease, injury, suffocation, and starvation.[13] The dead and diseased were later thrown overboard by the ship's crew; and, because most were attached by chains, it was not unusual for the healthy to skate across the wooden decks of the ship into the abyss along with the dead and diseased. When the threat of capture for the crime of piracy arose, in some instances and in a similar manner, crews would dispose of the evidence into the abyss.

Refusal to eat could result in sadistic torture for the captured souls. According to Falconbridge:

> Coals of fire, glowing hot, put on a shovel and placed so near their lips as to scorch and burn them. And this has been accompanied with threats of forcing them to swallow the coals if they any longer persisted in refusing to eat. These means have generally had the desired effect. I have also been credibly informed that a certain captain in the slave-trade poured melted lead on such of his Negroes as obstinately refused their food.[14]

Some of the Africans went mad in these gruesome conditions, while others managed to hurl themselves from the ship to a watery grave rather than face relentless torture and an unknown future. It has been estimated that more than 2 million Africans died during the Middle Passage alone, though a precise number is impossible to calculate.

Documented voyages represented only four-fifths of the slaves transported out of Africa. Europe, the Americas, the Caribbean, and Africa all participated. Europe was the starting point for at least half of the slave voyages since expanding empires reached into Africa for resources and human cargo. Brazil was consistently the largest destination for slaves. The Caribbean conducted more slavery expeditions than North America. While North America only absorbed about 4 percent of the Transatlantic Slave Trade, it also "imported" a great number of its slaves from the Caribbean and then benefitted from the population growth of slaves within the United States (according to law, subsequent generations were born into the condition of slavery).

Pursuant to law, King George III imposed slavery upon the American colonies and made it obligatory. In fact, Britain was the worst offender, responsible for the transport of nearly 2.5 million Africans, a number which represents only the survivors. While many colonists followed the letter of the law, many to increase their own prosperity, many more opposed the practice and indeed were offended by the mandate. From early in his legal career, Thomas Jefferson[15] denounced slavery. The man was indeed a mystery because he was a slave owner via inheritance. Still, he argued against the practice and in fact as a young attorney (in his twenties) defended a slave in court, saying:

> Under the law of nature, all men are born free; everyone comes into the world with a right to his own person, which includes the liberty of moving

> and using it at his own will. This is what is called personal liberty, and is given him by the Author of nature, because [it is] necessary for his own sustenance.[16]

His legal argument would become an indication of the direction of his latter Declaration of Independence. One of the earlier versions of Jefferson's Declaration denounced the practice of slavery and boldly charged King George III of what we now refer to as war crimes:

> He has *waged cruel war against human nature itself*, violating its most sacred rights of life and liberty in the persons of a distant people who never offended him, captivating and *carrying them into slavery in another hemisphere, or to incur miserable death in their transportation hither.* This piratical warfare, the opprobrium of INFIDEL powers, is the warfare of the CHRISTIAN king of Great Britain. Determined to keep open a market where MEN should be bought and sold, *he has prostituted his negative for suppressing every legislative attempt to prohibit or to restrain this execrable commerce.* And that this assemblage of horrors might want no fact of distinguished die, he is now exciting those very people to rise in arms among us, and to purchase that liberty of which he has deprived them, by murdering the people on whom he also obtruded them: thus paying off former crimes committed against the LIBERTIES of one people, with crimes which he urges them to commit against the LIVES of another.[17]

Unfortunately, Congress would strike out the entire paragraph, which may be considered its first major failure. Hence, slavery and the slave trade would to continue to exist in the young nation.

Slave Code

Throughout the country, as early as the mid-1600s, state legislatures passed statutes known as slave codes that regulated slavery. Slaves were not permitted to earn wages, own property, or move about freely. A child of a slave woman was deemed a slave.[18] Masters could not be charged with felonies related to the death of a slave. Slave codes permitted "lashes" for various infractions of their status of being a slave. Slaves were considered property and could be sold, seized, and mortgaged. They owed obedience to their masters, were not free to travel, and had no ownership or seller's rights. The codes controlled every aspect of the lives of slaves and free blacks. Completely dehumanized, slaves were without civil, legal, or human rights.

The Constitution of the United States was created in 1787 and ratified in 1788; and it is the Supreme Law of the Land. A mere five paragraphs into the Constitution, the Founding Fathers enshrined their belief that slaves did not have the value of a full person. This became America's first official sanctuary for dehumanization. At the time, members of the Constitutional Convention believed the "compromise" was necessary so that southern states would join the Union. According to Article 1, Section 2:

> Representatives . . . shall be apportioned among the several States which may be included within this Union, according to their respective Numbers, which shall be determined by adding to the whole Number of free Persons, including those bound to Service for a Term of Years, and excluding Indians not taxed, *three fifths of all other Persons.*[19]

In addition, Congress agreed to give the states control over importing "Persons" until 1808. Yet, Congress would retain the power to tax the importation of "each Person," as evidenced in Article I, Section 9:

> Migration or Importation of such Persons as any of the States now existing shall think proper to admit, shall not be prohibited by the Congress prior to the Year one thousand eight hundred and eight, but a Tax or duty may be imposed on such Importation, not exceeding ten dollars for each Person.[20]

The centers of the slave trade in the United States involved ports from Baltimore south along the east coast and around the Gulf of Mexico to Texas. Slavery was central to life in New Orleans with more than 100,000 human transactions conducted in the city between 1804 and 1862 alone. French and Spanish Code Noir ("Black Codes") governed slavery in New Orleans from the early 18th century through the 19th century.

Louisiana became a territory of the United States in 1803, approximately 100 years after its colonization by France; and in 1804, Congress established the Territory of Orleans and its government.[21] St. Bernard Parish was created in 1807, but tracts of farmland were granted to individuals from the Canary Islands (known as Isleños) in 1778 while Louisiana was still under Spanish rule.[22] The Canary Islands, a Spanish archipelago off the Moroccan coast, was a supply base for ships headed for the Spanish colonies in the West Indies.[23] Spain occupied Louisiana pursuant to a secret treaty following the Seven Year' War in 1762.[24] French nobles and military officers intermarried with the Spanish in Louisiana, creating a new ethnicity known in Louisiana as creoles; today, creoles trace their ancestry to these settlers, including those with a blended African ancestry.[25]

Canary Island natives and the Isleños speak Spanish. However, members of this ethnicity are not considered a Hispanic minority; rather, they are aligned with white Europeans because the islands belonged to Spain.[26] Hispanic Americans include individuals from the Spanish-speaking countries of Latin America, primarily Mexico, Puerto Rico, Cuba, Santo Domingo, and Columbia, and not those from Europe or Iberia.[27] Because Isleños owned plantations in St. Bernard Parish, they were considered white as opposed to nonwhite, with all of the legal rights and societal standing that "whiteness" provided. The history of the Isleños offers an important caveat for two main reasons:

1. Involvement with and prosperity as a result of the slave trade kept Isleños in a position of authority and power in Louisiana because many of these plantation owners also served in the state legislature and senate.[28]
2. Isleños have not been subjected to the racial discrimination that has historically affected Hispanic groups any other minority in the United States.

Just prior to becoming a state, Louisiana enacted the Code Noir, also known as the 1806 Black Code. This Code remained in force for nearly 60 years, until Reconstruction.[29] In its 40 sections of laws "prescribing the rules and conduct to be observed with respect to Negroes and other Slaves of this Territory," it provided a legal framework for slavery that was based on the codes of 1724.

New Orleans was the largest slave market in the United States. Slaves, like animals waiting to be sold, were kept in "pens" throughout the central business district. Slave yards filled downtown New Orleans and Algiers, also known as the 15th Ward in the city, while bizarre slave auctions were held at some of the finest hotels in the area.[30] Advertisements regarding the sale of slaves and rewards for runaway slaves littered the local newspaper, the *Daily Picayune*, like the following from 1845:

> $10 Reward – Ran away from the Louisiana state boat "Experiment" the boy W. M. Bradley, aged 28 or 30 years, light black, stout, built, joint of forefinger of the left hand off. The above named reward, of 10 dollars, will be paid by the State Engineer to the person who will lodge said negro in any jail in this state.[31]

By 1850, approximately, 300 slave traders operated in 25 downtown markets.[32] In contrast to other slave-holding states, Louisiana was a place where free men of color (including those of African descent) also held slaves; and many Asians and Native Americans were also enslaved within the state.[33]

Conditions of Slavery

The institution of slavery in the United States condemned slaves to impoverishment and created a slave's absolute dependence on his "master" and/or "mistress." In this manner, the masters' power was preserved: granted dominion over the entirety of slaves' lives. Slaveholders did not view or, more aptly put, did not verbalize—that the institution of slavery was one of "brute force." Instead, they portrayed slavery as "paternalistic," a responsibility over an inferior people to provide them with food, shelter, clothing, and (limited, if any) medical care. That responsibility, most unfortunately, was determined by a slaveholder's finances and temperament. Diaries of slaveowners evidence the contradiction of their paternalistic claims. Louisiana slave owner Bennet H. Barrow documented the near daily beatings and torture of slaves yet provided in his accounts "extensive moral explanations as to why such punishments were necessary."[34] Abolitionist Frederick Douglass, a former slave who escaped when he was 20 years old, wrote an account of what he witnessed during his own enslavement:

> Henrietta was about twenty-two years of age, Mary was about fourteen; and of all the mangled and emaciated creatures I ever looked upon, these two were the most so. [The master's] heart must be harder than stone, that [he] could look upon these unmoved. The head, neck, and shoulders of Mary were literally cut to pieces. I have frequently felt her head, and found it nearly covered with festering sores, caused by the lash of her cruel mistress. I do not know that her master ever whipped her, but I have been an eye-witness to the cruelty of Mrs. Hamilton [the mistress]. I used to be in Mr. Hamilton's house nearly every day. Mrs. Hamilton used to sit in a large chair in the middle of the room, with a heavy cow-skin always by her side, and scarce an hour passed during the day but was marked by the blood of one of these slaves.[35]

Slavery was pervasive during the 1800s in New Orleans. The booming economy of the sugar and cotton industries in New Orleans was built on the backs of slaves, making the city one of the wealthiest in the United States. Not only did private industry depend on slave labor, so did the government. The City of New Orleans itself owned slaves who dug drainage ditches, built roads, cleared forests, and prepared timber to be used in construction projects initiated by the French and Spanish.[36] During the 18th century, landowners were responsible for creating the levees; thus, slaves were used for that purpose in addition to their plantation work. Because the natural levees were only three feet in height, which was not high enough to protect the settlements on the banks of the Mississippi River from flooding, it would prove to be an eternal battle against nature. The first levee collapsed in 1735; and New Orleans suffered significant damage.[37] There are few tangible remnants of the New Orleans slave trade, though most notably Congo Square[38] and Banks Arcade[39] (on Magazine Street) remain.[40]

Although Congress prohibited importing new slaves at the time Louisiana became a U.S. territory, slavery as an institution was not outlawed. Despite the prohibition on importing slaves, Louisiana continued to import slaves illegally from Africa, the West Indies, Cuba, and Haiti.[41] By the 1840s, at least 10 sugar plantations were established in St. Bernard Parish in the former Isleño settlements.[42] Ten years later, New Orleans was the largest slave-trading center in the South.[43] This is not to say that all slaves coming into New Orleans were illegally imported, as New Orleans was also an important hub for the domestic slave trade.[44]

The bitter argument over slavery divided the nation from the lowly farmer to the greatest statesmen. John C. Calhoun, serving as the senator from South Carolina, addressed the U.S. Senate on February 6, 1837:

> We of the South will not, cannot surrender our institutions . . . Be it good or bad, [slavery] has grown up with our society and institutions, and is so interwoven with them, that to destroy it would be to destroy us as a people. But let me not be understood as admitting, even by implication, that the existing relations between the two races in the slaveholding States is an evil: - far otherwise; I hold it to be good, as it has thus far proved itself to be to both (races), and will continue to prove so if not disturbed by the fell spirit of abolition.[45]

Calhoun argued that the plight of the slaves was better than that of the poor in Europe or most of the working class in the United States because slaves were under the "kind superintending care of" their "master and mistress." Furthermore, Calhoun charged that emancipation would not satisfy "these fanatics" (those opposed to slavery); and

> the next step would be to raise the negroes to a social and political equality with the whites; and that being effected, we would soon find the present condition of the two races reversed. They and their northern allies would be the masters, and we the slaves.[46]

Calhoun made these claims as a Yale graduate and an attorney; he also served as vice president of the United States under John Quincy Adams and Andrew Jackson from 1825 until 1832.

Sixty-five years after the Declaration of Independence and following a 37-year hiatus from practicing before the Supreme Court, former president John Quincy Adams was inspired to take a case involving the illegal slave trade—*The Amistad* (40 U. S. 518 [1841]).[47] In his argument defending the Africans, he denounced the practice of slavery and the legal system that perpetuated it. While pointing to the Declaration of Independence on the wall of the Court, Adams eloquently addressed the Supreme Court of the United States:

> I know no law . . . except *that* law, *that law*, two copies which are ever before the eyes of your Honors, but the Law of Nature and of Nature's God on which our fathers placed our own national existence. That law . . . I trust will be the law on which the case will be decided by this Court . . . [slavery] is contrary to the Law of Nature . . . [slavery is] inhuman, cruel, odious, detestable . . . the Court must look to the legal standard of morality.[48]

Adams argued that the Africans, in this case, were kidnapped from Africa in violation of U.S. laws and brought to the United States contrary to the same. He then asked for the Court to order their return to the coast of Africa. The Court found the Africans were:

> natives of Africa . . . were kidnapped there, and were unlawfully transported to Cuba . . . [According to law] the African slave trade is utterly abolished; [and] the dealing in that trade is deemed a heinous crime . . . [as such and since there is no] ground for doubt . . . these negroes ought to be deemed free.[49]

Adams accurately predicted the issue of slavery would create a civil war for the nation.

The perpetuation of dehumanization continued and was deemed sociologically acceptable not only by government leaders and slaveholders, but also by the medical community. Dr. Samuel Cartwright, a well-respected and widely published doctor from the University of Louisiana, perpetuated and endorsed the dehumanization of those with African blood. In his 1851 report entitled *Diseases and Peculiarities of the Negro Race*, Cartwright "discovered" that slaves suffered from two distinct and uniquely slave "diseases": "drapetomania," which caused slaves to run away, and "dysaethesia aethiopica," also known as "rascality," which was cause of intentional acts of mischief committed by slaves. Illogically, he admitted these "diseases" were unknown to the medical community but could be confirmed by "planters and overseers." Treatment of "drapetomania" called for slaves to be:

> treated kindly, well fed and clothed, with fuel enough to keep a small fire burning all night—separated into families, each family having its own house—not permitted to run about at night to visit their neighbors, to receive visits or use intoxicating liquors, and not overworked or exposed too much to the weather, they are very easily governed—more so than any other people in the world." [Keeping slaves in such a state where they are] treated like children, with care, kindness, attention and humanity [would] prevent and cure them from running away.[50]

Dysaethesia," according to Cartwright, was found predominantly among "free negroes," but slaves were "symptom[atic]" if they exhibited:

> break[ing], waste[ing] and destroy[ing] everything they handle[d],—abuse horses and cattle,— [they] tear, burn or rend their own clothing, and, [paying] no attention to the rights of property, steal from others, to replace what they have destroyed. They wander about at night, and keep in a half nodding sleep during the day.[51]

Such "diseases" were "the natural offspring of negro liberty," and the recommended remedy for the "diseases" was "whipping."[52] The editor of *De Bow's Review Southern and Western States*, praised Cartwright's "discoveries" and stated "it ha[d] a direct and practical bearing upon over 3,000,000 people and $2,000,000,000 of property (slaves)."[53] Thoroughly dehumanized by the government, the law, slavery, politicking, and the medical community's pseudoscientists, those with African blood were societal outcasts. In Louisiana, "free blacks" had a few rights provided they carried a certificate validating their freedom. These rights included carrying weapons, being in charge of a plantation, and trial by jury. However, residency was restricted because "free blacks" were prevented from living within cities and towns per local ordinances.

There was only one way around the ordinances: free blacks must work for a white employer, and that employer had to agree to assume responsibility for the conduct of the employees.

The Migration of 1809, coupled with the exodus resulting from the revolution in Haiti in 1804, resulted in the addition of 2,731 whites; 3,102 free persons of African descent; and 3,226 enslaved persons of African descent to the population of New Orleans, which created a 63 percent black population. This was a larger percentage of blacks than in Charleston, South Carolina.[54] Given that the black population was larger than the white population in most slave-holding areas, whites believed statutes and societal rules were necessary to control the "black" and slave populace.

Although free blacks, also known as "free persons of color," may have had a few more rights than slaves, one must remember that slaves did have the value of a full person, held absolutely no rights, and had no semblance of citizenship. Free blacks could not vote, run for office, or marry a white person. Additionally, free blacks were restricted from owning or operating businesses where alcohol was sold, and their mobility was significantly restricted within the state. Between 1812 and 1865, Louisiana passed dozens of statutes and civil codes regulating lives of slaves and free blacks, and local governments were authorized to pass laws policing slavery as long as they were did not contradict state law.

In 1807, according to census records, there were 23,500 slaves and 4,000 free blacks in Louisiana. By 1860, the population swelled *more than 14 times that number* to 330,000 slaves. It is likely this increase in the number of slaves was due to the impact of the domestic slave trade as opposed to the importation of slaves from Africa. Slaves' and free blacks' freedom to travel was restricted by legislation in 1817 when those who had been convicted of a serious crime were prevented from entering Louisiana. In addition, these groups could not travel within the state without written authorization. Likewise, "free blacks" could not leave the state without the approval of Louisiana parish authorities.

Antimiscegenation laws in Louisiana were established in the Civil Code of 1825 stating that slaves and free persons of color could not marry whites.[55] The code continued the denial of property rights to slaves. Slave quarters were separate from those of their white masters and were mostly shacks.[56] Furthermore, according to the code, free blacks and slaves were prohibited from receiving religious instruction and gathering in public. Employment was restricted; and militias were segregated. It was criminal to teach slaves and blacks to read.[57]

New Orleans was, and still is, susceptible to severe flooding because southeast Louisiana is flanked by the mouth of the raging Mississippi River and the "wide water"[58] of Lake Pontchartrain.[59] Even regular rainfall could, and still does, flood the streets. The original settlement was placed upon the highest ground in the area, in what is now known as the French Quarter. Recall that slaves and free blacks were restricted from living within the city and therefore lived just outside the French Quarter in lower-lying areas, which were below sea level. Given the extensive flooding history, it is highly likely these residential areas were established deliberately. That New Orleans was vulnerable to the forces of nature was demonstrated by the Great Louisiana Hurricane of 1812,[60] which swept through the town[61] a little over 200 years before Katrina. By this time, Louisiana was admitted to the Union,[62] though just four months had passed. Most of New Orleans was under water; and, approximately, 100 people died as a result of the storm. The *Orleans Gazette* described the scene; and, unfortunately, it was one that would be repeated throughout Louisiana's history:

> The levee almost entirely destroyed; the beach covered from fragments of vessels, merchandize, trunks, and here and there the eye falling on a mangled corpse. In short, what a few hours before was life and property, presented to the astonished spectator only death and ruin.[63]

On a regular basis, hurricanes battered the Gulf Coast of Louisiana, New Orleans, and the surrounding areas from the beginning of its recorded history. Some of them were minor, but some were major and wreaked havoc and destruction. In 1831, the Great Barbados Hurricane ripped through Last Island (just west of Baton Rouge), killing 1,500 people. In addition, it destroyed sugar cane crops from Baton Rouge all the way through the south of New Orleans.[64] Numerous storms left death and apocalyptic scenes in their wakes, and the stench of rotting corpses of livestock, by the herds, and humanity filled the dense humid air of the bayou like the sagging Spanish moss on the live oaks. The hurricanes splintered the poorly constructed shanties of the slaves leaving what appeared to be stacks of toothpicks. Evacuation was impossible for slaves who had nowhere to go, lacked any warning system and, certainly, had no financial means to evacuate. Indeed they lacked even the permission to leave the plantations, as they were chained there (both figuratively and literally) by the necessity of a written pass to travel and because they were forbidden to travel after dark. Thus, many of them drowned like the "cargo" thrown off of the slave ships in the middle of the Atlantic Ocean.

In 1837, a hurricane named Racer's Storm destroyed 2,000 miles of land extending from Texas to Florida, and moved north into South Carolina and North Carolina. Louisiana—and particularly New Orleans—was devastated. The storm surge was eight feet above normal high tide on Lake Pontchartrain. The original wooden Bayou St. John Lighthouse was swept out to sea. Gale winds destroyed chimneys, awnings, and roofs of houses. The City Exchange on Lewis Street was severely damaged. The sugar cane and cotton crops of the plantations were whipped and ruined by the storm. All of the wharves along the Mississippi coastline "were washed away."[65] As had happened so many times before and would happen again in later storms, the lower portions of New Orleans were submerged, and "buildings were damaged or carried away" as were two miles of railroad tracks.[66] Just six people reportedly died in the storm's wake.[67]

Within 10 years of Racer's Storm, the Law of Slavery in the state of Louisiana was adopted. Promulgated in 1825, between the time of the Great Louisiana Hurricane of 1812 and the Great Barbados Hurricane in 1831, according to the Law of Slavery in the state of Louisiana:

1. Slaves belonged to their masters. Slaves could "do nothing, possess nothing, nor acquire anything."[68] All a slave possessed belonged to his master.[69] Slaves were entirely subject to the will of their masters[70] and were determined by law to be without capacity, as if they were insane.[71]
2. Slaves could not marry without the consent of their masters[72] and were deemed not to have the capacity to enter into marriages. Wedding celebrations were not permitted, and slave marriages were deemed void. The same incapacity and nullity applied to marriages between free whites and free people of color.[73] In fact, because of lack of capacity, a slave could not enter into any contract except one involving "his own emancipation."[74] The inability to enter into any contract would mean that such a person could not contract for the sale or rent of property.
3. Slaves could not transmit anything by devise or will.[75]
4. Slaves could not hold public office or positions of private trust, nor could a slave become an attorney. Because they were viewed as property, they had no right to judicial remedy or to be political participants. Nor could they be parties or witnesses at a trial or members of a jury.[76]
5. Most dehumanizing of all, masters had the right to "enjoy" the services of slaves (like animals) for the masters' "wants and those of his family," whatsoever that might be.[77]

Just before the Civil War began, in 1859, the state legislature passed a law providing that free blacks could renounce their freedom and become slaves for life. Then in 1864, all free blacks between the ages of 16 and 55 were drafted to the Confederate Army.[78]

The Fight for Human Dignity

Even if we did not have the diaries and records of plantation owners and recorded testimonies of slaves, it would be impossible to believe that slaves were treated well or were happy with their plight. Certainly the laws of this period directly opposed the theories of paternalism, Christianity, and basic human dignity. Slaves' resistance was not uncommon, as can be seen from the number of runaways (evidenced by the numerous newspaper advertisements and the passage of the Fugitive Slave Law) and slave revolts, most notably the revolts led by Nat Turner (Southampton County, Virginia, in 1831) and John Brown (Harpers Ferry, West Virginia, in 1859).

The earliest recorded slave revolt occurred in 1712 in Manhattan, New York. However, the largest slave revolt in American history was in Louisiana and is, ironically, the least well known. This revolt began on January 8, 1811, just one year before Louisiana became a state of the Union; and it "reverberated around the fledgling nation because of the large number of enslaved people involved [and] its military strategy . . . because it demonstrated that all was not well among those held in bondage."[79] Charles Deslondes and 200 slaves (some historians claim 500) fought with hoes, axes, and cane knives for their freedom. The revolt began in La Place, Louisiana, on Woodland Plantation; and they set out to capture New Orleans with the aim of setting up a "Black republic." While the revolutionaries came close to achieving their goal, they were defeated near present-day River Town in Kenner, the largest city in Jefferson Parish. After three days before a tribunal, 45 revolutionaries were convicted and sentenced to death or moved to New Orleans for further trials. Deslondes and the others "were executed by a firing squad and beheaded as punishment for their crime."[80] Their heads were impaled onto poles, which were then placed along a 40-mile stretch of the river levees from New Orleans to La Place.[81] This act of terror would serve as a deterrent for similar rebellions.[82]

In 1856, the Supreme Court of the United States, in what history calls one of the worst decisions ever made, cemented the notion that those of African descent were not "people or citizens" within the context of the

Constitution. The case was *Dred Scott v. Sandford.* The question before the Court was "simply this": could a "negro" of slave ancestry become a member of the citizenry of the United States and "be entitled to all the rights, and privileges, and immunities (including suing in a U.S. court)" guaranteed by the Constitution?[83] The Court held that the negro was not a citizen and that Congress—not any individual state—was the only authority that could grant citizenship. The Court stated that at the time the Constitution was drafted, negroes were "a subordinate and inferior class of beings who had been subjugated by the dominant race . . . remained subject to their authority, and had no rights (free or slave)."[84] To prove it, the Court cited a litany of law. Chief Justice Taney delivered the opinion of the Court. Beginning with the practice of slavery:

> [Negroes] had for more than a century before [the Declaration of Independence] been regarded as beings of an inferior order, and altogether unfit to associate with the white race either in social or political relations, and *so far inferior that they had no rights which the white man was bound to respect*, and that the negro might justly and lawfully be reduced to slavery for his benefit. He was bought and sold, and treated as an ordinary article of merchandise and traffic whenever a profit could be made by it.[85]

The Court further inventoried the catalogue of law and slave codes (which later became Jim Crow), which relegated negroes to a status that was less than human:

1. The Declaration of Independence. Slaves were not referred to at all in the Declaration.[86] "[W]hen in the course of human events it becomes necessary for one people to dissolve the political bands which have connected them with another, and *to assume among the powers of the earth the separate and equal station to which the laws of nature and nature's God entitle them, a decent respect for the opinions of mankind requires that they should declare the causes which impel them to the separation.*"[87]
2. The Articles of Confederation. Slaves were not included. "[T]hat the *free inhabitants* of each of the States, paupers, vagabonds, and fugitives from justice, excepted, should be entitled to all the privileges and immunities of free citizens in the several States."[88]
3. U.S. Constitution. Slaves were not included within the term "citizens."[89] It sanctioned the importation of slaves.[90] Thus, "the only two provisions which point to them and include them treat them as property and make it the duty of the Government to protect it."[91]

4. An act of Congress. "[T]the naturalization law, which was passed at the second session of the first Congress, March 26, 1790, and confines the right of becoming citizens "*to aliens being free white persons*."
5. English government and law (which was conferred upon its colonies). Took "Negroes" from Africa "as articles of merchandise."
6. Maryland, Ch. 13, s. 5 (1717). Antimiscegenation law.[92]
7. Massachusetts, Ch. 6 (1705). Antimiscegenation law and "[the] act for the better preventing of a spurious and mixed issue, . . . and it provides that "if any negro or mulatto shall presume to smite or strike any person of the English or other Christian nation, such negro or mulatto shall be severely whipped, at the discretion of the justices before whom the offender shall be convicted."[93]
8. Laws of slaveholding states. "Their statute books are full of provisions in relation to this class in the same spirit with the Maryland law which we have before quoted. They have continued to treat them as an inferior class, and to subject them to strict police regulations, drawing a broad line of distinction between the citizen and the slave races, and legislating in relation to them upon the same principle which prevailed at the time of the Declaration of Independence,"[94] which included prohibiting slaves:
   a. From traveling freely
   b. From reading, writing, and schools[95]
   c. From entering the militia[96]
   d. From holding nightly meetings "and other disorderly meetings of slaves, free negroes, and mulattoes"[97]
9. Finally, state courts that determined negroes were not citizens. "And this mark of degradation was renewed, and again impressed upon the race."[98]

Scott, a slave, wanted the courts to grant him his freedom because he and his master had resided in Illinois and Wisconsin (then a territory), where slavery was illegal. However, the highest court in the country endorsed nearly every bit of law from the preceding 200 years regarding the practice of subjugation and degradation of people with African blood. It would set the tone for another 150 years of slave code, Jim Crow, and white supremacy. Even worse, Scott was devastated to learn that he was not recognized as a human being by this Court or, for that matter, his own country.

Despite the fact that African Americans served in the Revolutionary War and the War of 1812, the United States Army prohibited the enlistment of "Negroes or Mulattoes" in 1820.[99] But in 1862, when New Orleans succumbed to Union troops, thousands of slaves sought refuge with the Union forces. Indeed, "historians say their numbers grew so large that they created a beachhead that influenced President Abraham Lincoln's strategies on slavery and led to Emancipation Proclamation."[100] This exodus destroyed the myth conjured by the slave owners and government officials that slaves were happy with their plight. By 1860, African Americans comprised more than 50 percent of the population in the Deep South, including Louisiana.[101]

Civil War

Louisiana reluctantly seceded from the Union in January 1861 because many businessmen were "Yankees." Additionally, its remote location kept many citizens from being interested in federal politics; however, the slave trade and the institution of slavery were so enmeshed in Louisiana's accumulation of wealth, the state seceded from the Union in an effort to keep its institution of slavery. In 1840, New Orleans was the wealthiest and third most populated city in the United States. Still, its geographic location as the gateway to the North American interior left Louisiana vulnerable not only to nature, but to military strategists. The Union Army invaded Louisiana through New Orleans and set up blockades along the Mississippi and on the lakes (a military coup that divided the Confederacy). As a result, trade evaporated, banks failed, and businesses closed. A mere 16 months after Louisiana's secession, it was occupied by the Union Army and came under federal rule. Once the richest state of the Union, Louisiana became the poorest; and that ranking persisted through the 21st century.[102]

Louisiana had more former slaves in the Union Army than any other state (24,000 out of the 180,000 African-American troop total). Emancipation granted former slaves permission to enlist in the Union Army. President Lincoln declared:

> by virtue of the power in me vested as Commander-in-Chief, of the Army and Navy of the United States in time of actual armed rebellion against the authority and government of the United States . . . I further declare and make known, that such persons of suitable condition, will be received into the armed service of the United States.[103]

The Fort Ward Museum in Alexandria, Virginia, has this to say with regard to black Union soldiers of the Civil War:

> [M]ilitary governor Gen. Benjamin Butler's 1st, 2nd and 3rd Louisiana Native Guards, the Corps D'Afrique, were formed from existing free black

> militia units and supervised by Gen. Daniel Ullmann. Major Francis E. Dumas and Paris-educated Captain Andre Cailloux, who proudly described himself as the blackest man in New Orleans, exemplified the affluent freeman who commanded these units. Many were to resign, however, because of tension in the ranks and the Army's official policy of excluding blacks from leadership positions and officer promotions.[104]

Of course, the Civil War was not about freeing 3.5 million slaves but rather preserving the Union in response to the secession of the southern states. In fact, the former slaves were permitted to serve in the Union Army because they were considered to be the confiscated property ("war contraband") of the secessionists. Their enlistment, however, set a precedent for paying the former slaves through a work contract from the Union Army because previously, only free persons could enter into contracts. Approximately 186,000 African Americans joined the Union Army during the war, 100 of them earned commissions, and 24 received the Congressional Medal of Honor for their heroism (this medal was first issued during the Civil War).

Unfortunately, when President Lincoln issued the Emancipation Proclamation, by Executive Order, the federally "occupied New Orleans and a handful of parishes were specifically exempted from the law." Those areas where slavery would continue specifically included "the Parishes of **St. Bernard, Plaquemines, Jefferson**, St. John, St. Charles, St. James Ascension, Assumption, **Terrebonne**, Lafourche, St. Mary, St. Martin, and **Orleans, including the City of New Orleans**."[105] In fact, the *Daily Picayune* continued to publish notices after the proclamation "seeking the capture of escaped slaves."[106]

The Civil War was America's bloodiest war and saw the deaths of approximately 620,000 soldiers, 260,000 of whom were southern men. Another estimated 460,000 were wounded in battle. One in four soldiers never returned home from the war; and, for every three soldiers killed, five died from disease. Moreover, the southern landscape was destroyed to the point of being unrecognizable. The Civil War severely damaged New Orleans's levee system, which was rebuilt—again—by slaves.[107] Because of the war's extensive violence, to this day, there are no final tallies on the casualties or financial costs.[108] Indeed, the financial costs of the war continue today as two elderly children of Civil War veterans are still receiving benefits.[109] Acts of terrorism, rooted in resistance to the verdict cast by the end of the war, ran rampant and persisted for decades. It has been said that the opening act of southern insurgency occurred a mere five days after the end of the Civil War with the assassination of President Lincoln.

Aware of southern states' resistance, Congress ratified the Thirteenth, Fourteenth, and Fifteenth Amendments to remove "the badge[s] of slavery"; establish citizens' rights and equal protection under law for recently freed slaves; and create voting rights, respectively. In defiant response, Louisiana created new black codes in 1865 that further restricted the rights of African Americans. Like a game of table tennis, Congress hit back with the passage of the Civil Rights Acts in 1866 and 1875 to establish that "all persons" would have the rights "as [those] enjoyed by white citizens."[110] These acts were then disgracefully overturned by the Supreme Court as unconstitutional law.[111]

The Reign of Terror

By the time Ulysses S. Grant assumed the presidency (1869–1877), violence by white supremacists against African Americans reached a fever pitch; and the Ku Klux Klan[112] was in full operation. On July 30, 1866, an angry mob of white citizens and policemen massacred Negroes at the Mechanics Institute. Radical Republican delegates and their supporters (who espoused liberal views), a large number of "Negroes" (some 225 in all), gathered at the Mechanics Institute to vote on retracting the Black Codes of 1865. However, they shortly found themselves under attack. Within minutes, nearly all of them were battered or dead (34 of the 37 killed were "Negroes"; 146 were wounded).[113] The message sent to the federal government was loud and clear: Louisiana would keep "their Negroes" in a "semi-slave state."[114]

Only in Louisiana did federal authorities "implement experimental Reconstruction policies during the Civil War."[115] These policies, including the establishment of the Freedmen's Bureau,[116] were met with violent hostility, most notably in Caddo and Bossier Parishes in 1868, where murders of free blacks were common. New Orleans became the headquarters of the Freedmen's Bureau in Louisiana. The bureau's investigative aims were obstructed by state and local governments as well as private entities.[117] The bureau found that freed blacks were "constantly being taken from their homes by desperadoes and either being killed or forced to leave their homes, crops and everything they possess, that no laws of any kind are enforced."[118] In addition, the bureau reported violent acts near Shreveport, Louisiana:

> [A] riot occurred caused by the lawless acts of desperadoes in which (2) two white men were shot and mortally wounded. Thirteen (13) freedmen and one (1) freedwoman killed and (2) two freedmen wounded. Latter advices in regard to the Bossier troubles state that some 8 or 10 freedmen more than the above reported were killed by the Arkansas Desperadoes and that after their departure the citizens of Bossier and the friends of the two murdered white men have been in constant pursuit of all freedmen implicated in the murder of the two whites and have killed all whom they have caught, from all the information that can be gleaned the number of freedmen killed, of which there are various statements, will reach (100) one hundred at least. It would be a matter of impossibility to ascertain the names of the killed or for an investigation to be made. Anyone that would attempt the task would share the fate of the rioting negroes.
>
> At Shreveport on October 16th a colored man named Robert Gray was shot and killed by a white man named Charles Wasson in a store on Texas St. The body of a negro was also found floating in Red River the same day in a far advanced state of decomposition.[119]

According to the Freedmen's Bureau 1867 annual report, 86 "freedmen" were killed by whites; and 210 were "shot at, whipped, stabbed, beaten." In comparison, only *one* white was murdered by a "freedman."[120] In Louisiana, in that one year alone, murders of African Americans occurred in more than two dozen towns, including Amite City,[121] Gretna,[122] Shreveport,[123] Alexandria,[124] St. Martinsville,[125] Flat Town,[126] Natchitoches,[127] Point Coupee,[128] Sparta,[129] Purchase,[130] Lake Providence,[131] Opelousas,[132] Monroe,[133] Jackson,[134] Baton Rouge,[135] Houma,[136] Vidalia,[137] Marksville,[138] Fausse Point,[139] and Carrolton.[140] Murders also occurred in various towns in St. Bernard, St. James, Bossier, Vermillion, and Plaquemine Parishes as well as—of course—in New Orleans.[141] What could probably be referred to as the worst crimes are those that were not listed—they were crimes committed by civil authorities who refused to protect and serve their citizens (specifically, the African-American community) and who would not pursue the criminals who committed the acts.

The aversion to the Freedmen's Bureau was manifested by Klansmen who whipped the teachers of the bureau's schools and burned the schoolhouses to the ground. Anyone who supported the policies was subject to the Klan's intimidation tactics of terror and murder.[142] Congressional responses included the Enforcement Acts that made it a crime to interfere in the political and voting processes to no avail. In 1871, Congress passed the Ku Klux Klan Act to give the federal government authority to act against this domestic terrorist organization. Within a decade, the Supreme Court of the United States would deliver another devastating blow to the issue by holding the Enforcement Act unconstitutional. Klan activities continued to increase: cross burnings; rallies; and parades that denigrated African Americans, immigrants, Catholics, Jews, and labor unions.[143] In 1871, one of the most heinous acts of violence by the KKK was carried out in South Carolina, where 500 hooded Klansmen attacked a county jail and lynched eight "Negroes."[144] Their thousands of terrorist acts throughout the entire South were virtually sanctioned by law enforcement, many of whom were either members of the Klan or sympathizers.

Racism, segregation, and disenfranchisement of rights were enforced outside the legal system through a reign of terror made up of ceremonious, sadistic acts of mob violence commonly known as lynching, which mainly targeted southern African Americans. Through "classification," "symbolization," "dehumanization," "organization," "polarization," and "preparation" effectively implanted in American society, the extermination of African Americans continued.[145] Between the Civil War and the Great Depression, the practice of lynching developed into a "widespread and stylized phenomenon."[146] During this period, no one in Louisiana supported the abhorrent practice more than "Major" Henry J. Hearsey, publisher of the *New Orleans Daily States*. Major Hearsey, the "chief ideologist of white supremacy politics in Louisiana"[147] and "the leading Negro hater of the state" endorsed lynchings. Hearsey stated in one of his articles that "if [negroes] listen to the screeds of agitators in the North ... the result will be a race war, and race war means extermination ... Then the negro problem of Louisiana at least will be solved—and that by extermination."[148]

These atrocities were often conducted like a carnival—they were premeditated events with notices of the anticipated sideshow printed in newspapers, and they generated large crowds.[149] From 1889 to 1930, over 3,700 men and women were reportedly lynched in the United States—mostly African Americans in the South.[150] Louisiana, Georgia, Alabama, Mississippi, and Texas—all states of the Deep South—led the nation in the number of recorded lynchings.[151] A lynching was a nightmarish event. The victim would be hanged, tortured, dismembered, and mutilated. Men, while still alive, were routinely castrated. The offenders would cut off the fingers and toes of their victims one at a time, passing to the onlookers these ghastly "souvenirs." Sometimes the lynchers cut the fetus out of a pregnant African-American woman's womb. In Louisiana, it was not unusual for a mob to consist of 1,000 people or more, sometimes as many as 2,000. Onlookers and participants routinely took photographs of lynchings, and the garish images were plastered on postcards for yet another souvenir of the sadistic event.[152] The U.S. Postal Service did not outlaw the mailing of the grotesque postcards until 1908.[153]

Hundreds of lynchings and acts of brutality against African Americans by white mobs occurred during this time, and most went unreported in the press. According to the Library of Congress, 1,145 African Americans were lynched in a 25-year period alone, from 1901 until 1925. In 1922, a federal antilynching bill was "killed by a filibuster in the United States Senate."[154] Most often, lynchings occurred after an African American violated some form of "social etiquette." Lynchings were also inflicted upon those charged with violating laws and those who fought against the "social customs." Regrettably, lynching was one of American society's malaises, particularly in the South, and continued into the modern era. White riots were widespread in urban areas where African Americans migrated after leaving the plantations. "In the single year of 1919, at least twenty-five incidents were recorded, with numerous deaths and hundreds of people injured. So bloody was this summer of that year that it is known as the Red Summer of 1919."[155]

The social and economic cost of the end of slavery was immense. Nearly half of the South's capital wealth disappeared immediately upon emancipation. The slave trade was a $2 billion industry, equal to $30 billion in today's currency; and, of course, New Orleans was the leader. While the war and subsequent amendments to the Constitution officially ended slavery, states, particularly Louisiana, had no intention of bringing social equality to the 4 million newly freed blacks.[156] Granting freedom to slaves meant that American society, especially southern society, must admit overnight that African Americans were human beings, not "livestock" or "property."

It is important to note that the definition of "Negro" included anyone who had "one drop" of Negro blood.[157] A fraction—one-sixteenth—was all that was necessary in most states.[158] In line with the extensive definitions of "hybridization, the Louisiana State Supreme Court determined that an 'octoroon' was not a "Negro."[159] However, the terms "colored" and "negro" were used interchangeably from the times of slavery through the modern era.[160]

Newly-freed blacks were subjected to a contemptible existence; they were terrorized, poverty-stricken, and landless for generations. This life was divorced from any definition of freedom. In their vulnerability, legally stripped of any semblance of an opportunity for self-sufficiency, they were the subjects of deprivation, racial tension, violence, and racial massacres in every state, city, and county of the South as the region fought to retain a source of free labor. It was, essentially, a second Civil War, and the reality of African Americans became a post–Civil War nightmare.

Louisiana was victimized by no less than six hurricanes during the Civil War (three in 1860, one in 1863, and two in 1865). All brought the same devastation, an obliteration of nearly everything in the lower laying areas. Black codes were instituted in the former slave-holding states even after the Civil War (an evolution of the slave codes). These codes regulated every aspect of African Americans' life and were designed to keep them in a state of de facto slavery. Once again, Louisiana instituted the Black Code of 1865 just eight months after the Civil War ended and, partially, in response to the obliteration of towns due to the series of storms from 1860 to 1865. With a swipe of the pen, "Negro[es]" would find themselves desperate to find a place to live:

> Sec. 3: No Negro shall be permitted to rent or keep a house within said parish. Any Negro violating this provision shall be immediately ejected and compelled to find an employer; and any person who shall rent, or give the use of any house to any Negro, in violation of this section, shall pay a fine of five dollars for each offence.
>
> Sec. 4: Every Negro is required to be in the regular service of some white person, to former owner, who shall be held responsible for the conduct of said Negro. But said employer or former owner may permit said Negro to hire his own time by special permission in writing, which permission shall not extend over seven days at any one time . . .[161]

Like their forebears who revolted against the institution of slavery, black citizens of New Orleans and those in other states decided to fight against the newly instituted Jim Crow. This time, instead of using violence, they used the court system to test the limitations of this second-class citizenship. Unfortunately, from the highest authorities of their country, no relief would be forthcoming. In *Pace v. Alabama* (106 U. S. 583 [1883]), Tony Pace (a "negro") and Mary J. Cox ("a white woman") were both indicted, tried, convicted, and sentenced to two years in prison for "living together in a state of adultery or fornication" in violation of Alabama law.[162] Incredibly, because the law was the same for both African Americans and whites, the Court found that there was no equal protection violation and upheld the antimiscegenation statute. Undoubtedly, the legal argument against adultery and fornication instead of the more personal right to marry was detrimental to the case.

Separate Is Equal

In 1896, *Plessy v. Ferguson* became the most famous—or more aptly infamous—case to test second-class citizenship. The case would be heard three years following the devastating Grand Isle Hurricane of 1893.[163] Grand Isle was located in Jefferson Parish; and the hurricane claimed the lives of over 1,150 people with its 16-foot storm surge. Cheniere Caminado; an island in the Baratania region of Louisiana, was completely obliterated; and the area would never be the same, nor would it be rebuilt.

In 1890, New Orleans established a "Separate Car law"[164] that prohibited white citizens and black citizens from riding in the same railroad cars. A group of citizens opposed to the black codes wanted to challenge the laws and wanted to test second-class citizenship. Homer Plessy was a willing participant as a free man of color who looked white. His great-grandmother was African.[165] Plessy purposefully boarded the 'white' car of the East Louisiana Railway on June 7, 1892, just one year prior to the Grand Isle Hurricane. Subsequently, he notified the conductor that he was one-eighth black and refused to move to the 'blacks only' car. He was arrested and paid a $500 bond to be released. The citizens of New Orleans hired Albion Winegar Tourgee, a white attorney from New York who was known for fighting for the rights of African Americans. He took the case though the court system in Louisiana for the four-year haul. Plessy was found guilty. Not to be dissuaded, they appealed the case to the Supreme Court of the United States, which reached the same devastating conclusion.[166] But this verdict would end up with more lasting consequences than simply upholding a guilty verdict.

The decision in *Plessy* provided the green light for de jure segregation in Louisiana and around the country. Astonishingly, the Court held that the Louisiana statute providing for separate railway cars for "white and colored races" did not violate the Constitution; and the Court cited the Civil Rights Cases of 1883 as precedent where "refusing accommodations to colored people" did not "impose a badge of slavery or servitude."[167] Condoning the separation of the "races," the Court said:

> A statute which implies merely a legal distinction between the white and colored races—a distinction which is founded in the color of the two races, and

> which must always exist so long as white men are distinguished from the other race by color—has no tendency to destroy the legal equality of the two races, or re-establish a state of involuntary servitude.

Justice Brown, writing for the majority, addressed the constitutionality of the law under the Fourteenth Amendment:

> [The purpose of the amendment] was undoubtedly to enforce the absolute equality of the two races before the law, but in the nature of things it could not have been intended to abolish distinctions based upon color, or to enforce social, as distinguished from political equality, or a commingling of the two races upon terms unsatisfactory to either. Laws permitting, and even requiring, their separation in places where they are liable to be brought into contact do not necessarily imply the inferiority of either race to the other, and have been generally, if not universally, recognized as within the competency of the state legislatures in the exercise of their police power.[168]

Detrimental to the case—and, consequently, to American society itself—were problems in the legal argument, including inter alia, challenging the law under an interstate commerce claim (this was not applicable because the train traveled only within the state), and claiming deprivation of property. In a ghastly description of what "property" actually included, the Court pronounced:

> If he be a white man, and assigned to a colored coach, he may have his action for damages . . . for being deprived of his so-called "property." Upon the other hand, if he be a colored man, and be so assigned, he has been deprived of no property, since he is not lawfully entitled to the reputation of being a white man.[169]

It is inconceivable that there would be a legal right, an entitlement, to the "reputation" of being a "white man" when it is clearly congenital, that is, outside one's ability to choose. The result and reality of the *Plessy* case was that African Americans (and consequently, as a result of distorted logic, it would later apply to "non-whites" overall) had gained freedom from slavery in name only. For all intents and purposes, they were relegated to a second-class level of citizenship sanctioned by the nation's highest Court authority. The decision is a major failure of the Supreme Court of the United States. Its only saving grace was the lone dissenting opinion penned by Justice Marshall Harlan:

> There is no caste here. Our constitution is color-blind, and neither knows nor tolerates classes among citizens. In respect of civil rights, all citizens are equal before the law. The humblest is the peer of the most powerful. The law regards man as man, and takes no account of his surroundings or of his color when his civil rights as guaranteed by the supreme law of the land are involved . . . The destinies of the two races, in this country, are indissolubly linked together, and the interests of both require that the common government of all shall not permit the seeds of race hate to be planted under the sanction of law. What can more certainly arouse race hate, what more certainly create and perpetuate a feeling of distrust between these races, than state enactments which, in fact, proceed on the ground that colored citizens are so inferior and degraded that they cannot be allowed to sit in public coaches occupied by white citizens? That, as all will admit, is the real meaning of such legislation as was enacted in Louisiana.[170]

Justice Harlan's discussion on the possible lengths to which segregationists might go was nearly prophetic:

> If a State can prescribe, as a rule of civil conduct, that whites and blacks shall not travel as passengers in the same railroad coach, why may it not so regulate the use of the streets of its cities and towns as to compel white citizens to keep on one side of a street and black citizens to keep on the other? Why may it not, upon like grounds, punish whites and blacks who ride together in streetcars or in open vehicles on a public road or street? Why may it not require sheriffs to assign whites to one side of a courtroom and blacks to the other? And why may it not also prohibit the commingling of the two races in the galleries of legislative halls or in public assemblages convened for the consideration of the political questions of the day? Further, if this statute of Louisiana is consistent with the personal liberty of citizens, why may not the State require the separation in railroad coaches of native and naturalized citizens of the United States, or of Protestants and Roman Catholics? The answer given at the argument to these questions was that regulations of the kind they suggest would be unreasonable, and could not, therefore, stand before the law.[171]

Sure enough, with white supremacy now firmly institutionalized and permanently branded into the American psyche by *Plessy*, this provided fertile ground for extensive Jim Crow laws to thrive across the nation and would serve as the model nearly the entire world used in its treatment of those who were socially undesirable.[172] The laws in Louisiana (and other southern states) were now all-encompassing.

In 1917, the Supreme Court of the United States addressed racial discrimination in housing, in *Buchanan v. Warley*, when it answered the question of whether a Louisville, Kentucky, ordinance restricting the sale of property from a white man "to a colored man" was constitutionally permissible.[173] The Court invalidated the ordinance as an illegitimate exercise of state police power with respect to a property owner's right to dispose of property and a violation of the Fourteenth Amendment.[174]

During this period (1900–1923), Louisiana was struck by nearly a dozen hurricanes and other storms, all of which repeated earlier tales of destruction. Two occurred in 1909. Three years later, in 1912, Louisiana passed housing statutes similar to the one at issue in the *Buchanan* decision, but, despite the Court's striking down the Kentucky ordinance, Louisiana continued the practice. After six more devastating storms (1915–1923), in 1924, Louisiana specifically denied permits to build "Negro houses in white communities," thus keeping its residential areas segregated.[175] Louisiana Act 117 of 1912 authorized municipalities to withhold permits for white or "Negro" houses under certain circumstances. Furthermore, Louisiana Act 118 of 1924 prohibited "white persons from establishing a home residence in a Negro community" and "negroes from establishing a home residence in a white community." Any person in violation of these laws was threatened with arrest and prosecution for the misdemeanor. The Constitution of Louisiana 1913 explicitly established separation of the black and white races. For example, Louisiana would provide "schools for white and colored races separately established by the General Assembly, throughout the State."[176] Later, the 1921 state constitution denied property ownership, including rental property, to noncitizens.[177] Additionally, it prohibited "the housing of Negro and white families in the same dwelling house."[178] In upholding the Acts, the Supreme Court of Louisiana, in *Tyler v. Harmon*, explained the law:

> The statute makes it unlawful, in such municipalities, for any white person to establish his residence on any property located in a negro community without the written consent of a majority of the negroes inhabiting the community, or for any negro to establish his residence on any property located in a white community without the written consent of a majority of the white persons inhabiting the community.[179]

In 1926, the law was challenged in *Land Development Co. of Louisiana v. City of New Orleans*, where the property owner/development company complained that New Orleans deprived it of use and enjoyment of property by refusing to allow rentals by "Negroes."[180] A temporary restraining order was issued. Unfortunately, because the federal court found the developer did not have standing to challenge the ordinance, the issue of constitutionality was not addressed. Instead, the court dismissed the case and found:

> The plaintiff corporation *does not declare itself composed of other than persons of the white race or of being discriminated against because of the color of its officers and stockholders*; nor is it charged that the ordinance deprives it of any right in or to its property, except only the right to rent it to third persons who are negroes . . .
>
> There is but a vague suggestion of complainant's clear right to obtain relief by injunction. If the case had been filed by a Negro tenant, whose right to occupancy of leased property was in jeopardy, the right to claim equitable relief would more clearly appear. There is presented here, however, what, in effect, amounts to a vicarious appearance by the owner of property, who seemingly pretends to champion the rights of undisclosed third persons, vaguely asserting, in itself, a right that is so doubtful that a court of equity should not assume to enforce or defend it by injunction. Complainant's interest seems too remote to give it a standing in court for such purpose.[181]

New Orleans, as it is well known, was and continues to be vulnerable to even heavy rains so much so that it lived in a time frame based on flood years not actual years. The city did not need a full-fledged hurricane to become inundated. In 1927, nature would again reclaim her land. After months of heavy rains that expanded the length of the Mississippi, many levees along its route were breached. Parts of Arkansas, Illinois, Kentucky, Mississippi, Missouri, Tennessee, and Louisiana were severely flooded, with the waters rising as high as 30 to 100 feet in various states to create lakes where previously there were none.[182]

Dubbed America's Greatest Flood, the flooding covered a total of 27,000 square miles; displaced 700,000 people; and killed 250.[183] Economic losses amounted to between $250 and $350 million.[184] Then, on a rainy day in April, on Good Friday, the New Orleans area soaked up an additional 15 inches of rain. Out of fear of levee breaches, it was decided by the powers that be to dynamite the Caernarvon levee but not before evacuating some 10,000 people. The rumbling of the thrashing water could be heard nearly one mile away.[185] New Orleans stood amidst four feet of water. But the segregated Lower Ninth Ward and most of St. Bernard and Plaquemines Parishes were decimated, an "unavoidable expense" to save the business districts and white neighborhoods on higher ground. These destitute communities were literally "hung out to dry." In what would become a familiar and nauseating scene, people by the *hundreds of thousands*, predominantly African Americans, desperately waited on their rooftops for rescue from the flood—some for days, some for weeks. Months would pass before the parishes were able to dry. Incredibly, African Americans were forced—yet again, just like the slaves before them—to rebuild the levee system, a system built and destroyed by man.[186]

In 1932, just five years after the "Great Flood," in a region where the search for housing was desperate, living accommodations for African Americans were further restricted by Louisiana's state code, which dictated that "no person or corporation shall rent an apartment in an apartment house or other like structure to a person who is not of the same race as the other occupants."[187] The Louisiana codes prohibited "Negro and White" families from living in the same dwelling place; and *40 years later*, in *McCain v. Davis*, the statutes were found to be in violation of the Equal Protection Clause and were finally repealed in 1972.[188]

Residential patterns were and continued to be very different in the New Orleans area compared to other cities in the United States because African Americans and whites lived in close proximity due to lack of space and the availability, or lack thereof, housing. Because of its status as a major slave port, New Orleans's population was predominantly African American (representing more than 50 percent of the population).[189] Therefore, the region did not have restricted neighborhoods in the usual sense of the term during this period. Daphne Spain explained: "The rigid caste/race system defined social distance when physical distance was lacking."[190] Historically, whites preferred to keep close watch over their slaves because African Americans were distrusted; and this created what is known as a "backyard pattern." For survival's sake, whites and African Americans lived in close proximity but by the 1940s, once freeways and highways were built, whites began leaving in droves to segregate themselves from the African-American community.[191]

History demonstrated that the rhetorical positions of the political theorists and government officials of the day controlled the citizens and greatly influenced social conduct. Indeed, they chiseled their viewpoints into the stone tablets of the law for the people to abide by lest they suffer the consequences. It was a rhetoric rooted in dehumanization and transmitted via white supremacy—the complete domination and subjugation of African Americans by relegating them to second-class citizenship by depriving them entirely of their status as human beings—a position totally contrary to the values of Christianity they claimed to espouse. Their thoughts, words, and deeds were in disharmony, as it was impossible for happiness and justice to survive. It instead allowed prejudice, inequality, and discrimination to thrive, which continues to persist.

Predating its birth, slavery and white supremacy deeply scarred probably no another nation on earth more greatly than the United States of America, a nation that continues to struggle with race relations. The official and traditional mottos adopted by the United States are paradoxical to its legal and cultural history: E Pluribus Unum (Latin for "Out of Many, One"—adopted by an act of Congress in 1782 but not codified into law) and In God We Trust (adopted by statute in 1956).[192] The failure of Reconstruction, the institution of Jim Crow laws, the decision in *Plessy*, African-American voter disenfranchisement, and acts of mob violence by whites reached a boiling point throughout the country, particularly in the South.

The 19th century showcased a complete domination of white males in American government. A mere 18 African Americans served in the U.S. House of Representatives during this era, though they did not begin serving until 1869 because prior to that time, African Americans were considered chattel and consequently were not deemed human. In the last 30 years of the 19th century, such representation (or rather lack thereof) *amounted to approximately one African-American representative every two years.* In this period, certainly, no African Americans served in the U.S. Senate. During this period, no African American was appointed as secretary of state or to any other cabinet position. No African American served on any jury or was a judge in *any court.* There were not even any African-American mayors of major American cities. To date, only white males have *ever* served as vice president of the United States, and, by the end of the 20th century, only white males held the highest government position: President of the United States.

At the time of *Plessy*, Justice Harlan—that lone dissenter—had a three-year-old grandson—his namesake, John Marshall Harlan II, who would follow in the justice's footsteps with his own appointment to the Supreme Court of the United States. Fifty-eight years after that devastating ruling, Harlan II would live to see his grandfather's opinion used to create new law: "separate was inherently unequal"[193] in the landmark case *Brown v. Board of Education.*[194]

Chapter 2

From Jim Crow to the Civil Rights Movement

I shall not undertake to interpret for Your Honors
the scope and weight of your own opinions . . . certainly
this Court has spoken in the most clear and unmistakable terms
to the effect that this segregation is not unlawful . . .
I respectfully submit to the Court,
there is no reason assigned here why this Court
or any other should reverse the findings of ninety years.[1]

—Attorney John W. Davis, representing the defense in
Brown v. Board of Education of Topeka, Kansas,
1952 argument before the Supreme Court of the United States to
let the ruling in Plessy *stand*

With the sanction of the "separate but equal" doctrine handed down from the Supreme Court of the United States, the road was paved for continued, extensive, and unfathomable levels of segregation. The Court would use the *Plessy* decision as precedent for the (lesser-known) 1908 case of *Berea College v. Kentucky*,[2] which dealt with a Kentucky statute that forbade the operation of schools that were not segregated.[3] The Court ruled in *Berea* that the state indeed had the authority to keep its schools segregated by race. Again, as in *Plessy*, Justice Harlan dissented. Perhaps indignant or sarcastic, he questioned state court precedent: "Are we to attribute such folly to legislators? . . . [that the] state [may] forbid *all* teaching of the two races together, in the same institution at the same time, no matter by whom the teaching was done." Harlan further pronounced: "I am of opinion that . . . the [Kentucky] statute is an arbitrary invasion of the rights of liberty and property guaranteed by the Fourteenth Amendment against hostile state action, and is therefore void."

The Battle against Separation

Unfortunately, in the years that followed *Plessy* and *Berea*, Louisiana (which, of course, was not existing in a vacuum within America), with the stamps of judicial approval, enacted additional statutes providing for the separation of races in education (1898), all public accommodations (1908), and prisons (1918).[4] The federal government also set out its own segregation programs in 1913 under Woodrow Wilson's administration, which initiated "government-wide segregation of work places, rest rooms, and lunch rooms."[5] The U.S. military continued to be segregated throughout World War I and World War II. It was not until 1948 that President Truman signed Executive Order 9981 to officially desegregate the armed forces. The world wars contributed to the increased number of enlisted African-American men.

Within Jim Crow society, which persisted legally until the end of the 1960s, African Americans were called by their first names, nigger, or colored and were never addressed as Mr., Mrs., or Miss. On the other hand, African Americans were expected to address whites formally—for example, Mr. Smith, Mrs. Jones, or Miss Grant—or to address white females by a title followed by the first name—for example, Miss Mary. Titles for authority figures were even more extensive—for example, Sir, Mr. Sheriff Sir. Utterly disrespected by whites, black adult men were often called boy and grown women girl, a continuation of the degradation from the time of slavery when adult runaways were sought after in newspapers describing them as such. African Americans were expected to step aside on sidewalks to let whites pass, give up their place in line, give up their seats on buses. They were relegated to the backs of restaurants and public transportation, and they were not to look whites directly in the eye as part of this degrading subservience, paradoxically referred to as social etiquette rooted in statutes. African Americans could not shake hands with whites because it implied social equality, and a black man could not physically touch a white woman lest he risk being charged with rape. Signs in city parks read "No dogs, No Negroes, No Mexicans"; restaurants posted signs directing "Colored served in the rear," if they would serve African Americans at all; and "White only" signs were the standard.

African-American musicians played to segregated audiences, which were separated by red velvet ropes or other markers, and that was only if they were allowed to play in front of whites at all. Those clubs and theaters that were designated for African Americans were said to be part of the "chitlin' circuit" (a name derived from the word "chitterlings," pig intestines, which were given to slaves to eat because the slave master and his family ate the pig—thus the negative connotation). All of this was part of the segregation that began in the 19th century. Many artists who worked the chitlin' circuit became well known and still perform today.[6] In New Orleans, the chitlin' circuit could be found on South Rampart Street.[7] Even the Catholic Church created a segregated parish in downtown New Orleans, the Congregation of Corpus Christi.[8] As these examples demonstrate, Jim Crow was fully cemented and all encompassing in the 20th century.

The effects of Jim Crow segregation and the social caste system were profound, indeed devastating. According to Delores Thompson Aaron, an African American and lifelong resident of New Orleans who was an educator during this period at Mc Donogh 35, the first high school for African Americans in Louisiana, a "competitive spirit" was drilled by parents and teachers, "always using white people as the standard." However, because of this system of perpetual and pervasive apartheid, even "middle-class black[s]" or "light-skinned blacks" believed they were superior to lower-class, darker African Americans and could be "condescending."[9] Still, people like Aaron knew they would not be accepted by whites or blacks.[10]

With public educational systems clearly separated by law in 17 southern states, Louisiana among them, the differences in funding, educational materials, and curricula prepared African Americans for a life subservient to whites for generations to come.[11] This existence motivated many African Americans to migrate north and to build schools in their own communities supported by their own limited funding, particularly historically black colleges and universities (HBCUs).[12] Still, even within the "black community," there was dissension. The two most prominent African-American educators of the time were Booker T. Washington[13] and W. E. B. Du Bois,[14] who openly demonstrated the polarities of the issues related to segregation and second-class citizenship. For civil rights activists of the day, challenging this pathological system, one that was engrained in both white and nonwhite society, would prove to be agonizing.

While *Plessy* is known for the giving green light to segregation, it can also be argued that the decision sparked the Civil Rights Movement during the 20th century (along with *Brown*). The National Association for the Advancement of Colored People (NAACP) was founded in 1909, just 13 years after *Plessy*, to advance civil rights.[15] The organization's Legal Defense and Educational Fund made the greatest impact in attacking the separate but equal doctrine. From the 1930s, psychologists and social scientists, most notably Howard University professor Charles H. Thompson, argued that segregation created a stigma for African Americans. Thompson's research was critical for NAACP attorneys. Determined to eradicate the doctrine throughout the South, the organization's legal strategy involved challenging segregation throughout the South (on a state and federal level) on the battlefield of higher education, where it would likely have the most success, and, hopefully, have a trickle-down effect. Other organizations such as the Congress of Racial Equality (CRE; established in 1942), the Southern Christian Leadership Conference (SCLC; established in 1957), and the Student Nonviolent Coordinating Committee (SNCC; established in 1960) were instrumental in bringing about societal changes during and following *Brown* with a commitment to nonviolence.[16]

Bit by bit, the NAACP began to chisel away at the unconstitutionality of segregation by setting important precedents. This was a necessary strategy because the courts traditionally base current decisions on previous opinions (known as stare decisis) and rarely step away from that to create new law. Once the NAACP established precedent, they would have the litany of case law necessary to argue the main issue, which was that separate was inherently unequal. Additionally, the organization strategized that if it appeared to be adhering to the separate but equal doctrine, it could force the states to create equal facilities or, more likely, to integrate facilities. It was a logical strategy because fiscally, it would be difficult for the states to perpetuate segregation. The best place to start the campaign would be in schools.

First, in 1938, the Supreme Court of the United States held in *Missouri ex rel. Gaines v. Canada* that "when a state furnish[ed] legal education" to whites and did not provide the same to "negroes," it was considered "discrimination repugnant to the Fourteenth Amendment."[17] Still, while schools were to "furnish substantially equal advantages to negro residents," the education did not have to be provided by "the same schools." Thus, that ruling did not eliminate separate facilities.

While the NAACP was focused on its desegregation campaign, other issues also concerned the organization, particularly lynching. In 1946, Alexander Pierre (A. P.) Tureaud,[18] the only African-American lawyer in Louisiana at the time, was asked to lead the NAACP's investigation of the lynching of Corporal John C. Jones, an honorably discharged World War II army veteran.

Tucked away in the piney woods of northwest Louisiana lays the town of Minden.[19] It was here that Jones was accused of "prowling" the house of a white female. Minden police released Jones and his 17-year-old cousin, Albert Harris Jr., to a mob—not an unusual practice in the South—who drove the two to a nearby creek. The mob stripped the two men, forced them to lie down naked, and beat them with sticks. Jones died at the scene; Harris survived. The incident sparked unprecedented federal support, the first of its kind in Louisiana; and the Federal Bureau of Investigations (FBI) conducted its own investigation. Unfortunately—but not surprisingly—"the trial failed to achieve any prosecutions."[20] With an all-white jury, Jim Crow prevailed.[21]

Additional cases were brought through the court system to challenge segregation in other areas. One of the landmark cases of the Supreme Court of the United States during this time was *Shelley v. Kraemer* in 1948. The case, combined two individual cases out of Missouri and Michigan, required the Court to answer the question of the constitutionality of court enforcement of private agreements (restrictive covenants), which excluded persons based on race or color.[22] The Court held that the restrictions were unconstitutional because although the contracts were between private individuals, there was *judicial enforcement* of the contracts amounting to a "state action" committing a violation of equal protection:

> It cannot be doubted that among the civil rights intended to be protected from discriminatory state action by the Fourteenth Amendment are the rights to acquire, enjoy, own and dispose of property. Equality in the enjoyment of property rights was regarded by the framers of that Amendment as an essential pre-condition to the realization of other basic civil rights and liberties which the Amendment was intended to guarantee.[23] . . . [Thus] in granting judicial enforcement of the restrictive agreements in these cases, the States have denied petitioners the equal protection of the laws and that, therefore, the action of the state courts cannot stand.[24]

Still, *Shelley* and other decisions did not stop state officials, judges, and law enforcement personnel (or society in general, for that matter) from perpetuating segregationist theory and policy. The earlier *Gaines* decision was reaffirmed in a short opinion by the Court 10 years later in the case of *Sipuel v. Regents of the University of Oklahoma* (332 U.S. 631 [1948]). Sipuel, a qualified applicant, was denied admission to the law school at the University of Oklahoma solely based on the color of her skin.

Despite some gains in college admission, after the *Sipuel* decision, segregation continued to persist pursuant to the mandate of state laws. Often state laws considered it a misdemeanor to maintain, operate, teach at, or attend a school where both whites and "Negroes" were enrolled or taught (a harkening back to the days of slavery wherein slaves were forbidden to learn how to read or write).[25] "Black" colleges and universities established by the states were inferior, lacking accreditation, a sufficient number of faculty, and appropriate educational materials. Some states continued to deny admission to "Negroes." Admitted "Negro" graduate students were often relegated to seats in rows marked "Reserved for Colored" and sat at separate tables in libraries and cafeterias: the foundation for the cases of *McLaurin v. Oklahoma State Board of Regents* (339 U. S. 637 [1950])[26] and *Sweatt v. Painter* (339 U. S. 629 [1950]),[27] respectively.

The Court held in *McLaurin* that restrictions found in the segregation of seating and social situations at the college level impaired and inhibited a student's "ability to study, to engage in discussions and exchange views with other students, and, in general, to learn his profession." Therefore, the policies and state law were found to be unconstitutional within the meaning of the Fourteenth Amendment.[28] Furthermore, in *Sweatt* (a Texas case), the Court did not "find substantial equality in the educational opportunities offered to white and 'Negro' law students by the State [of Texas]." There were significant differences, according to the Court, in "faculty, variety of courses and opportunity for specialization, size of the student body, scope of the library, [etc.]." The Court held that the colleges were substantially unequal and therefore, "the Equal Protection Clause of the Fourteenth Amendment requires that [Negroes] be admitted" to the "superior" school, which was white.[29] Just prior to *Brown*, in response to a pending lawsuit, Louisiana State University (LSU) abolished segregation and enrolled its first African-American student in 1953.[30] Those earlier cases created the foundation necessary for the case of *Brown v. Board of Education*, which almost immediately followed the *McLaurin* and *Sweatt* decisions.

Brown[31] (a "class-action"[32] suit) stemmed group of five individual cases from the states of Kansas, South Carolina, Virginia, and Delaware, and it challenged segregated elementary schools. "Negro" children were denied admission to public schools solely because of their race in each instance. The cases began in 1949 but were not heard by the Supreme Court of the United States until 1952. They were reheard in 1953 because the justices on the Court were divided on the issue and could not reach a decision.[33] The Court was forced to deal directly with the societal effects of segregation and the symptomology of dehumanization, rather than arguments over tangible issues such as buildings, seating, curriculum, and salaries.[34] Thurgood Marshall,[35] chief legal counsel for the NAACP, presented evidence relating to the psychological effects of segregation. This evidence included research on the issue by prominent social psychologist Kenneth Clark,[36] an African American. Clark's findings were endorsed by 35 leading social scientists of the day.[37]

Marshall would use leading modern studies and other findings to argue that segregated education was psychologically harmful to "black" children and amounted to "a denial of equal protection under law," which was mandated by the Fourteenth Amendment. In essence, Marshall argued that segregation is "inherently unequal." In a unanimous decision, the Court formally struck down the *Plessy* decision. Chief Justice Earl Warren delivered the opinion:

> Whatever may have been the extent of psychological knowledge at the time of *Plessy v. Ferguson*, this finding [that segregation is inherently unequal] is amply supported by modern authority. Any language[38] in *Plessy v. Ferguson* contrary to this finding is rejected. We conclude that, in the field of public education, the doctrine of "separate but equal" has no place. Separate educational facilities are inherently unequal . . . We have now announced that such segregation is a denial of the equal protection of the laws.[39]

Massive Resistance

The Court would later order that desegregation occur "with all deliberate speed"[40] because, despite the ruling that separate "was inherently unequal" and that segregation was "a denial of equal protection," Louisiana, demonstrating its insolence (along with other states) brazenly continued to pass segregationist policy. The plague encompassed America when "segregationists played on the fears and prejudices of their communities and launched a militant campaign of defiance and resistance," effective immediately.[41] With fervor, Louisiana state legislators drafted and instituted more statutes.

In 1954, Louisiana's state constitution provided that all elementary and other public schools would be operated separately for white and African-American children. The penalty for noncompliance was $500 to $1,000 and imprisonment from three to six months.

In 1956, two years after *Brown*, firms were prohibited from permitting integration on their premises that involved any dancing, social functions, other entertainment, athletic training, games, sports, or contests. Implausibly, at the same time, Louisiana revised its laws to pre-*Plessy* by requiring that common transportation carriers provide separate waiting rooms for white intrastate passengers and for "Negro" intrastate and interstate passengers. An employment statute provided that all persons, firms, and corporations create separate bathroom facilities for members of the "white and Negro races" employed by them or permitted to come upon their premises.

In addition, separate eating places in separate rooms as well as separate eating and drinking utensils were to be provided for members of the "white and Negro races." The penalty for violation was a misdemeanor; a fine of $100 to $1,000; and 60 days to one year imprisonment. All public parks, recreation centers, playgrounds, and so on were segregated. This provision was supposedly made "for the purpose of protecting the public health, morals and the peace and good order in the state and not because of race."[42]

By 1957, all public schools in Louisiana were *required* to be racially segregated. In fact, pursuant to statute, compulsory attendance was suspended in school systems where integration was ordered, that is, the state would not force students to attend integrated classrooms. Integrated schools were not entitled to state funding. Additionally, a unique component of the segregation laws in Louisiana required the consent of the majority of persons of the opposite race for residential integration.

In 1958, Louisiana even went so far as to dictate that all human blood to be used for transfusions was to be labeled "Caucasian," "Negroid," or "Mongoloid" so as to clearly indicate the race of the donor. If the blood was not labeled, it was not permitted to be used. Furthermore, in politics in 1960, candidates running for office were required to designate their race on the ballot. All of this may seem inconceivable—perhaps even absurd—to many people today.

Before Martin Luther King Jr. became famous for speeches, bus boycotts, marches, and sit-ins to oppose segregation and promotions of equality, there was Baton Rouge—the place of the first successful boycott in the 1950s.[43] According to the Hill Memorial Library at LSU, "this event became a blueprint for the more publicized boycott to take place two years later in Montgomery, Alabama, which involved Rosa Parks and Martin Luther King, Jr.; and it set the stage for desegregation in the Deep South."[44]

In the early 1950s, it was illegal for African Americans to own buses in Louisiana, which—along with enforced segregation on buses—led to the boycott.

Louisiana attorney A. P. Tureaud filed suit to desegregate New Orleans's city parks; and his winning cases against LSU in the 1950s (before *Brown*) forced the university to admit African-American students. He also represented three students in Baton Rouge who had been arrested for disturbing the peace during a sit-in; and his win legalized protests at segregated businesses.

The Louisiana legislature never attempted to hide its intent of racial discrimination; and, as late as 1960, it stated in a joint resolution that "Louisiana has always maintained a policy of segregation of the races; and . . . it is the intention of the citizens of this sovereign state that such a policy be continued."[45] Discriminatory intent was also addressed in court opinions, including that of the Supreme Court of the United States in the case of *Garner v. State of LA* (1961): *"Segregation is basic to the structure of Louisiana as a community; the custom that maintains it is at least as powerful as any law."*[46]

Massive resistance followed the *Brown* decision[47] as schools refused to desegregate throughout the country—including in Louisiana. In fact, Louisiana immediately began the process of building a greater legal structure *against* desegregation. In a 10-year period (from 1954 to 1964), the Louisiana state legislature set forth an unprecedented 130-plus acts and resolutions related to segregation—twice as many as any other state.[48] Opponents of *Brown* argued that the Court overextended its reach into states' rights and criticized the decision as judicial activism. Those at the highest rungs of government generated great public outcry over the Court's opinion. In 1956, members of Congress (both in the House of Representatives and the Senate) drafted and signed the Declaration of Constitutional Principles, commonly known as the Southern Manifesto.[49] Arguing that there was no violation of the Fourteenth Amendment (in *Brown*) and relying on centuries-old white supremacist values and the continued legal and social pathology of the nation and its states:

> [E]very one of the *26 States*[50] *that had any substantial racial differences among its people*, either approved the operation of segregated schools *already in existence* or subsequently established such schools . . . [and the] "separate but equal" [principle is] "within the discretion of the State in regulating its public schools and does not conflict with the 14th Amendment . . . there

> has been no constitutional amendment or act of Congress changing this established legal principle almost a century old.

Even more disturbing, the manifesto, which was almost identical to the views espoused by John Calhoun in the previous century, claimed that eliminating segregation "is destroying the amicable relations between the white and Negro races that have been created through 90 years of patient effort by the good people of both races. It has planted hatred and suspicion where there has been heretofore friendship and understanding." Signed by 19 members of the U.S. Senate (including both senators from Louisiana) and 63 members of the U.S. House of Representatives (eight from Louisiana), the document reeked of the warped sense of the so-called paternalistic values of slave masters past.

The Terrorism Continues

Racial violence in America reached its peak in the years after *Brown*. As civil rights activists used the decision as motivation to conduct nonviolent protests, segregationists used violence in an effort to terrorize African Americans and activists into subservience. Segregationists bombed houses and churches, killing scores of innocent people, including children. Civil rights activists paid the ultimate price—assassination by white supremacists.

The year after *Brown*, Emmett Till a 14-year-old African-American boy, traveled to visit relatives in Mississippi and was savagely lynched and murdered by Roy Bryant and Bryant's half-brother. Providing an example of the routine vigilante justice perpetuated by white supremacists, Till was killed for allegedly flirting with Bryant's wife. Bryant and his accomplice beat Till, gouged out an eye, and shot him in the head before using barbed wire to wrap a cotton gin fan around Till's neck and dumping his body in the Tallahatchie River. Both defendants were acquitted by an all-white jury and then admitted their guilt publicly without any remorse. Of course, the principle of double jeopardy would prevent the state from retrying the case.[51]

Similarly, the KKK murdered three young civil rights workers in Mississippi.[52] Referred to as the 1964 Freedom Summer killings, James Chaney, Andrew Goodman, and Michael Schwerner (then 21, 20, and 24 years old, respectively) were killed for their work in the civil rights movement that led to major reforms in access to voting, education, and public accommodations. A jury would convict Edgar Ray Killen of manslaughter in 2005, *more than 40 years after the murder.* At the time of his conviction, Killen was 80 years old. The original all-white jury, in 1967, deadlocked on the issue 11-1 in favor of conviction.

Medgar Evers, field secretary for the NAACP and civil rights activist, sought to change segregationist policies at the University of Mississippi. His application to the law school was rejected on the basis of race. In 1963, upon returning home from NAACP activities, he was shot in the back by Byron De La Beckwith, a member of the White Citizen's Council and later the KKK. Justice was not served in Evers's case until 1994, *more than 30 years after the murder*, when De La Beckwith was finally convicted for his crime.[53]

During the turbulent 1960s, the nation witnessed intense racially motivated brutality, from police attack dogs to fire hose– and baton-wielding police officers. Dozens of marchers were hospitalized after brutal assaults by police officers using tear gas, whips, and clubs.[54] The scenes provided present-day examples of tactics used by slave catchers of the past. State governors refused to desegregate schools, which prompted presidents to send in federal troops and the National Guard to support the mission of desegregation, most notably in Arkansas, Alabama, and Mississippi. When riots broke out in Mississippi because the state university admitted its first African-American student in 1962,[55] President Kennedy sent in 5,000 federal troops.

Alabama's governor George C. Wallace[56] championed white supremacist values publicly from the day of his inaugural address on January 14, 1963:

> Today I have stood, where once Jefferson Davis stood, and took an oath to my people. It is very appropriate then that from this Cradle of the Confederacy, this very Heart of the Great Anglo-Saxon Southland, that today we sound the drum for freedom as have our generations of forebears before us done, time and again down through history. Let us rise to the call of freedom-loving blood that is in us and send our answer to the tyranny that clanks its chains upon the South. In the name of the greatest people that have ever trod this earth, I draw the line in the dust and toss the gauntlet before the feet of tyranny ... and I say ... segregation now ... segregation tomorrow ... segregation forever ...
>
> And so it was meant in our racial lives ... each race, within its own framework has the freedom to teach ... to instruct ... to develop ... to ask for and receive deserved help from others of separate racial stations. This is the great freedom of our American founding fathers ... but if we amalgamate into the

> one unit as advocated by the communist philosophers . . . then the enrichment of our lives . . . the freedom for our development . . . is gone forever. We become, therefore, *a mongrel unit of one* under a single all powerful government . . . and we stand for everything . . . and for nothing.[57]

Six months later, Wallace stood in the doorway of the University of Alabama in an effort to prevent Vivian Malone and James Hood, "black students," from entering the institution. When he was confronted by federal marshals and the Alabama National Guard, he stepped aside.

Hundreds of examples reflect racial hatred, including murder, in the South during the mid-20th century. Almost all involved the KKK and Klan sympathizers within local law enforcement agencies.[58] Civil rights–era murder cases from Louisiana include Frank Morris of Ferriday,[59] Carrie Brumfield of Franklinton,[60] and O'Neal Moore of Varnado.[61] Frank Morris, a "shoe shop owner, died after the arson of his business in December 1964. An investigation by the *Concordia Sentinel* named the late Concordia Parish chief deputy Frank De Laughter, who was later convicted for police brutality in 1970, and quoted relatives fingering two men, one dead and the other from Rayville, Louisiana."[62]

Carrie Brumfield was "found shot to death in his car on September 12, 1967, on a deserted rural road, according to the Southern Poverty Law Center." O'Neal Moore was "one of two black deputies hired to appease civil rights demands in Washington Parish, according to the New Roads Daily. Moore and his partner, Creed Rogers, were shot on June 2, 1965, from another car while on patrol. Moore was killed and Rogers was wounded, losing the sight of one eye." The FBI reopened these cold cases in 2012, *nearly 50 years later*, in an effort to solve them.[63]

Not unlike the dissension between Du Bois and Washington some 50 years earlier, the African-American community was divided between advocating for nonviolent resistance and black nationalism. This time Martin Luther King Jr. and Malcolm X demonstrated the polarities. The suffering of those who had spent generations as second-class citizens was execrable as the struggle became a public disgrace in the media, and for the first time, instant visual evidence via television. The pain is best described in King's "Letter from a Birmingham Jail," which was written in 1963, nearly 10 years after the *Brown* decision:

> Perhaps it is easy for those who have never felt the stinging darts of segregation to say, "Wait." But when you have seen vicious mobs lynch your

> mothers and fathers at will and drown your sisters and brothers at whim; when you have seen hate-filled policemen curse, kick and even kill your black brothers and sisters; . . . see the vast majority of your twenty-million Negro brothers smothering in an airtight cage of poverty in the midst of an affluent society. . . . when you are forever fighting a degenerating sense of "nobodiness"—then you will understand why we find it difficult to wait.[64]

Successes of the period included the passages of the Twenty-Fourth Amendment,[65] the Civil Rights Act of 1964, and the Voting Rights Act of 1965. However, race riots continued around the country: Los Angeles, Detroit, New York, Newark, and, as expected, New Orleans. Outrage against abuses of African Americans poured out from communities and led to the rise of such movements as black nationalism, Afro-centrism, and black power. Malcolm X, considered one of the greatest leaders and activists of the 20th century, particularly decried the American pacifists, both black and white. During his tenure with the Nation of Islam,[66] Malcolm X referred to whites as "devils," and his descriptive terms for African Americans included "field negroes,"[67] "house negroes,"[68] and "Uncle Toms."[69] He would later recant his offensive terms describing whites and blacks.[70] Like many others who spoke forcefully against white supremacy, he was demonized and eventually paid the ultimate price—assassination. Though he was criticized and accused of being a reverse racist, he was never associated with actual violence. Still, Malcolm X sent an important message to the masses, an unapologetic truth that harkened back to the time when African Americans were deemed less than human. His was a haunting sentiment during the 1960s:

> We declare our right on this earth to be a man, to be a human being, to be respected as a human being, to be given the rights of a human being in this society, on this earth, in this day, which we intend to bring into existence by any means necessary.[71]

The Campaign for Equality

Admitting that legislation alone was not effective in maintaining equality, President Johnson issued Executive Order 11246, which enforced affirmative action for the first time. Government contractors were now required to take affirmative action in the hiring and employment of minorities. In addition, Johnson signed the Civil Rights Act of 1968 to prohibit discrimination in the sale, rental, and financing of housing to nonwhites. The same year, the Supreme Court of the United States decided *Jones v. Mayer Co.*, another Missouri case wherein a "Negro" was denied the opportunity to purchase a home because of his race.

In *Jones*, the Court would review whether the federal law, 42 U.S.C. 1982,[72] was constitutional but would not address the Fair Housing Act within the Civil Rights Act of 1968. Section 1982 provided: "All citizens of the United States shall have the same right, in every State and Territory, as is enjoyed by white citizens thereof to inherit, purchase, lease, sell, hold, and convey real and personal property."[73] Lower courts previously held that the statute did not reach individuals and applied only to state entities. The Court found otherwise and held that "*1982 bars all racial discrimination, private as well as public*, in the sale or rental of property, and that the statute, thus construed, is a valid exercise of the power of Congress to enforce the Thirteenth Amendment."

Any observer of the period would call the 1960s anarchic. Blood was shed at the highest levels—the assassinations of President John F. Kennedy, Malcolm X, Robert Kennedy, and Martin Luther King Jr. occurred during this period. A. P. Tureaud, the only practicing African-American attorney in Louisiana from 1937 until 1947 handled nearly all of the desegregation and other civil rights cases filed in in the state of Louisiana from the early 1940s through the 1960s. He successfully obtained equal pay for Louisiana's African-American teachers; worked for the college admission of qualified students regardless of color; fought against segregation in busing, parks, airports, and other public facilities; and successfully defended one of the first sit-in cases before the Supreme Court of the United States.[74] As a Louisiana attorney for nearly 50 years, Tureaud's contributions to desegregation and civil rights in Louisiana were massive. In 1969, he succeeded in the case of *Hubbard v. Tannehill*, thus banning Louisiana textbooks that supported white racial superiority. Tureaud's son explained the pain of living in segregated Louisiana:

> I left Louisiana in 1960 because I didn't want to be restricted in anything that I wanted to do as a person of color. Growing up in 1930s, 1940s, and 1950s, and having to travel and not have a place to stay, having to sit in segregated train cars, having to buy gasoline at the gas station and [then] go into the bushes to [relieve myself instead of] us[ing] the restroom, and go to back windows to buy food as we went from state to state, those were all demeaning experiences. We were segregated in every aspect of our lives.[75]

Orleans was the first parish to desegregate in Louisiana. In fact, it was here in 1960 that Ruby Bridges, then six years old, became the first African-American child to attend an all-white school in the entire South. The community response was deplorable. To protect her from the mobs, federal marshals escorted Ruby five blocks to the school. Immediately after "little Ruby" entered William Frantz Elementary School, white parents removed their children. Forty years later Ruby described her impressions:

> [White parents were] ... rushing their children out of the school. In the uproar I never got to my classroom ... I tried not to pay attention to the mob. Someone had a black doll in a coffin, and that scared me more than the nasty things people screamed at us [black children].[76]

Some teachers refused to remain at William Frantz Elementary School if an African-American child was enrolled. One educator, "Mrs. Henry," agreed to teach Ruby; and, for one year, Ruby was the only student in the class. Simultaneously, "three little black girls"—Leona Tate, Tessie Prevost, and Gail Etienne—on their way with the NAACP and a psychologist to integrating the all-white McDonogh No. 19 Elementary School survived the angry white mobs with their "the gauntlet of screaming, spitting racists trying to block [the children's path]." The white boycott that year "meant the girls would attend school by themselves, and the second year with only a couple dozen black children." Instead of being segregated officially by the state, African Americans remained segregated by mob rule. When Tate, Prevost, and Etienne entered third grade, their parents transferred them, integrating another Ninth Ward school, T. J. Semmes Elementary near the Industrial Canal.[77]

So hostile was the reaction from the community to desegregation and integration in New Orleans that dead animals and death threats were found in the home mailboxes of African-American first-grade students who were integrated into a Lower Ninth Ward school.[78] In some areas, whites hurled eggs at African-American students.[79] All white children were removed from the schools to boycott desegregation, but not before white mobs committed violent acts against the children.[80] According to Gail Etienne Netter, "We were all spit upon ... I had my dress ripped almost completely off of me. I was hit in the stomach with a baseball bat."[81]

As if segregationist policies and the community sentiment were not disturbing enough and the opposition to desegregation were not threatening enough, the ultimate condemnation of African Americans would be overlooked and undervalued for decades to come: "board discussions of that period include[d] speculation that black children would be better off in schools with lower test scores, so that 'they would not feel inferior.'" And that is the likely reason those schools were used to test desegregation.[82] It would prove to be fatal to the New Orleans school system into the new millennium. The lie perpetuated in the effort to make African-American children "feel [less] inferior" unequivocally resulted in the worst reality: *lower test scores became inherently linked with inferiority.* The educational system in New Orleans was doomed to complete and total failure and was a disgrace to the nation.

Self-Segregation

Following the desegregation of schools in the Lower Ninth Ward, whites moved in droves to neighboring St. Bernard Parish. White families opted out of the public school system, "abandoning it politically and economically." It was not that the public school system failed the people, but rather "the people failed the schools," according to Ken J. Saltman.[83] It left a legacy of underfunding the Orleans Public School system and contributed greatly to the failure of public education in the city. In 1950, public schools in New Orleans were segregated by law. Evidence of complete indoctrination of dehumanization was evidenced by the fact that the white population, on its own, *segregated itself* without a legal construct. Decades before President George W. Bush used the phrase, students in New Orleans were "left behind."

The "white flight" from New Orleans to this day reflects the effects of institutional segregation. More employment opportunities were available to whites in the suburbs because they packed up their businesses along with their families, thereby creating less need for low-income housing for white workers. The economic opportunities left town, effectively "shut[ting] out blacks from developing areas."[84]

While some may argue that other issues not related to desegregation were responsible for whites moving to suburbs, there is no denying that white supremacist values were at the root of it as they sought to continue the self-separation of whites and instituted regulations. Issues attributed to white flight around the nation included residential legal exclusion based on race and redlining; roads built via the National Interstate and Defense Highways Act (1956); blockbusting, which is a scheme wherein realtors would assist an African-American family in buying a house in a white neighborhood and then resell it to the *same* African-American family; urban decay; restrictive zoning committed by state entities and private developers; and, of course, desegregation policies and law.

African Americans who were financially able to move out of urban areas could not live in the suburbs, and a pervasive system known as redlining developed whereby banks and realtors refused to finance or sell homes to African Americans or, alternatively, charged African Americans more than whites for financing, providing insurance, renting, or selling residential properties. Households and businesses in these "red zones" could not get mortgages or business loans. This resulted in the devaluation of property, which in turn affected tax revenues, leaving little to cover the costs of maintaining or improving the infrastructure of African-American neighborhoods. White neighborhoods instituted racial covenants that shut African Americans out of "their" communities. Such types of racial profiling would be just as destructive as Jim Crow, perhaps even more so, since they made discrimination more difficult to prove.

In 1960, St. Bernard Parish established separate schools for whites who boycotted integration in New Orleans; and the U.S. Department of Justice targeted the parish's "political boss," Leander Perez, to halt the "evasive scheme."[85] Perez, an Isleño, served as a district judge, district attorney, and president of the Plaquemines Parish Commission Council. Known as the "Boss of the Delta," he dominated Plaquemines and St. Bernard Parishes for 50 years (from 1919 to 1969). In 1960 at a New Orleans rally in opposition to integrated schools, Perez declared: "Don't wait for your daughter to be raped by these Congolese.[86] Don't wait until the burrheads[87] are forced into your schools. Do something about it now."[88] Perez's speech inspired a hate attack on the school administration building by approximately 2,000 segregationists. Chased off by the police and fire hoses, the mob went on a rampage in the city and attacked African Americans in the streets.

Perez organized a school boycott by white residents and even threatened whites who allowed their children to attend desegregated schools. He arranged for poor whites to attend without charge a segregated private school and helped establish a whites-only private school in New Orleans. The invitation to the community sent throngs of whites from New Orleans into St. Bernard Parish schools. In 1965, *Time* magazine printed Perez's comments to the U.S. Senate Judiciary Committee as he described "what Negroes are really like." He said, "They are of immoral character ... their only interest is 'to get welfare checks ... [and] [t]hey are a low type of citizenship.' " In response to a question regarding giving African Americans the right to vote, Perez responded, "Poppycock . . . Why in a neighboring parish there were 800 registered Negroes and every damn election they've got to bribe them." Leander Perez was bold enough to say out loud what many in the apathetic racist masses could not; and he spewed: "Do you know what a Negro is? Animals right out of the jungle. Passion. Welfare. Easy life. That's the Negro. And if you don't know that, you're naïve."[89]

According to Perez, desegregation could be traced "back to all those Jews who were supposed to be cremated at Buchenwald and Dachau and weren't . . ."[90] These frightening and hateful statements by Perez and other segregationists of his time—like George Wallace, Ross Barnett, and Strom Thurmond—pandered to their audiences. Perez's tirade of hatred, segregationism, and white supremacy was unfiltered and was completely endorsed when St. Bernard Parish named a major thoroughfare in his honor, posthumously, in 1972. Today, the name of the road still remains Judge Perez Drive. Although locals say the intention changed in the 1990s to reflect the work of Judge Melvyn Perez, the signs remained the same, purportedly to avoid incurring a financial burden.[91]

By 1965, only five parishes in the entire state had submitted educational integration plans.[92] Not all members of the African-American community were happy with integration, especially when it meant closing down black schools and busing African-American children long distances into white schools like those in Baton Rouge, which is almost 37 miles from New Orleans.[93] Still, by 1967, 30 parishes made no plans to integrate their schools.[94] Until 1970, every school in Louisiana was under court order to integrate; and 45 parishes were ordered to draft and implement an integration plan.[95] It was not until the mid-1970s that all parishes submitted to integration,[96] but by that time, most white students had left New Orleans for surrounding parishes. In fact, 22 percent of the entire New Orleans population left.[97] All of these actions attributed to the disproportionate effects on African Americans, and Louisiana was no exception, particularly, following a hurricane.

In the midst of the storm of the Civil Rights Movement, a tropical cyclone developed and moved into the Gulf of Mexico. It would be the first ever tropical cyclone in America to cause $1 billion in damages; and it had a name as American as apple pie—Betsy. There would be nothing sweet about it. Nearly 45 miles south of the Mississippi Delta, Betsy's intensity peaked as a category 4 hurricane with maximum sustained winds of 155 miles per hour. Betsy made landfall at Grand Isle, Louisiana, on September 9, 1965. The eye wall covered southeastern Louisiana and New Orleans. Betsy's forces drove storm surge into Lake Pontchartrain; and the levees failed at Florida Avenue and along the Industrial Canal. Gentilly, the Upper and Lower Ninth Wards of New Orleans, Arabi, and Chalmette in St. Bernard Parish were inundated. The waves of water poured into the city; and the rooftops of houses appeared as rafts upon a river. Entire neighborhoods in St. Bernard and Plaquemines Parishes were completely wiped out. Seventy-five people were killed by the storm in Louisiana. The fishing villages of Yscloskey and Delacroix Island in St. Bernard were "washed away."[98] More than 160,000 homes were completely flooded; and it took 10 days for the waters to recede.

The day after the storm, President Johnson flew into New Orleans. He visited shelters and neighborhoods, and talked to the citizens personally. Holding a flashlight at his face and a megaphone to his lips, he promised, "My name is Lyndon Baines Johnson. I am your president. I am here to make sure you have the help you need." Johnson quickly initiated plans for an overdue levee system. Unfortunately, the U.S. Corps of Engineers did not follow through. The nation would learn, a little too late, that the design and construction were seriously flawed when they failed during Katrina, days before the fortieth anniversary of Betsy.[99]

The greatest tragedy in the wake of Betsy was neither the billions of dollars in damage nor the loss of life; rather, the greatest tragedy was the failure of the state, local, and federal governments and the members of society affected by these catastrophes to learn from the failures and effect positive and substantial changes in infrastructure and in the societal construct. Future generations, therefore, were doomed to suffer the same fate as a result of human-made problems, structural and societal, predating their own birth.

Soon after Betsy, Louisiana revived the "one drop [of Negro blood] rule," in an even stricter manner by using mathematical formulas via the "infamous" Act 46 of 1970 (LSA-R.S. 42:267), which provided:

> In signifying race, a person having one-thirty second or less of Negro blood shall not be deemed, described or designated by any public official in the state of Louisiana as "colored," a "mulatto," a "black," a "negro," a "griffe," an "Afro-American," a "quadroon," a "mestizo," a "colored person" or a "person of color."[100]

Having any more than 1/32 of "Negro" blood deemed a person as such, which included all of the degrees of hybridization. Naturally, this law was necessary to maintain segregationist policy. It was only a matter of time before it would be challenged; and, within three years, cases were brought to Louisiana's Fourth Circuit Court of Appeals.

The wife of a successful businessman wanted to change the racial classification on her birth certificate to white. She spent thousands of dollars in legal proceedings to prove it, but to no avail.[101] In 1973, in *Plaia v. Louisiana State Board of Health*, the designations would not completely fail again because the court was not faced with a constitutional question. Instead, the court found the state was unable to prove degrees of hybridization because prior to this statute, the degrees were not based on a mathematical formula. In Louisiana, no mathematical formula was used until 1970 because historically by law, "the only requirement for a designation of Negro race was that the Negro blood be traceable."[102]

The cases that challenged the formula law not only made local news, they also made national headlines. The law remained in force another 13 years, until it was repealed in 1983. It was during this time that experts determined "that the very concept of the racial classification of individuals, as opposed to that of a group, is scientifically insupportable."[103] Furthermore, research conducted by the Louisiana legislature in its efforts to repeal the law uncovered that the specific designation of race on official documents dating back to the 1700s was for the purpose of "keep[ing] control over land ownership, to keep the landowner from having to share his land with his illegitimate children who were family members.'"[104] Lee Frazier, a state legislator representing the district of New Orleans who wrote the law repealing LSA-R.S. 42:267, admitted that the attention drawn from the court cases made Louisiana "the laughingstock of the nation."[105]

Between 1965 and 1975, the residents of St. Bernard Parish were in the process of building the parish, particularly given white flight. Between 1975 and 1985, the parish expanded, and by the mid-1980s, the parish was "enjoying it[s] [growth], as everything fit together."[106] Under centuries of institutionalized dehumanization, society in its entirety manifested the symptomology of an inferiority complex. The social caste system was fully and firmly entrenched. Louisiana was among the first to deny African Americans the right to register to vote; and from birth to death, every segment of life in Louisiana (and among the southern states as a whole)—restaurants, hospitals, hotels, night clubs, street cars, amusement parks, playgrounds, schools, benches, beaches, pools, water fountains, marriages, housing, and cemeteries—was precisely segregated. Louisiana state law prohibited the cohabitation of African Americans and whites and the intermarriage (known as miscegenation[107]) of whites with those deemed nonwhite under La. Rev. Stat. § 14:79 (1950). In fact, interracial relationships with whites were criminalized in 16 states, all by statutes created between *1947 and 1966*, that is, they were not created many years ago.[108]

These directives[109] were not deemed unconstitutional until 1967 in the case of *Loving v. Virginia*,[110] when the Supreme Court of the United States held:

> Marriage is one of the "basic civil rights of man," fundamental to our very existence and survival. *Skinner v. Oklahoma*, 316 U. S. 535, 316 U. S. 541 (1942). *See also Maynard v. Hill*, 125 U. S. 190 (1888). To deny this fundamental freedom on so unsupportable a basis as the racial classifications embodied in these statutes, classifications so directly subversive of the principle of equality at the heart of the Fourteenth Amendment, is surely to deprive all the State's citizens of liberty without due process of law. The Fourteenth Amendment requires that the freedom of choice to marry not be restricted by invidious racial discriminations. Under our Constitution, the freedom to marry, or not marry, a person of another race resides with the individual, and cannot be infringed by the State.[111]

However, when the Court renders an opinion, or even when federal legislators change the law, societal opinion is unfortunately not changed overnight. In Louisiana, the antimiscegenation statute was not officially repealed until 1975, eight years after *Loving*.[112] Still, antimiscegenation sentiment remained. By the 1990s, many people who were involved in interracial marriages and other intimate relationships were ridiculed, threatened, assaulted, and often accused of having "jungle fever,"[113] a bigoted reference to the African American in the relationship being from the jungles of Africa.

By the mid-1980s, low-income African-American students made up 90 percent of the New Orleans School District.[114] The white students who boycotted the schools years earlier never returned; and the schools essentially remained all black. "The white people took their money, jobs, restaurants, and grocery stores with them. Most of them went to St. Bernard Parish . . . fewer than 3,000 white students remain in New Orleans Public schools."[115] With regard to higher education, on numerous occasions between 1965 and 2000, Louisiana was ordered to desegregate its colleges and universities. Almost 50 years after *Brown*, some school districts in

Louisiana were still refusing to fully comply.[116] Redlining paralyzed housing markets, reduced property values, and turned once thriving middle-class neighborhoods into slums. The Civil Rights Act of 1968 (also known as the Fair Housing Act) outlawed most housing discrimination and gave the U.S. Department of Housing and Urban Development (HUD) enforcement responsibility.[117] Furthermore, the Housing Act of 1968 established the Government National Mortgage Association (Ginnie Mae) to "expand availability of mortgage funds for moderate income families using government guaranteed mortgage-backed securities."[118] Unfortunately, the opportunity was lost in the New Orleans metropolitan area. From the 1930s through the 1980s, twice as many federally backed mortgages went to suburban residents as to Orleans Parish residents.[119] Housing discrimination continued.

To prove housing discrimination, plaintiffs also had to prove discriminatory intent. It took six years for the case of *Arlington Heights v. Metropolitan Housing Corp. [MHC]* to reach the Supreme Court of the United States in 1977.[120] Arlington Heights, a Chicago suburb, argued it did not allow rezoning in an effort to protect property values. The development company, MHC, and minority residents claimed discrimination and that rezoning disproportionately affected African Americans. The Court explained that MHC and the residents would have to prove "a racially discriminatory intent, as evidenced by such factors as disproportionate impact, the historical background of the challenged decision, the specific antecedent events, departures from normal procedures, and contemporary statements of the decisionmakers [sic] . . ."[121] The Court held, inter alia, that "[r]espondents simply failed to carry their burden of proving that discriminatory purpose was a motivating factor in the Village's decision."[122] However, because the lower court failed to determine whether "the Village's decision carried a discriminatory 'ultimate effect,' " the Court remanded the case back to the court of appeals for further consideration.[123]

By 1995, the Greater New Orleans Fair Housing Action Center (GNOFHAC) was established "to eradicate housing discrimination throughout the greater New Orleans area."[124] The federal government continued (from 1981 through 1997) to discriminate against tens of thousands of African Americans, for example, the Department of Agriculture (USDA) denied loans to African-American farmers that they would have provided to white farmers in similar circumstances.[125]

While some progress was made around the country with regard to desegregation of schools and communities, a phenomenon known as hypersegregation, which was fueled by white flight and discriminatory housing laws and practices, infiltrated America's largest metropolitan communities during the latter part of the 20th century. Examples include New Orleans (of course), Baltimore, Chicago, Cleveland, Detroit, Houston, Los Angeles, New York, Philadelphia, and Washington, DC. The construct of white supremacy took its toll on society and inevitably meant (and means) that anyone outside this group was deemed less than a citizen, in fact, less than human if not by law, then by society. Clearly, such persons were regarded as societal outcasts, denied respect and dignity, and deprived of the privileges under law in matters of voting rights, citizenship, property rights, literacy, immigration, and criminal procedure.

Some advances were made in the 20th century, mostly the official dismantling of Jim Crow. But "the proof is in the pudding." Even though Jim Crow statutes were struck down and the practice was criminalized, hate crimes continued. In the United States in the last four years of the 20th century, *tens of thousands* were victims of racial hatred. In the first statistical account of this trend, *Hate Crime*[126] *Statistics 1996: Uniform Crime Reports*, published by the FBI, in that one year alone, 10,706 incidents were reported against 11,309 victims.[127] Of these victims, 4,600 were "black"—nearly 42 percent of all victims. Meanwhile, white victims totaled 1,445, representing just over 13 percent of all victims. The unadulterated truth is that "blacks" were *more than three times* more likely to be victims of racial violence than whites.

That year, 5,396 violent attacks were racially motivated in the United States. Of these, 3,674 were "anti-black" (over 68 percent), with the greatest number of these committed at the victim's residence or home (2,734)—*nearly 75 percent*. The number of offenders was an astonishing 8,935. Approximately 5,891 of the offenders were white, that is, whites were responsible for *more than 65 percent* of these crimes. "Blacks" accounted for 1,826 of the offenders (just over 20 percent). Whites were *more than three times* more likely to commit a racially motivated crime than "blacks." Single bias incidents totaled 6,767; and 4,469 of those were "anti-black," *representing 66 percent of the total*. In Louisiana, 25 incidents were reported that year.

By the end of the century, racial violence persisted. In the blink of an historian's eye, between 1996 and 1999, there were *23,265* single bias incidents based on race in which *36,647* people were victimized. "Anti-black" crimes totaled 15,422, amounting to *66 percent* of the total. Approximately 15,893 victims were African American, more than 43 percent of all victims. Whites made up just over 12 percent of all victims.[128] More than 21,000 offenders were white, which is over 65 percent of all offenders. In those four years, Louisiana reported 52 racially motivated crimes.

No logical argument can deny that American culture has suffered from this pervasive xenophobia and the resulting racial stratification from the 17th century through today. No logical argument can deny that African Africans (and other groups) have been the victims of domestic violence and dehumanization in the United States. Key examples of such abuse include name-calling and putdowns (nigger, chattel, animal, mongrel, and other dehumanizing epithets); keeping a person from contacting their family or friends (kidnapping Africans, the Transatlantic and domestic slave trades, antimiscegenation laws and the practice of voiding marriages, travel permit requirements, the sale of family members, and segregation); withholding money (slavery, forced labor, and unequal pay); preventing a person from getting or keeping a job (denying housing, employment, and education); committing actual or threatened physical harm (drowning Africans during the Middle Passage; physical punishment of slaves such as whipping, the use of hunting dogs, shackling, and torture devices; lynching, assassinations of civil rights leaders, and police brutality; and hate crimes); committing sexual assault (the regular practice of the rape of female slaves either for punishment or breeding purposes and castration during lynchings); and stalking and intimidation (activities of white supremacists and their sympathizers).[129]

No more evidence is necessary. This extreme level of domestic violence against African Americans by their government and society did not happen to just a few—or 100 or 1,000—it happened to *tens of millions of people.* This domestic violence was not a "one-time thing." It did not last a couple of years or even a lifetime. Without any break at all, it has been happening for 600 years and counting!

Logical reasoning dictates that a pathology that has existed for more than half a millennia and has annexed the psyche of American society cannot be cured in a decade and a half (this new millennium). NAACP member and world-renowned scientist Albert Einstein called racism "America's worst disease," saying it could be cured only through "education" and "enlightenment."[130] Yet this history represents more than racism. It was complete dehumanization. The 20th century is often referred to as the nadir of American race relations—society hit rock bottom in committing antiblack violence, lynching, and legal segregation. In addition, there was an exponential increase in white supremacist values.[131]

The 20th century, a full 100 years, continued the domination of white male representation in government. Just 78 African Americans served in the U.S. House of Representatives during this century, which is an average of *less than one African-American representative per year*. No African American was appointed as secretary of state or attorney general during this century (or any previous time). The first and only female appointed as attorney general was Janet Reno in 1993. Four years later, the first female secretary of state was Madeline Albright. Both Reno and Albright were appointed by President Clinton.

In the history of the Supreme Court of the United States, incredibly, only *two* African Americans ever served, and both were appointed during the 20th century. They were *Brown* champion Thurgood Marshall, (appointed in 1967) and Clarence Thomas (appointed in 1991), but they did not serve together. It was not until 1981 that the first female Supreme Court justice, Sandra Day O'Connor, was appointed; the second, Ruth Bader Ginsburg, was appointed two years later.[132] In the 20th century, just two African Americans were U.S. senators—in 1967, Edward William Brooke (R-MA) and in 1993, Carol Moseley Braun (D-IL). They, like the African-American Supreme Court justices, never served together. By the end of the century, only one African American had been elected governor of a state—Lawrence D. Wilder (VA; 1990–1994). Only white males have ever served as vice president of the United States, and, by the end of the 20th century, only white males held the highest government position, president of the United States.

It is inexplicable that professionals and laypersons alike have the audacity to refer to this history as "great progress." Such a description only serves to further demonstrate the extent of the pathology and level of ignorance. The United States did not leap from 0 to 100; rather, it crawled from *0 to 2* on a scale of 0 to100. Racial stratification continues in the United States today in areas of government, employment, education, lending, criminal justice, and, of course, housing. On August 29, 2005, that reality was made all too clear when Hurricane Katrina's winds blew into New Orleans. Oddly enough, upon the onslaught of Katrina and its aftermath, the question was posed: *"How did this happen?"* Quite simply: *it has been happening*.

More than a century has passed since W. E. B. Du Bois famously remarked that the "problem of the Twentieth Century is the problem of the color line."[133] But Du Bois was wrong. The problem of the *17th, 18th, 19th, and 20th centuries* is the problem of the color line. It is no different in this new millennium.[134]

Chapter 3

Katrina's Scope and Devastation

Almost everyone I've talked to says, "we're gonna move to Houston."
What I'm hearing, which is sort of scary, is they all want to stay in Texas . . .
Everybody is so overwhelmed by the hospitality, and
so many of the people in the arenas here, you know,
were underprivileged anyway
so this[1] *(as she chuckles slightly) is working very well for them.*[2]

—Barbara Bush, former first lady to President George H. Bush and mother to President George W. Bush, in office during Hurricane Katrina (September 2005, Cable News Network)

Pre-Katrina Status

Before one can make sense of the post-Katrina devastation, in addition to knowing Louisiana's history, it is critical for one to understand the climatic conditions of New Orleans, the state, and across the nation just before Katrina. According to a majority of the locals, New Orleans "was already a failed city" with a bankrupt school system and a murder rate much higher than the national average.[3] In a community where the African-American population was 65 percent, by 2005, the student population in the city's schools was 95 percent black. That year, two-thirds of the public schools in the area were designated as failing; yet ironically, for 30 years, teachers in the system were given performance ratings of "satisfactory."[4] According to the 2000 census, Louisiana had the third highest rate of poverty in the nation, just behind the District of Columbia (first place) and Mississippi (second place). Louisiana's poverty rate was almost twice the national average.[5]

In 1994, "New Orleans was [the] country's murder capital."[6] A decade later, murder rates declined some, yet less than two weeks before Hurricane

Katrina, NBC News reported that the murder rate in New Orleans was 10 times greater than the national average (per capita): "We're going in the reverse of 46 of the top 50 cities in the United States. Almost everyone is going down, but we're going up," said criminologist Peter Scharf, executive director of the Center for Society, Law and Justice at the University of New Orleans. "There is something going on in New Orleans that is not going on elsewhere."[7] Despite its high murder rate, at that time "only one in four people arrested in the city for murder [was] eventually convicted, according to a recent study by the New Orleans Police Foundation."[8] The history of police brutality and corruption affected citizens of New Orleans so greatly that witnesses were reluctant to come forward to even report crime, never mind testify for the state. In the 1990s, when it was discovered that two New Orleans Police Department (NOPD) officers were actually killers in the community, African Americans' lack of trust in local police was cemented. In fact, in the months and weeks leading up to Katrina, police brutality was on the rise. Officers roughed up costumed African-American Mardi Gras entertainers; and just three weeks before the storm, two NOPD officers beat a man before dropping him off at a hospital.[9]

Drugs ran rampant in New Orleans for years before the storm. Peter Scharf "estimated that there were as many as 20,000 participants in the drug culture in the city" before Hurricane Katrina.[10] For decades, residents in the Lower Ninth Ward suffered from municipal neglect and increasing impoverishment; however, residents were able to develop "cross-generational neighborhood bonds that encouraged [the active] pursuit of better public services and nourished cultural traditions singular to New Orleans."[11] In 1970, the poverty rate was 28 percent, but by 2000, the poverty rate increased to 33 percent.[12] Although the Lower Ninth Ward was afflicted with high crime and poverty rates, home ownership rates were also high because the real estate was affordable. Yet, because of segregationist policies and practices, the Lower Ninth Ward was where African Americans were allowed to live since the 1800s.

Across the nation, segregation continued—although officially illegal and determined unconstitutional—as did crimes of racial hatred by the tens of thousands. In addition, sentiments of misogyny, homophobia, and intimidation infiltrated talk shows, news media, and the streets of nearly every major American city. Despite the high rates of race-related violence, few—with the exception of the most egregious—were reported by national media.

In Jasper, Texas, on a warm summer night in 1998, John William King, Shawn Berry, and Lawrence Brewer—all young white men—drove down a lonely country road and offered to give 49-year-old James Byrd,[13] an African American, a ride. It would be Byrd's last. Instead of allowing him to ride inside the vehicle, after the three men beat him, they chained Byrd to the back of their pick-up truck. The men climbed back into the truck, turned on the ignition, and began a sadistic two-mile "joyride" with Byrd dragging behind. Byrd's torso was shredded during the drive as the perpetrators weaved the truck from side to side, bouncing Byrd against the loose asphalt. Byrd's elbows were sheared to the bone, and his right arm was torn off. His living nightmare ended when he hit a sewer and was beheaded. At the end of the ride, the men unchained Byrd's remains, left him in the street, and went home to bed.[14] The incident sparked outrage across the nation that was stunned by an outright lynching this late in the 20th century.

With the prevalence of race-related church arsons and vandalism during the late 1990s, "President Clinton established the National Church Arson Task Force (NCATF) to pool law enforcement resources together to investigate these matters." Around the same time, the Magnolia (Louisiana) Police Officers' Association (MPOA) "began patrolling black and white churches" as a deterrent, and "developed and disseminated a manual" on the same for other agencies. The MPOA is "an organization of African-American law enforcement officers in Louisiana."[15]

The sentiment of racial hatred could be found at all levels. The president of the St. Bernard Parish Council in Louisiana at the time of Katrina, and until 2007, Henry "Junior" Rodriguez, is "foul mouthed [and] racially insensitive."[16] Rodriguez was not immune to spewing racial slurs when describing African Americans. As a councilman, he did so during at least two public meetings. On August 14, 1997, Rodriguez addressed the cost of federal mandates, saying, "It kind of smells like they've got a little nigger in the woodpile." Then he made a negative comment about Jews.[17] The following September, Rodriguez referred to Black Bay, the water zone of Delacroix Island located between the Mississippi River Gulf Outlet waterway to the north and the Mississippi River to the south,[18] as "nigger lake," justifying his statement by saying he was using a description from old maps.[19] Rodriguez offered an apology for the "nigger in the woodpile" comment but not for "nigger lake," saying, "I didn't name it . . . I can't rewrite history."[20]

Rodriguez, born in 1936, is of Isleño decent and is the sixth or seventh generation living in St. Bernard Parish, a living example of the deep-rooted trademark that makes up many residents of the parish.[21] Quite the local businessman, Rodriguez "owned a bar, ran a seafood business, trawled for shrimp, and ran heavy equipment."[22] More importantly, he also spent 33 years in local politics as a police juror, a councilman, and parish president.[23] What made Rodriguez's comments especially disturbing on the threshold of a new millennium is that they did not come from some "average Joe" but rather a person of political influence who then rose to the highest level of the parish council, which passes local ordinances. He has described the residents of his own community thus: "There may be racists here, but they're not violent."[24]

Segregation continued in Louisiana on different fronts. Recall that custom and law required every area of life to be segregated. In 1999, the U.S. Department of Justice filed a complaint against Richard Byron, who refused to serve African Americans in his nightclubs in Gueydan[25] and Mermentau.[26] The complaint charged Byron with "engag[ing] in a pattern and practice of denying to African-American persons, on the basis of race, the full use and enjoyment of the goods, services, facilities, privileges, advantages, and accommodations . . . of [the facilities where] such are provided to white members of the general public." Parties agreed to resolve their differences through a consent decree the following year.[27]

The Ku Klux Klan remained active. Just two years before Hurricane Katrina, in 2003, five Klan members pled guilty and were convicted in federal court in Louisiana for burning a five-foot cross at an African-American home in Longville[28] with the purpose of "get[ting] rid of them from the neighborhood."[29] Needless to say, all three of the victims moved out of the home they were renting.[30] According to the Invisible Empire, a faction of the KKK, its purpose is "to shield forever White homes and . . . to restore and preserve the right to segregate."[31] The leader of the group, Grand Titan David Anthony Fuselier (who was "promoted" from his previous title of Exalted Cyclops) was sentenced to 13 years in prison, a penalty that was upheld by the U. S. Court of Appeals for the Fifth Circuit in April 2004.[32] According to Greco-Roman mythology, a Cyclops has but one eye in the middle of his forehead.

In January 2004, two Louisiana facilities housing individuals with mental retardation or other developmental disabilities agreed to settle civil rights violations: Pinecrest Developmental Center and Hammond Developmental Center. The charge was: "vulnerable residents with developmental disabilities were repeatedly physically and verbally abused." The investigation, conducted by the U. S. Department of Justice, revealed that "various staff dragged a resident across the carpet, causing abrasions; kicked a resident; placed a blanket over a resident's head and hit him; slapped a 50-year-old resident on the head and put a rag over her nose and mouth; and pulled a resident's hair with such force that her head literally jerked from one side of the pillow to the other."[33] While there was no mention of race, the incidents were in violation of the Americans with Disabilities Act. People with disabilities are also victims of hate crimes. The U.S. Department of Justice opened *35* similar investigations after 2001.

Just one year prior to Katrina, the U.S. Department of Justice sued apartment owners in St. Bernard Parish for engaging in race discrimination against African Americans seeking housing. Using the segregationist practice of redlining, the owners of Foster Apartments were accused of discouraging "black persons from renting an apartment while encouraging white applicants to do so."[34] Similarly, on March 31, 2005, five months before Katrina, the Department of Justice settled with the owners and managers of more than *120* apartments in the towns of Chalmette and Violet in St. Bernard Parish, namely, B & S Properties of St. Bernard, FOSCO Enterprises, Berkely Foster, Selena Foster, Lonnie Foster, and Linda Foster, regarding discrimination against African-American apartment seekers. African-American renters were told no apartments were available for rent while whites were told apartments were available. Furthermore, "African-Americans were steered to Village Square, a largely black neighborhood. Chalmette is more than 90 percent white."[35]

On New Year's Eve 2004, racial tensions continued to be significant in New Orleans. On that day, a "black college student from Georgia" attempted to enter a bar on Bourbon Street, and the bouncers refused him entry. The white bouncers roughed the student up, pinned him to the ground, and killed him. Negligent homicide charges were filed and were still pending when Katrina hit eight months later. Furthermore, "a subsequent city survey showed that 60 percent of all bars in the French Quarter either overcharged black customers or refused them entrance for improper dress."[36]

These examples are by no means isolated incidents. Rather, they illustrate symptoms of the American pathology: *dehumanization*. There is a reason that more stories cannot be described in any one newspaper, book, or report: *sheer numbers*. If dehumanization were a medical pathology under the review of the Centers for Disease Control and Prevention (CDC), there would be, at least, a national warning of the epidemic. But the CDC does not acknowledge it as a health issue.

In the four years prior to Hurricane Katrina (2000–2004), FBI hate crime reports illustrated the insidious nature of the pathology. During that four-year period:

- 15,864 single-biased incidents based on race occurred
- 3,253 incidents were antiwhite incidents
- 10,685 incidents were antiblack incidents

Furthermore, of the 28,923 offenders who committed hate crimes, 18,062 of them were white (over 62 percent). The number of black offenders who committed hate crimes was much lower: 5,697 offenders comprising just over 19 percent. More important, 19,850 Americans were victims of race-related hate crimes. Of these, 4,023 were victims of antiwhite crime, while *13,236 were victims of antiblack crime, more than three times higher than antiwhite crime.* Victims of antiblack crime comprised over 66 percent of all victims of racial hatred.[37] These statistics merely scratch the surface of hate crime in 21st-century America as thousands of incidents related to misogyny, homosexuality, other racial or ethnic groups, and religious hatred are not included in these figures. Approximately 80 hate crimes were reported in Louisiana in the four years leading up to the storm. This is the America we created. This is the America we exported to the world. And this is the America Katrina entered.

Katrina Ravages the New Orleans Region

On August 29, 2005, Hurricane Katrina[38] devastated the U.S. Gulf Coast (Louisiana, Mississippi, Alabama, and parts of the Florida panhandle).[39] The day before landfall, it was recorded as a category 5 storm (the highest category) as it thrashed and covered the entire Gulf of Mexico with 175-mile-per-hour (mph) winds. By the time it landed in the New Orleans area, it was downgraded to category 3 with maximum winds reaching approximately 125 mph.[40] The damage was astronomical, initially estimated at $60 billion, nearly three times the amount incurred in Florida following Hurricane Andrew.[41] In particular, the danger posed to New Orleans would prove catastrophic because half of the city lies below sea level. It is often described as a city in a bowl; and it is nearly surrounded by water.

As unimaginable as the devastation was, scientists and politicians predicted the inevitable catastrophe for decades up until at least two months prior to the event.[42] Still, none of the predictions were really necessary considering the history of frequent devastation of New Orleans. For generations—from the time of its settlement—city residents were victimized. Evidently, given the experiences of centuries of brutality and humiliation and the continuation of inequality, dehumanization creates social amnesia.

Hours before the storm arrived in Louisiana, the Department of Homeland Security's National Infrastructure Simulation and Analysis Center (NISAC) delivered a 41-page report to the White House warning of a possible levee breach.[43] Although the eye of Katrina actually missed New Orleans, it is difficult to imagine a worse scenario: 80 percent of the area was under water within 24 hours when the levees, designed to protect the city, were breached.[44] The levees, particularly the one at the Industrial Canal, were neglected for generations because of municipal neglect of African-American communities. Economically, it was among the poorest neighborhoods in New Orleans. Floodwalls along Lake Pontchartrain shoreline collapsed and were responsible for the flooding and approximately 1,100 deaths.[45] Many areas of New Orleans were submerged under as much as nine to 20 feet of water.[46] The Federal Emergency Management Agency (FEMA) declared 88 counties as disaster areas.[47]

According to a Congressional Research Service (CRS) report, while 77 percent of population of Orleans Parish was affected by flooding, nearly *all* residents of St. Bernard Parish suffered:

> *"Property damage, loss of life, and sizeable displacement of population appear to have been largely concentrated within [a] 100-mile radius of where the storm made landfall [31 parishes in Louisiana] . . . St. Bernard Parish, to the southeast of New Orleans, was especially hard hit by flooding, with an estimated 65,000 people affected—nearly its entire population (97%)" [and] "many areas [were] assessed [as having] extensive to catastrophic damage."*[48]

The *Times-Picayune* listed the devastation in St. Bernard two weeks after the storm:

- "At least 45 homes were lifted off their foundations, and one was deposited on Judge Perez Drive."
- Shipping containers floated off Jackson Barracks and were deposited in the streets.
- "In the Carolyn Park[49] area, water is still draining."
- "Buccaneer Village also has some water still, as do some areas surrounding Chalmette Medical Center."
- Virtually all of the property in District B was flooded.

- Buildings in Village Square (a large African-American community) were destroyed.[50]

Consider that in a 2002 case against the St. Bernard Parish School Board, it was reported that "the total black population of the Parish is 5,112" out of approximately 65,000 (8.52 percent).[51] A study by Professor John Logan from Brown University provides an undeniable statistical account of the disproportionate effect of Katrina on African Americans in St. Bernard:

> more than one-third of the 1.7 million population lived in areas that suffered moderate to catastrophic flooding, 53,000 in St. Bernard Parish alone; damaged areas were 45.8 percent "Black" compared to 26.4 percent in undamaged areas; 45 percent of homes were occupied by renters; 20.9 percent of households had incomes below the poverty level; greater than 70 percent of the populations of St. Bernard Parish and Orleans Parish lived in heavily damaged areas; most significantly, if no one were able to return to the damaged areas, New Orleans would lose 80 percent of its African-American population.[52]

Little Irish Bayou is located in Eastern New Orleans in Slidell, Louisiana, and is separated from the city by undeveloped wetlands. Ground Zero during Hurricane Katrina, the saltwater, brought in by a tsunami-like wave, destroyed the vegetation and killed half of the population of native animal species. Battered piers remained in Little Irish Bayou following Hurricanes Katrina and Rita. (Liza Lugo, JD, May 2013)

Media images of people crammed into the Superdome, swimming through floodwaters, and waving from rooftops revealed the disproportionate effect on African Americans living in the devastated area. In New Orleans, more than 50 percent of persons in damaged areas were renters, and 30 percent of those lived below the poverty line.[53] More than half of the hundreds of thousands of people displaced by the storm were from New Orleans; and because of the socio-economic composition of this population, the storm heavily impacted the poor and African Americans.[54]

Before Katrina, approximately 49,000 people lived in public housing or received housing choice vouchers provided by the Housing Authority of New Orleans. Of these, more than 95 percent were African American, and only a fraction returned following Katrina.[55] Much of the public housing remains closed to this day. St. Bernard Parish received little media attention in the wake of Katrina.[56] The parish originally reported that approximately 70 percent of homes were unlivable.[57] However, of the 27,000 homes in the parish, only *50 homes* were not flooded. Certainly, the devastation was significantly greater than the original report. The significance of the property damage caused by Katrina is overwhelming, especially to poor and African-American populations, because areas hardest hit by Katrina "had a lower than average proportion of homeowners . . . only 55 percent in Katrina-impacted areas."[58] It is important to note that homeowners in these distressed areas lived there for decades: one-third had lived in their homes for 30 or more years, more than half of all homeowners lived in their homes for 20 or more years, and 29 percent of renters lived in their homes for ten years or more.[59]

Before Katrina, 46 percent of renters were paying more than 30 percent of their income for housing costs (a factor describing affordability), lived with more than one person in each room (overcrowding), or lacked complete plumbing and/or kitchen facilities (inadequacy).[60] Furthermore, over 70,000 apartments in the affected region suffered major damage or were completely destroyed.[61] Garland Robinette, Host of WWL Radio, said one year after the storm: "We are destroyed. I've seen Beirut; I've seen Calcutta; I've seen downtown Jakarta; I've seen [Banda] Aceh. They have nothing on us[62] . . . many neighborhoods do not have services . . . the entire Lower Ninth Ward . . . nobody lives there. That's because there's no electricity . . . no water . . . no gas. There is [sic] no services at all."

Citizens who spent those tortuous five days at the Superdome gave dramatic accounts: "it was the worst experience ever" and "the smell of death was everywhere."[63] The city scene represented that of a war-torn,

In 2013, a home in the Ninth Ward continues to bear markings from local and other government officials who searched the area for victims and survivors of Hurricane Katrina. (M. J. Clark, May 2013)

third-world nation. Almost immediately, the citizens became disillusioned and desperate. Media cameras captured it all in real time; and all of America watched from the safety of their own homes. One resident described the hopelessness she witnessed: a mother was so desperate on the I-10 bridge that in what appeared to be a personal haze, she quietly dropped her infant over the bridge and then followed suit herself.[64] Eerily, it was a ghostly re-creation of a scene from the Middle Passage when kidnapped Africans slid themselves over the side of the slave ship—preferring to perish in the depths of the ocean rather than face torture and an unknown future.

In Chalmette, St. Bernard Parish, the front yard of the Ninth Ward, an oil refinery spilled 1 million gallons of oil, which joined another 7 million gallons that contaminated Katrina's floodwaters. Those who were brave enough to wade through the floodwaters found that their clothes, soaked with toxins, were burning their skin. Many developed strange lesions on their bodies.[65]

As images of a drowning New Orleans flooded television screens, so did images of survivors, shell-shocked citizens asking the same questions over and again to television news reporters at Ground Zero. The film *The Axe in the Attic* covered a number of the pleas:

"Where is our government?"

"They knew this was going to happen . . . why isn't the government coming?"

"The [president, the mayor, the governor] have the power, how [could they] not know?"

And the fear was palatable:

"Please! Help us!"

"You don't see this in America—maybe in Iraq or Africa—but not in America."

"We're being forced into exile in our own country."

"They left us to die!"

"They think we're a bunch of riff-raff."

"We're left to live like animals!"

"Governor Blanco has issued a 'shoot-to-kill' order."

"They're gonna kill us all!"

"We are human beings!"[66]

Perhaps hindsight is 20-20. But perhaps the best predictor of *future* behavior is *relevant past behavior.* Quite predictably, the instant horror of Katrina and the chaotic aftermath eliminated any possibility of intellectual rationale in the moment. These simple questions may have been answered immediately if not for the shock of it all. The problem is that citizens of the affected area, and across the nation, are not fully aware of their own—America's own—personal history and therefore cannot completely understand their present circumstances. Hence the reactions of shock and disbelief. Therefore, I charge:

> So my fellow Americans . . . why did you think the government would come? They have not come to your immediate aid before. Yes, you do "see this in America," you've seen it many times before—you just forgot—lulled to sleep by some weak "honeymoon phase" dotted with "token" gifts in a cycle of domestic violence that allowed you to simply survive day by day; meanwhile, you walked around with some sort of amnesia. Why are you surprised that any or all of you are being forced into "exile" when Africans were kidnapped and enslaved, when Native Americans were tortured during Manifest Destiny and the Trail of Tears, exiled from their own land, and when Americans of Japanese descent were imprisoned in internment camps for nothing more than being found guilty of possession of a congenital lineage.
>
> Why are you shocked that they called you "refugees"[67] when you know that your entire American existence suffered the pathology via "second-class citizenship"? The Freedmen's Bureau, in reality, The Bureau of Refugees, Freedmen, and Abandoned Lands, christened itself in your "name" and referred to you as the same within mere minutes of the end of the Civil

War as measured in the time of human existence. More importantly, why do you need to plead that you are a human being and, as such, you live and die? Do you now realize the effect of centuries of dehumanization?

It is because of this pathology—because it is has metastasized to the American psyche and subconscious—because the truth is that for centuries you have been deemed less than human and instead referred to as "chattel," "someone else's possession" or "property," "war contraband," "refugee"—"-less-than" all because of "one-drop," all disguised as a legal system and social etiquette.

Maybe, just maybe, Katrina gave you a split-second of clarity, perhaps a passing thought or full realization that you are human. And when the wind and rain subsided and the shock and slumber wore off and you tried to tell the truth that Katrina was more than a natural disaster—that Katrina uncovered a national disaster—they told you that it was "not a race thing" because "whites" were affected too.

Well, time will tell.

The Aftermath

Whatever followed Katrina would be predictable. Hence, it would take more than a few bulldozers to clean up the social aftermath. Haley Barbour, governor of Mississippi, surveyed the disaster's impact on the region by air on August 30 and stated, "I can only imagine that this is what Hiroshima looked like sixty years ago."[68]

Racially motivated attacks ravaged African-American citizens of New Orleans almost immediately following the storm with a fury nearly equal to that of Katrina herself. On September 1, Roland Bourgeois Jr., a white male with friends, fired a shotgun at and wounded three African-American men who were evacuating the city, including Donnell Herrington, "because of their race" and because they were attempting to use public streets even though they did not "not live in the Algiers neighborhood." As he held up the blood-soaked baseball cap of one of his victims on that day, Bourgeois warned, "Any *thing* coming up this street darker than a brown paper bag is getting shot."[69] His mother maintained her son was "not a racist" despite her confirmation of the facts of the case.[70] Herrington was shot twice in the throat, which shredded his internal jugular vein. Miraculously, he survived. It took nearly four years for witnesses to come forward.[71] Bourgeois was charged by the U.S. Department of Justice five years after the incident and faces a life sentence.[72]

In those fateful days following Katrina, traumatized citizens suffered even more devastation from those who were supposed to uphold the highest duty to protect them. The mistrust of government authority stemming from centuries of dehumanization would now be nearly irretractable. On September 2, 2005, four days after the storm while New Orleans remained submerged, up to 20 feet in some areas, the brutality of the NOPD rose like a vengeful tide.

Former police officer David Warren was guarding a police substation located on the second floor of a strip mall in Algiers. Henry Glover, an unarmed citizen, approached the substation.[73] Warren stated he believed that Glover was a looter; and, even though Glover turned around and ran in the opposite direction, Warren took aim and shot Glover in the back.[74] Glover's friends put "the wounded [man] in his car" to "get medical attention for him." When they arrived at a makeshift police station seeking help, officer Greg McRae, along with other members of the NOPD, surrounded the men at gunpoint and handcuffed them. Officers made no move to assist the wounded Glover and let him die in the back seat of the car. Upon Glover's death, McRae then drove the car containing Glover's body to the Algiers levee. McRae exited the vehicle, lit a traffic flare, tossed the flare onto the car, and set it aflame, "burn[ing] both the body and the car." Former police lieutenant Travis McCabe then filed a false police report on the incident. All of the officers involved, including Warren, are white males. Glover and his friends were all African American. *Five years after the incident,* former officers David Warren and Greg McRae, along with former police lieutenant Travis McCabe were found guilty for their actions and civil rights violations.[75] Thomas E. Perez, assistant attorney general for the Civil Rights Division, later stated, "Instead of upholding their oath to protect and serve the people of New Orleans in the days after Hurricane Katrina, these officers violated the law and the public trust."[76]

The same day as the Glover murder, Mayor Nagin consented to an interview with Garland Robinette from the local radio station WWL-AM. Nagin was desperate. While it is not known whether Nagin was specifically aware of Glover's fate, we do know that the mayor was aware of the random shootings, police brutality, and the fact that the Superdome had become a death trap. New Orleans was rapidly descending into anarchy.

WWL: *What do you need right now to get control of this situation?*

NAGIN: I need reinforcements, I need troops, man. I need 500 buses, man. We ain't talking about—you know, one of the briefings we had, they were talking about getting public school bus drivers to come down here and bus people out here.

I'm like, "You got to be kidding me. This is a national disaster. Get every doggone Greyhound bus line in the country and get their asses moving to New Orleans." That's—they're thinking small, man. And this is a major, major, major deal. And I can't emphasize it enough, man. This is crazy. I've got 15,000 to 20,000 people over at the convention center. It's bursting at the seams. The poor people in Plaquemines Parish . . . We don't have anything, and we're sharing with our brothers in Plaquemines Parish. It's awful down here, man.

WWL: *Do you believe that the president is seeing this, holding a news conference on it but can't do anything until* [Louisiana Gov.] *Kathleen Blanco requested him to do it? And do you know whether or not she has made that request?*

NAGIN: I have no idea what they're doing. But I will tell you this: you know, God is looking down on all this, and if they are not doing everything in their power to save people, they are going to pay the price. Because, every day that we delay, people are dying; and they're dying by the hundreds; I'm willing to bet you.[77]

Two days after Mayor Nagin's desperate plea, on September 4, 2005, evacuated unarmed citizens waited for assistance on the Danziger Bridge. The citizens had been there for a total of six days in near 100-degree heat. Instead of receiving help, they were confronted by police officers who shot at them, creating panic, terror, and death. Officers of the NOPD took the life of 17-year-old James Brissette and wounded four others in one shooting on the east side of the bridge. On the west side of the bridge, other officers of the NOPD killed 40-year-old Ronald Madison, who had a severe disability and was trying to flee the scene. Lance Madison, Ronald's brother, was with him and was "was arrested on eight counts of [allegedly] attempting to kill police officers, but he was later released without indictment."[78] The process of investigating, indicting, trying, and sentencing the offending officers lasted *seven years.* "Former officer Robert Faulcon received a 65-year prison term; former sergeants Kenneth Bowen and Robert Gisevius received 40-year sentences."[79] Some pled guilty to the federal charges, including civil rights violations, and admitted "that the shootings were unjustified."[80] All of the officers involved were white, and all of the victimized citizens were African American. Even the sheriff of neighboring Plaquemines Parish "deputized shrimpers to help repel busloads of New Orleans evacuees trying to reach a U.S. naval reserve air station in the white suburb of Belle Chase."[81]

While housing has always been a critical issue for the citizens of New Orleans, following Katrina, it was a frantic scene, particularly for renters. Billions of dollars in renewal money was earmarked for housing aid in the devastated region; however, most of the aid would go to homeowners, leaving renters without access to these resources.[82] More significant and applicable to a legal analysis, all of the aforementioned incidents and statistics are evidence of the legacy of an extensive history of institutional discrimination and residential segregation that has continued to the present day. The current issues would leave no doubt.

The housing shortage disproportionately affected minorities in St. Bernard Parish, particularly considering the following factors:

> St. Bernard's population is "overwhelmingly white" (84.37 percent white, 7.6 percent black, and 5.09 percent Hispanic)[83]; 93 percent of all owner-occupied units are owned by whites; only 21 percent of whites reside in rental units compared to 45 percent of blacks and 31 percent of Hispanics. The damage from Katrina affected "97 percent of all rental units."[84]

Professor John Logan discussed the logical implications on future decisions in housing: "policy choices affecting who can return, to which neighborhoods, and with what forms of public and private assistance, will greatly affect the future character of the city."[85]

In Katrina's wake, St. Bernard Parish president "Junior" Rodriguez initially requested 5,000 trailers from FEMA and identified sites for them in St. Bernard. Some were "to be located at centralized areas and others to be distributed to homeowners who could park them in driveways while their homes are re-built."[86] Rodriguez is often credited with creating awareness about the loss of coastal wetlands in his parish; however, his social ignorance reappears without regard for who is listening to him. In the weeks following Katrina, he asked one female constituent, "How's your fine daughter, with the big boobs?"[87] His racist remarks continued. In mid-September, "before he realized a reporter was in his office, he was heard to use a slur for blacks. He did so in saying that many have the same names, drawing a comparison with the 90 German experts who are helping 'de-water' the parish, who, he said, are 'all called "Klaus." '"[88]

In an instant, a once lively and vibrant community was rendered silent. The people of New Orleans were scattered to neighboring states and makeshift shelters. Those who remained home found themselves living like caged animals with families of five crammed into 30-foot by 8-foot FEMA trailers. Ninety miles north of New Orleans, in the town of Baker, FEMA created the largest trailer park in the nation. If anyone had a job to return to in New Orleans, it would be nearly impossible to make such a trek on a daily basis. Renaissance Village consisted of over 500 trailers and 1,500 evacuees. Joseph Griffin, described his experience and his opinion of the mentality of New Orleans residents: the government was "supposed to do this for us" yet "they only allotted" the displaced "18 months" to rebuild their lives or else they would be relegated as "homeless." The sentiment was nearly reminiscent of the promise of "40 acres and a mule." Griffin was devastated by the aftermath of Katrina. He cringed that it was "graphic stuff" where "people were torn apart" and "bodies were mangled." Griffin was insulted by the simplistic FEMA "pamphlet" on "stress management" that, according to him, would help "nobody." His view echoed the sentiments of hundreds of thousands who survived the storm.[89]

Other survivors pleaded for understanding: "Imagine losing everything! Everything is soaked in chemicals . . . the only clothes you own are on your back and burning your skin . . . It's a pressure cooker."[90] Eighteen months after the storm, 13,000 people were still living in FEMA trailers. Some statistics showed the rates of depression and suicide in FEMA trailer parks were eight times greater than the national average.[91]

And despite the undeniable tragedy, a venomous spew of ignorance came from leaders in the community. The *Wall Street Journal* reported that Baton Rouge congressman Richard Baker told lobbyists, "We finally cleaned up public housing in New Orleans. We couldn't do it, but God did." Even HUD secretary Alphonso Jackson openly predicted a smaller, whiter city.[92] New Orleans was never a white city—for hundreds of years, African Americans and other people of color were the majority.

Undoubtedly, Hurricane Katrina's strength was unprecedented in North America. Tearing into the Mississippi Coast with 125 mph winds, Katrina railroaded the largest volume of water ever into Lakes Borgne and Pontchartrain with a storm surge of 28 feet and waves as high as 55 feet.[93] The surge and waves "greatly exceeded the intended design criteria of the Hurricane Protection System." There were an *incredible 50 major breaches* during the storm. However, major floodwall breaches in the outfall canals and the Inner Harbor Navigation Canal occurred well before water levels reached the top of the wall: 17th Street Canal; London Avenue Canal-South; London Avenue Canal-North; IHNC, West; and IHNC East Lower Ninth Ward and St. Bernard Parish. Flooding was unprecedented, and citizens found themselves amidst the swamp of the floodwaters with depths of 22 feet. The most severe flooding was in St. Bernard Parish, with the Lower Ninth Ward as its backyard. More than 85 percent of greater New Orleans was submerged, leaving more than 100,000 people homeless in a matter of hours.[94]

The floodwaters posed a likely death trap littered with innumerable hazards: collapsed bridges, large home construction debris containing lead and asbestos, glass, metals, vehicles, power lines, millions of gallons of oil and petrochemical compounds from damaged refineries, human corpses, sewage, bacteria,[95] poisonous snakes, rats, alligators, disoriented animals, and swarms of insects. According to one study, "concentrations of aldrin, arsenic, lead, and seven semi-volatile organic compounds in sediments/soils exceeded one or more United States Environmental Protection Agency (USEPA) thresholds for human health soil screening levels and high priority bright line screening levels."[96] Approximately 170 drinking water facilities were either destroyed or compromised.[97] Sewage treatment plants were destroyed; and within days, four major oil spills poured 1 million barrels of oil into the lakes and floodwaters. In St. Bernard Parish, Murphy Oil Field was a major source of contamination: "The force of the storm was so great that it picked up one of the storage tanks (with a capacity of about 250,000 barrels of oil), ripped it off the concrete pad, and moved the tank over, causing all the oil to spill into the water and the surrounding community."[98] The city was coated with fuel "from 2,200 fuel tanks and leaking gasoline from flooded cars and boats."[99]

Each day was more desperate than the last, and the world was scrutinizing every move. It took five days for search and rescue teams to successfully complete 62,000 water, roof, and attic rescues. Following Katrina, 78,000 survivors were lifted to higher ground and poured into shelters across the nation. According to the Army Corps of Engineers, for more than two weeks following the deluge, the city's pumps, including supplemental portable pumps, worked nonstop in efforts to return the water to Lake Pontchartrain. "As much as [100,642 gallons] of water were being pumped out of New Orleans every second."[100] It took 40 days to dry out New Orleans.

Economic costs of the natural disaster have been estimated to be near $100 billion. According to federal sources, housing damages totaled $67 billion, business property $20 billion, consumer durable goods

View of Lake Pontchartrain from the I-10 bridge in Orleans Parish in 2013. (M. J. Clark, May 2013)

$7 billion, and government property $3 billion.[101] Nearly 160,000 homes in Louisiana were destroyed during Katrina and the aftermath of raging floodwaters.[102] Approximately 90 percent of the public schools in New Orleans were damaged or destroyed, leaving 190,000 students displaced. The day Hurricane Katrina barreled into the New Orleans metropolitan area, nearly 230,000 citizens were housed in shelters, according to the Department of Homeland Security. The following day, the numbers dropped to approximately 180,000. Katrina's diaspora reached out to the state and federal government for assistance. More than 300,000 families and individuals applied for relief, with 270,000 of them from Louisiana.[103]

Damage to infrastructure was overwhelming. Whole communities were obliterated. According to a Department of Energy report, shutdowns of refineries cost the region 367,000 barrels per day between the period of Katrina's onslaught and December 15, 2005. The Louisiana Office of Conservation was required to address the operating status of producing wells in a 38-parish region. By December 27, 2005, Louisiana restored a little over 72 percent of its total production. Thirty-six percent of the wells in the region remained shut in. Katrina, along with Hurricane Rita (which followed less than a month later), damaged numerous natural gas processing facilities, which delayed recovery of natural gas production in the area.[104]

The New Orleans Recovery School District (RSD) was responsible for rebuilding schools following Katrina. Instead, many of the public schools were sold and became private charter institutions. In 2005, this public school in the Ninth Ward was submerged under 18 feet of water as a result of Hurricane Katrina. As of 2014, it remains closed, as do others in the area. (M. J. Clark, May 2013)

Even if pipelines were in operation, the gas could not flow into the market without treatment.[105]

In the fall of 2005, several wastewater treatment systems and water treatment systems remained inoperable. It has taken years to clean up the debris, and in many areas, particularly in the Lower Ninth Ward, nearly 10 years later, the cleanup continues. The skeletal remains of buildings and homes and empty concrete slabs stand as a grim reminder of the devastation. Housing quality, primarily the compromising of structural integrity and nearly a decade of growing mold pose significant risks.

Destruction to the power sources of the city created a major dilemma for the population of New Orleans. Several large hospitals were destroyed, and many others were rendered inoperable. Nearly all of the remaining health care facilities were forced to close, leaving citizens without access to basic medical services.[106] At least 10 major hospitals in New Orleans operated with emergency backup power.[107] Without power, it was impossible to maintain necessary services such as traffic lights, refrigeration, air conditioning, and communication systems. With citizens using generators for back-up power, several deaths following Katrina were related to carbon monoxide poisoning.

The Department of Energy (DOE) reported "unprecedented damage" to the U.S. energy sector and noted that 2.5 million customers in Alabama, Louisiana, and Mississippi reported power outages. Hurricane Katrina devastated communications infrastructure across the Gulf Coast, incapacitating telephone service, police and fire dispatch centers, and emergency radio systems. Almost 3 million customers' phone lines were knocked out. Telephone switching centers were seriously damaged and 1,477 cell phone towers were incapacitated. Most of the radio stations and many television stations in the New Orleans area were knocked off the air. Paul McHale, the assistant secretary of defense for homeland defense, summarized the damage by relaying that the magnitude of the storm was such that the local communications system was not simply degraded, it was destroyed for a period of time.[108]

Emergency services were crippled, and Katrina forced the closure of the Orleans Parish Emergency Operations Center. Local fire and police departments were completely destroyed, effectively closed down, or unable to reach out to those in need because government vehicles were lost or they were blocked from accessing routes throughout the area by 20-foot walls of water. Those that remained operable were ineffective. Command structures were nearly nonexistent or completely broke down, leaving officers to their own devices. Court systems entirely shut down. This lack of access to basic law and order services left citizens extremely vulnerable and abandoned. Warren J. Riley, the Superintendent of the NOPD, testified before Congress: "Much has been said about officers abandoning their position during the storm, and it is true that about 147 officers abandoned their positions." The officers were later suspended from their positions.[109] Nearly one week after the storm, the federal government deployed approximately 2,000 law enforcement officers to the region to assist in maintaining order.

Mayor Nagin reported to Congress that "primary and secondary power sources, sewerage and draining systems and communication and power lines were incapacitated."[110] With severed power sources, citizens could not communicate with the outside world and were in the dark, both literally and figuratively.

The National Disaster

Within a few short months, the Select Bipartisan Committee to Investigate the Preparation for and Response to Hurricane Katrina ("the Select Committee") was established by the U.S. House of Representatives. Soon after, the Select Committee reported to Congress: "It has become increasingly clear that local, state, and federal government agencies failed to meet the needs of the residents of Louisiana, Mississippi, and Alabama."[111] More important, it determined 12 major causes of the downward spiral:

1. Levees protecting New Orleans were not built for the most severe hurricanes.
2. The failure of complete evacuations led to preventable deaths, great suffering, and further delays in relief.
3. Critical elements of the National Response Plan were executed late, ineffectively, or not at all.
4. DHS and the states were not prepared for this catastrophic event.
5. Massive communications damage and a failure to adequately plan for alternatives impaired response, efforts, command and control, and situational awareness.
6. Command and control was impaired at all levels, which delayed relief.
7. The military played an invaluable role, but coordination was lacking.
8. The collapse of local law enforcement and lack of effective public communication led to civil unrest and further delayed relief.
9. Medical care and evacuations suffered from a lack of advanced preparations, inadequate communications, and difficulties coordinating efforts.
10. Longstanding weaknesses and the magnitude of the disaster overwhelmed FEMA's ability to provide emergency shelter and temporary housing.
11. FEMA logistics and contracting systems did not support a targeted, massive, and sustained provision of commodities.
12. Contributions by charitable organizations assisted many in need, but the American Red Cross and others faced challenges due to the size of the mission, inadequate logistics capacity, and a disorganized shelter process.[112]

The devastation and desperation were completely overwhelming for citizens, particularly those that were impacted disproportionately. On September 15, 2005, a little over two weeks after Katrina, President Bush acknowledged the connection between perpetual second-class citizenship and the current suffering: "As all of us saw on television, there is also some deep, persistent poverty in this region as well. *And that poverty has roots in a history of racial discrimination, which cut off generations from the opportunity of America.*"[113] Patricia Thompson, a New Orleans resident and evacuee, testified at the Select Committee Hearing on December 6, 2005, just three months after Katrina:

> We were abandoned. City officials did nothing to protect us. We were told to go to the Superdome, the Convention Center, [and] the interstate bridge for safety. We did this more than once. In fact, we tried them all for every day over a week. We saw buses, helicopters, and FEMA trucks, but no one stopped to help us. We never felt so cut off in all our lives. When you feel like this you do one of two things, you either give up or go into survival mode. We chose the latter. This is how we made it. We slept next to dead bodies; we slept on streets at least four times next to human feces and urine. There was garbage everywhere in the city. Panic and fear had taken over.[114]

The number of deaths in Louisiana related to Hurricane Katrina is disputed. No official final tallies exist, even nearly a decade after the disaster. According to the Department of Health and Hospitals (DHH) of the state Louisiana, 1,118 citizens perished (all in New Orleans and St. Bernard), with an additional 135 missing persons cases turned over to law enforcement.[115] The CDC identified 971 Katrina-related deaths in Louisiana.[116] Katrina claimed many lives across the Gulf Coast states: 14 in Florida, 15 in Alabama, and more than 230 in Mississippi.[117] Before Katrina approximately 14,000 people lived in the Lower Ninth Ward; in 2013 only 4,000 remain. Today no official list of victims is available.[118] Some sources calculate the total death toll from Katrina as high as 1,400 to 1,800 when considering all affected states. Over the years, the remains of Katrina's victims have appeared jutting out from under rubble and collapsed buildings. Still others have been found in marshes and open fields where they were carried and set aside by the raging floodwaters.

Whatever the exact number may be, the major causes of death were drowning (40 percent) and injury and trauma (25 percent). Nearly half of the dead were older adults (75 years old and older), and 70 percent were over the age of 60.[119] The average age of those who died was 69.[120] More than 500 bodies were found in their homes. At least 31 residents of St. Rita's Nursing Home in St. Bernard Parish drowned due to the great flood.[121] Today the eerie building, now empty and abandoned with an unkempt lawn surrounded by a high chain link fence, remains just hidden beyond tangled trees and shrubs in the background of the Isleño Museum. Hundreds of homes, trailers, and buildings still have the neon markings by their doorways made by search teams looking for victims on that fateful day.

More than half of the deceased were black, and 42 percent were white.[122] Mortality rates for blacks in Orleans Parish were between 1.7 and 4 times higher than for whites.[123] Whether victims were black or white was not a determining factor in the risk of death, as the wrath of nature sees no color. However, two significant factors determined the risk of life and death in the New Orleans area: (1) the ability to evacuate and (2) residential proximity to levee breaches.[124] Those two factors are the result of human social constructs. African-American communities line the floodwalls of New Orleans and St. Bernard, and the residences in these areas were no match for the massive force of the floodwaters that broke through and overtopped the levees. The ferocious waves smashed into buildings and knocked houses from their foundations. African Americans dominated these areas for a number of reasons. African Americans were there because they lived there for generations, and they lived there because of historically state-sanctioned segregationist policies. African Americans were there because of white flight and the later practice of redlining, which locked them out of geographically safer zones. With a majority living in poverty, many did not have the financial means to evacuate.[125] And because of discriminatory practices in housing, there was no place else to live—not before Katrina and even less after Katrina.

All of this is a direct result of the political power structure of the state of Louisiana, where the chief executives of the parishes and municipal governments by law have overall responsibility for not only the direction and control of policies and laws, but for emergency and disaster operations. The parishes have operated this way for generations with minimal oversight from the state government. And as Katrina showed, when those executives are committed to segregationist policies and practices, safety and lives are compromised.

Despite severed power and economic life lines and notwithstanding the drowning of property and lives in the depths of the floodwaters, segregationist policy would prove itself strong enough to re-emerge and take into its lungs a new breath of life. It would survive the wrath of Katrina, but one question would remain: Would it survive the aftermath?

Chapter 4

Hurricane Katrina's Winds Blow in New Ordinances

We got a serious situation in St. Bernard Parish. We got people living in tents and automobiles. We got people living in barns. We got people living in their houses in tents.[1]

Henry "Junior" Rodriguez, St. Bernard Parish President
December 13, 2005
3.5 months following Katrina

FOR IMMEDIATE RELEASE
August 29, 2005; 7:30 P.M. CST

Henry "Junior" Rodriguez
President
St. Bernard Parish, Louisiana

Dear President Bush,

My name is Henry "Junior" Rodriguez and I am president of St. Bernard Parish, Louisiana.

My parish is completely flooded from the recent passage of Hurricane Katrina. The eye of the hurricane passed directly over my parish and has caused mass destruction and complete flooding.

Of our community of 67,000 citizens, many are surrounded by water and have no place to go. We have NO food, NO water, NO sanitation, NO power, and NO communication.

We have no way to rescue or recover our citizens.

Absolutely no attempt has been made to communicate with me regarding the catastrophe that has occurred to the citizens I represent.

I cannot believe that in a country as sophisticated as the United States of America that the leadership in the White House cannot somehow communicate NOW with me and the local government that I represent.

This disaster is a direct outgrowth of the neglect of the Federal Government to address the coastal erosion problem of southern Louisiana.

I implore you to please contact me directly or have the appropriate federal agency respond IMMEDIATELY to this disaster. I am in danger of having many citizens die if they are not rescued now.

On behalf of the citizens of St. Bernard Parish, Louisiana I am begging for your help.

Sincerely,

Henry "Junior" Rodriguez, President, St. Bernard Parish, Louisiana

Cc: CNN, WWL, WDSU, WVUE, WGNO, Times-Picayune[2]

St. Bernard Parish Government
Official Hurricane Katrina Information
September 25, 2005; 11:00 AM CST

Return to St. Bernard to Resume Tomorrow:

St. Bernard Parish officials announce that beginning tomorrow September 26, 2005, at 6 AM CST, Parish business owners and residents may begin returning to St. Bernard in the areas that are clear of Hurricane Rita's flood waters.[3]

As of Noon on 9/25/05, there is standing water in the Arabi area, north of the Parish line to approximately Pakenham Drive in Chalmette, AND in the areas east of Verret. **IF YOUR BUSINESS OR RESIDENCE IS**

LOCATED IN ONE OF THESE AREAS, DO NOT PLAN ON RETURNING TO ST. BERNARD—YOU WILL NOT BE ABLE TO ACCESS YOUR PROPERTY.

The flood water is receding slowly, but it may take a few days to completely drain the effected [sic] areas.

To be eligible to return to St. Bernard, residents must present proof of residency. To protect homes and businesses from unwanted intrusion, we will strictly enforce this rule. **PLEASE BE SURE TO HAVE PROOF OF RESIDENCY.**

As was previously announced, when planning your return, please keep in mind that electrical power, telephone, and sanitation have not been restored in St. Bernard, and that water service is only available in limited areas. Moreover, presently there is no gasoline, food, water, or building material available. Thus, please plan accordingly. You should be totally self-sufficient with generators, tools, etc. to enable you to accomplish your planned tasks, and you must have sufficient gasoline to exit St. Bernard when you are finished.

A STRICT DAWN TO DUSK CURFEW will be enforced and **no person or vehicle will be allowed on the streets of St. Bernard Parish during the curfew.**

Please be aware that St. Bernard Parish Government does not have sufficient life sustaining supplies to support the general public, nor are 911 emergency telephone services available.

Further, you are advised to take precautions to ensure your personal safety when inside of St. Bernard Parish. We have posted the recommendations on the "News" link of: http://www.stbernardparishgovernment.com/. Scroll down to the September 14, 2005; 8:00 AM CST - Preparation to Return section.

We understand that traffic is very heavy on all routes available to gain access to St. Bernard. Please plan your travel accordingly. As of this time, all access from New Orleans is blocked. Thus, please do not attempt to return through those areas.

The latest flood water information will be posted later this afternoon or this evening.[4]

The Disproportionate Effect

According to a CRS report from November 2005, "*due to the city's social and economic composition*, the storm impacted heavily on the poor and African Americans.[5] CRS estimates that one-fifth of those displaced by the storm were likely to have been poor; and 30% of those who were displaced had incomes that were *below* 1½ times the poverty line." More than 310,000 African Americans in Orleans Parish were victims of the storm, and one-third of them were poor. More than 700,000 people in the New Orleans area were "acutely affected." And while overall there was a low rate of homeownership, the report provided an interesting hypothesis: "*Renters are more mobile and may have an easier time resettling in new communities than homeowners.*"[6] Well, that would be easier said than done.

The report made mention of the history of segregationist policy in the area, which is the reason African Americans were located in the most devastated areas. Reality would provide a good "kick in the pants." Beginning on day one, there was no way St. Bernard Parish was going to give renters "an easier time resettling." Authorities barricaded a main road by stacking huge metal shipping containers, and they purposefully "wrecked cars on another" on a thoroughfare "to keep anyone from entering the largely working-class, white suburban parish from the neighboring Ninth Ward of New Orleans."[7] The parish sheriff gave deputies a shoot-to-kill order. Dr. Lawrence Powell, a professor at Tulane University, commented one month after the hurricane:

> We're very fractured, and we have been for a long time, throughout our history. *The city prior to Katrina in terms of race, class and poverty was a manmade disaster*. It's one of the poorest big cities in the country. The economic foundations were rotting away. The main growth industry was tourism, but that's a Third World wage structure. And the school system was in the toilet.[8]

A total of 22,232 travel trailers were requested within the New Orleans area from FEMA. However, by November 2005, three months after Katrina, the agency provided just 16 percent of the requested housing. A federal court order halted evictions in the area at least until after the holidays but by November, "more than 3,000 renters, most of them black and lower-income, lost their apartments."[9] As time passed, those who sought shelter in hotels were also evicted by the tens of thousands.

The Ordinances

Despite the catastrophe and ensuing homelessness, with nearly all residents of St. Bernard Parish affected,[10] officials passed an ordinance on November 1, 2005, that "placed a *twelve-month moratorium* on the new construction of multi-family dwellings and prohibited the rehabilitation of any preexisting multi-family housing without first receiving the approval of the St. Bernard Parish Council."[11] Even though race was not mentioned, forbidding new construction of multifamily dwellings for one year and forbidding the restoration of damaged buildings without Parish approval, particularly in light of this housing catastrophe, smacks of segregation. There is no logical explanation for not building or rehabilitating dwellings in a parish that was "99.9 percent destroyed" with nearly all residential housing rendered unlivable.

By the following March, the St. Bernard Parish Council decided to pass a series of ordinances, including one restricting rentals of single-family homes, although initially the parish placed a complete moratorium on

Across the street from where the levees broke at the Industrial Canal in the Ninth Ward, homes were swept away in the floodwaters, leaving few remains of the homes' foundations. The foundation of this home is part of one of the hundreds of homes in the area that remain in their destroyed state eight years following Katrina. (M. J. Clark, May 2013)

renting these properties.[12] The ordinance proposed that the complete moratorium was necessary

> *to preserve the integrity of single family dwelling neighborhoods* by placing a moratorium on single-family homes becoming rental properties until such time as the post Katrina real estate market in St. Bernard Parish stabilizes.[13]

Despite the public hearing, according to council minutes: "NO ONE APPEARED TO SPEAK FOR THE PROPOSED ORDINANCE."[14]

But lack of attendance at the public hearings was likely due a number of issues, including:

1. Hundreds of thousands of citizens in the New Orleans metropolitan area were scattered before and after the storm.
2. Those who remained were still reeling from a storm that hit with the force of an atomic bomb, destroying everything in its wake.

The St. Bernard Parish Council, the local legislature, revised the parish housing ordinances several times over in the ensuing months, clearly in hopes of getting it just right. In the meantime, residents could not plan to restore properties with the constant evolution of housing ordinances (each within months of the other). On July 6, 2006, the council revised the ordinance "permitting owners to rent their single-family dwellings only if they obtained a conditional use permit from the Parish, but set no guidelines as to when the permits would be granted."[15]

An additional hurdle for residents was the terminology used in the ordinances. The council's reported intention of "preserving integrity of a neighborhood . . . until such time as the real estate market stabilizes" along with its failure to provide guidelines as to when a permit would be granted created confusion for residents because the wording was overbroad and vague. To prevent arbitrary and discriminatory enforcement, statutes must provide explicit standards for those who will apply them. "Overbreadth tests the constitutionality of legislation in terms of its potential applications."[16] In determining the overbreadth of a statute, the Supreme Court of the United States explained:

> There must be a realistic danger that the statute itself will significantly compromise [constitutional] protections of parties not before the Court for it to facially challenged on overbreadth grounds.[17]

However, because the overbreadth doctrine is "strong medicine," such challenges will "rarely, if ever ... succeed against a law or regulation that is not specifically addressed to speech or to conduct necessarily associated with speech."[18] In determining the vagueness of a statute, the Court held:

> Vague laws offend several important values. First, because we assume that man is free to steer between lawful and unlawful conduct, we insist that laws give the person of ordinary intelligence a reasonable opportunity to know what is prohibited, so that he may act accordingly. Vague laws may trap the innocent by not providing fair warnings. Second, if arbitrary and discriminatory enforcement is to be prevented, laws must provide explicit standards for those who apply them. A vague law impermissibly delegates basic policy matters to policemen, judges, and juries for resolution on an ad hoc and subjective basis, with the attendant dangers of arbitrary and discriminatory applications.[19]

But then on September 19, 2006, something more insidious developed. The council clarified the ordinance by amending it again. Ordinance SBPC#670-09-06 was introduced by Craig Tafarro.[20] This time, the council explained in more detail its intention and its rationale for the ordinance, referring to "long established neighborhoods," "the need to maintain the integrity ... of established neighborhoods," and retaining "their pre-existing neighborhoods." Section 1 R-1 stated:

> Considering the great social and economic need to encourage single family residence owners to return, rebuild, and resume living in the parish and to reoccupy their homes *in already long established neighborhoods*; Considering the public purpose, benefit and *need to maintain the integrity and stability of established neighborhoods as centers of family values and activities*; considering the public benefits to be obtained from *securing for the community the blessings of quiet enjoyment of their pre-existing neighborhoods*; and Considering the necessity to foster and encourage a community and family atmosphere in the neighborhood.[21]

Evidently, the council wanted to keep the neighborhoods as they were before Katrina. Some might ask, "What is wrong with wanting to maintain the integrity of the neighborhood?" Well, nothing is wrong with that intention, except for one thing: an intent to keep the neighborhoods in their pre-existing state meant the neighborhoods would remain segregated which was established by *previous law and practice*. And just in case there was any question of discriminatory intent, the parish, with the swipe of a pen,[22] made just one narrow exception in renting single family homes: *the blood-relatives of owners.*

> No person or entity shall *rent, lease, loan, or otherwise allow occupancy or use of any* single family residence located in an R-1 zone *by any person or groups of persons, other than a family member(s) related by blood* within the first, second, or third direct ascending or descending generation(s) without first obtaining a Permissive Use Permit from the . . . Council.

That's it—no renting, no lending, no leasing, no *occupying*, and certainly no *using*. Approximately 50 houses were available (according to some estimates, all but eight were rendered uninhabitable[23]) after Katrina, and not even sharing occupancy was permitted, unless one met the ancestry exception. And residents *still needed permission*, or they would suffer consequences under law. Lessors and lessees, owners and occupants, in violation of the ordinance would be subject to criminal prosecution and civil penalties, including a misdemeanor charge, a fine of between $50 and $250 per day for each day they were in violation of the ordinance, and a civil "penalty of $100 per day for each day of unpermitted rental . . . plus administrative costs, court costs, and attorney fees for investigation and prosecution of the civil matter."[24] In addition to other requirements, "the permissive use permit—often referred to as a PUP—allowed only two rental permits for every 500 linear feet of frontage for most contiguous single-family dwellings."[25] Almost immediately, the council denied residents permits to rent their properties to tenants because they were not blood relatives.

New law? Hardly. Maybe freshened up a bit, but still the same law. Recall that segregation was and is essential to the basic structure of Louisiana legally and socially. It is no surprise the ordinances passed in St. Bernard Parish following the storm echoed the segregationists' sentiments, which were enshrined in law following the Great Flood of 1932 when the search for housing was desperate in the New Orleans area:

> no person or corporation shall rent an apartment in an apartment house or other like structure to a person who is not of the same race as the other occupants.[26]

The St. Bernard Parish ordinance also smacked of Louisiana Act 118 of 1924, which:

- Withheld permits for white or "Negro" houses, under certain circumstances.
- Prohibited "white persons from establishing a home residence in a Negro community."
- Prohibited "negroes from establishing a home residence in a white community."

Any person in violation of these laws was threatened with arrest and prosecution, including tenants, for the misdemeanor.[27]

Additionally, the post-Katrina ordinance aligned with the Louisiana Constitution of 1921, which:

- Denied property ownership, including rental property, to noncitizens.[28]
- Prohibited "the housing of Negro and white families in the same dwelling house."[29]

To do differently would require "the written consent of a majority of the race inhabiting the community."[30]

Same intent, except now the phrase "who is not of the same race as the other occupants" was replaced with "*other than a family member(s) related by blood.*" Essentially, there is no difference between race and ancestry. Furthermore, recall that the Great Flood statute was in place for 40 years (and it was preceded by Jim Crow), and since its repeal, just one generation of citizens lived without a specific housing policy but certainly not without related societal practices. At the time Katrina hit, members of the new generation were approximately 30 years old (or younger), just about the age when one is married, has children, and needs a home for one's family. Their parents and grandparents lived under the Great Flood statute, so now it was the new generation's turn. What greater flood than that caused by Katrina could provide a perfect excuse for policymakers to emphasize their desire to maintain their "*long established . . . pre-existing neighborhoods.*"

The council simply substituted the word "blood" for the terms "Negro," "white," and "non-citizen." It substituted "Council's" written consent instead of the previous decision makers: the majority of the "race inhabiting the community," Now the decision was in the hands of just seven people. In further scrutinizing the ordinance, it appears as if the council was reviving the offensive one-drop rule:

> [The] "blood relative" must be within the first, second, or third direct ascending or descending generation(s)

Recall that the primary purpose in creating "degrees of hybridization" and the use of mathematical formulas to determine "blackness" was to keep control over land ownership. This was not ancient history but existed until it was repealed in 1983, just 22 years before Katrina.

On October 3, just three weeks following the passage of the blood relative ordinance, the Greater New Orleans Fair Housing Action Center (GNOFHAC) filed a lawsuit that argued the blood-relative designation constituted racial discrimination. The group requested an injunction against the parish council to halt enforcement of the ordinance pending the court's decision.[31] However, by December 2006, the council was holding fast to its position and again amended the ordinance. The reference to "blood relatives" was withdrawn, and now the council had to approve all rentals.[32] The council (a group of seven individuals) would now completely control permission, unlike years past when the "race of the community" was used. Furthermore, the council reserved the right to issue permits on a case-by-case basis with no indication of what criteria would need to be met other than "ensuring general compatibility with other *characteristics* of the neighborhood." The terms "integrity" and "characteristics of the neighborhood" were vague terms, leaving the council alone to decide what the criteria might be without spelling it out.

Chairman Lynn Dean,[33] who voted against the ordinance, revealed the council's intent and admitted that the ordinance was created "to block the blacks from living in these areas . . . Only we're doing it in a quiet manner, so you can't really say this . . . is what's happening. But I've watched it for years, and I know what they've been trying to do."[34] One month after Dean's comment, the council met in a private session to discuss the possibility of censuring Dean because his comments might affect the Council's strategy in the pending lawsuit. According to an article posted on the St. Bernard Parish website, council members "Craig Taffaro, Judy Hoffmeister, Kenny Henderson, and Ricky Melerine all said they believed it was imperative to preserve the parish's history of mostly owner-occupied neighborhoods."[35] Vice Chairman Joe DiFatta was quoted as saying the way "to preserve that atmosphere is to keep St. Bernard the way it was pre-Katrina."[36] Craig Taffaro, who initiated the ordinance, made a statement that the intent of the ordinance was *"to maintain the demographics."* Maintaining "the demographics" is clearly a reference to the racial make-up of the populace, which was and continues to be predominantly white due to segregationist policies and practices, thus de jure segregation existed.[37] Ricky Melerine said, "*We don't want to change the aesthetics of a neighborhood.*" Craig Taffaro argued, "This ordinance *restricts white people and non-white people the same.*" Taffaro's argument may lead one to suppose that because the ordinance affects everyone the same and does not single out a particular group, all residents are being treated equally. But Taffaro's argument is flawed. De jure segregation is "a current condition of segregation resulting from intentional state action."[38] "The differentiating factor between *de jure* segregation and so-called *de facto* segregation . . . is *purpose* or *intent* to segregate."[39] The parish and state setting official policies of racial segregation from the 1700s through 1983 and then calling for everyone to essentially remain in the properties that were in their possession is not equal treatment under law. Instead, it is a policy of keeping everyone in the place in which they have been set for hundreds of years, that is, segregated. Additionally, Taffaro and any advisory attorney for the parish overlooked *a very important caveat*: The government still may not pass or enforce any laws based on race or ancestry unless it can prove under strict judicial review three critical factors:

1. There must be a compelling governmental interest.
2. The law must be narrowly tailored to achieve the goal.
3. The law must be the least restrictive means.

Failure to meet these requirements serves as a fatal wound to the statute, and the statute will not be allowed to stand.

Local sentiment would provide additional evidence against the ordinance, particularly if legislators were listening to the voice of their constituents. The sharp tongues of many citizens of St. Bernard Parish spat racial hatred and went unfiltered, especially following Katrina. And when new housing projects finally began in St. Bernard Parish, the community not only jammed the voice mails of decision makers, they made their voices heard at construction sites. At a construction site for affordable apartments in Chalmette, someone spray-painted "No Niggers." A citizen who called Provident Realty Advisors pleaded in a voice mail to the developers: "We have enough rental garbage down here as it is. For 400 years, St. Bernard Parish has been white, French, Spanish. No niggers! We like no niggers. Please keep it that way! Please?" Another citizen spewed, "Don't build a nigger project in St. Bernard Parish." St. Bernard has deep roots—400-year-old roots—and today, the majority of families are at least three generations strong.[40] Many of its citizens and leaders would prove racial discrimination and dehumanization was a current practice that was centuries old, and no repeal of any discriminatory policy would change their customs or views.

The parish revised the blood relative ordinance and the conditional use permit ordinance by passing Ordinance 697-12-06, which took effect on January 4, 2007. The new requirement that the owner of any single family obtain a permissive use permit (PUP) from council to rent property to tenants. If the homeowner did not have the required permit, the offense was punishable by a daily fine of between $50 and $250 per day. Likewise, the renter would also be fined the same amount. While the elimination of the term "blood-relative" makes it appear that the law is facially neutral (appearance nondiscriminatory by the wording of the ordinance), in order to find a law discriminatory, the language need not be expressed or appear in the statute: "A statute, otherwise neutral on its face, must not be applied . . . invidiously to discriminate on the basis of race."[41] Via the PUP ordinance, the council could continue to maintain the desired discriminatory effect because all single-family residential rental property would have to be approved by the council members on a case-by-case basis. With no explanation as to how permits would be granted, there was a great threat that the ordinance would be applied in an arbitrary and capricious manner. More importantly, ". . . an invidious discriminatory purpose may often be inferred from the totality of the relevant facts, including the fact, if it is true, that the law bears more heavily on one race than another . . . a law, neutral on its face and serving ends otherwise within the power of government to pursue, is invalid under the Equal Protection Clause [of the Fourteenth Amendment] simply because it may affect a greater proportion of one race than of another."[42] For these reasons, the ordinance was more than likely unconstitutional.

Once the lawsuit was filed, the St. Bernard Parish Council backed itself into a corner and rather than repeal the ordinance, the council dug its heels into its marshlands and hired an attorney to defend its position. Two members of the council—Lynn Dean and Mark Madary—attempted to repeal the ordinance, but they were unsuccessful, failing with a 5–2 vote. Council members Craig Taffaro, Judy Hoffmeister, Kenny Henderson, Joey DiFatta, and "Ricky" Melerine refused to repeal the ordinance.[43] Even as late as January 2011, Craig Taffaro, who succeeded Junior Rodriguez and became president of the parish, stated, "Our stand has been challenged, mostly by *outside interests*. Our stand has been ridiculed, mostly by liberal media. And our stand has been eroded entirely by federal pressure."[44] Such espousals have been heard for centuries, having been voiced during secession, Reconstruction, the Civil Rights Movement, and massive resistance. Leaders in Louisiana (and in the Deep South overall) have often taken the position that "outsiders" are challenging their way of life, as if their states (or local governments) did not belong to this Union. The truth of the matter is that Louisiana *is* America—no one who resides there would deny he is an American. And because we are all Americans, there is no "outsider." As Americans, we all have an interest in protecting the constitutional rights of all citizens from government abuses, whether they come from federal, state, or local levels. We all have responsibilities to respond to our fellow citizens, to protect them, and to contain the pathology that allows for the abuse of fellow citizens, no matter where that citizen resides in this nation.

Years of financial mismanagement, segregation, and battles against hurricanes—particularly, Betsy, Katrina, and Rita—and resistance to the rule of law were breaking the parish's bank. After all, segregation does not allow for the full contribution of all citizens, creates ghettos, and reduces property values, which thus reduces tax revenue for the local government. Lynn Dean commented on the financial stresses created by the lawsuit, saying, "Our parish is broke. We don't have the money to fix roads. We are going to hire an attorney, and when it's all over with, we are going to lose."[45]

The council, by a vote of 6–1, decided to hire local attorney Francis B. Mulhall. Lynn Dean cast the lone dissenting vote. And while Mark Madary was opposed to the ordinance, he felt it necessary to vote to hire an attorney because the parish had "other priorities" and could not be left "defenseless."[46]

Meanwhile, 18 months after Katrina, "half of the homes in New Orleans still did not have electricity"; approximately 300,000 citizens had not returned; and "60,000 families in Louisiana [were still living] in 240 square-foot trailers." The Louisiana Hurricane Task forces called for an urgently needed "30,000 affordable rental apartments in New Orleans and another 15,000 around the rest of the state." More than "80 percent of the 5,100 occupied public-housing apartments in New Orleans remained closed by order of the US Department of Housing and Urban Development (HUD)."[47] Louisiana received *$10 billion* from the federal government to rebuild housing; yet 18 months after the aid was received, only 700 families received assistance. Renters received *nothing*.

Nearby, the Jefferson Parish Council, which represented another parish with a majority white population, "unanimously passed a resolution opposing all low-income, tax-credit, multifamily housing in the areas closest to New Orleans." The resolution "effectively [stopped] construction of a 200-unit apartment building on vacant land for people over the age of 62, and [blocked] any further assisted housing."[48] Jefferson Parish's resolution raised some eyebrows. According to former parish housing commissioners, "the Council as a group, and Councilman Chris Roberts in particular, have shown a pattern of 'racial animus' against low-income and minority residents in Jefferson Parish."[49] In fact, in July 2012, a federal audit revealed widespread mismanagement and more than $650,000 (of funds provided by HUD) in questionable expenses.[50] Racial animosity was also expressed in other areas surrounding New Orleans. The sheriff of St. Tammany Parish, Jack Strain, announced that "if you're going to walk the streets of St. Tammany Parish with dreadlocks and chee wee hairstyles then you can expect to be getting a visit from a sheriff's deputy." The American Civil Liberties Union issued an open letter to Strain "request[ing] an immediate retraction or clarification of [his] statements."[51] These examples collectively demonstrate the climate of discrimination in the southeastern parishes of Louisiana.

The stresses for citizens who suffered through Katrina and the aftermath became unbearable. According to the World Health Organization, serious and mild to moderate mental illness doubled among survivors in the year after Katrina.[52] Within 10 months, the suicide rate tripled, according to the New Orleans coroner's office.[53] Even more devastating was that New Orleans lost half of its mental health professionals following Katrina.

Adding to the pressure of finding affordable housing in St. Bernard Parish, "according to the Greater New Orleans Community Data Center, after appropriately adjusting for inflation ... median rental costs ... jumped from $609 in 2000 to $853 during the three-year period between 2007 and 2009."[54]

America continued to struggle against the legacy of dehumanization and the symptoms of discrimination and violence. In small doses, there were changes in federal government representation. Colin Powell was appointed as the first African-American secretary of state in 2001. And just seven months before Katrina hit, Condoleeza Rice was appointed as the first African-American female secretary of state. In other areas, the federal government remained the same. Clarence Thomas remained the sole African-American Supreme Court justice; no African Americans served in the U.S. Senate from 1999 until 2005, when Barack H. Obama—a Harvard-educated community organizer from Chicago—won a Senate seat representing Illinois. Obama was the sole African American in the Senate at the time of Katrina and its aftermath (2005–2009). There were 45 African Americans in the House of Representatives between 2000 and 2005, most of them by re-election. This was more than double the number of African-American representatives over the course of the entire 20th century.

Several years after Katrina, two more African Americans would be elected as governors of states: Deval Patrick (MA) in 2007 and David Paterson (NY) 2008. No racial changes to the presidency or vice presidency occurred. George W. Bush and Dick Cheney were elected in a controversial election in 2001, and they were re-elected in 2004, remaining in office until 2008. America was fighting a two-front war abroad in Iraq and Afghanistan. The fight in Afghanistan continues, as does the death toll. And, of course, the wars against terror, crime, drugs, poverty, racial hatred, and discrimination also continue.

From 2002 through 2011, the FBI reported that 89,715 Americans were victims of hate crime that were committed by 67,344 offenders. More than half of these attacks were based on race; and African Americans continued to be more than three times more likely than whites to be the victim of "anti-black crime."

While the St. Bernard Parish Council maintained it had no discriminatory intent, it is difficult to conceptualize such a position given the text of the statute in combination with a council president who uses racial epithets and admits that nonviolent racists exist in his district. In conjunction with the position of the council members, racist remarks, and police brutality from local sheriffs and deputies who enforce the local law and the unfiltered residential sentiment, along with the regular continuance of "anti-black hate crime," this whirlwind leaves the objective reviewer with a logical awareness that apartheid exists and segregation continues in the United States. In fact, when the ordinances are officially challenged in the legal arena, the council's comments are particularly relevant to the ordinance's passage. This is known as legislative intent. Furthermore, several versions of the ordinance were passed, which provided an additional and recent legislative history of the parish, which was in alignment with the legislation history of the state of Louisiana itself—segregationist policy. St. Bernard Parish in Louisiana boasted defiance to federal law, constitutional provisions, and Supreme Court holdings. It is the totality of these circumstances, including 400 continuous years of apartheid, disproportionate effects on non-whites, and the current socio-political climate, that is key in not only understanding the continuing establishment of segregationist policy, but in fighting against it and dismantling the policies. In Louisiana, the struggle for the dismantling of newer forms of segregationist policy and custom was just beginning. Those who fixed themselves to the ordinances would find themselves in the unsteady ground of their wetlands.

Chapter 5

The 21st Century and Legal Analysis

A lawyer's either a social engineer or . . . a parasite on society . . .
A social engineer [is] a highly skilled, perceptive,
sensitive lawyer who [understands]
the Constitution of the United States and [knows] how to explore its uses
in the solving of problems of local communities and
in bettering conditions of the underprivileged citizens.

—The credo of
Charles Hamilton Houston
Dean of Howard University School of Law (1930–1935)
and the attorney behind nearly every civil rights case before
the Supreme Court of the United States
between 1930 and 1954

It is important to demonstrate the legislative history of a particular state when evaluating a new law that is alleged to be unconstitutional. The legislative history provides evidence of the intent of the newly created law—and whether the law was promulgated for legitimate (and nondiscriminatory) purposes. From 1724 until 2006—a full 282 years—Louisiana created laws with the intent of segregating the races and subjugating blacks.[1] Prior to 1724, the French and Spanish Code Noir applied to the region.

The 2006 lawsuit by Greater New Orleans Fair Housing Action Center (GNOFHAC) requested a permanent injunction against the St. Bernard Parish and the council to prevent enforcement of the blood relative ordinances.[2] According to the complaint, the "ordinances have the intent and the effect of denying and making unavailable rental housing . . . based on race and national origin . . . permit[ting] re-occupancy . . . subject to case-by-case approval of the . . . Council."[3]

Wallace Rodrigue, who is white, always lived in St. Bernard Parish, owned three properties, and was in the process of renovating the properties for rental purposes when Hurricane Katrina hit. Rodrigue joined the suit after the original complaint was filed. The blood relative ordinance prohibited him from renting to nonrelatives and, according to Rodrigue, caused "a big financial hardship for him as he had no relatives in the area."[4]

Equal Protection and the Fourteenth Amendment

The Fourteenth Amendment to the U.S. Constitution was ratified in 1868 as part of the Reconstruction amendments, which also included the Thirteenth and Fifteenth Amendments. Its main purpose was to protect newly freed slaves from continued discrimination by state governments, particularly in former slave-holding states. In essence, it was to serve as a resolution to the controversy of the legal status of African Americans: persons or nonpersons and citizens or noncitizens under the law. Normally, when courts are "faced with ordinary social and economic legislation,"[5] they are usually deferential to political outcomes. But considering the history of the Supreme Court of the United States, it was unlikely that the judicial system would support discrimination targeting African Americans.[6] The Fourteenth Amendment serves as the impetus for discriminatory laws that applied to "both races." Additionally, past Supreme Court decisions essentially tied the hands of the government by refusing to protect citizens from discrimination between each other, emphasizing the Amendment only protected against infringement by state actors[7]—privately, segregation was permissible[8] as applied to African Americans and whites alike. Despite court errors and subsequent overruling of decisions, the primary purpose of the Equal Protection Clause of the Fourteenth Amendment is to prevent racial discrimination by a state entity.[9] It is applicable in the case of the blood relative ordinances developed by the St. Bernard Parish Council. According to Section 1 of the Fourteenth Amendment:

> All persons born or naturalized in the United States, and subject to the jurisdiction thereof, are citizens of the United States and of the State wherein they reside. No State shall make or enforce any law which shall abridge the privileges or immunities of citizens of the United States; nor shall any State deprive any person of life, liberty, or property, without due process of law; nor deny to any person within its jurisdiction the equal protection of the laws.[10]

Section 5 of the Fourteenth Amendment provides that "... Congress shall have power to enforce, by appropriate legislation, the provisions of this article," thus paving the way for federal statues such as the Civil Rights Acts of 1866 and 1964.

When statutes discriminate on the basis of race, the court applies strict scrutiny; and the legislation is struck down as a constitutional violation unless a compelling governmental interest is served. When a statute is facially neutral but there is an obvious pretext for racial discrimination, it is also subject to the court's strict scrutiny test. Neutral laws "with an invidious discriminatory purpose" that have a disproportionate impact on a racial minority may also be challenged, "but it is not the sole touchstone of an invidious racial discrimination forbidden by the Constitution."[11] To prove harm through disproportionate impact in cases of facially-neutral statutes, it is necessary to establish intent to discriminate, for example:

- "The historical background of the decision is one evidentiary source, particularly if it reveals a series of official actions taken for invidious purposes,"[12]
- "The legislative or administrative history may be highly relevant, especially where there are contemporary statements by members of the decision-making body, minutes of its meetings, or reports,"[13]
- "An invidious discriminatory purpose may often be inferred from the *totality of the relevant facts*, including the fact, if it is true, that the law bears more heavily on one race than another."[14]

In establishing the historical background of the council's decision to institute the new ordinances, one will find that the language, particularly that of the third version of the blood-relative ordinance, completely denies persons the ability to rent single-family homes unless they are related by certain degrees of ancestry. Given that the different ordinances were passed within a short time of each other and the slight changes to wording, it is likely the council was seeking to effectuate the same invidious purpose of the ordinance without it being facially discriminatory. Equally as important to the analysis, five years before Hurricane Katrina (in 2000), the Supreme Court of the United States held in the case of *Rice v. Cayetano* that "Distinctions between citizens *solely because of their ancestry* are by their very nature odious to a free people."[15] Within five months of Katrina's devastation, the council sought to put a halt to any activity that would likely change the composition of the area's "demographics," including placing a complete moratorium on rental properties despite the desperate need for housing in a parish where 90 percent of residences sustained significant damage. Furthermore, the language of the ordinances is eerily similar to those in effect during the Jim Crow era, when to live in white enclaves, African Americans needed special permission from members of the opposite race in the neighborhood.

In analyzing the ordinances' legislative history, particularly comments by council members, one will find that the intent of the ordinance was, indeed, to maintain the demographics of the population, not another characteristic of the neighborhoods, as single-family homes were not being rezoned for apartment complexes and the like. Councilman Dean's comments were critical in that he exposed the council's intent to "[keep] the blacks out" of St. Bernard Parish. The invidious purpose of the ordinance, therefore, can be inferred from the totality of the circumstances surrounding the passage of the ordinances, particularly because they would affect African Americans more heavily than whites. Whites owned 93 percent of the single family homes in the parish, yet, the majority of renters in St. Bernard Parish were predominantly African American. Only 21 percent of whites resided in rental units compared to 45 percent of blacks and 31 percent of Hispanics. The damage from Katrina affected nearly all rental units. Furthermore, at the time of the storm, Chalmette, the parish seat of St. Bernard, was 90 percent white. According to the St. Bernard Parish School Board, in 2002, the total black population of the Parish was 5,112 out of approximately 65,000. In 2005, at the time of Katrina, St. Bernard Parish was 84.37 percent white, 7.6 percent black, and 5.09 percent Hispanic.

State Action Required

To invoke a claim of violations under the Fourteenth Amendment, a litigant must be able to show that state action is involved in the denial of the constitutional rights.[16] Certainly states, including local governments, have wide authority to pass ordinances and other laws to promote the health, safety, and welfare of all of its citizens.[17] But they may not pass laws that run "counter to the limitations of the Federal Constitution," as held in *Buchanan v. Wharley* in 1920.[18] In the *Buchanan* case, blacks were forbidden from occupying homes in white neighborhoods pursuant to a Louisville, Kentucky, ordinance.[19] Buchanan, a white seller, and Warley, a black purchaser, entered into a real estate sales contract that contained a clause that Warley "shall not be required to accept a deed . . . or to pay for said property . . . unless [he had] the right under" state and city law to occupy the "property as a residence."[20] Considering the law in effect would forbid Warley from living in the neighborhood, Warley's essential argument was that the contract could not be enforced. But the Court held Buchanan was denied his constitutional right to dispose of his property and that the "attempt to prevent the alienation of the property in question to a person of color was not a legitimate exercise of the police power of the State, and is in direct violation of the fundamental law enacted in the Fourteenth Amendment."[21] The St. Bernard Parish Council's actions related to passing the ordinances (which were almost identical to what occurred in *Buchanan*, except in Louisiana they involved the rental of single-family homes) are considered state actions for the purposes of Fourteenth Amendment analysis because the council is the legislative entity for the parish.

Scrutiny by the Courts

Equal protection does not provide that all individuals are treated identically; rather, similarly situated individuals are treated similarly. Classifications "must be reasonable, not arbitrary."[22] Therefore, in deciding an equal protection claim, the court must determine whether the classification in question is "permissible," that is, what group is being treated differently, the goal or purpose behind different treatment, and the nexus between the government's "means" and its "ends."[23] The Supreme Court of the United States established a three-tier framework to answer these questions, which is also known as levels of scrutiny: rational scrutiny, intermediate scrutiny, and strict scrutiny.

Under rational scrutiny, legislation must be "rationally related to a legitimate governmental purpose."[24] Intermediate scrutiny applies to quasi-suspect classes (including gender and illegitimacy),[25] and the legislation "must serve important governmental objectives and must be substantially related to achievement of those objectives."[26] In 1985, in the case of *Cleburne v. Cleburne Living Center, Inc.*, a corporation sought to rent out a building for use as a "group home for the mentally retarded."[27] However, a city ordinance required a special use requirement for use in the care of such individuals and not other types of care. The Court found that even though individuals with developmental disabilities did not make up a quasi-suspect class, the state still needed to demonstrate at least a *legitimate* government interest. The Court held the ordinance invalid and added:

> The general rule gives way, however, when a statute classified by race, alienage, or national origin. *These factors are so seldom relevant to the achievement of any legitimate state interest that laws grounded in such considerations are deemed to reflect prejudice and antipathy—a view that those in the burdened class are not as worthy or deserving as others.* For these reasons and because such *discrimination is unlikely to be soon rectified by legislative means,* these laws are subjected to strict scrutiny and will be sustained only if they are suitably tailored to serve a compelling state interest.[28]

Strict scrutiny is the highest level and applies in two instances: (1) when fundamental interests[29] are implicated and (2) when a suspect classification (race, national origin, religion, and alienage[30]) is used by the government. Under strict scrutiny, government provisions must be "supported by a *compelling* state purpose and whether the means chosen to accomplish that purpose is narrowly tailored."[31] When the state distinguishes between individuals in an arbitrary and irrational manner, it violates the Equal Protection and Due Process clauses of the Fourteenth Amendment even under the Court's "most deferential standard of review."[32] Another case from Louisiana explains the principle. The Supreme Court of the United States held in *American Sugar Refining Co. v. Louisiana* (179 U.S. 89, 92 [1900]):

> If such discrimination were purely arbitrary, oppressive or capricious, and made to depend upon differences of color, race, nativity, religious opinions, political affiliations, or other considerations having no possible connection . . . [it] *would be pure favoritism, and a denial of the equal protection of the laws* to the less favored classes.

Around the country, there were challenges to segregation in housing. Plaintiffs in a case out of Illinois in 1977, *Metropolitan Hous. Dev. Corp. v. Village of Arlington Heights*, claimed the village's refusal to rezone property to allow construction of low-income housing was based on racial discrimination.[33] The case went to the Supreme Court of the United States, which returned it to the lower court for further analysis. The Seventh Circuit explained:

> Since the Village could supply no such compelling justification, we held that it had violated the Equal Protection Clause. 517 F. 2d 409, 412-415 (7th Cir. 1974). The Supreme Court reversed. Although the Court did not question our conclusion that the Village's zoning decision had a racially discriminatory effect, it noted that under *Washington v. Davis*, 426 U.S. 229, 48 L. Ed.

> 2d 597, 96 S. Ct. 2040 (1976), decided after we had issued our opinion in this case, *a showing of discriminatory intent was a prerequisite to establishing a violation of the Equal Protection Clause.*[34]

In the case at hand, involving the St. Bernard ordinances, there is evidence of both a discriminatory impact and effect given the composition of the population and the critical housing needs in the area that were caused by Hurricane Katrina. Whites own 93 percent of the single-family homes in St. Bernard Parish and comprise greater than 83 percent of the population; however, minority populations in St. Bernard Parish make up the majority of the rental population—and that is who is affected by the ordinances. There is also significant evidence of an intent to discriminate given comments by council members (one publicly admitted to being a racist, and another reported to the media the discriminatory intent of the council in developing the ordinances) and the historical significance of slavery and its codes, Black Codes, Jim Crow throughout this region, massive resistance to desegregation, and the evolution of the parish ordinances.

Equal Protection Analysis of Ordinances

The first ordinance placing a moratorium on single-family homes becoming rental properties would probably have been subject to the lowest level of scrutiny because there was no indication it was motivated by a protected class, such as race, and it was set for a period of time, perhaps vaguely, namely "until the post-Katrina real estate market stabilizes." Considering the scope of the devastation, the time needed to replace infrastructure and clean up, and the time needed to allow thousands of residents to return, the parish would have been able to argue a valid and rational concern related to wanting to protect residential integrity. St. Bernard Parish likely needed to articulate a rational basis for passage of the ordinance and set a reasonable time period in order to pass a court's muster.

Unfortunately, the second version of the ordinance went further, restricting owners from renting to "any person" without a special permit from the council. Again, it does not appear that any suspect classes are implicated and, therefore, a rational basis test would likely apply. There is, however, some ambiguity in the second version, as there is no explanation as to what the requirements would be to gain a special permit or how the ordinance would be applied. Considering the ambiguity, it is possible discrimination would be found to be arbitrary and therefore in violation of the Fourteenth Amendment. Furthermore, property rights are among those protected by the Fourteenth Amendment and may not be "invaded" by the state without due process of law, "includ[ing] the right to acquire, use, and dispose of [property]," as per *Buchanan*.

But it was the third version of the ordinance that became the target of the lawsuit. The council changed the wording to restrict rental to "any person" "other than a family member(s) related by blood within the first, second, or third direct ascending or descending generation(s) without first obtaining a Permissive Use Permit from the . . . Council"[35]

Because the third version required that a renter be related to the homeowner by blood, it is a classification based on national origin, ethnicity, or ancestry. Thus, the ordinance is automatically relegated to review under the strictest scrutiny because racial classification is so rarely tied with a legitimate government interest. In this case, St. Bernard Parish would have to demonstrate a *compelling* government interest for the ordinance to pass constitutional muster. The parish claimed it was necessary to maintain the aesthetics and integrity of the neighborhoods; however, simply restricting who can rent a property that is already zoned for single-family residency appears to be a cover for racial discrimination because use of the property would remain the same. In addition, there are likely other ways in which the parish could maintain the integrity of neighborhoods without using race or ancestry as a means to that end. In a parish where an overwhelming majority of the populace has ancestry that can be linked to the original white settlers of the area, it was likely that the reasons for the ordinance had nothing to do with the "aesthetics of the neighborhood" and more to do with maintaining the "demographics" of the predominantly white populace, which was an idea publicly espoused by council members. This is legally impermissible under equal protection.

Civil Rights Act of 1866 and 42 USCS §1981

Almost immediately following the passage of the Fourteenth Amendment, Congress passed the Civil Rights Act of 1866, making provisions for all citizens:

> That all persons born in the United States and not subject to any foreign power, excluding Indians not taxed, are hereby declared to be citizens of the United States; and such citizens, of every race and color, without regard to any previous condition of slavery or involuntary servitude . . . *shall have*

> *the same right, in every State and Territory in the United States, to make and enforce contracts, to sue, be parties, and give evidence, inherit, purchase, lease, sell, hold, and convey real and personal property,* and to full and equal benefit of all laws and proceedings for the security of person and property, as is enjoyed by white citizens, and shall be subject to like punishment, pains, and penalties, and to none other, any law, statute, ordinance, regulation, or custom, to the contrary notwithstanding.[36]

Currently, federal law similarly provides for all persons the same right "to make and enforce contracts . . . and equal benefit of all laws and proceedings for the security of persons and property as is enjoyed by white citizens" under 42 USCS §1981(a), the statute that provides for equal rights under the law. Additionally, Section C of the statute protects these rights from both the "impairment by non-governmental discrimination and impairment under color of State law." The St. Bernard Parish ordinance restricts individuals from renting single-family homes without obtaining a permit granted by the council only on a case-by-case basis, which directly violates the right "to lease real and personal property" and the right to "full and equal benefit of all laws and proceedings for the security of . . . property" regardless of any "ordinance . . . to the contrary." Therefore, in addition to it being applied in an arbitrary and capricious manner, the specific wording of the ordinance is in violation of the Civil Rights Act of 1866 and 42 USCS 1981.

The Fair Housing Act of 1968

The Fair Housing Act was enacted with a specific purpose: "to [prohibit] discrimination in the housing market based on race, color, religion, or national origin . . . so as to bar all racial discrimination, *private as well as public*, in sale and rental of real property."[37] Furthermore, "Congress passed [the] Fair Housing Act to ensure removal of artificial, arbitrary, and unnecessary barriers in housing when barriers operate invidiously to discriminate on [the] basis of impermissible characteristics."[38] The act provides a basis for a housing discrimination claim; and any state law that purports to require or permit actions that are discriminatory housing practices under the act is invalid.[39] One of the discriminatory practices prohibited by the act is found in Section 804(b), which makes it unlawful "[t]o discriminate against any person in the terms, conditions, or privileges of sale or rental of a dwelling, or in the provision of services or facilities in connection therewith, because of race, color, religion, sex, familial status, or national origin."[40] The Fair Housing Act applies to St. Bernard Parish and its ordinances.

Methods of enforcement of the act include filing a civil suit in an appropriate U.S. district court, or state or local court of general jurisdiction.[41] Standing to sue is intended to be broadly interpreted and may include "a white person upon whom discrimination against black persons has an impact."[42] "Aggrieved person(s) includes any person who (1) claims to have been injured by a discriminatory housing practice or (2) believes that such person will be injured by a discriminatory housing practice that is about to occur."[43] It is under this definition that GNOFHAC, Rodrigue, and housing developers would have standing. Mr. Rodrigue, one of the first plaintiffs, would have standing to sue on this issue because he did not have blood relatives to whom he could rent his property and would be unable to rent the property at all. Therefore, he would be injured by the practice. GNOFHAC and housing developers certainly had reason to believe that persons would be injured by the institution of the ordinance and any application that would ensue and therefore would also have standing.

Furthermore, the Fair Housing Act makes it unlawful:

- To refuse to sell or rent after the making of a bona fide offer, or *to refuse to negotiate for the sale or rental of, or otherwise make unavailable or deny, a dwelling to any person because of race, color... or national origin.*
- *To discriminate against any person in the terms, conditions, or privileges of sale or rental* of a dwelling, or in the provision of services or facilities in connection therewith, because of race, color ... or national origin.
- *To make, print, or publish, or cause to be made, printed, or published any notice, statement, or advertisement,* with respect to the sale or rental of a dwelling *that indicates any preference, limitation, or discrimination* based on race, color ... or national origin, or an intention to make any such preference, limitation, or discrimination.
- *To represent* to any person because of race, color, religion, sex, handicap, familial status, or national origin *that any dwelling is not available* for inspection, sale, or rental *when such dwelling is in fact so available.*[44]

Discrimination may be shown by providing evidence of overt racially discriminatory actions or statements incident to the denial of housing.[45] In the case involving St. Bernard Parish, evidence of overtly racial discriminatory action is found within the content of the third version of the ordinance; in the history of oppression and violence against African Americans; segregating them in the region; massive resistance to desegregation; and in council members' public comments regarding the intent of the ordinance; and the acts of residents, without police or council intervention, who affixed signs to properties stating "No Niggers." Remedies for violation of the Fair Housing Act include injunctive relief, damages for emotional distress, punitive damages, and attorney's fees.

Conclusions of Law

Although the current ordinance is facially neutral, given the evolution of the St. Bernard ordinance and the history of residential segregation within the state of Louisiana, the ordinance should be found to have a discriminatory intent and is arbitrary and capricious. Furthermore, it would have a disparate impact against nonwhites, predominantly affecting African Americans. After several revisions to the ordinance, the parish settled on a clause prohibiting owners from renting to anyone who was not a blood relative and specifically those relatives who were direct ancestors or descendants. Following a lawsuit filed by the Greater New Orleans Fair Housing Action Center, the parish revised the ordinance so that it was facially neutral but would have the same effect because the rental of all single-family residential property would have to be approved by the parish on a case-by-case-basis. In essence, the parish, in an effort to avoid a lawsuit, simply erased the non–blood relative reference but retained the right to approve or deny permits on a case-by-case basis without any direction as to what standard would be required to receive approval. This decision leaves approval solely to the discretion of the seven members of the council, which raises the risk of arbitrary and capricious application.

In light of the extensive history of institutional racial discrimination in St. Bernard Parish and the surrounding New Orleans area (where it was customary to require special written permission for blacks to move around the state or into white neighborhoods), it can be seen that the current ordinances mirror the customary practice. Finally, the discriminatory intent of council members, the inevitable disproportionate impact on African Americans, and the lack of a compelling—or for that matter, rational—government interest are critical to making the determination that the St. Bernard Parish ordinance would have been struck down as unconstitutional.

As if the St. Bernard Parish ordinance is not sufficient evidence of continued segregation, in March 2009, the U.S. District Court Eastern District of Louisiana "found that a September 2008 moratorium on the construction of multi-family housing of more than five units violated the Fair

Housing Act, 42 U.S.C. §3604(a), and the 2008 Consent Order . . . because the moratorium was racially discriminatory in intent and effect.[46] By 2009 in New Orleans, 5,670 Katrina-damaged structures were torn down with $53 million in FEMA money; but in St. Bernard Parish, Unified Recovery Group demolished more than 7,000 buildings costing $241 million of FEMA money." In addition, half of the buildings were sold to the state through Road Home buyouts. At least 12 St. Bernard Parish homes that were up to code were "mistakenly demolished."[47] At that time, St. Bernard Parish president Craig Taffaro, who authored the discriminatory ordinance, "said the parish was still reviewing about 800 condemned properties," but he refused "to provide a list of upcoming demolitions, saying the parish was still reviewing many cases."[48] According to the Greater New Orleans Data Center, between September 2010 and March 2011, approximately 8,000 properties affected by Katrina were "repaired or rebuilt," and still 21 percent of all properties were "blighted."[49]

Most recently, on June 25, 2013, the Supreme Court of the United States ruled on issues related to the constitutionality of certain provisions in the Civil Rights Act of 1965 in the case of *Shelby County, Alabama v. Holder, Attorney General, et al.* Parts of the act specifically covered certain states because of their implementation of voter tests and devices: Alabama, Georgia, Virginia, Mississippi, South Carolina, and—once again—Louisiana. Tests and devices included, inter alia, literacy and knowledge tests, good moral character requirements, and the need for vouchers from registered voters.[50]

Chief Justice Roberts delivered the opinion of the Court, acknowledging that "[the Civil Rights Act of 1965 was] strong medicine, but Congress determined it was needed to address entrenched racial discrimination in voting, 'an insidious and pervasive evil which had been perpetuated in certain parts of our country through unremitting and ingenious defiance of the Constitution,' [citing *South Carolina* v. *Katzenbach*, 383 U. S. 301, 309 (1966)]. As we explained in upholding the law, 'exceptional conditions can justify legislative measures not otherwise appropriate.' "[51] Congress extended the Civil Rights Act of 1965 to the year 2031. According to the Court, "the Act imposes current burdens and must be justified by current needs."[52]

In a 5–4 vote, the court held that distinguishing the affected states based on 40-year-old data violated states' rights to equal sovereignty and was therefore unconstitutional:

> Our decision in no way affects the permanent, nationwide ban on racial discrimination in voting found in §2. We issue no holding on §5 itself, only on the coverage formula. Congress may draft another formula based on current conditions. Such a formula is an initial prerequisite to a determination that exceptional conditions still exist justifying such an "extraordinary departure from the traditional course of relations between the States and the Federal Government." *Presley*, 502 U. S., at 500–501. *Our country has changed, and while any racial discrimination in voting is too much, Congress must ensure that the legislation it passes to remedy that problem speaks to current conditions.*[53]

The simplistic beliefs that "racism is no longer a basis" and that "our country has changed" belie hundreds of years of history to the contrary, including the present date, rolling the clock backward from *today*. In the case of St. Bernard Parish, the battle would prove to be long and costly—an impossible mission.

Chapter 6

The Lawsuits

[The goal is] to block blacks from living in these areas.
Only we're doing it in a quiet manner so you can't really
say this is what is happening.
But I've watched it for years, and I know what they've been trying to do.[1]

—Lynn Dean
Former St. Bernard council member, resident of St. Bernard
Parish for over 70 years,
and one of two council members who voted against the ordinance

A lawsuit was filed by the Greater New Orleans Housing Action Center (GNOFHAC) against St. Bernard Parish on October 3, 2006, requesting a permanent injunction to prevent the parish from enforcing the "non–blood relative" ordinances.[2] No clients were listed as parties to the suit; rather, the GNOFHAC claimed itself as a victim of the ordinance: "injured by St. Bernard's discriminatory housing practices through the diversion of its resources to enforcing fair housing laws violated by . . . discriminatory zoning practices."[3] The original and amended complaints listed as causes of action violations of the Fair Housing Act, 42 U.S.C. §3604(a); Equal Rights Under Law, 42 U.S.C. §1981; Property Rights of Citizens, 42 U.S.C. §1982; Civil Action for Deprivation of Rights, 42 U.S.C. §1983; the equal protection clause; and the Fourteenth Amendment to the U.S. Constitution.[4]

The parish already paid $32,500 to settle an antidiscrimination lawsuit related to the ordinance, which was conceived by council president Craig Taffaro when he was a parish council member in 2006. It would cost St. Bernard Parish an additional $123,000 in attorney fees to the Greater New Orleans Fair Housing Action Center, which filed the suit. These amounts do not include the parish's own legal bills, which were also rising as officials dealt with another lawsuit against an amended rental restriction, this one filed by Florida investors.

The GNOFHAC sued because the St. Bernard Parish law required council permission to rent homes to anyone who was not a blood relative of the owner, in effect restricting rentals to minorities in the overwhelmingly white parish. The council dropped that provision in late 2006, but it still required homeowners to get a permit to rent homes that were not rentals before Katrina by passing additional ordinances. That prompted the second lawsuit.[5] The parish would inevitably lose all court battles in which they had to defend the discriminatory law. U.S. district court judge Ginger Berrigan ruled that a 2008 moratorium on multifamily housing was intentionally discriminatory. These legal defeats were foreseeable from the beginning even to members of the council. Then councilman Lynn Dean chastised his colleagues for creating policies with the intent to discriminate and for using taxpayer dollars to defend themselves. He said, "Our parish is broke. We are going to hire an attorney, and when it's all over with, we are going to lose." Dean had good common sense because that is exactly what occurred.

Parish taxpayers paid for the stubbornness of their government. St. Bernard spent another $153,000 to settle the second lawsuit related to the 2006 rental ordinance alone. The next case would cost more. Judge Berrigan ruled that St. Bernard Parish was liable for the housing developers' attorney fees. By March 2008, those fees totaled almost $770,000. Judge Berrigan acknowledged that no other parish in Louisiana was more devastated by Katrina than St. Bernard, but the parish's relentless discriminatory campaign threatened to block investment.[6]

Discriminatory Intent and Contempt of Court

Berrigan issued the parish three contempt of court rulings within a span of six months (March through September 2009) for its actions that blocked construction of mixed-income apartment complexes by Provident Realty Advisors of Dallas, particularly because the ordinances were revised nearly every three to six months. In October 2009, the parish approved the Provident building permits but by December, it passed "sweeping new zoning laws that eliminated 99.3 percent of the land available for multi-family housing in the parish."[7]

The *Times-Picayune* reported that Judge Berrigan "found that St. Bernard officials acted with a discriminatory intent as the parish continued to obstruct Provident from building the apartments. Berrigan advised the political leaders to 'display mature leadership and dispense with the demagoguery they'd been using to keep their constituents frenzied.' "[8] Berrigan would issue six more contempt motions against the parish for continued violation of "federal Fair Housing laws, in connection with housing and zoning decisions."[9]

Adding to the pressure, the U.S. Department of Housing and Urban Development (HUD) had enough of the stonewalling of the Provident development project and threatened to withhold $91 million in funding that HUD had stipulated for the parish, part of which was designated for a proposed hospital. On January 28, 2011, HUD filed a complaint against the parish that focused broadly on 2009 zoning ordinances, which eliminated most multifamily housing as a permitted use. HUD was aware that such a complaint could result in a referral to the U.S. Department of Justice (DOJ) for further action. Sure enough, the same month, DOJ filed suit seeking a general court order that would prevent the parish council from making unavailable or denying housing on the basis of race. It would also require the parish to take actions to prevent any similar discriminatory conduct in the future. In addition, the lawsuit sought a civil penalty and monetary damages for people harmed by the parish's actions.

Then the Department of Justice charged the parish with violating the Fair Housing Act for "engaging in a multi-year campaign to limit rental housing opportunities for African-Americans." Based on the two Taffaro-introduced ordinances, Berrigan issued a three-year federal consent decree barring St. Bernard from further violating the Fair Housing Act. Several of Berrigan's rulings stated that the actions of the parish intentionally segregated African Americans. As late as October 2011, Berrigan continued to chastise St. Bernard Parish, ruling it in contempt of court for the same reasons over and over again. Judge Berrigan charged that it was illegal for the parish council to "doggedly [attempt] to preserve the pre-Katrina demographics." In late December 2011, Berrigan ordered the council to issue occupancy permits for the apartments or be subjected to a fine of $50,000 per day.

The council conceded and provided Provident with the building permit necessary to construct the four 72-unit mixed-income apartments. Some officials remained stubborn, though, and Councilman Ray Lauga stated that "he was willing to forsake the federal help the parish needs for the hospital if he could keep out the apartments."[10] By March 2011, the council called a meeting to repeal the restrictive ordinances. Residents packed the chambers of the St. Bernard Parish government and were described as "raucous." Many wore red shirts to demonstrate their opposition to building the multifamily units. Before the vote, parish president Taffaro "urged the parish council to join him in an all-out stand against the 'federal agenda' imposed on the citizens and [to] reject 'an inappropriate insertion into our community.' "[11]

Finally, residents began moving into the complexes in January 2012. In July 2012, Provident and GNOFHAC filed a motion for summary judgment. The motion argued that "the conduct at issue in the relevant time period involved issuing repeated cease and desist orders, withholding the release of critical municipal services, refusing to provide feedback and information on construction specifications, refusing to issue renewed building permits, and delaying construction by seeking to enforce inapplicable codes." This conduct, the motion argued, was sufficient for the plaintiffs to win the case and for St. Bernard Parish to lose. The plaintiffs would wait for the court's response, which would come in the fall.[12]

The "Feds" Step In

When the Department of Justice became involved with the case, and as part of the "ongoing discovery phase of a long-running housing discrimination case," the agency requested parish documents in July 2012. The matter was set for trial on February 19, 2013. St. Bernard Parish failed—or ignored the request—to produce four boxes of documents related to the permit issues in question. U.S. magistrate judge Sally Shushan ordered the parish to produce the documents. The continued failure by the parish to produce the evidence resulted in the issuance of a search warrant; and in October 2012, St. Bernard Parish deputies who were armed with the warrant retrieved 19 boxes of copies of parish documents from Taffaro's old storage unit in Chalmette. According to Taffaro's attorney, the parish government was always in possession of the documents because Taffaro "scanned them into the parish government's computer server and left the original documents in his parish president's office."[13]

Undoubtedly influenced by the pressures of the lawsuits and investigations, the new council took a giant leap into the 21st century by proposing an amendment to the parish's charter in October 2012, just before the election. For the first time in its 400 years of existence, the parish proposed to establish an ethics board. The proposition called the Parishwide Proposition (Charter Amendment) Summary: Amendment to Article VIII, to

Amend Section 8-04 (Ethics Board) for Selection of Board Members for St. Bernard Parish.

Accordingly, the question for voters was:

> Shall Article VIII, Section 8-04 of the Home Rule Charter of the Parish of St. Bernard, State of Louisiana, be amended to read as follows: (a) The St. Bernard Parish Ethics Board (hereinafter referred to as the ethics board) shall be composed of (5) five members; (b) The members shall be selected from nominations submitted by the presidents/chancellors from the following institutions of higher learning: 1. University of New Orleans; 2. Loyola University; 3. Tulane University; 4. Xavier University; 5. Nunez Community College. The members of the Board of Ethics shall serve a term of four years?[14]

Despite all of the tension and their fight to stick to their guns, voters evidently knew something had to change, and they overwhelmingly approved the measure. Previous attempts to create an ethics board had been thwarted by voters, supposedly "because of fears that the board [would] become politicized." Perhaps there was a change of heart once voters knew that universities would be "in charge of appointing the board." Tulane University nominated St. Bernard resident Chris Holmes, "a writer, law clerk, and notary public actively involved in environmental and outdoors issues [who] also writes a monthly outdoor column in The St. Bernard Voice." Loyola University chose Adele Faust as their nominee. Faust is also "a St. Bernard native and lawyer based in Chalmette known for her active role in the local business community." The University of New Orleans chose one from its own ranks. John Keifer is the director of the university's master's program in political science and is also the president of the Greater New Orleans chapter of the American Society for Public Administration. Nunez Community College selected the chairman of its foundation board, Frank Auderer Jr., who was formerly the Ssuperintendent of the St. Bernard School Board and a former member of the parish council. Xavier University has yet to provide a nominee.[15]

By the end of 2012, the parish had a $3 million bigotry bill on its hands. St. Bernard residents largely supported parish officials and allowed themselves to be misguided. Judge Berrigan granted GNOFHAC its summary judgment and ordered the parish to pay $625,153 (in addition to its previous costs of $2 million) in fees, costs, and damages related to its opposition to Provident Realty's efforts to construct apartments in the parish. Judge Berrigan based her ruling in part on:

1. the transcripts of public meetings and determined that racial animus was the driving force behind the opposition and the ordinances,
2. that officials repeatedly defied the federal court orders she issued
3. and her repeated findings of the parish in contempt.

St. Bernard Parish was now definitely broke, so much so that parish officials imposed a $32 monthly fee on residents for fire service. Furthermore, the parish council "introduced an ordinance that would allow the parish to take out a $5 million bond because its members fear they might need it to plug holes in the parish budget." The newly-elected parish president David Peralta took a different stance from his predecessors, Rodriquez and Taffaro—one that was desperately necessary. Peralta was formerly the chief administrative officer under parish president Henry "Junior" Rodriguez. When Craig Taffaro became parish president, he fired Peralto. Ironically, Taffaro would lose re-election to Peralta, who "pushed for a parish inspector general, a parish ethics board and said he would create easier access to both himself and parish government records."[16] With regard to the housing debate, Peralta stated, "I have seen no problem with the apartments. I don't see any now, nor do I anticipate any."[17]

When led by Taffaro, St. Bernard Parish incurred approximately $3 million in legal fees, costs, and damages throughout their uphill battle in favor of what ultimately amounted to a policy of segregation. And the parish lost big. Yet it would lose even more in the case that involved the Department of Justice, which it was forced to settle. Judge Berrigan approved a civil settlement between St. Bernard Parish and the DOJ on May 10, 2013. Despite its agreement to settle, St. Bernard Parish failed to admit any liability.[18] However, both sides stipulated the following:

1. Prior to the landfall of Hurricane Katrina, the population of St. Bernard Parish was approximately 86 percent white and 10 percent African American, while the population of neighboring Orleans Parish was approximately 29 percent white and 67 percent African American.
2. In September 2006, the parish imposed rental permitting requirements on all persons seeking to rent single-family dwellings but exempted homeowners who rented to persons "related by blood" from the permitting requirements and fines for noncompliance.
3. In January 2007, the parish enacted a replacement permissive use permit requirement for single-family rentals in districts zoned for single-family use and thereafter limited the density of rentals to two per 500 feet of frontage.

4. In December 2009, the parish made comprehensive revisions to its zoning ordinances that eliminated multifamily housing as a use allowed by right in four zones (A-1, C-2, C-2, and I-1) and entirely eliminated the RO zone, which also allowed multifamily residential use.[19]

The settlement will cost St. Bernard Parish another $2.5 million as follows:

1. Seventeen individuals who were harmed by the restrictions will receive more than $1 million.
2. The parish will pay $275,000 to eight aggrieved persons identified by the United States and $15,000 to the United States as a civil penalty.
3. The parish also must establish a new Office of Fair Housing within 90 days of the settlement and hire a fair housing coordinator with an annual salary of at least $40,000.
4. The parish must spend $25,000 a year for three years, (2013–2016) in a marketing campaign to attract renters and developers of multifamily rental housing to the parish.
5. The parish must create a rental land grant program through which the parish would transfer lands in its possession, free of cost, to qualified persons, or entities, who are willing to create or rehabilitate housing for rental purposes.
6. The land grant program, which requires the parish to offer lands worth up to $83,000 each year, will last for five years (2013–2018).

The *St. Bernard Voice* reported the additional terms of the settlement, which includes an extensive list of requirements the Parish must meet:

- Greater New Orleans Fair Housing Action Center will be receiving $900,000.
- NOLA Capital Group—a land owner who sought to rent its property and was denied—will be receiving $775,000.
- A Department of Treasury civil penalty of $15,000.
- The Office of Fair Housing will be required to promote homeownership and will be required to conduct home buying clinics three times a year
- Each clinic will include, at a minimum, a presentation by the Office of Fair Housing about services offered by the office, financial incentives available to home buyers and renters in St. Bernard Parish (including information about the Rental Land Grant Program), and the fair housing rights of prospective home buyers and renters.
- The parish must apply for Community Development Block Grant funding to pay for the new fair housing initiatives.[20]

Finally, all parish council members, planning commission members, "and several parish department heads must attend training sessions with a DOJ-approved Housing of Urban Development Official on the requirements of the settlement agreement and the requirements of the Fair Housing Authority." This training will be conducted annually.[21]

With the settlement in place, it was time for St. Bernard Parish to comply with the terms. On August 8, 2013, Pharissa Robinson began her task as the fair housing coordinator for St. Bernard Parish. Robinson, who has a law degree from Loyola University, has experience from her former position as a compliance consultant for the Housing Authority of New Orleans. Her role is to "receive and process all housing discrimination complaints against the parish government."[22] Her position is independent of the parish government. Robinson has an incredible responsibility and will play a major role in the parish because she is to:

- "[C]oordinate fair housing training activities for elected officials and employees"
- "[P]romote fair housing practices and help ensure the parish's compliance with all applicable fair housing laws"
- Assist in publicizing "rental housing and affordable home ownership opportunities in the parish"
- Prepare two reports per year "on fair housing activities in the parish"[23]

The parish's ethics board seems to be running smoothly, and the council approved all of the nominees on June 4, 2013 (with the exception of a nominee from Xavier University, which the university has yet to provide). Whether the ethics board will be successful depends on its willingness to investigate issues that arise and then impose appropriate sanctions for failure to comply.

The incredible stubbornness of the council lasted seven years and bankrupted the parish. There is an old saying that the only ones who really win in a lawsuit are the lawyers. St. Bernard Parish obviously lost financially. Yet sadly, the parish may have "won" something in the short term by keeping African Americans out of the parish for at least six years following Katrina. The real losers in the tug-of-war of segregation are the citizens who remained homeless during the fight; the loss of revenue for the parish, which increased the risk of poverty for the citizens of the community when businesses could not thrive or even exist; and the taxpayers who footed the bill of segregationist policy instead of paying for desperately needed infrastructure. Segregationist policy taxes citizens—all citizens—not only on a financial level but on a civil, mental, and emotional level—reduced property values, a strain on community relations, tension and violence, depression and anxiety, the desperation of being deprived of the most basic of needs, the threat of arrest and conviction, and the confusion of changing law in rapid succession. The cost of ignorance and abuse is way too high, and Americans simply cannot afford the bill anymore.

Chapter 7

The Current State of Affairs

We hold these truths to be self-evident, that all men are created equal,
that they are endowed by their Creator with certain unalienable Rights,
that among these are Life, Liberty and the pursuit of Happiness.
That to secure these rights Governments are instituted among Men,
deriving their just powers from the consent of the governed.
That whenever any Form of Government becomes destructive of these ends,
it is the Right of the People to alter or abolish it,
and to institute new Government,
laying its foundation on such principles and organizing its powers in such form,
as to them shall seem most likely to effect their Safety and Happiness.

—*The Declaration of Independence. July 4, 1776*

In determining what work is still necessary to ensure civil liberties and full rights to citizenship, in addition to looking at the past, we must consider the current state of affairs in our nation. While we may give gratitude for not being where we used to be, we are far from where we need to be. The land in southern Louisiana "is slowly sinking and quickly eroding away. Nowhere is the sinking more evident than in the New Orleans metropolitan area. Back in 1718, the levee system was only 3 feet high; today, the levees are 17 feet high."[1] Virtually the only way out of New Orleans is via Interstate 10, which means that the amount of time needed to evacuate is extremely high.

Following Katrina, corruption continued in New Orleans, and disaster fraud started. In 2007, Raul Miranda, a former contract employee for the U.S. Army Corps of Engineers, pled guilty to bribery for agreeing to accept nearly $300,000 from a local sand and gravel subcontractor in 2006. The bribe was "in connection to the $16 million hurricane protection project for the reconstruction of the Lake Cataouatche Levee, south of New Orleans . . . Miranda reviewed construction projects" necessary to community recovery from Hurricane Katrina.[2] On January 21, 2013, former

The Hotel St. Marie faces The Olivier House on Toulouse Street and corners on Bourbon Street. Although surrounding buildings are hundreds of years old, the Hotel St. Marie was built in 1970, purposefully designed to mimic its surroundings. (Liza Lugo, JD, May 2013)

New Orleans mayor Ray Nagin was indicted on 21 counts of "bribery (from December 2004 through the present), honest service wire fraud[3] (2005 to 2008), money laundering and conspiracy (2005 to 2008), and filing false tax returns (2005 to 2008)."[4] Witness preparation began on August 12, 2013. Nagin filed a motion to dismiss the indictment but Judge Berrigan, the judge who handled the lawsuits against St. Bernard Parish, rejected Nagin's petition. Nagin's trial was scheduled to begin in October 2013, and he petitioned the court for an indefinite delay by claiming that U.S. prosecutors anonymously posted online derogatory comments about him and two other mayors of New Orleans (Sidney Barthelemy and Marc Morial, who are both African American). According to Nagin's filing, the messages stated: "You three stooges have wrought upon this city one disaster after another. This is just more evidence of your collective racism and incompetence."[5] His request was denied. Nagin then asked for a delay so that he could properly prepare his defense, which was granted until January 27, 2014.[6]

Following Katrina, antiblack attacks continued to occur in Louisiana. A 19-year-old from Natchitoches Parish pleaded guilty to civil rights violations for dressing in KKK garb and screaming racial obscenities to an African-American family who recently moved into a (nearly) all-white neighborhood in Lena.[7] Out of fear, the victims sold their home and moved.

Hate crime offenders can be frighteningly young. The pathology of dehumanization has proven to be contagious and passed onto subsequent generations as evidenced by continued threats and violence in Louisiana. In 2007, 18-year-old Jeremiah Munsen intimidated African-American marchers who participated in a civil rights rally in Jena, Louisiana. Munsen "displayed two hangman's nooses, fashioned from extension cords, from the back of a pick-up truck." According to the federal hate crime statute, "[i]t is a violation of federal law to intimidate, oppress, injure or threaten people because of their race," stated U.S. attorney Donald W. Washington.[8] But despite official federal opposition, the pathology continues in Louisiana and around the country.

On June 15, 2008, 47-year-old Johnny Mathis fired shots at the home of three Hispanic men who lived across the street from him in Lecompte, Louisiana. He admitted shooting at the victims because of their race and national origin. Mathis pleaded guilty to two federal crimes: criminal interference with the right to fair housing and using a firearm during a crime of violence. The victims ran into the woods during the shooting and were not injured.[9]

On January 21, 2010, Daniel Earl Danforth was convicted and sentenced to four years in prison and three years of supervised release for committing federal hate crimes and obstructing justice. Danforth and others carried out a cross burning near the home of an interracial couple in Athens, Louisiana. The victims were his cousin and her African-American husband[10] along with other relatives who supported the relationship. Thomas E. Perez, assistant attorney general of the Civil Rights Division of the U. S. Department of Justice, remarked, "Driven only by bigotry and hate, the defendant threatened members of his own family with violence because they associated with persons of another race. Incidents of this kind have no place in this country, and they are a reminder of the civil rights challenges we still face."[11]

At the end of 2011, Craig Taffaro bid farewell to his position as president of St. Bernard Parish to move onto his appointment as the head of Hazard Mitigation Programs and Recovery Coordination in the Office of Community Development, under Governor Bobby Jindal.[12] Paul Rainwater, the commissioner of administration, welcomed Taffaro as an asset to the administration. According to Rainwater, Taffaro

> has proven in his years leading St. Bernard Parish's recovery that he's skilled at working with federal funds and cutting through red tape to get projects done. We're excited that he is bringing this expertise not only to our state Hazard Mitigation program, but also to helping local leaders access their own HMGP funds, so that all of Louisiana's coastal communities will be better protected from damage in future storms.[13]

Evidently, Taffaro's financial waste in defending the segregationist policy he introduced did not make him a questionable candidate, nor did it disqualify him from the position.

Current Status of African Americans

The current status of African Americans as a population is disturbing. Currently, one in three African-American males are under the control of the criminal justice system—either in jail, on probation, or on parole.[14] More African Americans have gone to jail than have graduated from college.[15] African-American men have "borne the brunt of the rise in mass incarceration."[16] Currently, there are more than 2 million people in America's prisons and jails, and 40 percent of them are African American. Their representation in the system is *more than three times greater* than their representation in the general populace.[17]

In 2011, Hispanics—who represented a slightly smaller percentage in the general populace than do African Americans—comprised 21 percent of America's prison population. The combination of African Americans and Hispanics in the prison population represents nearly 60 percent of all inmates in America's prisons. They make up 25 percent of the general population. There is something odd going on in the calculation aside from the obvious disproportionate effect. The U.S. Bureau of Justice admits that the "white" prison population *includes* American Indians, Alaska Natives, Asians, Native Hawaiians, other Pacific Islanders, *and persons identifying as two or more races.*[18] While previously and in other legal constructs "one drop" automatically designated a person as nonwhite, that is not so in the prison population. This perpetuates a false reality that there is less discrimination in the criminal justice system than people think. The reality is that the number of nonwhite prisoners greatly exceeds the number of whites in comparison to their numbers in the general population. According to Ralph Richard Banks, professor of law at Stanford Law School, "Our nation's prisons have become the destination for so many of the black boys who drop out of high school that researchers and activists have coined the term the 'school-to prison pipeline.' In some urban areas, three out of four African-American boys drop out of high school."

The African-American middle class is fragile because it achieved some wealth relatively recently in American history. Unlike whites, African Americans on the whole had no intergenerational wealth to pass.[19] Most sociologists agree that home and property ownership play vital roles in determining wealth.[20] However, the reality of America's past and present legal and social construct is that the African-American community generally has been shut out of America's wealth. Furthermore, those who have been incarcerated do not fare well economically. The disproportionate effect on African-American education is palpable:

- Only 50 percent of "black" males graduate from high school.[21]
- Only 25 percent of "black" males graduate high school in New York.[22]
- "Black" male high school dropouts are nearly 25 percent less likely to have a job now than in 1979.[23]

Education is directly related to employability; and employability is directly related to generated income. The truth of the matter is that the battle for equal opportunities in education continues. America must see the big picture. African Americans were legally dehumanized for centuries. Likewise, there is a constant struggle for the right to become literate and then the right to access education, home ownership, and employment. Moreover, there is a lack of African-American representation in government and the legal profession. This is compounded by violent attacks, domestic terrorism, and the criminalization of people based on race—all of which make the chances for mobility nearly nonexistent for this segment of the population.

The unemployment rate for African Americans at the beginning of the 21st century was 11.2 percent. The unemployment rate of whites at the same time was just than half of that, at 5.1 percent.[24] With the passing of only one decade, the unemployment rate for African Americans has gone from bad to worse. By 2010, the U.S. Department of Labor statistics revealed that the unemployment rate for African Americans was 16.1 percent, and whites still have half that unemployment rate (8 percent). African Americans' unemployment rates continue to increase; by 2011, African-American unemployment was the highest it had been since 1984.[25]

The disparity is not limited to that among whites and African Americans but other ethnic groups that are nonwhite. At the beginning of the 21st century, only 10 percent of whites lived in poverty, while 25 percent of Native Americans did.[26] Today, the white poverty level has remained relatively stable, but minorities suffer at much higher rates. Census Bureau statistics report that "*[b]lacks experienced the highest poverty rate, at 27 percent, up from 25 percent in 2009*, and Hispanics rose to 26 percent from 25 percent . . . Asians were unchanged at 12.1 percent."[27]

While laws that blatantly prohibit the socialization of blacks and whites are unconstitutional, in many areas of the country, particularly the Deep South, the practice is still in effect socially – de facto segregation, although the likelihood of racially-motivated arrests or terrorist attacks is less likely. Laws prohibiting interracial marriage were stricken from the books courtesy of *Loving* but there are still many who would not date or marry a member of another race or ethnicity, a practice rooted in antimiscegenation law perpetuated over numerous generations.[28]

For those who assume that times have changed and the country now embraces individuals from all walks of life, we must not forget that until 1964, discrimination against African Americans was sanctioned by the state. That means throughout the nation's history (1776 to the present), nearly 80 percent of the time has been plagued by a legal construct favoring dehumanization. And if lawyers are indeed "social engineers," as articulated by Charles Hamilton Houston, then the legal profession failed miserably. There is some saving grace for the legal community because numerous lawsuits were filed in opposition to this practice and new legislation has been created over recent decades to break the back of the practice. But, as we know, segregationist policy continues in the 21st century—from the St. Bernard ordinances to the more than 200 segregation cases around the country that are under the scrutiny of the U.S. Department of Justice.

Hate crimes are evidence of the transmission of the dehumanization pathology. Such evidence and *the absence of any reduction* in hate crimes from 1996 to 2011 debunk the myth of tolerance or acceptance. Many experts believe that the number of hate crimes is greatly underreported. Heidi Beirich, director of research for the Southern Poverty Law Center's

Intelligence Project, told ABC News: "[T]he truth is that the FBI's data severely undercount the number of hate crimes each year."[29] The Bureau of Justice Statistics conducted a victimization study in 2005 and reported that "an average of 191,000 hate crime incidents involving one or more victims occurred annually."[30] The FBI determined that "only 44 percent of hate crimes were reported to police."[31]

Across the country, the U.S. Department of Justice now actively pursues civil rights violations. Recent examples include:

- The fatal beating of a Mexican immigrant during which the offenders shouted racial epithets and told him he did not belong in their town
- The father and son team in South Carolina who, with a friend, pled guilty to chasing an African-American man from a convenience store, threatening him with a chainsaw, and then attacking others who tried to help the victim
- The arson of the Islamic Center of Columbia by three men who spray-painted the mosque with racist symbols and used Molotov cocktails to destroy it[32]

From 2006 to 2011, hate crime reports from the FBI[33] illustrate that within this six-year period, tens of thousands of hate crimes occurred in America:

- Single-biased incidents totaled 42,562.
- 21,207 were based on race alone, which accounted for nearly 50 percent of all hate crimes.[34]
- "Anti-black" crime accounted for approximately 65 percent of all hate crimes based on race, with more than 60 percent committed by white offenders.

"Blacks" continue to be *more than three times* as likely to be victims of racial hatred crimes than whites, and the greatest number of incidents occur at or near the victim's residence, factors that have not changed in 17 years. As a nation, we cannot continue to keep our heads in the sand when faced with these raw and disturbing facts. On the fifth anniversary of Katrina's strike, Houston mayor Annise Parker stated: "We put out the welcome mat and stepped in to lend a hand to our neighbors in need but Katrina was not our disaster."[35] Here is a news flash: Katrina was *America's* disaster and so is the issue of race relations.

The major positive change in the United States is that federal and state governments took action to strike down de jure segregation, passed explicit civil rights laws, and are now pursuing offenders, whereas America's past evidenced the complete opposite. While many who value segregationist policy and practice, whether de jure or customary, may believe that they have a right to privately act upon their beliefs, the federal government legislated that neither is acceptable in the United States, even among private citizens. The Department of Justice has and will continue to pursue investigations, indictments, and lawsuits against perpetrators of civil rights violations such as racial or religious discrimination; use of excessive force or police misconduct; and involuntary servitude or slavery. Other discriminatory actions may amount to violations of the Voting Rights Act of 1965, the Civil Rights Act of 1964, the Equal Credit Opportunity Act, the Freedom of Access to Clinic Entrances Act, and the Civil Rights of Institutionalized Persons Act. The Department of Justice stated:

> Federal laws prohibit discrimination based on a person's national origin, race, color, religion, disability, sex, and familial status. Laws prohibiting national origin discrimination make it illegal to discriminate because of a person's birthplace, ancestry, culture or language. This means people cannot be denied equal opportunity because they or their family are from another country, because they have a name or accent associated with a national origin group, because they participate in certain customs associated with a national origin group, or because they are married to or associate with people of a certain national origin.
>
> [The Civil Rights Division] also enforces laws that prohibit discrimination on the basis of disability, protects the civil rights of persons who are institutionalized in certain state or local facilities, and prosecutes crimes that are motivated by a crime victim's race, color, or national origin.[36]

In March 2010, the Department of Justice announced a settlement of more than $6 million with two subsidiaries of AIG to resolve allegations of discrimination against African-American borrowers by brokers with whom the subsidiaries contracted.[37] This "settlement marked the first time that the Department of Justice has held a lender accountable for failing to monitor its brokers to ensure that borrowers are not charged higher fees because of their race."[38]

Police departments in Louisiana and across the country are increasingly subjected to scrutiny by the Department of Justice. In a speech delivered at the University of Tennessee Diversity and Quality Conference in Knoxville, Tennessee, on November 15, 2012, Assistant Attorney General Thomas E. Perez promised "to hold law enforcement accountable when they abuse their power and violate the public trust." In addition, he provided an account of the progress, saying, "During the past four months alone we have reached agreements with Portland, Seattle, and New Orleans." To this resolve, more than two dozen investigations are currently open. In 2010, specifically addressing the New Orleans Police Department (NOPD) violations, Perez explained that reforming the department would serve as an example to the nation:

> [Post-Katrina] New Orleans Mayor Mitch Landrieu[39] invited the Division to conduct a pattern or practice investigation of the NOPD. In his letter to the Division, Mayor Landrieu wrote that "nothing short of a complete transformation [of the New Orleans Police Department] is necessary and essential to ensure safety for the citizens of New Orleans."
>
> Shortly thereafter, we notified Mayor Landrieu that the Division would begin an independent, comprehensive review of the Department under our pattern or practice enforcement authority. That investigation ultimately led to a comprehensive agreement for reform, reached in July, [which] will reduce crime, ensure constitutional policing, and enhance public confidence in the New Orleans Police Department. It will serve as a blueprint for reform for departments across the country—and the Division currently has several similar investigations underway.[40]

In four years, from 2009 to 2012, the Department of Justice convicted 140 people of federal hate crimes. The Matthew Shepard and James Byrd Jr., Hate Crimes Prevention Act was passed in 2009, and, for the first time, the words "lesbian, gay, bisexual and transgender" appeared in U.S. Code. Under this new law, 13 cases were filed "against 36 defendants ... in Arkansas, Kentucky, Michigan, Minnesota, New Mexico, New York, Ohio, Texas, and Washington."[41] And for those who believe segregation is dead, the Department of Justice provides a much needed wake-up call. Currently, the department is "engaged in efforts to dismantle racial segregation in nearly *200* desegregation cases across the country."[42]

The cleanup continues in New Orleans and the surrounding parishes affected by Katrina. Severely damaged structures still stand, people are still displaced, and many more want to return but do not have the financial means to do so or do not have access to housing. The levees are still under construction and repair, as they have been for 400 years; and many schools still have not reopened. Drive through the Lower Ninth Ward to see one closed school after another. The streets are unnervingly silent. But the greatest work yet to be completed is in the area of respecting the rights "retained by the people" and living up to our constitutional values.

In 2012, the Department of Justice acknowledged the work remaining in New Orleans:

> Much of the focus has necessarily been, and continues to be, on bricks and mortar reconstruction—literally putting this city back together, rebuilding its infrastructure and its communities. *Today is about rebuilding a core part of the fundamental infrastructure of democracy*—an effective, accountable police department that reduces crime, ensures respect for the Constitution, and earns the trust of the public it is charged with protecting.[43]

Fifty years after the Civil Rights Movement, minorities in the United States have yet to achieve equal economic representation, educational access, and social acceptance. With regard to representation in government, for this new millennium (and centuries past), the facts are clear: white males have dominated government in the United States. However, Barack H. Obama was elected as the first African-American president in 2008 and re-elected in 2012. Following the 2012 election, President Obama was joined by two African-American senators and and 45 African Americans in the House of Representatives.[44] It only took from 1789 to 2012 for America to "get there."

The Pathology of Dehumanization

Since the birth of our nation, each generation brings with it a heaviness, and yet they also bring with them some progression and hope. The pathology of dehumanization and the methods of transmission, past and present, do not allow for a collective contribution of citizens, which is a critical component of a country's development and success. Dehumanization (which is the treatment of persons as if they were less than human by depriving them of inherent human qualities), which I refer to as a pathology, did not occur hundreds of years ago as a historical event distant in place and time; rather, *it has been happening for hundreds of years* as a continued and unfortunate phenomenon. Perhaps it has existed since the beginning of humankind.

It has been said that half of any solution comes in defining the problem. Admitting the dehumanization has been a long-term issue for U.S. society. Next, we must acknowledge the methods of transmission and then recognize the symptoms. When medical scientists are fighting an epidemic, they must not only relieve the symptoms, but also identify the disease and address the modes of transmission to prevent its spread. If they can find the cure, usually some kind of antitoxin, the disease can be completely eradicated. But it will not be eradicated by treating the symptoms alone. Sociologists, anthropologists, and mental health professionals have struggled to address dehumanization. As late as 2006, according to Nick Haslam of the University of Melbourne, "The concept of dehumanization lack[ed] a systematic theoretical basis, and research that addresse[d] it ha[d] yet to be integrated."[45] Others posit that "little is known about the origins of dehumanization or the mechanisms through which dehumanization impacts . . . prejudice."[46] While the *academic study* of dehumanization may be relatively new, the concept reaches back millennia, much further than is possible to document within the scope of this book. It is possible that it has become a sort of chicken or the egg discussion.

Still, the history books are filled with examples of revolutions against tyranny (including in our own nation); and tyranny is inextricably tied to dehumanization. Perhaps the lack of understanding of political theory interferes with the study of dehumanization, or maybe the enormous scope of dehumanization—particularly acts during the 20th and 21st centuries—overwhelms researchers. It is likely that the failure to understand dehumanization in full is a result of the *individual* disciplinary approach (political theory, law, psychology, sociology, anthropology, etc.) rather than approaching it from a collective or multidisciplinary view. Perhaps we need to simply get back to basics. Consider Figure 7.1 which describes the pathology of dehumanization, the methods of transmission, and the symptomology, particularly in light of the subjugation of African Americans in the United States.

Dehumanization Defined

Dehumanization is currently defined by some as the "deprivation of human qualities, personality, or spirit"[47]; "to deprive [a person] of human... attributes; divestment of [a] person's individuality."[48] It is "the process of losing altruistic or individual qualities, as may occur in some psychotic states or in environments that produce emotional trauma . . . It may be influenced by external forces."[49] More important, dehumanization is "the stripping of human qualities from people or from situations involving people, as an expediency that allows the policy makers (in a totalitarian state) to justify untenable situations, as the persons of interest are 'less than human.' "[50] This is what happened to and within America. We have no immunity.

Before understanding dehumanization on the macro level within the context of society, government, and the greater global context, it may be

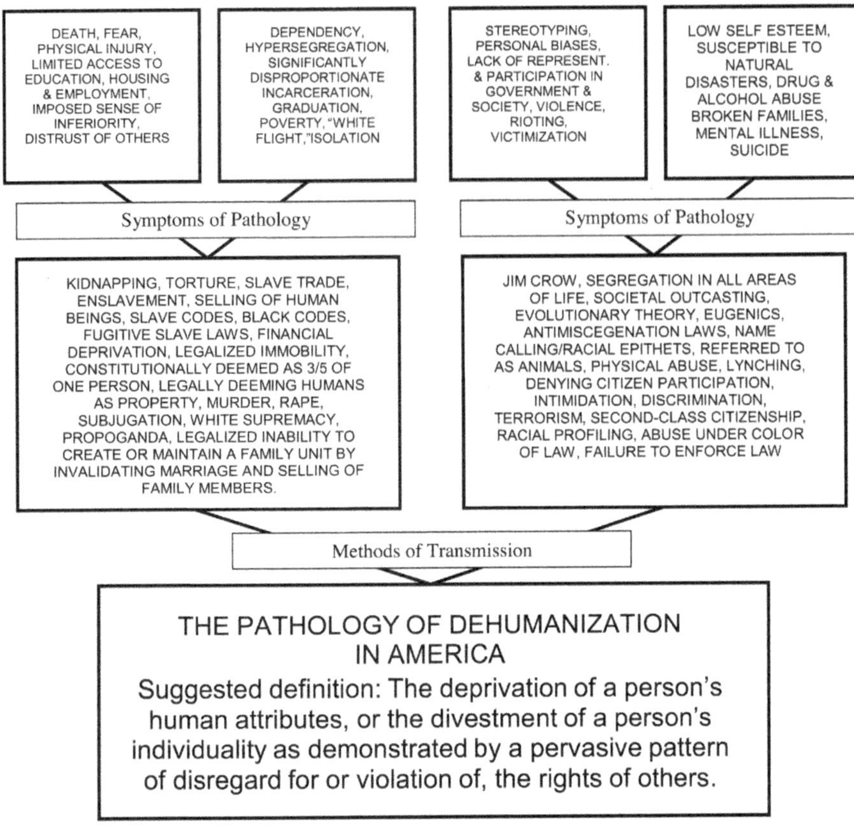

FIGURE 7.1 The Pathology of Dehumanization by Liza Lugo, JD.

easier to comprehend dehumanization on a micro level or, even better, a personal level. If we can make sense of it when it happens personally, then surely the picture becomes clearer with smaller groups of perpetrators and victims, or the larger context of governmental abuses of citizens.

Domestic Violence: The Micro Level of Dehumanization

For more than 35 years, much progress has been made with regard to understanding domestic violence. According to the National Coalition against Domestic Violence (NCADV), "In one year alone 12.7 million men and women in the U.S. are physically abused, raped or stalked by their partners."[51] Even the Centers for Disease Control and Prevention (CDC) addresses the issue: "Intimate partner violence (IPV) is a serious, preventable public health problem that affects millions of Americans."[52] Nearly all research concurs that domestic abuse and marital/IPV rape have nothing to do with the victim personally (the act of sex or otherwise); rather, they occur because one person believes he or she is entitled to gain and maintain power over another. That may come in the form of IPV or other familial violence. Most commonly in all cultures, this involves a male perpetrator and a female victim who is often dependent on the male. The dependency factor is certainly applicable in instances of child abuse. According to the World Health Organization, "The fact that women are often emotionally involved with and economically dependent on those who victimize them has major implications for both the dynamics of abuse and the approaches to dealing with it."[53] It is also common for children who witness abusive relationships to believe that such abuse is "normal," as they repeat the behavior in their adult lives as either victim or abuser. Prior victimization is the strongest predictor of perpetration.[54]

According to the CDC, there are a myriad of risk factors including:

- low self-esteem, low income, low academic achievement,
- young age, aggressive or delinquent behavior as a youth,
- heavy alcohol and drug use,
- depression, anger and hostility,
- antisocial personality traits, borderline personality traits,
- prior history of being physically abusive,
- having few friends and being isolated from other people,
- unemployment, emotional dependence and insecurity,
- belief in strict gender roles, (power and control)
- psychological aggression and
- a history of experiencing poor parenting [or] physical discipline as a child (See Figure 7.3).[55]

Domestic violence is also cyclical, as can be seen in Figure 7.2.

The beginning of this cycle evidences dehumanization, that is, divesting the victim of human qualities, personality, and individuality. Most often this occurs by isolating the victim (financially and socially) and stripping her of her self-esteem and self-worth through intimidation, fear, and threats. At the center of it all is power and control. Research provides insight: domestic violence is "*intrinsically connected to . . . societal oppression.*"[56] That societal oppression is most often rooted in the *law.*

Predating American history and later adopted into the colonies, English law provided:

> The husband cannot be guilty of a rape committed by himself upon his lawful wife, for by their mutual matrimonial consent and contract the wife hath given up herself in this kind unto her husband, which she cannot retract.[57]

From before the founding of the United States through the 20th century,[58] a wife was legally considered the property of her husband. Whatever she owned became his once she married him. Additionally, the law provided either no legal construct regarding marital rape or specifically exempted the husband from criminal prosecution for the act. North Carolina, for example, maintained the following law until 1993:

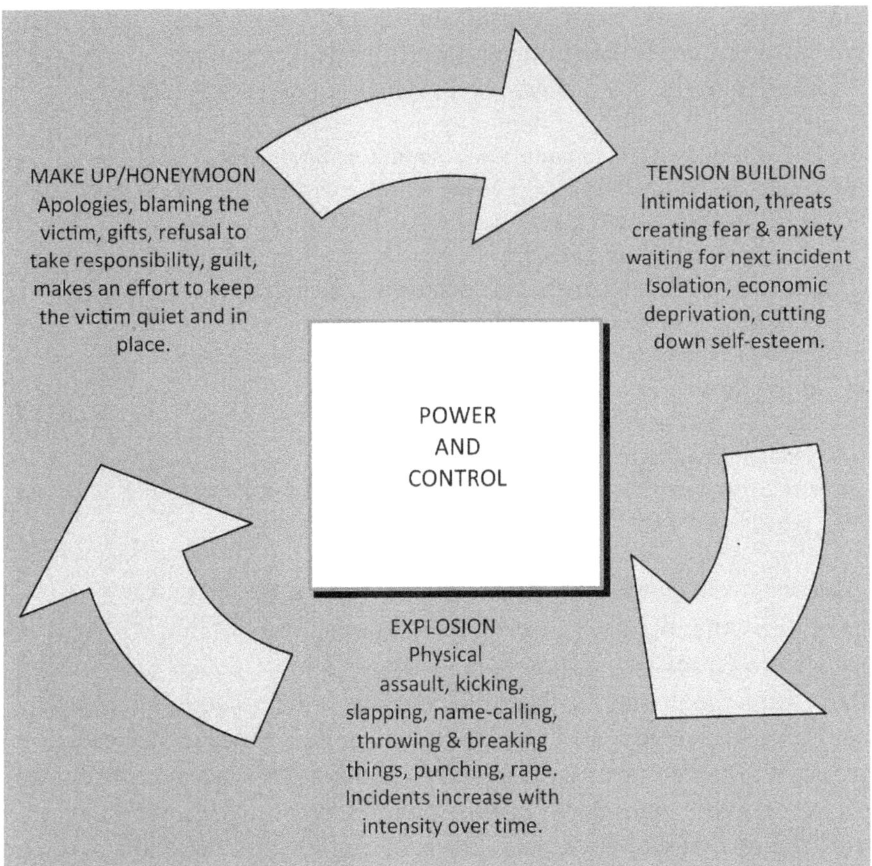

FIGURE 7.2 The Cycle of Domestic Violence by Liza Lugo, JD.

> A person may not be prosecuted under this article [rape] if the victim is the person's legal spouse at the time of the commission of the alleged rape or sexual offense, unless the parties are living separate and apart.[59]

As late as 2003, in 20 states, it still was not a crime for a husband to have nonconsensual sex with his wife. The theory was that she was his property to do with as he saw fit. Police refused to assist in such matters because the law made no such provision. This is the legal construct that went unchallenged until the 1970s.

Socially, a wife was considered subordinate to her spouse through vows to obey him. With legal and societal constructs firmly in place, justification was provided for the perpetrator to continue to abuse. Likewise, and unfortunately, if the victim is left to feel the degradation is sanctioned by law and by societal values that enforces that belief, or if she has witnessed it among others like her, or has been subjected to abuse from other persons in her life, she undoubtedly comes to believe that she must somehow deserve it. The abnormal, because of its frequency, becomes the new normal. The legal sanction keeps her in her place because she has neither a legal remedy nor the personal resources to escape the environment.

In the face of disaster, such as Hurricane Katrina, the rate of domestic violence increases greatly. The NCADV reported that in the aftermath of Hurricane Katrina, "at least seven domestic violence shelters, transitional housing programs, and outreach organizations were impacted by the storm's severity." Furthermore, before Katrina:

> Battered women's shelters and programs across the country struggled on a daily basis to meet battered women's basic imminent safety, emotional and physical needs. Shortages in funding, staffing, resources, and time place undue constraints on programs' abilities to advocate for battered women's safety. A disaster such as Katrina accentuates these constraints . . . The state of chaos and devastation in the City of New Orleans and other impacted regions afforded little solace to battered women—many of whom fled their abusive homes for the protection of the shelter only to find themselves displaced from the shelter in the aftermath of the storm.[60]

Abuse includes the following actions by the perpetrator: controlling finances, lying, using children to manipulate emotions, intimidation, isolation, fear, shame, criticism, physical violence, creating confusion, rape and sexual assault, yelling, rages, harassment, neglect, abandonment, silent treatment, destroying personal property, name-calling, brainwashing, public humiliation, preventing access to medical care, ridicule, restraining, threats with weapons, threats or violence against children or animals, and death threats.[61]

The costs of the epidemic of domestic violence are enormous. The CDC, estimates:

- IPV costs exceeded $8.3 billion, which included $460 million for rape, $6.2 billion for physical assault, $461 million for stalking, and $1.2 billion for the value of lost lives.
- The increased annual health care costs for victims of IPV *can persist as long as 15 years after the cessation of abuse.*
- Victims of severe IPV lose nearly 8 million days of paid work—the equivalent of more than 32,000 full-time jobs—and almost 5.6 million days of household productivity each year.
- Women who experience severe aggression by men (e.g., not being allowed to go to work or school, or having their lives or their children's lives threatened) are more likely to have been unemployed in the past, have health problems, and be receiving public assistance.[62]

The greater cost to the victim, and to society at large, involves the psychological and emotional effects of the abuse, including "anxiety, depression, post-traumatic stress disorder (PTSD), antisocial behavior, suicidal behavior, low self-esteem, inability to trust others, especially in intimate relationships, fear of intimacy, emotional detachment, sleep disturbances, and flashbacks."[63] Victims have a higher incidence of "engaging in high-risk sexual behavior," "using harmful substances" such as alcohol and drugs, and "unhealthy diet-related behaviors" such as anorexia, bulimia, and obesity.[64] Again, there is a high probability of passing on the victim/perpetrator cycle to the next generation because children grow up believing that behavior is normal. The perpetrator often lacks remorse, blames the victim, and refuses to take responsibility, including citing the law as justification for his actions. Figure 7.3 combines the preceding information to provide another view of domestic violence.

Genocide: The Macro Level of Dehumanization

While domestic violence illustrates the micro level of dehumanization, genocide does so on a macro level. The term "genocide" comes from the Greek and Latin words *geno*, meaning "race or tribe" and *cide*, which means "killing." According to Raphael Lemkin, a Jewish-Polish attorney, genocide describes "a coordinated plan of different actions aiming at the destruction of essential foundations of the life of national groups, with the aim of annihilating the groups themselves." Following World War II, particularly in response to the holocaust perpetrated by the Nazi regime, the United Nations established the Convention on the Prevention and Punishment of the Crime of Genocide. The convention established genocide as an international crime, not limited to killing. Unlike other crimes, genocide includes a special intent. Further:

> Genocide means *any of the following* acts committed with *intent to destroy, in whole or in part*, a national, ethnical, racial or religious group, as such:
>
> a. Killing members of the group;
> b. Causing serious bodily or mental harm to members of the group;
> c. Deliberately inflicting on the group conditions of life calculated to bring about its physical destruction in whole or in part;
> d. Imposing measures intended to prevent births within the group;
> e. Forcibly transferring children of the group to another group.[65]

According to Gregory H. Stanton, president of Genocide Watch, genocide develops in eight stages: "classification, symbolization, *dehumanization*,

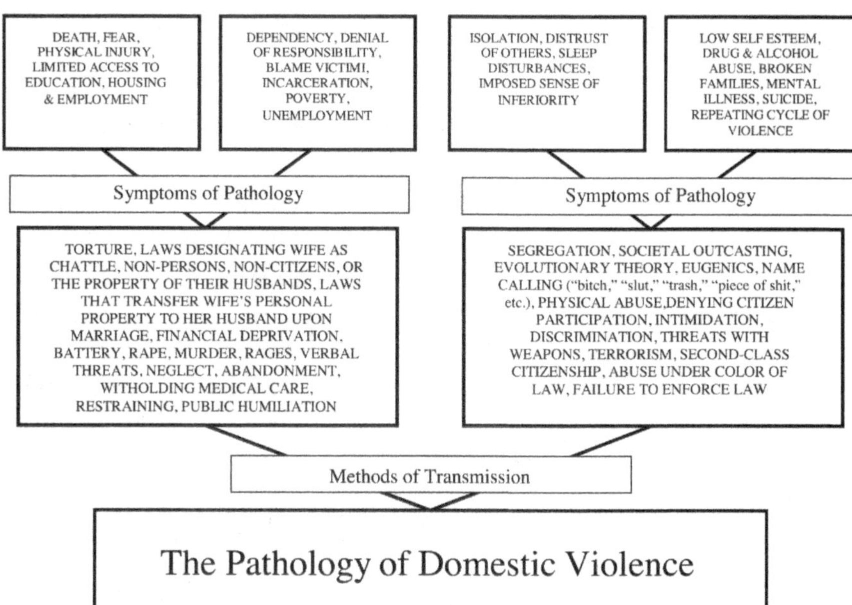

FIGURE 7.3 The Pathology of Domestic Violence by Liza Lugo, JD.

organization, polarization, preparation, extermination, and denial."[66] Classification is the way societies differentiate each other, whether by race, religion, ethnicity, and so on and thus create an "us and them" perspective. Symbols are then used to define members of those groups, including the use of hate symbols (e.g., yellow stars for Jews, flags, and even more invasive methods such as tatooing, branding, or mutilation). However, the processes are not necessarily linear, and mere classification and symbolization alone do not necessarily lead to genocide "*unless they lead to the next stage, dehumanization.*"[67] According to Stanton, "One group denies the humanity of the other group. Members of it are equated with animals, vermin, insects or diseases. Dehumanization overcomes the normal human revulsion against murder."[68] Stanton finalizes his analysis with "denial," which

> always follows a genocide [and] is among the surest indicators of further genocidal massacres. The perpetrators of genocide dig up the mass graves, burn the bodies, try to cover up the evidence and intimidate the witnesses. They deny that they committed any crimes, and often blame what happened on the victims. They block investigations of the crimes.[69]

Perpetrators lack remorse and a sense of responsibility, and they often cite the law as having provided their justification for their actions.

Antisocial Personality Disorder: The Individual Level of Dehumanization

In an attempt to bring individual disciplines to a collective understanding of dehumanization, one cannot ignore the impact of modern psychology. Antisocial personality disorder (ASPD), or psychopathology, is the most thoroughly researched personality disorder. In an effort to define the disorder, psychological professionals renamed the disorder many times. In the 19th century, psychopathology was called moral insanity.[70] The genocide witnessed during World War II forced psychologists to re-evaluate their theories. Instead of attributing the psychopathic behavior to genes, psychologists took a serious look at social factors such as discrimination, deprivation, and poor modeling. They decided to abandon the term "psychopath" altogether to avoid links to the past and renamed a person with this disorder a sociopath, which reflected society's concerns related to the disorder.[71]

The latest term in use is the much milder "antisocial personality disorder (ASPD)," though even the most violent and chilling criminals fall under this category. Without the intention of dismissing the seriousness of the crimes, one of the reasons given for this shift away from the use of the words "psychopath" or "sociopath" was that personality traits are difficult to measure reliably. It was easier to agree on *behaviors* that typify a disorder than on the reasons they occur. While the diagnostic category is reliable, it lacks the well-established conceptions of psychopathy. But professionals agree that antisocial personality disorder is a lifelong disorder; and men are at greater risk of developing the disorder, which often begins in childhood.

According to the Mayo Clinic:

> Antisocial personality disorder is a type of chronic mental condition in which a person's ways of thinking, perceiving situations and relating to others are dysfunctional—and destructive. People with antisocial personality disorder typically *have no regard for right and wrong and often disregard the rights, wishes and feelings of others.*
>
> Those with antisocial personality disorder tend to *antagonize, manipulate or treat others either harshly or with callous indifference. They may often violate the law, landing in frequent trouble, yet they show no guilt or remorse. They may lie, behave violently or impulsively,* and have problems with drug and alcohol use.[72]

The *Diagnostic and Statistical Manual of Mental Disorders*, fourth edition (DSM-IV),[73] published by the American Psychiatric Association (APA), attempts to make the diagnosis as objective and nonprejudicial as possible in order to omit presumed etiologies. According to the DSM-IV, the essential feature of ASPD is "*a pervasive pattern of disregard for, and violation of, the rights of others* that begins in childhood or early adolescence and continues into adulthood."

The complete diagnostic criterion for ASPD, according to the DSM-IV, consists of four major areas:

1. There is a pervasive pattern of disregard for and violation of the rights of others occurring since age 15 years, as indicated by three or more of the following:
   a. Failure to conform to social norms with respect to lawful behaviors as indicated by repeatedly performing acts that are grounds for arrest;
   b. Deceitfulness as indicated by repeated lying, use of aliases, or conning others for personal profit or pleasure;

c. Impulsivity or failure to plan ahead;
d. Irritability and aggressiveness, as indicated by repeated physical fights or assaults;
e. Reckless disregard for safety of self or others;
f. Consistent irresponsibility, as indicated by repeated failure to sustain consistent work behavior or honor financial obligations;
g. Lack of remorse, as indicated by being indifferent to or rationalizing having hurt, mistreated, or stolen from another.

2. The individual is at least 18 years old.
3. There is evidence of Conduct Disorder with onset before age 15 years.
4. The occurrence of antisocial behavior is not exclusively during the course of Schizophrenia or a Manic Episode.

Since the 2000 publication of the DSM-IV, there have been updates to the criteria of ASPD. It is also characterized by the following: superficiality, grandiosity, manipulation, lack of remorse, lack of empathy, impulsiveness, poor behavior control, and disavowal of responsibility.[74]

Part of the problem in understanding and treating the disorder is that the DSM-IV requires that only three out of the seven criteria be met to diagnose someone with ASPD, that is, an individual can be diagnosed while meeting less than half of the criteria. That determinant would have many people fall into this category, including thieves, con artists, corrupt government officials, even people who operate shady businesses. Critics argue that the DSM-IV focuses more on irresponsible behavior than personality, that children may be improperly diagnosed before their personality is formed, and that the diagnosis does not help professionals as they work to develop treatment plans.[75] The DSM-IV also notes that "only when antisocial personality traits are inflexible, persistent, maladaptive and cause significant functional impairment or subjective distress do they constitute Antisocial Personality Disorder."

Initially, these individuals can make a friendly and intelligent impression, but they lack empathy and tend to be callous and cynical. They may have an inflated and arrogant self-appraisal and may be excessively opinionated. Individuals with ASPD are extremely irresponsible; and they are completely indifferent to their crimes. More important, they blame the victims for being foolish or deserving of their fate. What remains problematic is that psychopathic traits such as egocentricity, superficiality, and manipulation are increasingly tolerated by society, perhaps even valued. The abnormal is becoming increasingly—and inappropriately—normal. This validation contributes to their ability to camouflage themselves within society for long periods of time.

The list of risk factors for violent behavior is broad. According to the American Academy of Child and Adolescent Psychiatry (AACAP), such factors are a "complex interaction" of physiological and sociological issues, including prior victimization, exposure to violence, genetic factors, drug or alcohol abuse, stressful socioeconomic situations, or brain damage or brain injury.[76]

What is extremely significant about persons with ASPD is their inability to trust, to empathize, to feel, and to learn. They have no remorse. The worst of them, serial killers, live without reasoning capabilities on the other side of social boundaries.

Parents who provide an abusive and discordant environment are more likely to produce antisocial children; but it is equally possible that children's personality traits can lead parents to provide an unstable, unhappy home life where they drink, fight, and abuse their children. It is difficult to separate environment from genetics in early childhood. Children who live in abusive, dysfunctional homes; are exposed to antisocial models; and have a genetic tendency toward low arousal and compensatory sensation seeking are at a high risk of developing ASPD.[77] Most data shows that societal issues are the major component in the risk factors for psychopathology: inadequate mental health services, unresponsive schools, child maltreatment, economic inequality, spiritual emptiness, and psychoactive substances.[78] Medications have not proven to be effective. The behavior will stop only when the individual is caught or dies.

Comparing Disciplines to Understand Dehumanization

Herein lay the challenges of developing an understanding of the inseparable component of genocide and the often overlooked factor in domestic violence: dehumanization. However, dehumanization is clearer within the scope of ASPD, although the word is not even mentioned. The destructive actions or modes of transmission cannot occur without dehumanization, either on a societal or individual level. Once dehumanization is imbedded into a perpetrator's psyche and perhaps even into the victim's psyche, then to organize destructive campaigns, polarize the population, and finally exterminate groups of people becomes par for the course; and anything is possible. In fact, logic would follow that when one believes something (or someone) is not human (or is less than human), there is no entitlement to any rights, including the right to exist.

The difference between domestic violence and genocide is intent. The intent of domestic violence is power and control, whereas genocide has the special "intent to destroy . . . a group." But the conversation of domestic violence often leaves out the dehumanization component, and the debate on genocide often omits the idea of power and control. Undoubtedly, it can be substantiated that with genocide, *particularly within the structure of government*, the intent to destroy the group is *most often rooted in an effort to gain physical and political control of a populace* no matter the size of the populace. For example, the Nazi regime sought to conquer all of Europe, and then the world, to establish an empire (the Third Reich). Likewise, a spouse cannot gain power and control over his partner without first dehumanizing his victim and then using various methods of abuse to enforce his power and control. Finally, persons with ASPD disregard the rights of others, and varying methods of abuse are indicative of their disorder. However, there is no real mention of the power and control mechanism in the diagnosis. Consistent themes in domestic violence, genocide, and ASPD include abuse, disregard of the rights of others, lack of remorse or failure to assume responsibility, and justifications for their actions.

Compare and then combine the definition of dehumanization—"the deprivation of a person's human attributes or the divestment of a person's individuality"—with the essential feature of ASPD—"a pervasive pattern of disregard for, and violation of, the rights of others."[79] In this way, perhaps, we can gain a greater understanding of the pathology of dehumanization (and its role in domestic violence, genocide, ASPD, and subjugation), which has plagued the entire world. Add to the phenomenon the importation of the law, which provides a license, and society will see the perfect ingredient in a recipe for disaster.

The Destructiveness of the Pathology

Instead of evolving, families, governments, and societies of the world at large are currently in a critical state of de-evolution, which reached its peak in the 20th century as evidenced by the increase in crime, domestic abuse, and genocide. Over 180 million people died as a result of genocide in the 20th century.[80] In the United States, a woman is assaulted or beaten every nine seconds. Worldwide, at least one in every three women has been abused during her lifetime; and "domestic violence is the leading cause of injury to women" who are between the ages of 15 and 44.[81] Studies have shown that approximately 10 million children per year witness domestic violence.[82] In the United States, more than three women are murdered by their boyfriends or husbands every day.[83] Annually, tens of thousands of people in the United States are victims of hate crimes. In 2011 alone, more than 1.2 million violent crimes were committed in the United States (compared to 288,460 in 1960).[84] What we are now witnessing in the 21st century is the fracture or complete breakdown of families, societies, and governments as a result of centuries of dehumanization that have taken a toll. More natural disasters (tsunamis, earthquakes, hurricanes, tornados, etc.) merely uncover the reality of the national disasters we have created by granting sanctuary to dehumanization via the law.

Just like local policy can never trump state or federal law, dehumanization must never be allowed to trump the natural state of humans nor their right to civil liberties. Second-class citizenship cannot be tolerated on any level (micro or macro, de facto, de jure or customary), for it is a twisted root that stems from the greatest evil, the destruction of the essence of humanity. It destroys us all—our hope, our trust, our self-worth, and most certainly our very lives. Constitutional protections mean nothing without a government (local, state, and federal) willing to enforce the law and secure the liberties, freedoms, and guarantees to humane treatment of all of its citizens. We know all too well what happens when the government fails to do so. It is simply not enough to be tolerant or to embrace diversity; it is imperative to respect the sanctity of human life and embrace civility.

Treating the Pathology of Dehumanization

The antitoxin for dehumanization is humanism in the manner of ensuring a system, thoughts, or actions where human interests, value, and dignity predominate our society. Ironically, humanity had it all along. Nearly every culture, whether through religion, philosophy, and/or political theory, espoused the ideas of humanism over several millennia. Jewish tradition is rooted in the Ten Commandments handed down by Moses, which include prohibitions on covetousness, murder, theft, lying, and adultery. The early Christians avowed the major principle to "love your neighbor as you love yourself." The ancient Greeks believed in the natural rights granted to man by God, which existed before government, and that these rights were granted at birth and exist for all time. Basic principles have been worth repeating.

The Magna Carta (1297) provided liberties "to have and to hold . . . us and our heirs in perpetuity." Those liberties include the right to property, separation of church and state, the right to witnesses at trial, and the right to due process. One of the most influential theories comes from John Locke's Two Treatises of Government. Locke, like the ancient Greeks, believed that natural rights were given by God and included the right to life, liberty, and property. The natural state of men, according to Locke:

> is a state of perfect freedom of acting and disposing of their own possessions and persons as they think fit within the bounds of the law of nature. People in this state do not have to ask permission to act or depend on the will of others to arrange matters on their behalf. The natural state is also one of equality in which all power and jurisdiction is reciprocal and no one has more than another. It is evident that all human beings—as creatures belonging to the same species and rank and born indiscriminately with all the same natural advantages and faculties—are equal amongst themselves.[85]

Furthermore, in Locke's Second Treatise, he lists more specific liberties:

- "The state of nature has a law of nature to govern it, which obliges every one: and reason, which is that law, teaches all mankind, who will but consult it, that being all equal and independent, *no one ought to harm another in his life, health, liberty, or possessions* . . ." (Ch 2., Sec. 6).
- ". . . *that all men may be restrained from invading others rights*, and from doing hurt to one another . . ." (Ch 2, Sec. 7)
- ". . . a liberty for everyone to do what he lists, to live as he pleases . . ." (Ch. 4, Sec. 22)
- ". . . freedom from absolute, arbitrary power . . ." (Ch. 4, Sec. 23)
- ". . . the power [over] of his own life . . ." (Ch. 4, Sec. 23)

According to Locke, it is absolutely because of the existence of these inherent rights that man is able to create a "social contract" with his government to "have a standing rule to live by, common to everyone of that society."

Largely influenced by the theories of Locke, Thomas Jefferson drafted the Declaration of Independence, which states "*We hold these truths to be self-evident that all men are created equal, that they are endowed by their Creator with certain unalienable Rights . . . among these are life, liberty, and the pursuit of happiness . . .*" Later, in the preamble to the Constitution, the Founding Fathers drafted, "*We the People . . . in Order to form a more perfect Union, establish Justice, insure domestic Tranquility, provide for the common defence, promote the general Welfare, and secure the Blessings of Liberty to ourselves and our Posterity . . .*" But more important, because it is impossible to list all of the rights of humans in a simple bill of rights, the U.S. Constitution provides in the Ninth Amendment: "The enumeration in the Constitution, of certain rights, shall not be construed to deny or disparage others retained by the people." These basic tenets must be internalized. Anything less flies in the face of basic human decency and self-government. On a personal level, victims of dehumanization must find safe ways of eliminating violators from their life. When persons violently violate the basic principles and sanctity of humanity, they should be removed from the community (incarcerated) to ensure the safety of society. And if the government abuses its power and violates human liberties, there is political philosophy that provides a right to revolution (or rebellion) to ensure the safety of all citizens.[86] In the case of America, the best way to resolve abusive government practices is to hold political leaders to a standard of accountability through the judicial system, remove leaders through an impeachment process, or vote in leaders who will respect basic human dignity. Not only should we do this from a moral standard but this is the duty of citizens in a self-governing society. In addition, citizens cannot remain complacent and must stand up to violations of their rights not only under "equal protection under law," but under the Ninth Amendment and their powers under the Tenth Amendment.

Many have attempted to deconstruct racism and discrimination. That may be impractical because what we are really facing is the *pathology of dehumanization*. That pathology is transmitted in numerous ways. Racism and discrimination are mere methods of transmission, and dehumanization is the true sickness. Other methods of transmission can be seen in numerous examples, including slavery, segregation, white supremacy, second-class citizenship, societal outcasting, and even evolutionary theory.[87] Current methods include restrictive covenants, verbal and physical abuse, racial profiling, and segregationist policies that are still developing. It matters not if the action is committed by a private citizen or under color of law.

Unfortunately, what we debate today, in government and society and even in our individual families, is not the pathology of dehumanization; rather, we are scratching at the surface of *the methods of transmission*:

abuse, segregationist policy, and second-class citizenship. We are fighting battles against the *symptomology* of dehumanization, for example, disproportionate rates of incarceration, graduation, poverty, unemployment, and mortality; lack of representation in government; violence and rioting; limited access to education, housing, and employment; and depression and mental illness. Simply put, we are attempting to treat a headache with aspirin when the cause is a brain tumor. An aspirin will not do.

Government, society, and each individual citizen must understand the dynamics of the pathology of dehumanization, the methods of transmission, and the symptomology. We must all understand the history and relate it to the present via a multidisciplinary approach. Only then can we apply humanism to our daily lives and encourage others to take a stand against dehumanization publicly. The task remains daunting, particularly when those with political power refuse to address it. Frank Hargrove, a white Virginia legislator, is one example of a lack of political will. In February 2007, Hargrove stated that "black citizens should get over" slavery. This is a common theme in dehumanization, whether domestic or related to government: Get over it. *Time* magazine succinctly described the impact of Hargrove's statement: "That notion invalidates the black reality."[88] There is no getting over it when the legacy continues to this day—while we are still symptomatic. Instead of putting the weight on the victims to get over it, take the perpetrators out of the game. The issues of slavery, segregation, and discrimination cannot be viewed within their own individual time capsules. To gain proper perspective, these issues must be viewed collectively as devastating our culture and threatening our democracy.

We have treated the symptoms of dehumanization with some public policy but have struggled in finding the cure. Some forms of policy have been effective in reducing the transmission of dehumanization, such as dismantling Jim Crow and the recent efforts of the Department of Justice to pursue civil rights violators and beef up law enforcement to reduce crime. Also, the court system has been relatively consistent when actions rise to the level of a "hostile work environment" or are emotionally or psychologically abusive under Title VII of the Civil Rights Act of 1964.[89] But we need to do more. Whether we need more law may be subject to debate. The greater necessity is to make government officials accountable for the law they create and to hold law enforcement accountable for failures to protect. Why should we not? Even under basic family law principles, parents can be held liable for abuse, neglect, and failure to protect.

Therefore, it is imperative to hold government officials accountable for the same.

The Department of Justice's call for the "reconstruction" of the "infrastructure of democracy" is a deeply significant and proper goal.[90] Though its premise was within the context of New Orleans, the goal should be instituted nationally. It includes three basic factors:

1. Reducing crime
2. Ensuring respect for the Constitution
3. Enhancing public confidence in law enforcement[91]

While the New Orleans Police Department (and law enforcement in general) certainly needed an overhaul, evidently so do Louisiana's parish governments. Louisiana (and other states) must police the actions of the parish councils (local government) to ensure two necessary objectives:

1. That the actions of the local government *do not conflict* with state or federal law, especially constitutional law
2. That the actions of the local government *do not violate* the civil and human rights of its citizens

While government certainly has an important role in developing good citizens and economic success, all levels of socialization are critically important:

1. Parents need to build their child's confidence level and self-esteem and provide for their needs, which are more than material.
2. Public and private schools need to be committed to providing a quality education that prepares their students for *reality.*
3. Employers need to implement various recruitment methods in order to receive the best qualified candidates and develop a diverse workplace and be active in dismantling "hostile work environments."
4. Government's primary mission should be to protect its citizens from injustice, violence and attack, and violations of personal liberty—to keep its citizens free of dehumanization, especially, from government itself.[92]

As of 2009, seven state legislatures officially expressed remorse for their participation in slavery: Alabama, Arkansas, Florida, Maryland, New Jersey, North Carolina, and Virginia. Other states have similar measures pending or proposed: Georgia, Missouri, New York, Nebraska, and Tennessee. For the first time on a federal level, in 2009, the U.S. Senate passed a nonbinding resolution that "acknowledges the fundamental injustice, cruelty, brutality and inhumanity of slavery and Jim Crow laws," and "apologizes to African-Americans on behalf of the people of the United States for the wrongs committed against them and their ancestors who suffered under slavery and Jim Crow laws."[93] During his Senate tenure, Barack H. Obama was one of many co-sponsors of the resolution. As for St. Bernard Parish—and to a greater extent, Louisiana—leaders should seriously consider apologizing for the errors of their predecessors. This will likely start healing in the entire community because such an apology sets the tone for all who have held on to (false) beliefs of superiority and serves to heal and provide for those who have suffered under the color of law and from the symptoms of dehumanization.

On the other hand, some believe such an apology is unnecessary. According to Roger Clegg of the Center for Equal Opportunity, "The success of the Obama candidacy underscores the irrelevance of an apology because it shows enormous progress. Haven't we already moved beyond it?"[94] But statements such as this demonstrate the essence of ignorance—somehow even *the nomination* of one African American for the presidency (in a 232-year-old government) erases a 400-year-old legacy and the current practices of segregationist policy. Assuredly, it does not.

Additionally, a bill to form a commission to study the history and legacy of slavery and its aftermath and possible reparations or other remedies has been introduced by Representative John Conyers (D-MI) into the House in each Congress since 1989. This bill, known as H.R. 40: Commission to Study Reparation Proposals for African-Americans Act, was the subject of a hearing before a House Judiciary subcommittee in December 2007. On January 25, 2013, the bill was again referred to the Subcommittee on the Constitution and Civil Justice.[95]

Undoubtedly, reparations are a tense subject. Opponents usually argue that individually, they bear no responsibility for the actions of their forebears. This is a logical position. However, some people currently bear personal responsibility for *their own* actions, for example, the members of the St. Bernard Parish Council. Aside from suits against the state, individuals who abuse their position under law should be held liable under criminal and civil penalty rather than be allowed to retire on government pensions paid for by the same taxpayers they abuse. Both the government and the individuals harmed by an individual's abuse of power should have a claim against the individual holding the office of public trust. Furthermore, institutionally, government cannot deny such responsibility in the creation of a sanctuary for dehumanization. Reparations are necessary and can come to fruition with the establishment of government programs that can at least promote human dignity, the punishment of other institutions or individuals for official misconduct, and investment in educational systems across the nation. The indictment of Ray Nagin "should serve as a reminder to current and former public officials that, in the interest of full accountability, the FBI pursues corruption even after an official leaves office," according to Michael Anderson, special agent in charge of the FBI's New Orleans Field Office.[96]

Leaders who have inherited the unfortunate legacy of institutional discrimination have a responsibility—an overwhelming one—to work steadily to overcome it by creating transparency in government as well as independent offices of ethics and equality. St. Bernard Parish is on its way; and the new administration appears to recognize the value of doing so. The parish has this window of opportunity in its grasp and, if successful, it may serve as a model for the nation. David Peralta, the current parish president, is committed to "a new wind of progress, transparency and equal treatment to all. I work hard every day to counter the negative activity of my predecessor."[97]

On June 27, 2013, President Barack Obama and his family began their African pilgrimage at Goree Island, where enslaved Africans first laid eyes on the ocean and the slave ships that would mark the beginning of the Middle Passage. Deeply moved, President Obama told reporters, "It was a very powerful moment to be able to come here and to fully appreciate the magnitude of the slave trade, to get a sense in a very intimate way of the incredible inhumanity and hardship that people faced before they made the Middle Passage and that crossing . . . Obviously, for an African-American president to be able to visit this site, gives me even greater motivation in terms of human rights around the world."[98] The ruins of Goree Island stand as a monument to what can occur when we fail to vigilantly defend humanity.

Inspired by the emotional visit, First Lady Michelle Obama wrote an essay that was posted on the White House website. She reminded humanity as a whole that:

> People who came through this island could never have imagined how history would unfold. And they certainly could never have imagined that someone like me—a descendant of slaves—would come here with her own family, and look out through that door of no return. And maybe, in the end, that is an argument for hope even in the face of the most unspeakable horrors, because time and again—both in America and around the world—we have

> seen that cruelty and oppression are no match for people of conscience who commit themselves to the cause of freedom. So I hope that in your own lives, instead of being overwhelmed by the tragedies of our past, you will take inspiration from the triumphs of history's heroes—and I hope you will follow in their footsteps to create a better future.[99]

Should the creation of new law be necessary, it must be underscored with values of maintaining the sanctity of human dignity no matter what other human characteristic may be involved. This is not a call for color blindness, which serves to reinforce denial of our current state; rather, remedies must include opportunities to allow for a collective contribution of all citizens and an allowance for remediation at every level of citizenry. A focus on multiculturalism is one way to combat the pathology: from grade school curriculums to the highest levels of education; from the home to the workplace; from the private citizen or activist to the government leader.

There are consequences for failing to include every member and section of society into the whole.

> If a class of people is not allowed to participate culturally, we fail to understand and appreciate our differences and similarities. We become increasingly ethnocentric. We fail to develop socially, unable to get along with our fellow man. No matter how hard a society might try to separate classes or races, the bottom line is that, eventually, we will share the same space. The reality is we may never eliminate discrimination and racism through public policy. Consider, sometimes legislation serves to hide discrimination. That is, people will find a way to practice it. Employers may say one person is more qualified than another but could be, in reality, favoring one race or ethnicity over another. Laws cannot force people to allow their children to play and socialize with the children of a race for which they may feel is inferior.[100]

Affirmative action, obviously without quotas, is another method of treatment. Yet, the subject causes great controversy; and many statistics demonstrate that it is a failure. Rhetoric from both sides reduces its importance. However, while some may cite statistics to prove affirmative action is a failure, that view is problematic because of two main principles: "(1) discrimination is extremely difficult to prove, and (2) the socio-economic problems in the United States are much more complex than civil rights activists would like to admit."[101]

No person "should be denied a job, housing, salary increases, college admission, *et cetera*, on the basis of sex or skin color"[102] or, for that matter, any human quality. In theory, that is fair, but in reality, it has often shut out people who are not white, most significantly in education, which is where affirmative action is most appropriate. After all:

> education is perhaps the most important function of state and local governments. Compulsory school attendance laws and the great expenditures for education both demonstrate our recognition of the *importance of education to our democratic society. It is required in the performance of our most basic public responsibilities ... It is the very foundation of good citizenship.* Today it is a principal instrument in awakening the child to cultural values, in preparing him for later professional training, and in helping him to adjust normally to his environment. In these days, it is doubtful that any child may reasonably be expected to succeed in life if he is denied the opportunity of an education.[103]

There is a need to actively seek to include those citizens who were and are effectively denied their "unalienable rights."

As Americans we stand at a precipice. The world's sole hegemon and currently the world's greatest influence, we must realize that leading by example is more important than leading by speeches or rhetoric. While some may say that we are hated by other countries because of our freedom, it might be worth considering that perhaps we are hated for our hypocrisy in the piecemeal granting of freedoms to certain Americans. We must gain a thorough understanding that if we fail to protect our own citizens, that if we fail to garner the trust of our own citizens, we will fail miserably as we seek to protect citizens of the world; and we will lose the trust of the nations of the world. And even if it is too great a responsibility to be the world's leader, instead of being some great experiment, the United States could find itself destined to be the great failure of democracy. As *human beings*, we stand at a precipice; collectively, we are the world's greatest influence. If we fail to protect each other, if we fail to garner the trust of each other, humanity itself will pay the greatest price. The time for action in combating the dehumanization of slavery was in the 18th and 19th centuries. The time for action in combating the dehumanization of segregation was in the 20th century. The time for action in combating dehumanization in any arena is now, head on.

Author's Note

As far back as I can remember, I have always believed that there is but one race—the human race. Just as clearly, I recall my time in elementary school at PS 22 in Yonkers, New York, when I challenged the theory that three races exist. Part of the curriculum taught in the early 1970s was that there were three races: Caucasian (white), Negroid (black), and Mongoloid (referring predominantly to Asians).[1] According to that theory, differences in race were attributed to certain physical characteristics that supposedly occurred during the "evolution of man," where physical attributes evolved to accommodate certain climates around the world. This theory may seem archaic by today's standards, or at least by my own. And though I could not articulate it at the time, I knew that evolutionary theory, in its equation of humans to animals, was dehumanizing.

Having lived in Florida for more than a decade, I know all too well the risks associated with living in paradise on the Gulf of Mexico. I was transfixed watching Hurricane Katrina grow into a monster that encompassed the entire Gulf. My gut, along with Doppler radar, projected a hit near New Orleans. Though in the safety of my own home, along with friends who evacuated the Panhandle to my place (one of them a New Orleans native who survived Betsy), I was crushed with the images I saw, in full awareness of the social problems leading up to Katrina. We all cried that day. A first-year law student, I became a bit obsessed with the aftermath, watching Katrina-related television; reading and researching everything I could get my hands on; and relating (in my mind) almost every law class to the issues in New Orleans (criminal law, torts, constitutional law, property law, human rights law, critical race theory, and the list goes on). Together, it became a law school thesis and now, this book.

I knew that in being able to write this with clarity and fairness, I would need to visit the region, which I did, in May 2013—eight years following the disaster. In many ways, both structurally and in the sentiments of the natives, nothing has changed. And despite all that I already knew, I was shocked. Scores of schools in the Lower Ninth Ward remain closed, surrounding by high chain-link fences, and there were homes with faded markings from scores of search teams, along with neighborhoods that remain completely and eerily desolate. Locals talked to me about their continuous fear (likely post-traumatic stress disorder) of another flood and abandonment, even during periods of light rain. They expressed their disappointment in local and federal government, and some actually had deep perceptions of being hated because of their race. They said, "They hate us." Some Isleños reported to me that the community was trying to be more inclusive by inviting different cultures in the area to participate in multicultural events but still had no takers. Older residents talked about days gone by—the effects of *Plessy* and Jim Crow—admitted to a sense of shame, and hoped for change.

Because the French Quarter is the highest mass of land in New Orleans, it did not suffer the same devastation from Hurricane Katrina as other areas. As of 2013, more than 90 percent of the businesses have reopened and recovered. The Olivier House, built in 1838, remains intact despite the extensive exposure to the wrath of Mother Nature. This great mansion, one of the first built and located on Toulouse Street, was turned into a hotel in the 1970s. (Liza Lugo, JD, May 2013)

The French Quarter was beautiful and lively—for me, there was no sense, really, of the tragedy that the surrounding area suffered under the wrath of Katrina. Locals were loaded with a sense of "southern hospitality" no matter whether I was in the Quarter, the Lower Ninth Ward, or St. Bernard Parish. Therein lays the dichotomy—the sense of welcoming me, an outsider, contrasted with the way they have related to each other. And yet I found in my conversations with blacks, whites, Isleños, and Creoles that all of them held in their hearts a yearning to heal from the past. But they were unsure as to how to do so. Just like a family—with all its dysfunction—there was a heartfelt desire to understand the other member of the family.

The city, along with its surrounding parishes, is one of America's precious gems. After all, even diamonds have flaws. While it has its share of conflict and strife, the character of New Orleans is unique and valuable to the world. It is an example of the true spirit of the survivalist—both naturally and socially. In the worst of times, those in the area remained steadfast in their positions, perhaps even stoically. In the best of times, they are free in their manner and speech. They are real folks. And they know how to throw a party even in the midst of sorrow. Not only do they survive . . . they *live*.

This book is dedicated to all of those who fought the battles of civil rights before me and for those who will come afterward. It is because of their early and recent battles that I have the privilege of writing a book on such a critical and timely issue. My humblest appreciation goes out to the natives of New Orleans, those who remained and those who have moved elsewhere but carry a Mardi Gras spirit wherever they are, and to all of my teachers—professionals and laypersons—along the way. Your time, efforts, and sacrifices have all been worth it.

Appendix A

African-American Representation in Congress, 1870–Present

These lists are based on information drawn from the *Biographical Directory of the United States Congress*. Within each Congress, representatives and senators are listed in alphabetical order.

(D) = Democrat; (R) = Republican; (I) = Independent.

Senate

41st (1869–1871)	REVELS, Hiram Rhodes (R-MS)
44th (1875–1877)	BRUCE, Blanche Kelso (R-MS)
45th (1877–1879)	BRUCE, Blanche Kelso (R-MS)
46th (1879–1881)	BRUCE, Blanche Kelso (R-MS)
90th (1967–1969)	BROOKE, Edward William, III (R-MA)
91st (1969–1971)	BROOKE, Edward William, III (R-MA)
92nd (1971–1973)	BROOKE, Edward William, III (R-MA)
93rd (1973–1975)	BROOKE, Edward William, III (R-MA)
94th (1975–1977)	BROOKE, Edward William, III (R-MA)
95th (1977–1979)	BROOKE, Edward William, III (R-MA)
103rd (1993–1995)	MOSELEY BRAUN, Carol (D-IL)
104th (1995–1997)	MOSELEY BRAUN, Carol (D-IL)
105th (1997–1999)	MOSELEY BRAUN, Carol (D-IL)
109th (2005–2007)	OBAMA, Barack (D-IL)
110th (2007–2009)	OBAMA, Barack (D-IL)[1]
111th (2009–2011)	BURRIS, Roland (D-IL)[2]
113th (2013–2015)	COWAN, William ("Mo") (D-MA)[3]
113th (2013–2015)	SCOTT, Tim (R-SC)

House of Representatives

41st (1869–1871)	LONG, Jefferson Franklin (R-GA)
41st (1869–1871)	RAINEY, Joseph Hayne (R-SC)
42nd (1871–1873)	DE LARGE, Robert Carlos (R-SC)
42nd (1871–1873)	ELLIOTT, Robert Brown (R-SC)
42nd (1871–1873)	RAINEY, Joseph Hayne (R-SC)
42nd (1871–1873)	TURNER, Benjamin Sterling (R-AL)
42nd (1871–1873)	WALLS, Josiah Thomas (R-FL)
43rd (1873–1875)	CAIN, Richard Harvey (R-SC)
43rd (1873–1875)	ELLIOTT, Robert Brown (R-SC)
43rd (1873–1875)	LYNCH, John Roy (R-MS)
43rd (1873–1875)	RAINEY, Joseph Hayne (R-SC)
43rd (1873–1875)	RANSIER, Alonzo Jacob (R-SC)
43rd (1873–1875)	RAPIER, James Thomas (R-AL)
43rd (1873–1875)	WALLS, Josiah Thomas (R-FL)
44th (1875–1877)	HARALSON, Jeremiah (R-AL)
44th (1875–1877)	HYMAN, John Adams (R-NC)
44th (1875–1877)	LYNCH, John Roy (R-MS)
44th (1875–1877)	NASH, Charles Edmund (R-LA)
44th (1875–1877)	RAINEY, Joseph Hayne (R-SC)
44th (1875–1877)	SMALLS, Robert (R-SC)
44th (1875–1877)	WALLS, Josiah Thomas (R-FL)
45th (1877–1879)	CAIN, Richard Harvey (R-SC)
45th (1877–1879)	RAINEY, Joseph Hayne (R-SC)
45th (1877–1879)	SMALLS, Robert (R-SC)
47th (1881–1883)	LYNCH, John Roy (R-MS)
47th (1881–1883)	SMALLS, Robert (R-SC)
48th (1883–1885)	O'HARA, James Edward (R-NC)
48th (1883–1885)	SMALLS, Robert (R-SC)
49th (1885–1887)	O'HARA, James Edward (R-NC)
49th (1885–1887)	SMALLS, Robert (R-SC)
51st (1889–1891)	CHEATHAM, Henry Plummer (R-NC)
51st (1889–1891)	LANGSTON, John Mercer (R-VA)
51st (1889–1891)	MILLER, Thomas Ezekiel (R-SC)
52nd (1891–1893)	CHEATHAM, Henry Plummer (R-NC)
53rd (1893–1895)	MURRAY, George Washington (R-SC)
54th (1895–1897)	MURRAY, George Washington (R-SC)
55th (1897–1899)	WHITE, George Henry (R-NC)
56th (1899–1901)	WHITE, George Henry (R-NC)
71st (1929–1931)	DE PRIEST, Oscar Stanton (R-IL)
72nd (1931–1933)	DE PRIEST, Oscar Stanton (R-IL)
73rd (1933–1935)	DE PRIEST, Oscar Stanton (R-IL)

74th (1935–1937)	MITCHELL, Arthur Wergs (D-IL)
75th (1937–1939)	MITCHELL, Arthur Wergs (D-IL)
76th (1939–1941)	MITCHELL, Arthur Wergs (D-IL)
77th (1941–1943)	MITCHELL, Arthur Wergs (R-IL)
78th (1943–1945)	DAWSON, William Levi (R-IL)
79th (1945–1947)	DAWSON, William Levi (R-IL)
79th (1945–1947)	POWELL, Adam Clayton, Jr. (D-NY)
80th (1947–1949)	DAWSON, William Levi (D-IL)
80th (1947–1949)	POWELL, Adam Clayton, Jr. (D-NY)
81st (1949–1951)	DAWSON, William Levi (D-IL)
81st (1949–1951)	POWELL, Adam Clayton, Jr. (D-NY)
82nd (1951–1953)	DAWSON, William Levi (D-IL)
82nd (1951–1953)	POWELL, Adam Clayton, Jr. (D-NY)
83rd (1953–1955)	DAWSON, William Levi (D-IL)
83rd (1953–1955)	POWELL, Adam Clayton, Jr. (D-NY)
84th (1955–1957)	DAWSON, William Levi (D-IL)
84th (1955–1957)	DIGGS, Charles Coles, Jr. (D-MI)
84th (1955–1957)	POWELL, Adam Clayton, Jr. (D-NY)
85th (1957–1959)	DAWSON, William Levi (D-IL)
85th (1957–1959)	DIGGS, Charles Coles, Jr. (D-MI)
85th (1957–1959)	NIX, Robert Nelson Cornelius, Sr. (D-PA)
85th (1957–1959)	POWELL, Adam Clayton, Jr. (D-NY)
86th (1959–1961)	DAWSON, William Levi (D-IL)
86th (1959–1961)	DIGGS, Charles Coles, Jr. (D-MI)
86th (1959–1961)	NIX, Robert Nelson Cornelius, Sr. (D-PA)
86th (1959–1961)	POWELL, Adam Clayton, Jr. (D-NY)
87th (1961–1963)	DAWSON, William Levi (D-IL)
87th (1961–1963)	DIGGS, Charles Coles, Jr. (D-MI)
87th (1961–1963)	NIX, Robert Nelson Cornelius, Sr. (D-PA)
87th (1961–1963)	POWELL, Adam Clayton, Jr. (D-NY)
88th (1963–1965)	DAWSON, William Levi (D-IL)
88th (1963–1965)	DIGGS, Charles Coles, Jr. (D-MI)
88th (1963–1965)	HAWKINS, Augustus Freeman ("Gus") (D-CA)
88th (1963–1965)	NIX, Robert Nelson Cornelius, Sr. (D-PA)
88th (1963–1965)	POWELL, Adam Clayton, Jr. (D-NY)
89th (1965–1967)	CONYERS, John, Jr. (D-MI)
89th (1965–1967)	DAWSON, William Levi (D-IL)
89th (1965–1967)	DIGGS, Charles Coles, Jr. (D-MI)
89th (1965–1967)	HAWKINS, Augustus Freeman ("Gus") (D-CA)
89th (1965–1967)	NIX, Robert Nelson Cornelius, Sr. (D-PA)
89th (1965–1967)	POWELL, Adam Clayton, Jr. (D-NY)
90th (1967–1969)	CONYERS, John, Jr. (D-MI)

(*continued*)

90th (1967–1969)	DAWSON, William Levi (D-IL)
90th (1967–1969)	DIGGS, Charles Coles, Jr. (D-MI)
90th (1967–1969)	HAWKINS, Augustus Freeman ("Gus") (D-CA)
90th (1967–1969)	NIX, Robert Nelson Cornelius, Sr. (D-PA)
90th (1967–1969)	POWELL, Adam Clayton, Jr. (D-NY)[4]
91st (1969–1971)	CHISHOLM, Shirley Anita (D-NY)
91st (1969–1971)	CLAY, William Lacy, Sr. (D-MO)
91st (1969–1971)	COLLINS, George Washington (D-IL)
91st (1969–1971)	CONYERS, John, Jr. (D-MI)
91st (1969–1971)	DAWSON, William Levi (D-IL)
91st (1969–1971)	DIGGS, Charles Coles, Jr. (D-MI)
91st (1969–1971)	HAWKINS, Augustus Freeman ("Gus") (D-CA)
91st (1969–1971)	NIX, Robert Nelson Cornelius, Sr. (D-PA)
91st (1969–1971)	POWELL, Adam Clayton, Jr. (D-NY)
91st (1969–1971)	STOKES, Louis (D-OH)
92nd (1971–1973)	CHISHOLM, Shirley Anita (D-NY)
92nd (1971–1973)	CLAY, William Lacy, Sr. (D-MO)
92nd (1971–1973)	COLLINS, George Washington (D-IL)
92nd (1971–1973)	CONYERS, John, Jr. (D-MI)
92nd (1971–1973)	DELLUMS, Ronald V. (D-CA)
92nd (1971–1973)	DIGGS, Charles Coles, Jr. (D-MI)
92nd (1971–1973)	FAUNTROY, Walter Edward (D-DC)
92nd (1971–1973)	HAWKINS, Augustus Freeman ("Gus") (D-CA)
92nd (1971–1973)	METCALFE, Ralph Harold (D-IL)
92nd (1971–1973)	MITCHELL, Parren James (D-MD)
92nd (1971–1973)	NIX, Robert Nelson Cornelius, Sr. (D-PA)
92nd (1971–1973)	RANGEL, Charles B. (D-NY)
92nd (1971–1973)	STOKES, Louis (D-OH)
93rd (1973–1975)	BURKE, Yvonne Brathwaite (D-CA)
93rd (1973–1975)	CHISHOLM, Shirley Anita (D-NY)
93rd (1973–1975)	CLAY, William Lacy, Sr. (D-MO)
93rd (1973–1975)	COLLINS, Cardiss (D-IL)
93rd (1973–1975)	CONYERS, John, Jr. (D-MI)
93rd (1973–1975)	DELLUMS, Ronald V. (D-CA)
93rd (1973–1975)	DIGGS, Charles Coles, Jr. (D-MI)
93rd (1973–1975)	FAUNTROY, Walter Edward (D-DC)
93rd (1973–1975)	HAWKINS, Augustus Freeman ("Gus") (D-CA)
93rd (1973–1975)	JORDAN, Barbara Charline (D-TX)
93rd (1973–1975)	METCALFE, Ralph Harold (D-IL)
93rd (1973–1975)	MITCHELL, Parren James (D-MD)
93rd (1973–1975)	NIX, Robert Nelson Cornelius, Sr. (D-PA)
93rd (1973–1975)	RANGEL, Charles B. (D-NY)
93rd (1973–1975)	STOKES, Louis (D-OH)

93rd (1973–1975)	YOUNG, Andrew Jackson, Jr. (D-GA)
94th (1975–1977)	BURKE, Yvonne Brathwaite (D-CA)
94th (1975–1977)	CHISHOLM, Shirley Anita (D-NY)
94th (1975–1977)	CLAY, William Lacy, Sr. (D-MO)
94th (1975–1977)	COLLINS, Cardiss (D-IL)
94th (1975–1977)	CONYERS, John, Jr. (D-MI)
94th (1975–1977)	DELLUMS, Ronald V. (D-CA)
94th (1975–1977)	DIGGS, Charles Coles, Jr. (D-MI)
94th (1975–1977)	FAUNTROY, Walter Edward (D-DC)
94th (1975–1977)	FORD, Harold Eugene (D-TN)
94th (1975–1977)	HAWKINS, Augustus Freeman ("Gus") (D-CA)
94th (1975–1977)	JORDAN, Barbara Charline (D-TX)
94th (1975–1977)	METCALFE, Ralph Harold (D-IL)
94th (1975–1977)	MITCHELL, Parren James (D-MD)
94th (1975–1977)	NIX, Robert Nelson Cornelius, Sr. (D-PA)
94th (1975–1977)	RANGEL, Charles B. (D-NY)
94th (1975–1977)	STOKES, Louis (D-OH)
94th (1975–1977)	YOUNG, Andrew Jackson, Jr. (D-GA)
95th (1977–1979)	BURKE, Yvonne Brathwaite (D-CA)
95th (1977–1979)	CHISHOLM, Shirley Anita (D-NY)
95th (1977–1979)	CLAY, William Lacy, Sr. (D-MO)
95th (1977–1979)	COLLINS, Cardiss (D-IL)
95th (1977–1979)	CONYERS, John, Jr. (D-MI)
95th (1977–1979)	DELLUMS, Ronald V. (D-CA)
95th (1977–1979)	DIGGS, Charles Coles, Jr. (D-MI)
95th (1977–1979)	FAUNTROY, Walter Edward (D-DC)
95th (1977–1979)	FORD, Harold Eugene (D-TN)
95th (1977–1979)	HAWKINS, Augustus Freeman ("Gus") (D-CA)
95th (1977–1979)	JORDAN, Barbara Charline (D-TX)
95th (1977–1979)	METCALFE, Ralph Harold (D-IL)
95th (1977–1979)	MITCHELL, Parren James (D-MD)
95th (1977–1979)	NIX, Robert Nelson Cornelius, Sr. (D-PA)
95th (1977–1979)	RANGEL, Charles B. (D-NY)
95th (1977–1979)	STOKES, Louis (D-OH)
95th (1977–1979)	YOUNG, Andrew Jackson, Jr. (D-GA)
96th (1979–1981)	CHISHOLM, Shirley Anita (D-NY)
96th (1979–1981)	CLAY, William Lacy, Sr. (D-MO)
96th (1979–1981)	COLLINS, Cardiss (D-IL)
96th (1979–1981)	CONYERS, John, Jr. (D-MI)
96th (1979–1981)	CROCKETT, George William, Jr. (D-MI)
96th (1979–1981)	DELLUMS, Ronald V. (D-CA)
96th (1979–1981)	DIGGS, Charles Coles, Jr. (D-MI)[5]

(continued)

96th (1979–1981)	DIXON, Julian Carey (D-CA)
96th (1979–1981)	EVANS, Melvin Herbert (R-VI)
96th (1979–1981)	FAUNTROY, Walter Edward (D-DC)
96th (1979–1981)	FORD, Harold Eugene (D-TN)
96th (1979–1981)	GRAY, William Herbert, III (D-PA)
96th (1979–1981)	HAWKINS, Augustus Freeman ("Gus") (D-CA)
96th (1979–1981)	LELAND, George Thomas (Mickey) (D-TX)
96th (1979–1981)	MITCHELL, Parren James (D-MD)
96th (1979–1981)	RANGEL, Charles B. (D-NY)
96th (1979–1981)	STEWART, Bennett McVey (D-IL)
96th (1979–1981)	STOKES, Louis (D-OH)
97th (1981–1983)	CHISHOLM, Shirley Anita (D-NY)
97th (1981–1983)	CLAY, William Lacy, Sr. (D-MO)
97th (1981–1983)	COLLINS, Cardiss (D-IL)
97th (1981–1983)	CONYERS, John, Jr. (D-MI)
97th (1981–1983)	CROCKETT, George William, Jr. (D-MI)
97th (1981–1983)	DELLUMS, Ronald V. (D-CA)
97th (1981–1983)	DIXON, Julian Carey (D-CA)
97th (1981–1983)	DYMALLY, Mervyn Malcolm (D-CA)
97th (1981–1983)	FAUNTROY, Walter Edward (D-DC)
97th (1981–1983)	FORD, Harold Eugene (D-TN)
97th (1981–1983)	GRAY, William Herbert, III (D-PA)
97th (1981–1983)	HALL, Katie Beatrice (D-IN)[6]
97th (1981–1983)	HAWKINS, Augustus Freeman ("Gus") (D-CA)
97th (1981–1983)	LELAND, George Thomas ("Mickey") (D-TX)
97th (1981–1983)	MITCHELL, Parren James (D-MD)
97th (1981–1983)	RANGEL, Charles B. (D-NY)
97th (1981–1983)	SAVAGE, Gus (D-IL)
97th (1981–1983)	STOKES, Louis (D-OH)
97th (1981–1983)	WASHINGTON, Harold (D-IL)
98th (1983–1985)	CLAY, William Lacy, Sr. (D-MO)
98th (1983–1985)	COLLINS, Cardiss (D-IL)
98th (1983–1985)	CONYERS, John, Jr. (D-MI)
98th (1983–1985)	CROCKETT, George William, Jr. (D-MI)
98th (1983–1985)	DELLUMS, Ronald V. (D-CA)
98th (1983–1985)	DIXON, Julian Carey (D-CA)
98th (1983–1985)	DYMALLY, Mervyn Malcolm (D-CA)
98th (1983–1985)	FAUNTROY, Walter Edward (D-DC)
98th (1983–1985)	FORD, Harold Eugene (D-TN)
98th (1983–1985)	GRAY, William Herbert, III (D-PA)
98th (1983–1985)	HALL, Katie Beatrice (D-IN)
98th (1983–1985)	HAWKINS, Augustus Freeman ("Gus") (D-CA)
98th (1983–1985)	HAYES, Charles Arthur (D-IL)

98th (1983–1985)	LELAND, George Thomas ("Mickey") (D-TX)
98th (1983–1985)	MITCHELL, Parren James (D-MD)
98th (1983–1985)	OWENS, Major Robert Odell (D-NY)
98th (1983–1985)	RANGEL, Charles B. (D-NY)
98th (1983–1985)	SAVAGE, Gus (D-IL)
98th (1983–1985)	STOKES, Louis (D-OH)
98th (1983–1985)	TOWNS, Edolphus (D-NY)
98th (1983–1985)	WASHINGTON, Harold (D-IL)
98th (1983–1985)	WHEAT, Alan Dupree (D-MO)
99th (1985–1987)	CLAY, William Lacy, Sr. (D-MO)
99th (1985–1987)	COLLINS, Cardiss (D-IL)
99th (1985–1987)	CONYERS, John, Jr. (D-MI)
99th (1985–1987)	CROCKETT, George William, Jr. (D-MI)
99th (1985–1987)	DELLUMS, Ronald V. (D-CA)
99th (1985–1987)	DIXON, Julian Carey (D-CA)
99th (1985–1987)	DYMALLY, Mervyn Malcolm (D-CA)
99th (1985–1987)	FAUNTROY, Walter Edward (D-DC)
99th (1985–1987)	FORD, Harold Eugene (D-TN)
99th (1985–1987)	GRAY, William Herbert, III (D-PA)
99th (1985–1987)	HAWKINS, Augustus Freeman ("Gus") (D-CA)
99th (1985–1987)	HAYES, Charles Arthur (D-IL)
99th (1985–1987)	LELAND, George Thomas ("Mickey") (D-TX)
99th (1985–1987)	MITCHELL, Parren James (D-MD)
99th (1985–1987)	OWENS, Major Robert Odell (D-NY)
99th (1985–1987)	RANGEL, Charles B. (D-NY)
99th (1985–1987)	SAVAGE, Gus (D-IL)
99th (1985–1987)	STOKES, Louis (D-OH)
99th (1985–1987)	TOWNS, Edolphus (D-NY)
99th (1985–1987)	WALDON, Alton R., Jr. (D-NY)
99th (1985–1987)	WHEAT, Alan Dupree (D-MO)
100th (1987–1989)	CLAY, William Lacy, Sr. (D-MO)
100th (1987–1989)	COLLINS, Cardiss (D-IL)
100th (1987–1989)	CONYERS, John, Jr. (D-MI)
100th (1987–1989)	CROCKETT, George William, Jr. (D-MI)
100th (1987–1989)	DELLUMS, Ronald V. (D-CA)
100th (1987–1989)	DIXON, Julian Carey (D-CA)
100th (1987–1989)	DYMALLY, Mervyn Malcolm (D-CA)
100th (1987–1989)	ESPY, Alphonso Michael ("Mike") (D-MS)
100th (1987–1989)	FAUNTROY, Walter Edward (D-DC)
100th (1987–1989)	FLAKE, Floyd Harold (D-NY)
100th (1987–1989)	FORD, Harold Eugene (D-TN)
100th (1987–1989)	GRAY, William Herbert, III (D-PA)

(*continued*)

100th (1987–1989)	HAWKINS, Augustus Freeman ("Gus") (D-CA)
100th (1987–1989)	HAYES, Charles Arthur (D-IL)
100th (1987–1989)	LELAND, George Thomas ("Mickey") (D-TX)
100th (1987–1989)	LEWIS, John R. (D-GA)
100th (1987–1989)	MFUME, Kweisi (D-MD)
100th (1987–1989)	OWENS, Major Robert Odell (D-NY)
100th (1987–1989)	RANGEL, Charles B. (D-NY)
100th (1987–1989)	SAVAGE, Gus (D-IL)
100th (1987–1989)	STOKES, Louis (D-OH)
100th (1987–1989)	TOWNS, Edolphus (D-NY)
100th (1987–1989)	WHEAT, Alan Dupree (D-MO)
101st (1989–1991)	CLAY, William Lacy, Sr. (D-MO)
101st (1989–1991)	COLLINS, Cardiss (D-IL)
101st (1989–1991)	CONYERS, John, Jr. (D-MI)
101st (1989–1991)	CROCKETT, George William, Jr. (D-MI)
101st (1989–1991)	DELLUMS, Ronald V. (D-CA)
101st (1989–1991)	DIXON, Julian Carey (D-CA)
101st (1989–1991)	DYMALLY, Mervyn Malcolm (D-CA)
101st (1989–1991)	ESPY, Alphonso Michael ("Mike") (D-MS)
101st (1989–1991)	FAUNTROY, Walter Edward (D-DC)
101st (1989–1991)	FLAKE, Floyd Harold (D-NY)
101st (1989–1991)	FORD, Harold Eugene (D-TN)
101st (1989–1991)	GRAY, William Herbert, III (D-PA)
101st (1989–1991)	HAWKINS, Augustus Freeman ("Gus") (D-CA)
101st (1989–1991)	HAYES, Charles Arthur (D-IL)
101st (1989–1991)	LELAND, George Thomas ("Mickey") (D-TX)
101st (1989–1991)	LEWIS, John R. (D-GA)
101st (1989–1991)	MFUME, Kweisi (D-MD)
101st (1989–1991)	OWENS, Major Robert Odell (D-NY)
101st (1989–1991)	PAYNE, Donald Milford (D-NJ)
101st (1989–1991)	RANGEL, Charles B. (D-NY)
101st (1989–1991)	SAVAGE, Gus (D-IL)
101st (1989–1991)	STOKES, Louis (D-OH)
101st (1989–1991)	TOWNS, Edolphus (D-NY)
101st (1989–1991)	WASHINGTON, Craig Anthony (D-TX)
101st (1989–1991)	WHEAT, Alan Dupree (D-MO)
102nd (1991–1993)	BLACKWELL, Lucien Edward (D-PA)
102nd (1991–1993)	CLAY, William Lacy, Sr. (D-MO)
102nd (1991–1993)	CLAYTON, Eva M. (D-NC)[7]
102nd (1991–1993)	COLLINS, Barbara-Rose (D-MI)
102nd (1991–1993)	COLLINS, Cardiss (D-IL)
102nd (1991–1993)	CONYERS, John, Jr. (D-MI)
102nd (1991–1993)	DELLUMS, Ronald V. (D-CA)

102nd (1991–1993)	DIXON, Julian Carey (D-CA)
102nd (1991–1993)	DYMALLY, Mervyn Malcolm (D-CA)
102nd (1991–1993)	ESPY, Alphonso Michael ("Mike") (D-MS)
102nd (1991–1993)	FLAKE, Floyd Harold (D-NY)
102nd (1991–1993)	FORD, Harold Eugene (D-TN)
102nd (1991–1993)	FRANKS, Gary A. (D-CT)
102nd (1991–1993)	GRAY, William Herbert, III (D-PA)[8]
102nd (1991–1993)	HAYES, Charles Arthur (D-IL)
102nd (1991–1993)	JEFFERSON, William Jennings (D-LA)
102nd (1991–1993)	LEWIS, John R. (D-GA)
102nd (1991–1993)	MFUME, Kweisi (D-MD)
102nd (1991–1993)	NORTON, Eleanor Holmes (D-DC)
102nd (1991–1993)	OWENS, Major Robert Odell (D-NY)
102nd (1991–1993)	PAYNE, Donald Milford (D-NJ)
102nd (1991–1993)	RANGEL, Charles B. (D-NY)
102nd (1991–1993)	SAVAGE, Gus (D-IL)
102nd (1991–1993)	STOKES, Louis (D-OH)
102nd (1991–1993)	TOWNS, Edolphus (D-NY)
102nd (1991–1993)	WASHINGTON, Craig Anthony (D-TX)
102nd (1991–1993)	WATERS, Maxine (D-CA)
102nd (1991–1993)	WHEAT, Alan Dupree (D-MO)
103rd (1993–1995)	BISHOP, Sanford Dixon, Jr. (D-GA)
103rd (1993–1995)	BLACKWELL, Lucien Edward (D-PA)
103rd (1993–1995)	BROWN, Corrine (D-FL)
103rd (1993–1995)	CLAY, William Lacy, Sr. (D-MO)
103rd (1993–1995)	CLAYTON, Eva M. (D-NC)
103rd (1993–1995)	CLYBURN, James Enos (D-SC)
103rd (1993–1995)	COLLINS, Barbara-Rose (D-MI)
103rd (1993–1995)	COLLINS, Cardiss (D-IL)
103rd (1993–1995)	CONYERS, John, Jr. (D-MI)
103rd (1993–1995)	DELLUMS, Ronald V. (D-CA)
103rd (1993–1995)	DIXON, Julian Carey (D-CA)
103rd (1993–1995)	ESPY, Alphonso Michael (Mike) (D-MS)[9]
103rd (1993–1995)	FIELDS, Cleo (D-LA)
103rd (1993–1995)	FLAKE, Floyd Harold (D-NY)
103rd (1993–1995)	FORD, Harold Eugene (D-TN)
103rd (1993–1995)	FRANKS, Gary A. (R-CT)
103rd (1993–1995)	HASTINGS, Alcee Lamar (D-FL)
103rd (1993–1995)	HILLIARD, Earl Frederick (D-AL)
103rd (1993–1995)	JEFFERSON, William Jennings (D-LA)
103rd (1993–1995)	JOHNSON, Eddie Bernice (D-TX)
103rd (1993–1995)	LEWIS, John R. (D-GA)

(continued)

103rd (1993–1995)	MCKINNEY, Cynthia Ann (D-GA)
103rd (1993–1995)	MEEK, Carrie P. (D-FL)
103rd (1993–1995)	MFUME, Kweisi (D-MD)
103rd (1993–1995)	NORTON, Eleanor Holmes (D-DC)
103rd (1993–1995)	OWENS, Major Robert Odell (D-NY)
103rd (1993–1995)	PAYNE, Donald Milford (D-NJ)
103rd (1993–1995)	RANGEL, Charles B. (D-NY)
103rd (1993–1995)	REYNOLDS, Mel (D-IL)
103rd (1993–1995)	RUSH, Bobby L. (D-IL)
103rd (1993–1995)	SCOTT, Robert Cortez (D-VA)
103rd (1993–1995)	STOKES, Louis (D-OH)
103rd (1993–1995)	THOMPSON, Bennie (D-MS)
103rd (1993–1995)	TOWNS, Edolphus (D-NY)
103rd (1993–1995)	TUCKER, Walter R., III (D-CA)
103rd (1993–1995)	WASHINGTON, Craig Anthony (D-TX)
103rd (1993–1995)	WATERS, Maxine (D-CA)
103rd (1993–1995)	WATT, Melvin L. (D-NC)
103rd (1993–1995)	WHEAT, Alan Dupree (D-MO)
103rd (1993–1995)	WYNN, Albert Russell (D-MD)
104th (1995–1997)	BISHOP, Sanford Dixon, Jr. (D-GA)
104th (1995–1997)	BROWN, Corrine (D-FL)
104th (1995–1997)	CLAY, William Lacy, Sr. (D-MO)
104th (1995–1997)	CLAYTON, Eva M. (D-NC)
104th (1995–1997)	CLYBURN, James Enos (D-SC)
104th (1995–1997)	COLLINS, Barbara-Rose (D-MI)
104th (1995–1997)	COLLINS, Cardiss (D-IL)
104th (1995–1997)	CONYERS, John, Jr. (D-MI)
104th (1995–1997)	CUMMINGS, Elijah Eugene (D-MD)
104th (1995–1997)	DELLUMS, Ronald V. (D-CA)
104th (1995–1997)	DIXON, Julian Carey (D-CA)
104th (1995–1997)	FATTAH, Chaka (D-PA)
104th (1995–1997)	FIELDS, Cleo (D-LA)
104th (1995–1997)	FLAKE, Floyd Harold (D-NY)
104th (1995–1997)	FORD, Harold Eugene (D-TN)
104th (1995–1997)	FRANKS, Gary A. (R-CT)
104th (1995–1997)	FRAZER, Victor O. (I) VI
104th (1995–1997)	HASTINGS, Alcee Lamar (D-FL)
104th (1995–1997)	HILLIARD, Earl Frederick (D-AL)
104th (1995–1997)	JACKSON, Jesse L., Jr. (D-IL)
104th (1995–1997)	JACKSON LEE, Sheila (D-TX)
104th (1995–1997)	JEFFERSON, William Jennings (D-LA)
104th (1995–1997)	JOHNSON, Eddie Bernice (D-TX)
104th (1995–1997)	LEWIS, John R. (D-GA)

104th (1995–1997)	MCKINNEY, Cynthia Ann (D-GA)
104th (1995–1997)	MEEK, Carrie P. (D-FL)
104th (1995–1997)	MFUME, Kweisi (D-MD)[10]
104th (1995–1997)	MILLENDER-MCDONALD, Juanita (D-CA)[11]
104th (1995–1997)	NORTON, Eleanor Holmes (D-DC)
104th (1995–1997)	OWENS, Major Robert Odell (D-NY)
104th (1995–1997)	PAYNE, Donald Milford (D-NJ)
104th (1995–1997)	RANGEL, Charles B. (D-NY)
104th (1995–1997)	REYNOLDS, Mel (D-IL)[12]
104th (1995–1997)	RUSH, Bobby L. (D-IL)
104th (1995–1997)	SCOTT, Robert Cortez (D-VA)
104th (1995–1997)	STOKES, Louis (D-OH)
104th (1995–1997)	THOMPSON, Bennie (D-MS)
104th (1995–1997)	TOWNS, Edolphus (D-NY)
104th (1995–1997)	TUCKER, Walter R., III (D-CA)[13]
104th (1995–1997)	WATERS, Maxine (D-CA)
104th (1995–1997)	WATT, Melvin L. (D-NC)
104th (1995–1997)	WATTS, Julius Caesar, Jr. ("J. C.") (R-OK)
104th (1995–1997)	WYNN, Albert Russell (D-MD)
105th (1997–1999)	BISHOP, Sanford Dixon, Jr. (D-GA)
105th (1997–1999)	BROWN, Corrine (D-FL)
105th (1997–1999)	CARSON, Julia May (D-IN)
105th (1997–1999)	CHRISTENSEN, Donna Marie (D-VI)[14]
105th (1997–1999)	CLAY, William Lacy, Sr. (D-MO)
105th (1997–1999)	CLAYTON, Eva M. (D-NC)
105th (1997–1999)	CLYBURN, James Enos (D-SC)
105th (1997–1999)	CONYERS, John, Jr. (D-MI)
105th (1997–1999)	CUMMINGS, Elijah Eugene (D-MD)
105th (1997–1999)	DAVIS, Danny K. (D-IL)
105th (1997–1999)	DELLUMS, Ronald V. (D-CA)[15]
105th (1997–1999)	DIXON, Julian Carey (D-CA)
105th (1997–1999)	FATTAH, Chaka (D-PA)
105th (1997–1999)	FLAKE, Floyd Harold (D-NY)[16]
105th (1997–1999)	FORD, Harold, Jr. (D-TN)
105th (1997–1999)	HASTINGS, Alcee Lamar (D-FL)
105th (1997–1999)	HILLIARD, Earl Frederick (D-AL)
105th (1997–1999)	JACKSON, Jesse L., Jr. (D-IL)
105th (1997–1999)	JACKSON LEE, Sheila (D-TX)
105th (1997–1999)	JEFFERSON, William Jennings (D-LA)
105th (1997–1999)	JOHNSON, Eddie Bernice (D-TX)
105th (1997–1999)	KILPATRICK, Carolyn Cheeks (D-MI)
105th (1997–1999)	LEE, Barbara (D-CA)[17]

(continued)

105th (1997–1999)	LEWIS, John R. (D-GA)
105th (1997–1999)	MCKINNEY, Cynthia Ann (D-GA)
105th (1997–1999)	MEEK, Carrie P. (D-FL)
105th (1997–1999)	MEEKS, Gregory W. (D-NY)
105th (1997–1999)	MILLENDER-MCDONALD, Juanita (D-CA)
105th (1997–1999)	NORTON, Eleanor Holmes (D-DC)
105th (1997–1999)	OWENS, Major Robert Odell (D-NY)
105th (1997–1999)	PAYNE, Donald Milford (D-NJ)
105th (1997–1999)	RANGEL, Charles B. (D-NY)
105th (1997–1999)	RUSH, Bobby L. (D-IL)
105th (1997–1999)	SCOTT, Robert Cortez (D-VA)
105th (1997–1999)	STOKES, Louis (D-OH)
105th (1997–1999)	THOMPSON, Bennie (D-MS)
105th (1997–1999)	TOWNS, Edolphus (D-NY)
105th (1997–1999)	WATERS, Maxine (D-CA)
105th (1997–1999)	WATT, Melvin L. (D-NC)
105th (1997–1999)	WATTS, Julius Caesar, Jr. ("J. C.") (R-OK)
105th (1997–1999)	WYNN, Albert Russell (D-MD)
106th (1999–2001)	BISHOP, Sanford Dixon, Jr. (D-GA)
106th (1999–2001)	BROWN, Corrine (D-FL)
106th (1999–2001)	CARSON, Julia May (D-IN)
106th (1999–2001)	CHRISTENSEN, Donna Marie (D-VI)
106th (1999–2001)	CLAY, William Lacy, Sr. (D-MO)
106th (1999–2001)	CLAYTON, Eva M. (D-NC)
106th (1999–2001)	CLYBURN, James Enos (D-SC)
106th (1999–2001)	CONYERS, John, Jr. (D-MI)
106th (1999–2001)	CUMMINGS, Elijah Eugene (D-MD)
106th (1999–2001)	DAVIS, Danny K. (D-IL)
106th (1999–2001)	DIXON, Julian Carey (D-CA)
106th (1999–2001)	FATTAH, Chaka (D-PA)
106th (1999–2001)	FORD, Harold, Jr. (D-TN)
106th (1999–2001)	HASTINGS, Alcee Lamar (D-FL)
106th (1999–2001)	HILLIARD, Earl Frederick (D-AL)
106th (1999–2001)	JACKSON, Jesse L., Jr. (D-IL)
106th (1999–2001)	JACKSON LEE, Sheila (D-TX)
106th (1999–2001)	JEFFERSON, William Jennings (D-LA)
106th (1999–2001)	JOHNSON, Eddie Bernice (D-TX)
106th (1999–2001)	JONES, Stephanie Tubbs (D-OH)
106th (1999–2001)	KILPATRICK, Carolyn Cheeks (D-MI)
106th (1999–2001)	LEE, Barbara (D-CA)
106th (1999–2001)	LEWIS, John R. (D-GA)
106th (1999–2001)	MCKINNEY, Cynthia Ann (D-GA)
106th (1999–2001)	MEEK, Carrie P. (D-FL)

106th (1999–2001)	MEEKS, Gregory W. (D-NY)
106th (1999–2001)	MILLENDER-MCDONALD, Juanita (D-CA)
106th (1999–2001)	NORTON, Eleanor Holmes (D-DC)
106th (1999–2001)	OWENS, Major Robert Odell (D-NY)
106th (1999–2001)	PAYNE, Donald Milford (D-NJ)
106th (1999–2001)	RANGEL, Charles B. (D-NY)
106th (1999–2001)	RUSH, Bobby L. (D-IL)
106th (1999–2001)	SCOTT, Robert Cortez (D-VA)
106th (1999–2001)	THOMPSON, Bennie (D-MS)
106th (1999–2001)	TOWNS, Edolphus (D-NY)
106th (1999–2001)	WATERS, Maxine (D-CA)
106th (1999–2001)	WATT, Melvin L. (D-NC)
106th (1999–2001)	WATTS, Julius Caesar, Jr. ("J. C.") (R-OK)
106th (1999–2001)	WYNN, Albert Russell (D-MD)
107th (2001–2003)	BISHOP, Sanford Dixon, Jr. (D-GA)
107th (2001–2003)	BROWN, Corrine (D-FL)
107th (2001–2003)	CARSON, Julia May (D-IN)
107th (2001–2003)	CHRISTENSEN, Donna Marie (D-VI)
107th (2001–2003)	CLAY, William Lacy, Jr. (D-MO)
107th (2001–2003)	CLAYTON, Eva M. (D-NC)
107th (2001–2003)	CLYBURN, James Enos (D-SC)
107th (2001–2003)	CONYERS, John, Jr. (D-MI)
107th (2001–2003)	CUMMINGS, Elijah Eugene (D-MD)
107th (2001–2003)	DAVIS, Danny K. (D-IL)
107th (2001–2003)	FATTAH, Chaka (D-PA)
107th (2001–2003)	FORD, Harold, Jr. (D-TN)
107th (2001–2003)	HASTINGS, Alcee Lamar (D-FL)
107th (2001–2003)	HILLIARD, Earl Frederick (D-AL)
107th (2001–2003)	JACKSON, Jesse L., Jr. (D-IL)
107th (2001–2003)	JACKSON LEE, Sheila (D-TX)
107th (2001–2003)	JEFFERSON, William Jennings (D-LA)
107th (2001–2003)	JOHNSON, Eddie Bernice (D-TX)
107th (2001–2003)	JONES, Stephanie Tubbs (D-OH)
107th (2001–2003)	KILPATRICK, Carolyn Cheeks (D-MI)
107th (2001–2003)	LEE, Barbara (D-CA)
107th (2001–2003)	LEWIS, John R. (D-GA)
107th (2001–2003)	MCKINNEY, Cynthia Ann (D-GA)
107th (2001–2003)	MEEK, Carrie P. (D-FL)
107th (2001–2003)	MEEKS, Gregory W. (D-NY)
107th (2001–2003)	MILLENDER-MCDONALD, Juanita (D-CA)
107th (2001–2003)	NORTON, Eleanor Holmes (D-DC)
107th (2001–2003)	OWENS, Major Robert Odell (D-NY)

(*continued*)

107th (2001–2003)	PAYNE, Donald Milford (D-NJ)
107th (2001–2003)	RANGEL, Charles B. (D-NY)
107th (2001–2003)	RUSH, Bobby L. (D-IL)
107th (2001–2003)	SCOTT, Robert Cortez (D-VA)
107th (2001–2003)	THOMPSON, Bennie (D-MS)
107th (2001–2003)	TOWNS, Edolphus (D-NY)
107th (2001–2003)	WATERS, Maxine (D-CA)
107th (2001–2003)	WATSON, Diane Edith (D-CA)[18]
107th (2001–2003)	WATT, Melvin L. (D-NC)
107th (2001–2003)	WATTS, Julius Caesar, Jr. ("J. C.") (R-OK)
107th (2001–2003)	WYNN, Albert Russell (D-MD)
108th (2003–2005)	BALLANCE, Frank W., Jr. (D-NC)[19]
108th (2003–2005)	BISHOP, Sanford Dixon, Jr. (D-GA)
108th (2003–2005)	BROWN, Corrine (D-FL)
108th (2003–2005)	BUTTERFIELD, George Kenneth, Jr. ("G. K.") (D-NC)
108th (2003–2005)	CARSON, Julia May (D-IN)
108th (2003–2005)	CHRISTENSEN, Donna Marie (D-VI)
108th (2003–2005)	CLAY, William Lacy, Jr. (D-MO)
108th (2003–2005)	CLYBURN, James Enos (D-SC)
108th (2003–2005)	CONYERS, John, Jr. (D-MI)
108th (2003–2005)	CUMMINGS, Elijah Eugene (D-MD)
108th (2003–2005)	DAVIS, Artur (D-AL)
108th (2003–2005)	DAVIS, Danny K. (D-IL)
108th (2003–2005)	FATTAH, Chaka (D-PA)
108th (2003–2005)	FORD, Harold, Jr. (D-TN)
108th (2003–2005)	HASTINGS, Alcee Lamar (D-FL)
108th (2003–2005)	JACKSON, Jesse L., Jr. (D-IL)
108th (2003–2005)	JACKSON LEE, Sheila (D-TX)
108th (2003–2005)	JEFFERSON, William Jennings (D-LA)
108th (2003–2005)	JOHNSON, Eddie Bernice (D-TX)
108th (2003–2005)	JONES, Stephanie Tubbs (D-OH)
108th (2003–2005)	KILPATRICK, Carolyn Cheeks (D-MI)
108th (2003–2005)	LEE, Barbara (D-CA)
108th (2003–2005)	LEWIS, John R. (D-GA)
108th (2003–2005)	MAJETTE, Denise L. (D-GA)
108th (2003–2005)	MEEK, Kendrick B. (D-FL)
108th (2003–2005)	MEEKS, Gregory W. (D-NY)
108th (2003–2005)	MILLENDER-MCDONALD, Juanita (D-CA)
108th (2003–2005)	NORTON, Eleanor Holmes (D-DC)
108th (2003–2005)	OWENS, Major Robert Odell (D-NY)
108th (2003–2005)	PAYNE, Donald Milford (D-NJ)
108th (2003–2005)	RANGEL, Charles B. (D-NY)
108th (2003–2005)	RUSH, Bobby L. (D-IL)

108th (2003–2005)	SCOTT, David (D-GA)
108th (2003–2005)	SCOTT, Robert Cortez (D-VA)
108th (2003–2005)	THOMPSON, Bennie (D-MS)
108th (2003–2005)	TOWNS, Edolphus (D-NY)
108th (2003–2005)	WATERS, Maxine (D-CA)
108th (2003–2005)	WATSON, Diane Edith (D-CA)
108th (2003–2005)	WATT, Melvin L. (D-NC)
108th (2003–2005)	WYNN, Albert Russell (D-MD)
109th (2005–2007)	BISHOP, Sanford Dixon, Jr. (D-GA)
109th (2005–2007)	BROWN, Corrine (D-FL)
109th (2005–2007)	BUTTERFIELD, George Kenneth, Jr. ("G. K.") (D-NC)
109th (2005–2007)	CARSON, Julia May (D-IN)
109th (2005–2007)	CHRISTENSEN, Donna Marie (D-VI)
109th (2005–2007)	CLAY, William Lacy, Jr. (D-MO)
109th (2005–2007)	CLEAVER, Emanuel, II (D-MO)
109th (2005–2007)	CLYBURN, James Enos (D-SC)
109th (2005–2007)	CONYERS, John, Jr. (D-MI)
109th (2005–2007)	CUMMINGS, Elijah Eugene (D-MD)
109th (2005–2007)	DAVIS, Artur (D-AL)
109th (2005–2007)	DAVIS, Danny K. (D-IL)
109th (2005–2007)	FATTAH, Chaka (D-PA)
109th (2005–2007)	FORD, Harold, Jr. (D-TN)
109th (2005–2007)	GREEN, Al (D-TX)
109th (2005–2007)	HASTINGS, Alcee Lamar (D-FL)
109th (2005–2007)	JACKSON, Jesse L., Jr. (D-IL)
109th (2005–2007)	JACKSON LEE, Sheila (D-TX)
109th (2005–2007)	JEFFERSON, William Jennings (D-LA)
109th (2005–2007)	JOHNSON, Eddie Bernice (D-TX)
109th (2005–2007)	JONES, Stephanie Tubbs (D-OH)
109th (2005–2007)	KILPATRICK, Carolyn Cheeks (D-MI)
109th (2005–2007)	LEE, Barbara (D-CA)
109th (2005–2007)	LEWIS, John R. (D-GA)
109th (2005–2007)	MCKINNEY, Cynthia Ann (D-GA)
109th (2005–2007)	MEEK, Kendrick B. (D-FL)
109th (2005–2007)	MEEKS, Gregory W. (D-NY)
109th (2005–2007)	MILLENDER-MCDONALD, Juanita (D-CA)
109th (2005–2007)	MOORE, Gwendolynne S. (Gwen) (D-WI)
109th (2005–2007)	NORTON, Eleanor Holmes (D-DC)
109th (2005–2007)	OWENS, Major Robert Odell (D-NY)
109th (2005–2007)	PAYNE, Donald Milford (D-NJ)
109th (2005–2007)	RANGEL, Charles B. (D-NY)
109th (2005–2007)	RUSH, Bobby L. (D-IL)

(continued)

109th (2005–2007)	SCOTT, David (D-GA)
109th (2005–2007)	SCOTT, Robert Cortez (D-VA)
109th (2005–2007)	THOMPSON, Bennie (D-MS)
109th (2005–2007)	TOWNS, Edolphus (D-NY)
109th (2005–2007)	WATERS, Maxine (D-CA)
109th (2005–2007)	WATSON, Diane Edith (D-CA)
109th (2005–2007)	WATT, Melvin L. (D-NC)
109th (2005–2007)	WYNN, Albert Russell (D-MD)
110th (2007–2009)	BISHOP, Sanford Dixon, Jr. (D-GA)
110th (2007–2009)	BROWN, Corrine (D-FL)
110th (2007–2009)	BUTTERFIELD, George Kenneth, Jr. ("G. K.") (D-NC)
110th (2007–2009)	CARSON, André (D-IN)
110th (2007–2009)	CARSON, Julia May (D-IN)[20]
110th (2007–2009)	CHRISTENSEN, Donna Marie (D-VI)
110th (2007–2009)	CLARKE, Yvette Diane (D-NY)
110th (2007–2009)	CLAY, William Lacy, Jr. (D-MO)
110th (2007–2009)	CLEAVER, Emanuel, II (D-MO)
110th (2007–2009)	CLYBURN, James Enos (D-SC)
110th (2007–2009)	CONYERS, John, Jr. (D-MI)
110th (2007–2009)	CUMMINGS, Elijah Eugene (D-MD)
110th (2007–2009)	DAVIS, Artur (D-AL)
110th (2007–2009)	DAVIS, Danny K. (D-IL)
110th (2007–2009)	EDWARDS, Donna F. (D-MD)
110th (2007–2009)	ELLISON, Keith (D-MN)
110th (2007–2009)	FATTAH, Chaka (D-PA)
110th (2007–2009)	FUDGE, Marcia L. (D-OH)[21]
110th (2007–2009)	GREEN, Al (D-TX)
110th (2007–2009)	HASTINGS, Alcee Lamar (D-FL)
110th (2007–2009)	JACKSON, Jesse L., Jr. (D-IL)
110th (2007–2009)	JACKSON LEE, Sheila (D-TX)
110th (2007–2009)	JEFFERSON, William Jennings (D-LA)
110th (2007–2009)	JOHNSON, Eddie Bernice (D-TX)
110th (2007–2009)	JOHNSON, Hank (D-GA)
110th (2007–2009)	JONES, Stephanie Tubbs (D-OH)[22]
110th (2007–2009)	KILPATRICK, Carolyn Cheeks (D-MI)
110th (2007–2009)	LEE, Barbara (D-CA)
110th (2007–2009)	LEWIS, John R. (D-GA)
110th (2007–2009)	MEEK, Kendrick B. (D-FL)
110th (2007–2009)	MEEKS, Gregory W. (D-NY)
110th (2007–2009)	MILLENDER-MCDONALD, Juanita (D-CA)[23]
110th (2007–2009)	MOORE, Gwendolynne S. (Gwen) (D-WI)
110th (2007–2009)	NORTON, Eleanor Holmes (D-DC)
110th (2007–2009)	PAYNE, Donald Milford (D-NJ)

110th (2007–2009)	RANGEL, Charles B. (D-NY)
110th (2007–2009)	RICHARDSON, Laura (D-CA)[24]
110th (2007–2009)	RUSH, Bobby L. (D-IL)
110th (2007–2009)	SCOTT, David (D-GA)
110th (2007–2009)	SCOTT, Robert Cortez (D-VA)
110th (2007–2009)	THOMPSON, Bennie (D-MS)
110th (2007–2009)	TOWNS, Edolphus (D-NY)
110th (2007–2009)	WATERS, Maxine (D-CA)
110th (2007–2009)	WATSON, Diane Edith (D-CA)
110th (2007–2009)	WATT, Melvin L. (D-NC)
110th (2007–2009)	WYNN, Albert Russell (D-MD)[25]
111th (2009–2011)	BISHOP, Sanford Dixon, Jr. (D-GA)
111th (2009–2011)	BROWN, Corrine (D-FL)
111th (2009–2011)	BUTTERFIELD, George Kenneth, Jr. ("G. K.") (D-NC)
111th (2009–2011)	CARSON, André (D-IN)
111th (2009–2011)	CHRISTENSEN, Donna Marie (D-VI)
111th (2009–2011)	CLARKE, Yvette Diane (D-NY)
111th (2009–2011)	CLAY, William Lacy, Jr. (D-MO)
111th (2009–2011)	CLEAVER, Emanuel, II (D-MO)
111th (2009–2011)	CLYBURN, James Enos (D-SC)
111th (2009–2011)	CONYERS, John, Jr. (D-MI)
111th (2009–2011)	CUMMINGS, Elijah Eugene (D-MD)
111th (2009–2011)	DAVIS, Artur (D-AL)
111th (2009–2011)	DAVIS, Danny K. (D-IL)
111th (2009–2011)	EDWARDS, Donna F. (D-MD)
111th (2009–2011)	ELLISON, Keith (D-MN)
111th (2009–2011)	FATTAH, Chaka (D-PA)
111th (2009–2011)	FUDGE, Marcia L. (D-OH)
111th (2009–2011)	GREEN, Al (D-TX)
111th (2009–2011)	HASTINGS, Alcee Lamar (D-FL)
111th (2009–2011)	JACKSON, Jesse L., Jr. (D-IL)
111th (2009–2011)	JACKSON LEE, Sheila (D-TX)
111th (2009–2011)	JOHNSON, Eddie Bernice (D-TX)
111th (2009–2011)	JOHNSON, Hank (D-GA)
111th (2009–2011)	KILPATRICK, Carolyn Cheeks (D-MI)
111th (2009–2011)	LEE, Barbara (D-CA)
111th (2009–2011)	LEWIS, John R. (D-GA)
111th (2009–2011)	MEEK, Kendrick B. (D-FL)
111th (2009–2011)	MEEKS, Gregory W. (D-NY)
111th (2009–2011)	MOORE, Gwendolynne S. (Gwen) (D-WI)
111th (2009–2011)	NORTON, Eleanor Holmes (D-DC)
111th (2009–2011)	PAYNE, Donald Milford (D-NJ)

(continued)

111th (2009–2011)	RANGEL, Charles B. (D-NY)
111th (2009–2011)	RICHARDSON, Laura (D-CA)
111th (2009–2011)	RUSH, Bobby L. (D-IL)
111th (2009–2011)	SCOTT, David (D-GA)
111th (2009–2011)	SCOTT, Robert Cortez (D-VA)
111th (2009–2011)	THOMPSON, Bennie (D-MS)
111th (2009–2011)	TOWNS, Edolphus (D-NY)
111th (2009–2011)	WATERS, Maxine (D-CA)
111th (2009–2011)	WATSON, Diane Edith (D-CA)
111th (2009–2011)	WATT, Melvin L. (D-NC)
112th (2011–2013)	BASS, Karen (D-CA)
112th (2011–2013)	BISHOP, Sanford Dixon, Jr. (D-GA)
112th (2011–2013)	BROWN, Corrine (D-FL)
112th (2011–2013)	BUTTERFIELD, George Kenneth, Jr. ("G. K.") (D-NC)
112th (2011–2013)	CARSON, André (D-IN)
112th (2011–2013)	CHRISTENSEN, Donna Marie (D-VI)
112th (2011–2013)	CLARKE, Hansen (D-MI)
112th (2011–2013)	CLARKE, Yvette Diane (D-NY)
112th (2011–2013)	CLAY, William Lacy, Jr. (D-MO)
112th (2011–2013)	CLEAVER, Emanuel, II (D-MO)
112th (2011–2013)	CLYBURN, James Enos (D-SC)
112th (2011–2013)	CONYERS, John, Jr. (D-MI)
112th (2011–2013)	CUMMINGS, Elijah Eugene (D-MD)
112th (2011–2013)	DAVIS, Danny K. (D-IL)
112th (2011–2013)	EDWARDS, Donna F. (D-MD)
112th (2011–2013)	ELLISON, Keith (D-MN)
112th (2011–2013)	FATTAH, Chaka (D-PA)
112th (2011–2013)	FUDGE, Marcia L. (D-OH)
112th (2011–2013)	GREEN, Al (D-TX)
112th (2011–2013)	HASTINGS, Alcee Lamar (D-FL)
112th (2011–2013)	JACKSON, Jesse L., Jr. (D-IL)
112th (2011–2013)	JACKSON LEE, Sheila (D-TX)
112th (2011–2013)	JOHNSON, Eddie Bernice (D-TX)
112th (2011–2013)	JOHNSON, Hank (D-GA)
112th (2011–2013)	LEE, Barbara (D-CA)
112th (2011–2013)	LEWIS, John R. (D-GA)
112th (2011–2013)	MEEKS, Gregory W. (D-NY)
112th (2011–2013)	MOORE, Gwendolynne S. ("Gwen") (D-WI)
112th (2011–2013)	NORTON, Eleanor Holme (D-DC)
112th (2011–2013)	PAYNE, Donald Milford (D-NJ)[26]
112th (2011–2013)	PAYNE, Donald, Jr. (D-NJ)
112th (2011–2013)	RANGEL, Charles B. (D-NY)
112th (2011–2013)	RICHARDSON, Laura (D-CA)

112th (2011–2013)	RICHMOND, Cedric (D-LA)
112th (2011–2013)	RUSH, Bobby L. (D-IL)
112th (2011–2013)	SCOTT, David (D-GA)
112th (2011–2013)	SCOTT, Robert Cortez (D-VA)
112th (2011–2013)	SCOTT, Tim (R-SC)
112th (2011–2013)	SEWELL, Terri (R-AL)
112th (2011–2013)	THOMPSON, Bennie (D-MS)
112th (2011–2013)	TOWNS, Edolphus (D-NY)
112th (2011–2013)	WATERS, Maxine (D-CA)
112th (2011–2013)	WATT, Melvin L. (D-NC)
112th (2011–2013)	WEST, Allen (R-FL)
112th (2011–2013)	WILSON, Frederica (D-FL)
113th (2013–2015)	BASS, Karen (D-CA)
113th (2013–2015)	BEATTY, Joyce (D-OH)
113th (2013–2015)	BISHOP, Sanford Dixon, Jr. (D-GA)
113th (2013–2015)	BROWN, Corrine (D-FL)
113th (2013–2015)	BUTTERFIELD, George Kenneth, Jr. ("G. K.") (D-NC)
113th (2013–2015)	CARSON, André (D-IN)
113th (2013–2015)	CHRISTENSEN, Donna Marie (D-VI)
113th (2013–2015)	CLARKE, Yvette Diane (D-NY)
113th (2013–2015)	CLAY, William Lacy, Jr. (D-MO)
113th (2013–2015)	CLEAVER, Emanuel, II (D-MO)
113th (2013–2015)	CLYBURN, James Enos (D-SC)
113th (2013–2015)	CONYERS, John, Jr. (D-MI)
113th (2013–2015)	CUMMINGS, Elijah Eugene (D-MD)
113th (2013–2015)	DAVIS, Danny K. (D-IL)
113th (2013–2015)	EDWARDS, Donna F. (D-MD)
113th (2013–2015)	ELLISON, Keith (D-MN)
113th (2013–2015)	FATTAH, Chaka (D-PA)
113th (2013–2015)	FUDGE, Marcia L. (D-OH)
113th (2013–2015)	GREEN, Al (D-TX)
113th (2013–2015)	HASTINGS, Alcee Lamar (D-FL)
113th (2013–2015)	HORSFORD, Steven (D-NV)
113th (2013–2015)	JACKSON LEE, Sheila (D-TX)
113th (2013–2015)	JEFFRIES, Hakeem (D-NY)
113th (2013–2015)	JOHNSON, Eddie Bernice (D-TX)
113th (2013–2015)	JOHNSON, Hank (D-GA)
113th (2013–2015)	KELLY, Robin L. (D-IL)[27]
113th (2013–2015)	LEE, Barbara (D-CA)
113th (2013–2015)	LEWIS, John R. (D-GA)
113th (2013–2015)	MEEKS, Gregory W. (D-NY)
113th (2013–2015)	MOORE, Gwendolynne S. (Gwen) (D-WI)

(continued)

113th (2013–2015)	NORTON, Eleanor Holmes (D-DC)
113th (2013–2015)	PAYNE, Donald, Jr. (D-NJ)
113th (2013–2015)	RANGEL, Charles B. (D-NY)
113th (2013–2015)	RICHMOND, Cedric (D-LA)
113th (2013–2015)	RUSH, Bobby L. (D-IL)
113th (2013–2015)	SCOTT, David (D-GA)
113th (2013–2015)	SCOTT, Robert Cortez (D-VA)
113th (2013–2015)	SEWELL, Terri (D-AL)
113th (2013–2015)	THOMPSON, Bennie (D-MS)
113th (2013–2015)	VEASEY, Marc (D-TX)
113th (2013–2015)	WATERS, Maxine (D-CA)
113th (2013–2015)	WATT, Melvin L. (D-NC)
113th (2013–2015)	WILSON, Frederica (D-FL)

Contact Information:

Office of the Historian: history@mail.house.gov

Office of Art & Archives, Office of the Clerk: art@mail.house.gov, archives@mail.house.gov

Located online at: http://history.house.gov/Exhibitions-and-Publications/BAIC/Historical-Data/Black-American-Representatives-and-Senators-by-Congress/

Appendix B

African-American Firsts

Government

Local elected official: John Mercer Langston (1855), town clerk of Brownhelm, Ohio.

State elected official: Alexander Lucius Twilight (1836) of the Vermont legislature.

Mayor of major city:

Carl Stokes (1967–1971), Cleveland, Ohio.
The first African-American woman to serve as mayor was Sharon Pratt Dixon Kelly (1991–1995) of Washington, DC.

Governor (appointed): P. B. S. Pinchback (1872–1873) as a result of impeachment proceeding against the elected governor.

Governor (elected): L. Douglas Wilder (1990–1994), Virginia.

U.S. Representative:

Joseph Rainey (1870), South Carolina. Rainey was re-elected four more times.
The first African-American woman elected to the House was Shirley Chisholm (1969–1983), New York.

U.S. Senator:

Hiram Revels (Feb. 25, 1870 to March 4, 1871), Mississippi.
The first African-American female senator was Carol Mosely Braun (1992–1998) Illinois.

U.S. cabinet members:

Robert C. Weaver (1966–1968) as Secretary of the Department of Housing and Urban Development.

The first African-American female to be appointed to a cabinet position was Patricia Harris (1977) also as secretary of the Department of Housing and Urban Development.

Gen. Colin Powell (2001–2004) as U.S. secretary of state.

The first African-American female appointed as secretary of state was Condoleezza Rice (2005–2009).

Major party nominee for president: Senator Barack H. Obama (2008) of the Democratic Party.

President of the United States: Barack H. Obama, who began his term of office in January 2009, and re-elected in 2012.

Law

President, *Harvard Law Review*: Barack H. Obama (1990).

Editor, *Harvard Law Review*: Charles Hamilton Houston (1919).

Federal judge: William Henry Hastie (1946); the first African-American female federal judge was Constance Baker Motley (1966).

U.S. Supreme Court Justice: Thurgood Marshall (1967–1991). Clarence Thomas was the second when he was appointed in 1991.

Diplomacy

U.S. diplomat: Ebenezer D. Bassett (1869) as minister-resident to Haiti; the first African-American female ambassador was Patricia Harris (1965), ambassador to Luxembourg.

U.S. representative to the United Nations: Andrew Young (1977–1979).

Nobel Peace Prize winner: Ralph J. Bunche (1950) for mediating an Arab-Israeli truce. The second was Martin Luther King Jr., in 1964.

Military

Combat pilot: Eugene Jacques Bullard (1917). He was, however, denied entry into the U.S. Army Air Corps because of the color of his skin.

First Congressional Medal of Honor winner: Sgt. William H. Carney for bravery during the Civil War. But he did not receive the medal until 1900.

General: Benjamin O. Davis Sr. (1940–1948).

Chairman of the Joint Chiefs of Staff: Colin Powell (1989–1993).

Science and Medicine

First patent holder: Thomas L. Jennings (1821), for the dry-cleaning process.

MD degree: James McCune Smith (1837) from the University of Glasgow.

Inventor of the blood bank: Dr. Charles Drew (1940).

Heart surgery pioneer: Daniel Hale Williams (1893).

First astronaut: Robert H. Lawrence Jr. (1967). However, he did not make a space flight because he died in a plane crash. Guion Bluford (1983) was the first African American to travel in space.

Scholarship

College graduate (BA): Alexander Lucius Twilight (1823) from Middlebury College.

PhD: Edward A. Bouchet (1876) from Yale University.

Rhodes scholar: Alain L. Locke (1907).

College president: Daniel A. Payne (1856) of Wilberforce University, Ohio.

Ivy League president: Ruth Simmons (2001) of Brown University.

Literature

Novelist: Harriet Wilson, *Our Nig* (1859).

Poet: Lucy Terry (1746), “Bar's Fight.”

Poet (published): Phillis Wheatley (1773), *Poems on Various Subjects, Religious and Moral.*

Pulitzer Prize winner: Gwendolyn Brooks (1950), in poetry.

Pulitzer Prize winner in drama: Charles Gordone (1970), for the play *No Place to Be Somebody.*

Nobel Prize winner in literature: Toni Morrison (1993).

Poet laureate: Robert Hayden (1976–1978).

Music and Dance

Member of the New York City Opera: Todd Duncan (1945).

Member of the Metropolitan Opera Company: Marian Anderson (1955).

Male Grammy Award winner: Count Basie (1958).

Female Grammy Award winner: Ella Fitzgerald (1958).

Principal dancer in a major dance company: Arthur Mitchell (1959), New York City Ballet.

Film

First Oscar: Hattie McDaniel (1940), Best Supporting Actress, *Gone with the Wind.*

Oscar, Best Actress Nominee: Dorothy Dandridge (1954), *Carmen Jones.*

Oscar, Best Actor/Actress: Sidney Poitier (1963), *Lilies of the Field*; Halle Berry (2001), *Monster's Ball.*

Film director: Oscar Micheaux (1919), *The Homesteader.*

Hollywood director: Gordon Parks (1969), *The Learning Tree.*

Television

Network television show host male/female: Nat King Cole (1956), *The Nat King Cole Show*; Oprah Winfrey (1986), *The Oprah Winfrey Show.*

Star of a network television show: Bill Cosby (1965), *I Spy.*

Sports

Major league baseball player: Jackie Robinson (1947), Brooklyn Dodgers.

Elected to the Baseball Hall of Fame: Jackie Robinson (1962).

NBA:

Chuck Cooper (1950) for Boston, first player to be drafted.
Nat "Sweetwater" Clifton (1950) for New York, first to sign an NBA contract.
Earl Lloyd Washington (October 31, 1950) for Washington, first to play an NBA game.

NFL quarterback: Willie Thrower (1953).

NFL football coach: Fritz Pollard (1922–1937).

Golf champion: Tiger Woods (1997), the Masters Golf Tournament.

NHL hockey player: Willie O'Ree (1958) for the Boston Bruins.

World cycling champion: Marshall W. "Major" Taylor (1899).

Tennis champion: Althea Gibson—Wimbledon (1957); Arthur Ashe was the first and only African-American male player to win the U.S. Open (1968) and Wimbledon (1975). Ashe was also the first African-American player to be ranked number 1 in the world and the first black American to be inducted into the International Tennis Hall of Fame (1985).

Heavyweight boxing champion: Jack Johnson (1908).

Olympic medalist (Summer games): George Poage (1904) for two bronze medals in the 200-meter (m) hurdles and 400-m hurdles.

Olympic gold medalist (Summer games): John Baxter "Doc" Taylor (1908), for a gold medal as part of the 4 x 400-m relay team.

Olympic gold medalist (Summer games; individual): DeHart Hubbard (1924) in the long jump.

Olympic medalist (Winter games): Debi Thomas (1988), bronze medal in figure skating.

Olympic gold medalist (Winter games): Vonetta Flowers (2002) in bobsled.

Olympic gold medalist (Winter games; individual): Shani Davis (2006) in the 1,000-m speed skating.

Other Firsts

Licensed pilot: Bessie Coleman (1921).

Millionaire: Madame C. J. Walker (1867–1919) for Madam Walker's Wonderful Hair Grower, a scalp conditioning and healing formula and Walker's Salon.

Billionaire: Robert Johnson (2001), owner of Black Entertainment Television (BET); Oprah Winfrey (2003).

Portrayal on a postage stamp: Booker T. Washington (1940 and 1956).

Miss America: Vanessa Williams (1984) for New York.

Explorer, North Pole: Matthew A. Henson (1909).

Explorer, South Pole: George Gibbs (1939–1941).

Flight around the world: Barrington Irving (2007) starting from Miami Gardens, Florida.

Appendix C

"Diseases and Peculiarities of the Negro Race" by Dr. Cartwright (in *DeBow's Review*)

DRAPETOMANIA, OR THE DISEASE CAUSING NEGROES TO RUN AWAY.

It is unknown to our medical authorities, although its diagnostic symptom, the absconding from service, is well known to our planters and overseers . . .

In noticing a disease not heretofore classed among the long list of maladies that man is subject to, it was necessary to have a new term to express it. The cause in the most of cases, that induces the negro to run away from service, is as much a disease of the mind as any other species of mental alienation, and much more curable, as a general rule. With the advantages of proper medical advice, strictly followed, this troublesome practice that many negroes have of running away, can be almost entirely prevented, although the slaves be located on the borders of a free state, within a stone's throw of the abolitionists.

If the white man attempts to oppose the Deity's will, by trying to make the negro anything else than "the submissive knee-bender," (which the Almighty declared he should be), by trying to raise him to a level with himself, or by putting himself on an equality with the negro; or if he abuses the power which God has given him over his fellow-man, by being cruel to him, or punishing him in anger, or by neglecting to protect him from the wanton abuses of his fellow-servants and all others, or by denying him the usual comforts and necessaries of life, the negro will run away; but if he keeps him in the position that we learn from the Scriptures he was intended to occupy, that is, the position of submission; and if his master or overseer be kind and gracious in his hearing towards him, without condescension, and at the sane time ministers to his physical wants, and protects him from abuses, the negro is spell-bound, and cannot run away.

According to my experience, the "genu flexit"—the awe and reverence, must be exacted from them, or they will despise their masters, become rude and ungovernable, and run away. On Mason and Dixon's line, two classes of persons were apt to lose their negroes: those who made themselves too familiar with them, treating them as equals, and making little or no distinction in regard to color; and, on the other hand, those who treated them cruelly, denied them the common necessaries of life, neglected to protect them against the abuses of others, or frightened them by a blustering manner of approach, when about to punish them for misdemeanors. Before the negroes run away, unless they are frightened or panic-struck, they become sulky and dissatisfied. The cause of this sulkiness and dissatisfaction should be inquired into and removed, or they are apt to run away or fall into the negro consumption. When sulky and dissatisfied without cause, the experience of those on the line and elsewhere, was decidedly in favor of whipping them out of it, as a preventive measure against absconding, or other bad conduct. It was called whipping the devil out of them.

If treated kindly, well fed and clothed, with fuel enough to keep a small fire burning all night-separated into families, each family having its own house-not permitted to run about at night to visit their neighbors, to receive visits or use intoxicating liquors, and not overworked or exposed too much to the weather, they are very easily governed-more so than any other people in the world. When all this is done, if any one of more of them, at any time, are inclined to raise their heads to a level with their master or overseer, humanity and their own good require that they should be punished until they fall into that submissive state which it was intended for them to occupy in all after-time, when their progenitor received the name of Canaan or "submissive knee-bender." They have only to be kept in that state and treated like children, with care, kindness, attention and humanity, to prevent and cure them from running away.

DYSAETHESIA AETHIOPICA, OR HEBETUDE OF MIND AND OBTUSE SENSIBILITY OF BODY-A DISEASE PECULIAR TO NEGROES-CALLED BY OVERSEERS, "RASCALITY."

Dysaesthesia Aethiopica is a disease peculiar to negroes, affecting both mind and body in a manner as well expressed by dysaesthesia, the name I have given it, as could be by a single term. There is both mind and sensibility, but both seem to be difficult to reach by impressions from without. There is a partial insensibility of the skin, and so great a hebetude of the intellectual faculties, as to be like a person half asleep, that is with difficulty aroused and kept awake. It differs from every other species of mental disease, as it is accompanied with physical signs or lesions of the body discoverable to the medical observer, which are always present and sufficient to account for the symptoms. It is much more prevalent among free negroes living in clusters by themselves, than among slaves on our plantations, and attacks only such slaves as live like free negroes in regard to diet, drinks, exercise, etc. It is not my purpose to treat of the complaint as it prevails among free negroes, nearly all of whom are more or less afflicted with it, that have not got some white person to direct and to take care of them. To narrate its symptoms and effects among them would be to write a history of the ruins and dilapidation of Hayti, and every spot of earth they have ever had uncontrolled possession over for any length of time. I propose only to describe its symptoms among slaves.

From the careless movements of the individuals affected with the complaint, they are apt to do much mischief, which appears as if intentional, but is mostly owing to the stupidness of mind and insensibility of the nerves induced by the disease. Thus, they break, waste and destroy everything they handle,—abuse horses and cattle,—tear, burn or rend their own clothing, and, paying no attention to the rights of property, steal others, to replace what they have destroyed. They wander about at night, and keep in a half nodding sleep during the day. They slight their work,—cut up corn, cane, cotton or tobacco when hoeing it, as if for pure mischief. They raise disturbances with their overseers and fellow-servants without cause or motive, and seem to be insensible to pain when subjected to punishment. The fact of the existence of such a complaint, making man like an automaton or senseless machine, having the above or similar symptoms, can be clearly established by the most direct and positive testimony. That it should have escaped the attention of the medical profession, can only be accounted for because its attention has not been sufficiently directed to the maladies of the negro race. Otherwise a complaint of so common an occurrence on badly-governed plantations, and so universal among free negroes, or those who are not governed at all,—a disease radicated in physical lesions and having its peculiar and well marked symptoms and its curative indications, would not have escaped the notice of the profession. The northern physicians and people have noticed the symptoms, but not the disease from which they spring. They ignorantly attribute the symptoms to the debasing influence of slavery on the mind without considering that those who have never been in slavery, or their fathers before them, are the most afflicted, and the latest from the slave-holding South the least. The disease is the natural offspring of negro liberty-the liberty to be idle, to wallow in filth, and to indulge in improper food and drinks.

De Bow's Review
Southern and Western States
Volume XI, New Orleans, 1851
AMS Press, Inc., New York, 1967

Appendix D

Famous American Civil Rights Leaders and Activists

Ralph Abernathy (1926–1990)
John Quincy Adams (1767–1848)
Susan B. Anthony (1820–1906)
Ella Baker (1903–1986)
James Baldwin (1924–1987)
Daisy Bates (1914–1999)
Dana Beal (1947–)
James Bevel (1936–2008)
Claude Black (1916–2009)
Antoinette Brown Blackwell (1825–1921)
Julian Bond (1940–)
John Brown (1800–1859)
Lucy Burns (1879–1966)
Stokely Carmichael (1941–1998)
Carrie Chapman Catt (1859–1947)
Cesar Chavez (1927–1993)
Claudette Colvin (1939–)
Marvel Cooke (1903–2000)
Humberto "Bert" Corona (1918–2001)
Dorothy Cotton (1930–)
Norris Wright Cuney (1846–1898)
Ossie Davis (1917–2005)
Eugene Debs (1855–1926)
Ruby Dee (1924–)
Frederick Douglass (1818–1895)
W. E. B. Du Bois (1868–1963)
Charles Evers (1922–)

Medgar Evers (1925–1963)
James Farmer (1920–1999)
Louis Farrakhan (1933–)
Jane Fonda (1937–)
James Forman (1928–2005)
Abby Kelley Foster (1811–1887)
Marie Foster (1917–2003)
Betty Friedan (1921–2006)
William Lloyd Garrison (1805–1879)
Dick Gregory (1932–)
Prathia Hall (1940–2002)
Fannie Lou Hamer (1917–1977)
Harry Hay (1912–2002)
Lola Hendricks (1932–)
Gordon Hirabayashi (1918–2012)
Myles Horton (1905–1990)
T. R. M. Howard (1908–1976)
Julia Ward Howe (1818–1910)
Dolores Huerta (1930–)
John Peters Humphrey (1905–1995)
Jesse Jackson (1941–)
John Jay (1745–1829)
Thomas Jefferson (1743–1826)
Nellie Stone Johnson (1905–2002)
Abby Kelley (1811–1887)
Coretta Scott King (1927–2006)
Bernard Lafayette (1940–)
Martin Luther King Jr. (1929–1968)
James Lawson (1928–)
John Lewis (1940–)
Abraham Lincoln (1809–1865)
Joseph Lowery (1921–)
Clara Luper (1923–2011)
James Madison (1751–1836)
George Mason (1725–1792)
James Meredith (1933–)
Mamie Till Bradley Mobley (1921–2003)
Charles Morgan Jr. (1930–2009)

Harvey Milk (1930–1978)
Bob Moses (1935–)
Diane Nash (1938–)
Edgar Nixon (1899–1987)
Barack H. Obama (1961–)
James Orange (1942–2008)
Rosa Parks (1913–2005)
Alice Paul (1885–1977)
Elizabeth Peratrovich (1911–1958)
A. Philip Randolph (1889–1979)
Amelia Boynton Robinson (1911–)
Jo Ann Robinson (1912–1992)
Eleanor Roosevelt (1884–1962)
Bayard Rustin (1912–1987)
Al Sharpton (1954–)
Charles Sherrod (1937–)
Judy Shepard (1952–)
Fred Shuttlesworth (1922–2011)
Elizabeth Cady Stanton (1815–1902)
Gloria Steinem (1934–)
Lucy Stone (1818–1893)
Harriet Beecher Stowe (1811–1896)
Sojourner Truth (Isabella Baumfree) (1797–1883)
Harriet Tubman (1820–1913)
A. P. Tureaud (1899–1972)
C. T. Vivian (1924–)
Wyatt Tee Walker (1929–)
Booker T. Washington (1856–1915)
Ida B. Wells (1862–1931)
Walter Francis White (1895–1955)
Roy Wilkins (1901–1981)
Frances Willard (1839–1898)
Hosea Williams (1926–2000)
Robert F. Williams (1925–1996)
Victoria Woodhull (1838–1927)
Malcolm X (1925–1965)
Andrew Young (1932–)
Whitney M. Young Jr. (1921–1971)

American Civil Rights Organizations of Historical Significance

American Anti-Slavery Society
American and Foreign Anti-Slavery Society
American Woman Suffrage Association
Congress of Racial Equality
Friends of Universal Reform
League of Women Voters and International Alliance of Women
Mattachine Society
Nation of Islam
National American Woman Suffrage Association
National Association for the Advancement of Colored People
National Urban League
New York Manumission Society
Pennsylvania Abolition Society
Regional Council of Negro Leadership
Southern Christian Leadership Conference (SCLC)
Student Nonviolent Coordinating Committee (SNCC)

International Human Rights Organizations

The Advocacy Project
Amazon Watch
Amnesty International
Anti-Slavery International
Article 19
Avocats Sans Frontières
Breakthrough (human rights)
Carter Center
CCJO René Cassin
Center for Economic and Social Rights
Center for Human Rights and Humanitarian law
Centre on Housing Rights and Evictions (COHRE)
Committee to Protect Journalists
Commonwealth Human Rights Initiative
CryptoRights Foundation
Cultural Survival
Disabled Peoples' International
Enough Project
Ensemble contre la peine de mort

Equality Now
Every Human Has Rights
Forum 18
Free the Slaves
Freedom from Torture
Freedom House
Freedom Later on after Dinner
Friends of Peoples Close to Nature
Genocide Watch
GIRCA
Global Rights
Global Peace Promoters
Habitat International Coalition
Helsinki Committee for Human Rights
Helsinki Watch
Hindu American Foundation
Hindu Human Rights
Hirschfeld Eddy Foundation
Human Life International
Human Rights Defence
Human Rights First
Human Rights Foundation
Human Rights Internet
Human Rights Observers
Human Rights Watch
Human Rights Without Frontiers
Institute for War and Peace Reporting
Institute on Religion and Public Policy
Inter-American Association for Environmental Defense
International Alliance of Women
International Association of Jewish Lawyers and Jurists
International Center for Transitional Justice
International Centre for Human Rights and Democratic Development
International Centre for Human Rights Research
International Coalition against Enforced Disappearances
International Commission of Jurists
International Committee of the Red Cross
International Crisis Group
International Federation for Human Rights

International Foundation for Human Rights and Tolerance
International Freedom of Expression Exchange
International Human Rights Administration (IHRA)
International Human Rights Association of American Minorities (IHRAAM)
International Humanist and Ethical Union
International Institute of Human Rights
International League for Human Rights
International Partnership for Human Rights (IPHR)
International Progress Organization
International Property Rights Index
International Rehabilitation Council for Torture Victims
International Rescue Committee
International Service for Human Rights
International Society for Human Rights
International Tibet Support Network
International Work Group for Indigenous Affairs
Islamic Human Rights Commission
JUSTICE
MindFreedom International
National Labor Committee in Support of Human and Worker Rights
Network for Education and Academic Rights
No Peace Without Justice
No Sweat
Norwegian Refugee Council
Peace Brigades International
People & Planet
Physicians for Human Rights
Point of Peace Foundation
Protection International
Redress Trust
Refugees International
Release International
Reporters Without Borders
Reprieve
Scholar Rescue Fund
Scholars at Risk
The Sentinel Project for Genocide Prevention
Society for Threatened Peoples
Survival International

Tahirih Justice Center
UNITED for Intercultural Action
United Nations
UN Watch
Witness (human rights group)
Womankind Worldwide
Women's Learning Partnership for Rights, Development, and Peace
World Council of Churches
World Future Council
World Organisation Against Torture
Youth for Human Rights International

Appendix E

Louisiana's Deadliest Storms

Louisiana's Deadliest Atlantic Tropical Cyclones

Areas of Greatest Loss	Dates	Notes
Louisiana	September 12–13, 1722	"During a hurricane . . . a large number of unidentified ships were sunk at and near New Orleans."
Louisiana	September 2, 1772	*El Principe de Orange* "was struck by a hurricane . . . and wrecked at the entrance of the Mississippi River, where she quickly went to pieces, only six survivors."
Louisiana	August 18, 1779	All but one of a fleet of Spanish warships sunk by a hurricane. "Slaves were drowned in ditches."

See National Hurricane Center. "The Deadliest Atlantic Tropical Cyclones, 1492–1996." http://www.nhc.noaa.gov/pastdeadlyapp2.shtml. Access date: July 8, 2013

Louisiana's Deadliest Hurricanes

Dates	Name of Storm	Fatalities
8/10–12/1856	Isle Demieres	218+
8/11/1860	Number 1 SE Louisiana	47
10/12/1886	Number 10 Sabine Pass	110
10/1–2/1893	Number 10 Mouth of MS	2000
9/20/1909	Number 8 Thibodaux	353
9/29/1915	Number 2 Galveston	275
9/19–20/1947	Number 4 New Orleans	51
6/27/1957	Audrey	526
10/3/1964	Hilda	81
8/29/2005	Hurricane Katrina	1,577 (death toll as of August 10, 2006)

See Roth, David. "Louisiana Hurricane History." National Weather Service. http://www.srh.noaa.gov/images/lch/tropical/lahurricanehistory.pdf. Access date: July 8, 2013.

Recommended Reading

Laws

The Constitution of the United States (1789)
Louisiana Purchase (1803)
Law of Slavery in the State of Louisiana (1847)
The Emancipation Proclamation: An Executive Order from the President of the United States (1863)
Louisiana Black Code (1865)
The Civil Rights Act of 1866
Louisiana Constitution (1913)
Louisiana Constitution (1921)
Louisiana No. 8037. Commission Council Series. September 16, 1924.
36 USC §302.

Cases

Dred Scott v. Sandford, 60 U.S. 393 (1856)
Fenn v. Carr, 19 La. Ann. 106 (1867)
Dejean v. Arnaud, 25 La. Ann. 521 (1873)
Civil Rights Cases, 109 U.S. 3 (1883)
Plessy v. Ferguson, 163 U.S. 537, 543 (1896)
State v. Treadaway et al., 126 La. 300, 52 So. 500 (1910)
Buchanan v. Warley, 245 U.S. 60, 75 (1917)
Tyler v. Harmon, 158 La. 439 (La. 1925)
Land Development Co. of Louisiana v. City of New Orleans, 13 F.2d 898 (1926)
McCain v. Davis, 217 F. Supp. 661, (1963)

Books and Articles

Allen, James. *Without Sanctuary: Lynching Photography in America.* Santa Fe, NM: Twin Palms, 2000.
Badger, Richard G. *The Mulatto in the United States, Including a Study of the Role of Mixed-Blood Races throughout the World.* Boston: Gorham, 1918. Online

availability by the Cornell University Library through the Library of Congress at: http://www.archive.org/stream/mulattoinamerica00reutrich/mulattoinamerica00reutrich_djvu.txt. 6/13/2013.

Brinkley, Douglas. *The Great Deluge: Hurricane Katrina, New Orleans, and the Mississippi Gulf Coast.* New York: Harper Perennial, 2007.

Campanella, Richard, and Marina Campanella. *New Orleans Then and Now.* Gretna, LA: Pelican, 1999.

De Jong, Greta. *A Different Day: African-American Struggles for Justice in Rural Louisiana 1900-1970.*Chapel Hill: University of North Carolina Press, 2002

Falconbridge, Alexander. *An Account of the Slave Trade on the Coast of Africa.* London: J. Phillips, 1788.

Foner, Phillip S. *The Life and Writings of Frederick Douglass: Vol. 2. Pre–Civil War Decade, 1850–1860.* New York: International Publishers, 1950.

Kottak, Conrad Phillip. *Mirror for Humanity: A Concise Introduction to Cultural Anthropology.* New York: McGraw-Hill, 2009.

Quigley, Bill, and Maha Zaki. "The Significance of Race: Legislative Racial Discrimination in Louisiana, 1803–1865." 24 S.U.L. Rev. 145, 147 (1997).

Torr, James D., ed. *Opposing Viewpoints in World History: Slavery.* Farmington Hills, MI: Greenhaven, 2004.

Resources

Accessible Archives, Inc.
Mr. Tom Nagy, Chief Operating Officer
5 Great Valley Parkway, Suite 216
Malvern, PA 19355
Tel.: 866-296-1488 (toll-free) or 610-296-7441
Fax: 610-725-1745
Email: tnagy@accessible.com
Website: http://www.accessible-archives.com

AMS Press, Inc.
David Ramm, Editor-in-Chief
Brooklyn Navy Yard
63 Flushing Ave., Unit 221
Brooklyn, NY 11205-1073
Tel.: 718-875-8100
Fax: 718-875-3800
Email: editorial@amspressinc.com
Website: http://amspressinc.com

Anti-Slavery International
Thomas Clarkson House
The Stableyard
Broomgrove Road
London SW9 9TL
Tel.: +44 (0)20 7501 8920
Fax: +44 (0)20 7738 4110
Email: info@antislavery.org
Website: http://www.antislavery.org/english

Genocide Watch
Coordinator of the International Alliance to End Genocide
P.O. Box 809
Washington, D.C. 20044
Tel.: 1-202-643-1405
E-mail: communications@genocidewatch.org
Website: http://www.genocidewatch.org

Lake Pontchartrain Basin Foundation
Mailing Address:
P.O. Box 6965
Metairie, LA 70009
Physical Address:
New Canal Lighthouse Museum and Education Center
8001 Lakeshore Drive
New Orleans, LA 70122
Pontchartrain Beach Office
2045 Lakeshore Drive, Suite 339
New Orleans, LA 70122
Tel.: 504-836-2215
Fax: 504-836-7070
Website: http://www.saveourlake.org

National Center for Public Policy Research
501 Capitol Court NE
Washington, DC 20002
Tel.: (202) 543-4110
Fax: (202) 543-5975
Email: info@nationalcenter.org
Website: http://nationalcenter.org

NOAA/National Weather Service
National Centers for Environmental Prediction
National Hurricane Center
11691 SW 17th Street
Miami, FL 33165-2149
E-mail: nhcwebmaster@noaa.gov
Website: http://www.nhc.noaa.gov/

Pelican Publishing Company
1000 Burmaster Street
Gretna, LA 70053-2246
Tel.: (504) 368-1175; Toll-free: 1 (800) 843-1724; 1 (888) 5-PELICAN
Fax: (504) 368-1195
Email: office@pelicanpub.com
Website: http://www.pelicanpub.com

Roy Rosenzweig Center for History and New Media
Department of History and Art History
George Mason University
4400 University Drive, MSN 1E7
Fairfax, VA 22030
Tel.: 703-993-9277
Fax: 703-993-4585
Email: chnm@gmu.edu
Website: http://chnm.gmu.edu

Schomburg Center for Research in Black Culture
Research and Reference Division
A research unit of The New York Public Library
515 Malcolm X Boulevard
New York, NY 10037-1801
Tel.: (212) 491-2200
Email: scgenref@nypl.org
Website: http://www.inmotionaame.org/home.cfm

Southern University Law Review
Southern University Law Center
P.O. Box 9294
Baton Rouge, LA 70813
Tel.: (225) 771-2223
Fax: (225) 771-6253
Email: lawreview@sulc.edu
Website: http://www.sulc.edu/Student/StudentOrgs/StudentJournals/LawReview/index.html

The University of North Carolina Press
116 South Boundary Street
Chapel Hill, NC 27514-3808
Website: http://uncpress.unc.edu

U.S. National Archives & Records Administration
8601 Adelphi Road
College Park, MD 20740-6001
Tel: 1-86-NARA-NARA, 1-866-272-6272

Notes

Introduction

1. Phillipe d'Orléans was the head of state of France at the time of the founding of New Orleans.

2. Sugar cane was the largest export of New Orleans.

3. Fussell, Elizabeth. "Constructing New Orleans, Constructing Race: A Population History of New Orleans." *J. of Amer. History* 94 (December 2007): 846–855. http://www.journalofamericanhistory.org/projects/katrina/Fussell.html. Access date: June 27, 2013.

4. Lake Pontchartrain connects to Lake Borgne, which leads into the Gulf of Mexico.

5. "Napoleonic Code." Encylopædia Britannica, 2013. http://www.britannica.com/EBchecked/topic/ 403196/Napoleonic-Code. Access date: August 2, 2013. See also La-Legal.com. "How the Code Napoleon Makes Louisiana Law Different: Louisiana Law; A Short History Lesson." http://la-legal.com/history_louisiana_law.htm. Access date: August 2, 2013.

6. Los Isleños Heritage and Cultural Society. *A Louisiana Local Legacy: Los Isleños*. Library of Congress. 2000.

7. In 1970, there was a 5.4 percent decrease; in 1980, a decrease of 6.1 percent; and in 1990, a decrease of 10.9 percent.

8. The population of New Orleans in 2010 was 343,829; the population of New Orleans in 1910 was 339,075.

9. See Rastogi, Sonya, Tallese D. Johnson, et al. "The Black Population, 2010: 2010 Census Briefs." U.S. Census Bureau, September 2011. http://www.census.gov/prod/cen2010/briefs/c2010br-06.pdf. Access date: August 2, 2013. The federal government still uses the terms "white" (or "non-Hispanic white") and "black." Terms for other groups include "Hispanic/Latino," "American Indian or Alaskan Native," "Asian," "Native Hawaiian or Pacific Islander," and "mixed race." The Office of Management and Budget (OMB) defines the term "black or African-American" as "refer[ing] to a person having origins in any of the Black racial groups of Africa.

The black racial category includes people who marked the "Black, African Am., or Negro" checkbox. It also includes respondents who reported entries such as African American; Sub-Saharan African entries such as Kenyan and Nigerian; and Afro-Caribbean entries such as Haitian and Jamaican. Sub-Saharan African entries are classified as black or African American, with the exception of Sudanese and Cape Verdean because of their complex heritage.

North African entries are classified as white, as OMB defines white as a person having origins in any of the original peoples of Europe, the Middle East, or North "Africa." Furthermore, as of 1997, OMB required federal agencies to use a minimum of five race categories: White; Black or African American; American Indian or Alaska Native, Asian; and Native Hawaiian or Other Pacific Islander. Individuals who are unable to identify with any of the race categories, were permitted to use the Census Bureau's sixth category—Some Other Race—on the Census 2000 and 2010 Census questionnaires. OMB standards also allowed respondents to identify themselves as a member of more than one race.

10. The population of Alabama is 26.2 percent African American.

11. The population of Washington, DC, is 50.1 percent African American.

12. The population of Georgia is 30.5 percent African American.

13. The population of Maryland is 29.4 percent African American.

14. The population of Mississippi is 37 percent African American.

15. The population of South Carolina is 27.9 percent African American.

16. Rastogi, Johnson, et al. "The Black Population, 2010."

17. P. B. S. Pinchback served as governor of Louisiana from December 9, 1872, until January 13, 1873, a position he garnered by default because he had been lieutenant governor. Pinchback was considered an "octoroon" under Louisiana law at the time. His mother was a "mulatto" slave, and his father was the plantation owner. They lived together as husband and wife because a legal marriage was impermissible under Louisiana's antimiscegenation statutes at the time. He was the only governor of Louisiana to have African-American blood. The term "octoroon" is an epithet, and the offensive "degrees of hybridization" are detailed in Chapter 1.

18. Douglas Wilder served as governor of Virginia from 1990 until 1994.

19. Obviously, half of African-American state governors were elected *following Katrina* but none representing a southern state.

20. The three lieutenant governors were Oscar J. Dunn, P. B. S. Pinchback, and Ceasar Carpetier ("C. C.") Antoine, respectively. Oscar J. Dunn served as lieutenant governor from 1868 until 1872. In 1893, Dunn was described by the *New York Times* as "Jamaican, well educated, and pure African." The next year, the *Times* described him as having "pure negro blood." However, in Louisiana, he was known as a griffe—an epithet for being the son of a mulatto and a negro. Note that "mulatto" is an epithet for being the child of a negro and a white person. Caesar Carpetier ("C. C.") Antoine served as a delegate to the Louisiana Constitutional

Convention of 1867 until 1868. Following his service in the Louisiana Senate, he served as lieutenant governor from 1872 until 1876 under governors William Pitt Kellogg and P. B. S. Pinchback. A captain in the U.S. Army, Antoine created Company 1 of the Seventh Louisiana Colored Regiment after Union troops invaded New Orleans. He was from a racially-mixed background and was considered a mulatto under Louisiana law at the time. A significant part of his life was dedicated to social equality for African Americans, including advocating for tax reforms, an extensive bill of rights, and the extension of the Freedmen's Bureau, which was abolished in 1872. Antoine was vice president of the Comité des Citoyens (Citizens' Committee) and engaged Homer Plessy to test provisions of Louisiana Jim Crow law. The case became *Plessy v. Ferguson* (1896). The committee also challenged Louisiana's antimiscegenation law but failed.

21. Charles Edmund Nash (R-LA) (one term from 1875 to 1877).

22. William Jefferson Jennings (D-LA) (consecutive terms from 1991 until 2007). Cleo Fields (D-LA) (consecutive terms from 1993 to 1997).

23. William Jefferson Jennings (D-LA) (served from 2000 until 2007). Cedric Richmond (D-LA) was first elected in 2011 and is currently serving.

24. The eight U.S. senators (from earliest to most recent) are: Hiram Rhodes Revels (R-MS) (1869–1871); Blanche Kelso Bruce (R-MS) (1875–1881); Edward Brooke III (R-MA) (1967–1979); Carol Elizabeth Moseley Braun (D-IL) (1979–1983), who was the first African-American female elected as a U.S. senator; Barack Hussein Obama (D-IL) (2005–2008); Roland Wallace Burris (D-IL) (2008–2010); Timothy Eugene Scott (R-SC) (2013–present); and William Maurice Cowan (D-MA) (2013–present). African Americans were completely unrepresented in the U. S. Senate for 188 years out of America's 237-year history. Representation by an African American existed for eight years during the 19th century and 16 years during the 20th century. Interestingly, 86 years passed—from 1881 until 1967—until the next African American appeared in the Senate. After Carol Braun, it took an additional 22 years for Barack Obama to become elected to the U.S. Senate. Half of all African-American representatives in the House were elected into office *following Katrina.*

25. Currently serving in the U.S. Senate are William "Mo" Cowan (D-MA) and Tim Scott (R-SC). They are set to serve from 2013 until 2015.

26. President Obama was born in Hawaii on August 4, 1961. He was first elected president on November 4, 2008, with 365 electoral votes. He was re-elected for a second term on November 6, 2012, with 332 electoral votes. Only 270 electoral votes are necessary for election. His mother, who was white, was born in Kansas. His father, of the Luo ethnic group, was born in Kenya. President Obama is also the first president from the state of Hawaii.

27. Currently, 45 African Americans serve in the House of Representatives, two in the Senate, and one as president of the United States. Currently, there are 17 African-American justices within the U.S. Court of Appeals. One African American, Justice Clarence Thomas, sits on the bench of the U.S. Supreme Court.

28. Encylopædia Britannica. "Conspiracy." 2013. http://www.britannica.com/EBchecked/topic/133670/conspiracy. Access date: September 11, 2013.

29. *Dred Scott v. Sandford*, 60 U.S. 393 (1856).

30. Cornell University Law School. Legal Information Institute. "Conspiracy: Definition from Nolo's Plain-English Law Dictionary." August 19, 2010. http://www.law.cornell.edu/wex/conspiracy. Access date: December 2, 2013.

31. This is also known as the Great October Storm.

32. See National Oceanic Atmospheric Administration (NOAA). "Top 10 Deadliest Hurricanes in U.S. History, 1900–1996." http://www.nhc.noaa.gov/pastdead.html; "Economic Costs of the Top 10 Most Expensive Hurricanes from 1980 to 2011." http://stateofthecoast.noaa.gov/insurance/hurricanetopten.html. Access date: June 12, 2013. The National Oceanic Atmospheric Administration is hereinafter referred to as NOAA.

33. Supra. NOAA. "Top 10 Deadliest Hurricanes." See also "The Deadliest, Costliest, and Most Intense United States Tropical Cyclones from 1851–2006 (And Other Frequently Requested Hurricane Facts). NOAA Technical Memorandum NWS TPC-5, April 15, 2007. http://www.nhc.noaa.gov/pdf/NWS-TPC-5.pdf. Access date: June 12, 2013. Death tolls were as follows: Cheniere Caminada, LA (1893), 2,000 deaths; Grand Isle, LA (1905), 350 deaths; Southwest Louisiana (1918), 34 deaths; New Orleans (1915), 275 deaths; Hurricane Hilda (1964), 38 deaths; Hurricane Camille (1965), 256 deaths; Hurricane Betsy (1965), 75 deaths; and Hurricane Katrina (2005), 1,836 deaths.

34. Ordinance SBPC #370-09-06, Summary No. 1911. September 19, 2006. Throughout this introduction, italics have been added for emphasis.

35. Preamble to the U.S. Constitution.

36. Declaration of Independence, July 4, 1776.

Chapter 1

1. Foner, Phillip S. *The Life and Writings of Frederick Douglass. Vol. 2: Pre-Civil War Decade, 1850–1860*. New York: International Publishers, 1950. See also "The Meaning of July Fourth for the Negro." *Africans in America*. PBS. http://www.pbs.org/wgbh/aia/part4/4h2927t.html. Access date: June 8, 2013.

2. According to the *Oxford Dictionary of Politics*, "apartheid" is an Afrikaans (from South Africa) word meaning "separateness." Although it is normally used to reference the 20th century system of segregation in South Africa, *Roget's Thesaurus* defines apartheid as "the policy or practice of political, legal, economic, or social discrimination, as against the members of a minority group." Undoubtedly, apartheid was a condition suffered by African Americans in America well into the modern era.

3. See Schomburg Center for Research in Black Culture. "The Black Republic and Louisiana." *In Motion: The African-American Migration Experience*. New

York Public Library, 2005. http://www.inmotionaame.org/migrations/topic.cfm;jsessionid=f8305713913872572O7838?migration=5&topic=3&bhcp=1. Access date: June 12, 2013.

4. For a comprehensive definition of the origin of the term "Jim Crow" and its usage in America, see Njemanze, Paul Obiyo Mbanaso. "Jim Crow Laws." *Affirmative Action: An Encyclopedia. Vol. 2*, edited by James Beckman. Westport, CT: Greenwood, 2004, 524–526.

5. In the 16th century, Charles V of Spain granted license to a Fleming to import 4,000 "Negroes" per year to the West Indies. The Fleming eventually turned over his license to a Genoese (Italian). John Hawkins received permission from Queen Elizabeth I, which engaged England in the trade. In rapid succession, the Portuguese, French, and Dutch would join the slave trade. Slaves were introduced to the English colonies in 1619 when 20 Africans were brought into Jamestown. In the 1660s, colonies created laws regarding slaves, the most important of which was that children assumed the status of their mothers (free or slave). In 1681, Maryland passed the first antimiscegenation law in the colonies. In 1770, King George ordered the colonies not to obstruct the institution of slavery or the slave trade; his mandate, along with other "crimes" against the colonies, would be the impetus for the Declaration of Independence and the American Revolution.

6. PBS. "The Terrible Transformation Part 1: The African Slave Trade and the Middle Passage." http://www.pbs.org/wgbh/aia/part1/1narr4_txt.html. Access date: May 14, 2013.

7. According to *The American Heritage Dictionary of the English Language*, 4th ed. Houghton Mifflin, 2000, "barrracoons" were barracks (or cages) where slaves were temporarily confined until transferred to the slave ships. The word is derived from the Spanish word *barraca* meaning "hut."

8. Supra. PBS. "The Terrible Transformation Part 1."

9. UN Organization for Education, Science and Culture (UNESCO). "Virtual Visit of Goree Island, Dakar, Senegal: The House of Slaves." http://webworld.unesco.org/goree/en/screens/0.shtml. Access date: June 29, 2013. The first "slave house" was built in 1536 by the Portuguese. The last, Goree Island, was built in 1776 by the Dutch. Europeans first arrived on Goree Island in 1444. Goree Island remained a slave post until the 1840s. Currently, the Senegalese government maintains the island and "The House of Slaves" as a museum.

10. Falconbridge, Alexander. *An Account of the Slave Trade on the Coast of Africa*. London: J. Phillips, 1788. New Calabar is located in the Bight of Biafra, in today's eastern Nigeria. Falconbridge served on slave trips that began in Angola, which was a principal port in the African slave trade established by the Portuguese in the late 15th century.

11. Eltis, David. "A Brief Overview of the Trans-Atlantic Slave Trade." Transatlantic Slave Trade Database, Emory University, 2007. http://slavevoyages.org/tast/index.faces. Access date: May 14, 2013. Note: Depending on the organization, the

Transatlantic Slave Trade is referred to as the "Trans-Atlantic Slave Trade." This author uses the unhyphenated term in alignment with the United Nations.

12. Supra. PBS. "The Terrible Transformation Part 1."

13. Supra. Eltis. "Brief Overview of the Trans-Atlantic Slave Trade."

14. Supra. Falconbridge. *Account of the Slave Trade on the Coast of Africa.*

15. Thomas Jefferson (1743–1826) was the third president of the United States (1801–1809) and served two terms. He was vice president from 1797 to 1801 under President John Adams (father of John Quincy Adams). Jefferson was the first secretary of state (1790–1793) under the first president, George Washington.

16. Jefferson, Thomas. Legal Argument, 1770. FE 1:376. April 1770. "Quotations on Slavery and Emancipation." *Th. Jefferson Encyclopedia.* http://wiki.monticello.org/mediawiki/index.php/Quotations_on_Slavery_and_Emancipation#_note-0. Access date: July 5, 2013.

17. Jefferson, Thomas. "Rough draught of the Declaration of Independence." Princeton, NJ: Princeton University Press, 1776/1950.http://jeffersonpapers.princeton.edu/selected-documents/jefferson%E2%80%99s-%E2%80%9Coriginal-rough-draught%E2%80%9D-declaration-independence-0#notes11b. Access date: July 5, 2013.

Jefferson's denunciations can be found in many of his papers, which survive, including "A Summary View of the Rights of British America," "Draft of Virginia Constitution," "Bill to Prevent the Importation of Slaves," "Revisal of Virginia Laws: Jefferson's emancipation plan," "Notes on the State of Virginia," "Revised report of the Committee on ordinance for the Western territory," Article, and on the United States in the Encyclopidie Methodique. His position is also stated in numerous letters to friends and members of the government. *See also* Jefferson, Thomas. "Quotations on Slavery and Emancipation." Th. Jefferson Encyclopedia. Charlotesville: University of Virginia. http://www.monticello.org/site/jefferson/quotations-slavery-and-emancipation. Access date: July 5, 2013.Throughout this chapter, italics added for emphasis.

18. Law of Slavery in the State of Louisiana, 1847, Article 183. http://www.accessible-archives.com/2011/08/law-of-slavery-in-the-state-of-louisiana/. Access date: May 16, 2013. The statute stated: "Children born of a mother then in a state of slavery, whether married or not, follow the condition of their mother; they are consequently slaves, and belong to the master of their mother."

19. U.S. Const. Art. I, Sec. 2. This section of the Constitution was changed by the ratification of the Fourteenth Amendment in 1868.

20. Id. at Sec. 9. This section of the Constitution was changed by the ratification of the Thirteenth Amendment in 1865.

21. Quigley, Bill, and Maha Zaki. "The Significance of Race: Legislative Racial Discrimination in Louisiana 1803-1865." Southern University Law Review 24 (Spring 1997). 145—205. http://billquigley.files.wordpress.com/2013/01/racialdiscrimination louisianalegislative1803to1865.pdf. Access date: December 17, 2013.

22. Genealogical Information for the State of Louisiana. "St. Bernard Parish History and Information." http://mylouisianagenealogy.com/la_county/sb.htm. 11/3/07. "Isleños" means "islanders" in Spanish. Many of the descendants from the original settlers remain in St. Bernard Parish and continue to call themselves Isleños to the present day. The Isleños have made great efforts in maintaining their culture and roots in St. Bernard, including the formation of the Los Isleños Heritage and Cultural Society and an expanding Los Isleños Museum.

23. Anti-slavery.org. "Breaking the Silence: Learning about the Transatlantic Slave Routes; Spain." http://www.antislavery.org/breakingthesilence/slave_routes/slave-routes_spain.shtml. 12/9/07. The establishment of the supply bases in the Canary Islands coincided with Christopher Columbus's first voyage to the "New World" in 1492 and continued throughout the Transatlantic Slave Trade, as the islands were an ideal location on the slave route out of Africa. "Merchants and sailors (from the Canaries) prospered greatly by investing in slavery in the Americas." Slavery was part of Spain's culture even before Spain colonized the Americas. Sugar cane was carried to the Caribbean and the Americas for cultivation; and shipments were sent back to Spain as early as the 1500s. It would not be long before African slaves were included in the shipments.

24. Perez, Lizette. "Manumission and Gender in 18th-Century Spanish Louisiana: The Role of Women in the Establishment of a Free Black Society." *San Diego State University McNair Journal*. http://www.sci.sdsu.edu/mcnair/ejournal/Volume%20XI/perez.pdf. Access date: June 13, 2013.

25. Owens, Maida. "Louisiana's Traditional Cultures: An Overview." Louisiana's Living Traditions. http://www.louisianafolklife.org/LT/Maidas_Essay/main_introduction_onepage.htm. Access date: December 9, 2007.

26. Supra. Anti-slavery.org. "Breaking the Silence." Spain conquered the Canary Islands in 1483.

27. Merriam-Webster Online Dictionary. http://www.merriam-webster.com/. Access date: December 9, 2007.

28. Supra. Genealogical Information for the State of Louisiana. "St. Bernard Parish History and Information." That plantation owners were also political officials is not unique to Louisiana. Only wealthy male property owners were allowed to hold political office and vote throughout the United States.

29. Supra. Quigley.

30. See also Deyle, Steven. *Carry Me Back: The Domestic Slave Trade in American Life*. Oxford University Press, 2005. At the time, the St. Charles and the St. Louis hotels held the "most celebrated auction rooms."

31. *Times-Picayune*. http://photos.nola.com/4500/gallery/1845_slavery_in_new_orleans/index.html#/3. Access date: May 14, 2013. Note that the advertisement refers to the runaway, W.M. Bradley, as "the boy" despite the fact that he is the age of a man. W.M. has been used as the abbreviation for William. Now known as the *Times-Picayune*, the newspaper has been in publication for more than 175 years.

32. Campanella, Richard, and Marina Campanella. *New Orleans Then and Now*. Gretna, LA: Pelican, 1999.

33. Midlo Hall, Gwendolyn. *The Louisiana Slave Database and the Louisiana Free Database, 1719–1820*. http://www.afrigeneas.com/library/louisiana/. Access date: July 6, 2013. See also Midlo Hall, Gwendolyn. *The African Diaspora in the Americas: Regions, Ethnicities, and Cultures*. Chapel Hill: University of North Carolina Press, 2000.

34. PBS. "The Slave Experience: Living Conditions." *Slavery and the Making of America*. Thirteen/WNET New York: Educational Broadcasting Corp., 2004. http://www.pbs.org/wnet/slavery/experience/living/history.html. Access date: May 15, 2013.

35. Douglass, Frederick. *The Narrative of the Life of Frederick Douglass*. Boston: Anti-Slavery Office, 1845. http://www.pagebypagebooks.com/Frederick_Douglass/The_Narrative_of_the_Life_of_Frederick_Douglass/index.html. Access date: May 15, 2013.

36. Pope, John. "Slave Trade in New Orleans Was a Thriving Business." *Times-Picayune*, April 13, 2010. http://www.nola.com/politics/index.ssf/2010/04/slave_trade_in_new_orleans.html. Access date: May 14, 2013. See also Fussel, Elizabeth. "Constructing New Orleans, Constructing Race: A Population History of New Orleans." *Journal of American History* 94, no. 3 (2007): 846–855.

37. Colten, Craig E. *An Unnatural Metropolis: Wresting New Orleans from Nature*. Baton Rouge: Louisiana State University Press, 2005, 19.

38. See also Branley, Edward. "NOLA History: Congo Square and the Roots of New Orleans Music." GoNOLA.com, July 2, 2012. http://www.gonola.com/2012/07/02/nola-history-congo-square-and-the-roots-of-new-orleans-music.html. Access date: June 22, 2013. Originally called the Place des Negres, it was commonly called Place Congo. It was an area outside the city north of Rampart Street where slaves were able to congregate on Sunday afternoons (a day of rest). Unique to Louisiana, slaves were not mandated to assimilate into American or Creole culture. After the American Civil War, it was called Congo Square. For a period of time following the Civil War, it was named Beauregard Square in honor of the Confederate general. The area is now named Louis Armstrong Park and is host to an annual jazz festival.

39. Banks Arcade was a prominent slave mart in the South.

40. Supra. Campanella and Campanella. *New Orleans Then and Now*.

41. Louisiana State Museum. "The Cabildo: Antebellum Louisiana: Immigration." http://lsm.crt.state.la.us/cabildo/cab8.htm. Access date: October 27, 2007.

42. "St. Bernard Parish's History: How We began; Louisiana's Spanish Treasure." LosIsleños.org. http://www.losisleños.org/history.htm. Access date: November 3, 2007.

43. Id.

44. "The Domestic Slave Trade." *New York Times*, July 26, 1852. http://query.nytimes.com/gst/abstract.html:res_950DE2D71531E13BBC4E51DFB1668389649FDE. Access date: December 9, 2007. Because the number of slaves in Virginia, Maryland, Kentucky, and Missouri had grown "to an inconvenient extent," it was necessary to "dispose" of them further south. Not only was it important to continue the slave trade in the southern states because of its economic dependency on slavery, but the southern states wanted to—at the very least—maintain their numbers of slaves in the south for purposes of political representation (slaves were counted as three-fifths of a person).

45. Calhoun, John C. "Slavery is a Positive Good." (Address to the U.S. Senate, February 6, 1837) *Opposing Viewpoints in World History: Slavery*, edited by James D. Torr. Greenhaven Press. 2004.

46. Id.

47. John Quincy Adams (1767–1848) was the sixth president of the United States (1825–1829), a member of the House of Representatives for Massachusetts for 13 years (1833–1848), and secretary of state (1817–1825) under President James Monroe. John Adams and John Quincy Adams were the first set of presidents who were father and son. George H. Bush and George W. Bush were the second.

48. Adams, John Quincy. Argument before the Supreme Court of the United States in the case of *United States v. Cinque and Others, Africans Captured on the Schooner Amistad by Lieut. Gedney*. February 24 and March 1, 1841. http://books.google.com/books?hl=en&lr=&id=LZIsAAAAIAAJ&oi=fnd&pg=PA1&dq=John+Quincy+Adams+Amistad+address&ots=ZmXBewfGkB&sig=xsMefBY1SPx6sYky5nfcNWI2sjs. Access date: July 5, 2013. See also *The United States v. The Libellants and Claimants of the Schooner Amistad, Her Tackle, Apparel, and Furniture, Together with Her Cargo, and the Africans Mentioned and Described in the Several Libels and Claims*. 40 U.S. 518; 10 L. Ed. 826. (1841). http://www.law.cornell.edu/background/amistad/opinion.html. Access date: July 5, 2013.

49. Id.

50. Cartwright, Samuel. "Drapetomania, or the Disease Causing Negroes to Run Away: Dyaethesia Aethiopios, or the Hebitude of the Mind and Obtuse Sensibility of Body; A Disease Peculiar to Negroes Called by Overseers Rascality." *New Orleans Medical and Surgical Journal* 2 (1846): 694–731. See also Cartwright, Samuel. "Diseases and Peculiarities of the Negro Race." *De Bow's Review Southern and Western States*. Vol. 11. New Orleans, 1851. AMS Press, Inc. New York, 1967.

Note: In this chapter, the terms "disease," "Drapetomania," "rascality," "Dysaethesia," and "symptomatic" are placed in quotations because they are quoted from Dr. Cartwright's work. It is important to note that his findings were unfounded and are considered as pseudoscience.

51. Id.

52. Id.

53. Supra. Cartwright. "Diseases and Peculiarities of the Negro Race," 64.

54. See Schomburg Center for Research in Black Culture. "The Black Republic and Louisiana." "Haitian Immigration: 18th and 19th Century." *In Motion: The African-American Migration Experience.* New York: New York Public Library, 2005. http://www.inmotionaame.org/migrations/topic.cfm;jsessionid=f830104318137 1029872686?migration=5&topic=3&bhcp=1. Access date: June 12, 2013. At that time, it was generally estimated that 53 percent of the population in Charleston, South Carolina, was "black."

55. Louisiana Civil Code of 1825. Article 95. The code provided that "Free persons and slaves are incapable of contracting marriage together; the celebration of such marriages is forbidden, and the marriage is void; there is the same incapacity and the same nullity with respect to marriages contracted by free white persons with free people of color." Furthermore, according to Art. 182 of the same: "Slaves cannot marry without the consent of their masters, and their marriages do not produce any of the civil effects which result from such contract." See also Tennessee Department of State. "Miscegenation." http://www.tn.gov/tsla/exhibits/blackhistory/pdfs/Miscegenation%20laws.pdf. Access date: June 29, 2013. The word "miscegenation" is derived from the Latin words *miscere* (to mix) and *genus* (type, family, or descent). The following states never implemented antimiscegenation laws: Alaska, Connecticut, Minnesota, New Hampshire, New Jersey, New York, Vermont, Wisconsin, Hawaii, and Alaska. The following list of states includes the year in which antimiscegenation laws were repealed: Illinois, 1818; Iowa, 1846; Kansas, 1861; Maine, 1820; Massachusetts, 1788; Michigan, 1837; New Mexico, 1912; Ohio, 1803; Pennsylvania, 1787; Rhode Island, 1790; and Washington State. On their own, without Supreme Court influence, the following states repealed antimiscegenation statutes between 1948 and 1967: Arizona, California, Colorado, Idaho, Indiana, Maryland, Montana, Nebraska, Nevada, North Dakota, Oregon, South Dakota, Utah, and Wyoming.

56. Louisiana Civil Code of 1825. Article 175. The code provided that "All that a slave possesses, belongs to his master; he possesses nothing of his own, except . . . that is to say, the sum of money, or movable estate, which his master chooses he should possess."

57. "An act to punish the crimes therein mentioned, and for other purposes," Acts of Jan. 4, 1830 of Ninth Legislature of Louisiana, Mar. 16, 1830, 2nd Sess. Section 3, at 96 (1830).

58. See Lake Pontchartrain Basin Foundation. "History of the Pontchartrain Basin." http://www.saveourlake.org/basin-history.php. Access date: July 7, 2013. Native Americans called this body of water Okwata, meaning "wide water." It was renamed Pontchartrain in 1699 "after the French Minister of the Marine at the time, the Comte de Pontchartrain." Its delta became the parishes of St. Bernard, Orleans, and Plaquemines.

59. Lake Pontchartrain is not an actual lake. It is an estuary consisting of wetlands covering 630 square miles and is thus part of six parishes: Orleans, Jefferson, St. Tammany, St. John the Baptist, Tangipahoa, and St. Charles.

60. The Great Louisiana Hurricane of 1812 occurred on August 19, 1812.

61. Previous hurricanes did occur; however, they were forgotten as time passed and records were not kept well, or they may have been destroyed. It is therefore difficult to reconstruct the meteorological history of hurricanes in this region.

62. Louisiana was admitted to the Union on April 30, 1812.

63. NBC News Digital. "Louisiana's Great Hurricane of 1812 Reconstructed." February 8, 2011. http://www.nbcnews.com/id/41473917/ns/technology_and_science-science/t/louisianas-great-hurricane-reconstructed/. Access date: July 7, 2013.

64. Hurricane information gathered from the National Weather Service office in Lake Charles. www.srh.noaa.gov/lch. 7/7/2013. See also Kingery, Don. "Louisiana's Hurricanes: State has centuries-old history of damaging storms." American Press. www.louisiana101.com/Louisiana-hurricanes.doc. Access date: July 7, 2013.

65. Roth, David. "Louisiana Hurricane History." National Weather Service. http://www.srh.noaa.gov/images/lch/tropical/lahurricanehistory.pdf. Access date: August 6, 2013.

66. Id.

67. Id.

68. Law of Slavery in the State of Louisiana – 1847, Article 35. http://www.accessible-archives.com/2011/08/law-of-slavery-in-the-state-of-louisiana/. Access date: May 16, 2013. "A slave is one who is in the power of a master to whom he belongs. The master may sell him, dispose of his person, his industry, and his labor; he can do nothing, possess nothing, nor acquire anything, but what must belong to his master."

69. Id. at Art. 175. "All that a slave possesses belongs to his master; he possesses nothing of his own, except his *peculium*—that is to say, the sum of money or movable estate which his master chooses he should possess."

70. Id. at Art. 173. "The slave is entirely subject to the will of his master, who may correct and chastise him, though not the unusual rigor, nor so as to maim or mutilate him, or to expose him to the danger of loss of life, or to cause his death."

71. Id. at Art. 1584. "The following persons are absolutely incapable of being witnesses to testaments: 1. Women, of what age soever; 2. Male children who have not attained the age of sixteen years; complete; 3. Persons insane, deaf, dumb, or blind; 4. Persons whom the criminal laws declare incapable of exercising civil functions; 5. Slaves." Furthermore, Article 1775 stated: "All persons have the capability to contract, except those whose incapacity is specially declared by law. These are—persons of insane mind, slaves, those who are interdicted, minors, or married women."

72. Id. at Art. 182. "Slaves cannot marry without the consent of their masters, and their marriages do not produce any of the civil effects which result from such contract."

73. Id. at Art. 95. "Free persons and slaves are incapable of contracting marriage together; the celebration of such marriages is forbidden, and the marriage is void. There is the same incapacity and the same nullity with respect to marriages contracted by free white persons with free people of color."

74. Id. at Art. 174. "The slave is incapable of making any kind of contract, except those which relate to his own emancipation."

75. Id. at Art. 176. "They can transmit nothing by succession or otherwise."

76. Id. at Art. 177. "The slave is incapable of exercising any public office or private trust; he cannot be tutor, curator, executor, nor attorney; he cannot be a witness in either civil or criminal matters. He cannot be a party in any civil action, either as plaintiff or defendant, except when he has to claim or prove his freedom."

77. Id. at Art. 631. "He who has the use of one or more slaves or animals has the right to enjoy their service for his wants and those of his family."

78. Supra. Quigley, 203.

79. Bacon-Blood, Littice. "The Largest Slave Revolt in U.S. History Is Commemorated." *Times-Picayune*, January 3, 2011. http://www.nola.com/politics/index.ssf/2011/01/the_largest_slave_revolt_in_us.html. Access date: May 14, 2013.

80. Id.

81. Id.

82. Rasmussen, Daniel. "1811 Slave Revolt Can't Be Forgotten." *Times-Picayune*, January 4, 2011. http://www.nola.com/opinions/index.ssf/2011/01/1811_slave_revolt_cant_be_forg.html. Access date: May 14, 2013.

83. *Dred Scott v. Sandford*, 60 U.S. 393, 407 (1856). Scott was owned by Dr. John Emerson, an army surgeon. When Emerson died, Scott offered to buy his freedom (and that of his own wife) from Emerson's widow for $300, but his offer was declined. After his offer was declined, Scott sought his freedom through the courts, a process that lasted 10 years. Scott lost his initial case on a technicality because he could not prove the widow owned him. The Missouri Supreme Court allowed a retrial; and subsequently, the St. Louis circuit court set Scott and his wife free. The Missouri Supreme Court again intervened and reversed the decision. Taking the case to federal court, Scott again lost when the court affirmed the Missouri Supreme Court's decision. Scott then decided to take the case to the Supreme Court of the United States. He named the widow's brother in the suit and claimed that they were citizens of different states so that the Supreme Court of the United States would hear the case. Therefore, the Court had to determine only whether it had jurisdiction and subsequently, it found that Scott could not bring forward a suit because he was not a citizen. The sons of Peter Blow (Scott's first master) were childhood friends and paid for Scott's legal fees. Later, they

bought Scott and his wife and granted them their freedom, but it was short-lived for Scott since he died nine months later.

Note: The term "negro" is lowercase in quotations from the Court. Because African-Americans were not considered full persons under law, the use of the lowercase "n" demonstrates their diminution of value. This is legally significant.

84. Id. at 405.

85. Id. at 408.

86. Id. at 407.

87. Id. at 410.

88. Id. at 419.

89. Id. at 407.

90. Id. at 412.

91. Id. at 426.

92. Id. at 409.

93. Id.

94. Id. at 413.

95. Id. at 415.

96. Id. at 416.

97. Id. at 422.

98. Id. at 414.

99. Fort Ward Museum & Historic Site. "Fighting for Freedom: Black Union Soldiers of the Civil War." Apr. 12, 2012. http://alexandriava.gov/historic/fortward/default.aspx?id=40018. Access date: May 14, 2013.

100. Associated Press. "New Orleans Fall in 1862 Created Emancipation Beachhead." *Times-Picayune*, May 28, 2012. http://www.nola.com/175years/index.ssf/2012/05/new_orleans_fall_in_1862_creat.html. Access date: May 14, 2013.

101. "U.S. African-American Population, 1860." Grolier Online Atlas. http://go.grolier.com/atlas?id=mh00117. Access date: July 7, 2013.

102. Supra. Campanella. See also "America's Poorest States." Huffington Post, September 15, 2011. http://www.huffingtonpost.com/2011/09/15/americas-poorest-states-_n_964058.html#slide=362416. Access date: May 18, 2013. Louisiana and Mississippi have alternated in their rankings. In 2011, Louisiana was ranked fourth worst state in the nation and was listed in fourth place regarding lowest median income, with a poverty rate of 18 percent.

103. Lincoln, Abraham. "The Emancipation Proclamation." January 1, 1863. http://www.archives.gov/exhibits/featured_documents/emancipation_proclamation/transcript.html. Access date: May 14, 2013.

104. Fort Ward Museum & Historic Site. "Fighting for Freedom: Black Union Soldiers of the Civil War." April 12, 2012. http://alexandriava.gov/historic/fortward/default.aspx?id=40018. Access date: May 14, 2013.

105. Supra. Lincoln. "Emancipation Proclamation." The New Orleans metropolitan area is comprised of the parishes of St. Charles, St. John, Jefferson,

Plaquemines, and St. Bernard. The parishes placed in bold are among those most hard hit by Hurricane Katrina in 2005, more than 140 years after the Emancipation Proclamation, which kept slavery intact.

106. Karst, James. "Our Times: New Orleans and the Emancipation Proclamation." *Times-Picayune*, September 15, 2012. http://www.nola.com/175years/index.ssf/2012/09/our_times_new_orleans_and_the.html. Access date: May 14, 2013.

107. Colten, Craig E. *An Unnatural Metropolis: Wresting New Orleans from Nature*. Baton Rouge: Louisiana State University Press, 2005, 30.

108. See also Civil War Trust. "Civil War Casualties." http://www.civilwar.org/education/civil-war-casualties.html. Access date: June 9, 2013.

109. Notte, Jason. "US Is Still Paying Civil War Benefits." MSN Money. March 20, 2013. http://money.msn.com/now/post.aspx?post=dcac55b0-93d0-4fb1-9fde-26bee1aa7081. Access date: June 9, 2013.

110. The Civil Rights Act of 1866 provided inter alia that ". . . all persons born in the United States and not subject to any foreign power, excluding Indians not taxed . . . shall have the same right, in every State and Territory in the United States, to make and enforce contracts, to sue, be parties, and give evidence, to inherit, purchase, lease, sell, hold, and convey real and personal property, and to full and equal benefit of all laws and proceedings for the security of person and property, as enjoyed by white citizens, and shall be subject to like punishment, pains, and penalties, and to none other, any law, statute, ordinance, regulation, or custom, to the contrary notwithstanding."

111. See Civil Rights Cases, 109 U.S. 3 (1883).

112. "Rise of the Ku Klux Klan." PBS.org. http://www.pbs.org/wgbh/americanexperience/features/general-article/grant-kkk/. Access date: July 7, 2013. The KKK was also called the Invisible Empire of the South. Its first leader (Grand Wizard) was General Nathan Bedford Forrest. Forrest served the Confederacy during the Civil War.

113. Louisiana State Museum: The Cabildo. "Reconstruction: A State Divided." http://www.crt.state.la.us/museum/online_exhibits/Cabildo/11.aspx. Access date: July 7, 2013. Some sources claim the death toll was as high as 46; and some historians say it was much higher. It is difficult to determine the exact number because by the time the federal troops arrived from the neighboring Jackson Barracks, families were removing the dead from the streets. Jackson Barracks is located in St. Bernard Parish just three miles from the site of the massacre.

114. Reynolds, Donald. "The New Orleans Riot of 1866: Reconsidered." *Louisiana History: The Journal of the Louisiana Historical Association* 5, no. 1 (Winter 1964): 5–27.

115. Supra. Louisiana State Museum. "Reconstruction." Compared to other states, Louisiana strongly resisted reconstruction policies because Louisiana's cities were not destroyed during the war. Therefore, the population was not desperate for an end to the war.

116. See also National Archives and Records Administration. *Bureau of Refugees, Freedmen, and Abandoned Lands (Freedmen's Bureau) for Louisiana, 1865–1872.* http://www.archives.gov/research/african-americans/freedmens-bureau/louisiana.pdf. Access date: July 5, 2013. The Bureau of Refugees, Freedmen, and Abandoned Lands (1862–1872) was the actual government agency under the Department of War, which was simply referred to as the Freedmen's Bureau. President Andrew Jackson opposed—and indeed eventually vetoed—the creation of the department and its purpose because he believed it was unconstitutional. The bureau provided food, clothing, and medical care, though limited to the newly-freed families. urged freed slaves to gain employment, encouraged an employer-employee relationship between former masters and slaves, encouraged the rebuilding of plantations, assisted in finding lost family members of freed slaves, built schools to educate freed slaves (at that time, no state-supported educational system existed in the South), provided relocation transportation, and provided legal advocates and negotiated labor contracts for the same. It was an impossible mission given that in 1860, the slave population in New Orleans alone exceeded 300,000.

117. De Jong, Greta. *A Different Day: African-American Struggles for Justice in Rural Louisiana, 1900–1970.* University of North Carolina Press, 2002. http://uncpress.unc.edu/chapters/dejong_different.html. Access date: November 3, 2007.

118. Freedmen's Bureau Online. *Synopsis of Murder & c. (crimes) Committed in Parishes of Caddo and Bossier September and October 1868.* Records of the Bureau of Refugees, Freedmen, and Abandoned Lands. http://freedmensbureau.com/louisiana/outrages/bossierandcaddo.htm. Access date: July 5, 2013.

119. Id.

The use of the lowercase "negro" by some newspapers is significant because African-Americans during this era did not have the value of a full person.

120. Bureau of Refugees, Freedmen, and Abandoned Lands. *Miscellaneous Reports and Lists Relating to Murders and Outrages, Mar. 1867–Nov. 1868.* http://freedmensbureau.com/louisiana/outrages/outrages4.htm. Access date: July 5, 2013.

121. Amite City is located in St. Tammany Parish.

122. Gretna is located in Jefferson Parish.

123. Shreveport is located in Caddo Parish and is the parish seat.

124. Alexandria is located in Rapides Parish and is the parish seat.

125. St. Martinsville is located in St. Martin Parish and is the parish seat.

126. Flat Town is located in Washington Parish.

127. Natchitoches is located in Natchitoches Parish and is the parish seat.

128. Point Coupee is located in Point Coupee Parish. It is one of the oldest settlements on the Mississippi River, having been established in the 1720s by the French.

129. Sparta is located in Bienville Parish.

130. Purchase is located in Bienville Parish.

131. Lake Providence is located in East Carroll Parish and is the parish seat.

132. Opelousas is located in St. Landry Parish and is the parish seat.

133. Monroe is located in Ouachita Parish and is the parish seat.

134. Jackson is located in East Feliciana Parish.

135. Baton Rouge is located in East Baton Rouge Parish and is the parish seat.

136. Houma is located in Terrebonne Parish and is the parish seat.

137. Vidalia is located in Concordia Parish and is the parish seat.

138. Marksville is located in Avoyelles Parish and is the parish seat.

139. Fausee Point is located in Iberia Parish.

140. Carrolton is a neighborhood in uptown New Orleans.

141. Supra. Bureau of Refugees, Freedmen, and Abandoned Lands. "Miscellaneous Reports and Lists."

142. Supra. "Rise of the Ku Klux Klan." PBS.org.

143. "Ku Klux Klan." History Channel. http://www.history.com/topics/ku-klux-klan. Access date: July 7, 2013.

144. Id.

145. See Stanton, Gregory H. "The 8 Stages of Genocide." Genocide Watch. http://www.genocidewatch.org/aboutgenocide/8stagesofgenocide.html. Access date: June 9, 2013. According to Stanton, president of Genocide Watch, there are eight stages of genocide: classification, symbolization, dehumanization, organization, polarization, preparation, extermination, and denial. It can be charged that the United States experienced all of the eight. America is currently in its final stage, denial. This work was originally presented as a briefing paper at the U.S. State Department in 1996.

146. Buckser, Andre S. "Lynching as Ritual in the American South." *Berkeley Journal of Sociology* 37 (1992): 11–28.

147. Hair, William I. "Henry J. Hearsey and the Politics of Race." *Louisiana History: The Journal of the Louisiana Historical Association* 17, no. 4 (Autumn 1976): 393–400.

148. Hair, William I. *Carnival of Fury: Robert Charles and the New Orleans Race Riot of 1900*. Baton Rouge: Louisiana State University Press, 2008, 91.

149. One such "notice" was on the front page of the newspaper *New Orleans States* on June 26, 1919. John Hartfield, a black man accused of assaulting a white girl, was set to be turned over by officers to a mob for lynching in Ellisville, Mississippi, at 5:00 p.m. Then-governor Bilbo said he could not prevent the event; and a reverend asked the mob to "use discretion" during the lynching.

150. Id. See also Davis, Ronald L.F. "Creating Jim Crow: In-Depth Essay." http://www.jimcrowhistory.org/history/creating2.htm. Access date: February 13, 2012.

151. Though lynching occurred in almost every state of the Union, the highest number of recorded incidents occurred in the following states: Alabama (347),

Arkansas (284), Florida (282), Georgia (531), Kentucky (205), Mississippi (581), Missouri (122), North Carolina (101), Oklahoma (122), South Carolina (160), Tennessee (251), Texas (493), Virginia (100) and, of course, Louisiana (391), especially, in New Orleans. While African Americans made up the largest number of victims, whites who sympathized with the plight of African Americans were also targeted. In addition, other minorities suffered similar fates: Native Americans, Chinese, Italians, and Mexicans. However, lynchings against African Americans were particularly sadistic. Not one person was ever brought to justice for their participation in lynching. A list of recorded lynchings by state and race from 1882 until 1968 compiled by the Archives of Tuskegee can be located at http://www.legendsofamerica.com/ah-lynching11.html. 6/8/2013.

152. See Allen, James. *Without Sanctuary: Lynching Photography in America*. Twin Palms Publishers, 2000. See also the Without Sanctuary website at http://withoutsanctuary.org/main.html. Access date: June 9, 2013.

153. See "Lynching Postcard Sold for $240." Associated Press, October 8, 2008. http://www.kare11.com/news/news_article.aspx?storyid=526422. Access date: July 7, 2013. In 2008, one of these postcards was auctioned and brought in $240. It was sold to an unidentified buyer in Duluth, Minnesota.

154. Allen, *Without Sanctuary*. See also the Without Sanctuary website at http://withoutsanctuary.org/main.html.

155. Supra. Davis, " History of Jim Crow."

156. Approximately half of southerners were slaves or family members of slaves.

157. So firmly entrenched was the prejudice against those who had even "one drop" of "negro blood" that an extensive list of terms was used to describe each individuals' "degree of hybridization." Defining individuals in this manner was critical to imposing precise codes of discrimination (i.e., slave codes, Black Codes, and Jim Crow). Those with negro blood were treated as subordinate to whites; it was a system of "hypodescent" where children of mixed heritage were automatically assigned status in the subordinate group. The following list is historically accurate within the context of the law, at that time, which defined those with mixed ancestry. Recently, anthropologists agreed that no distinct human characteristics (e.g., skin color) can be allocated to different races. Consequently, there are no "races." Therefore, these terms are considered archaic and offensive in today's society: Mulatto = white and negro. Derived from Spanish *mulatto* meaning "mule"; a cross-breeding of a horse and a donkey. Quadroon = white and mulatto. Derived from Spanish *cuateron* meaning "quarter." Octoroon = quadroon and white. Spanish designation *terceron* meaning "three quarters." Other designations are quintroon or hexadecaroon. Griffe = negro and mulatto. French word meaning "claw." Sambo = negro and mulatto. Spanish designation *zambo* and *cholo* for members of the "half-caste" society. Metif = white and Quadroon. Sacatra = griffe and negress. Marabon = mulatto and griffe. "Meamelouc" = white

and metif "Quarteron" = white and meamelouc. Sangmele = white and quarteron. French designation meaning "half-blood." Cascos = mulatto and mulatto. Mango = sambo and negro. Mustifec = octoroon and white. Mustifino = mustifec and white. See Badger, Richard G. *The Mulatto in the United States Including a Study of the Role of Mixed-Blood Races throughout the World.* Boston: Gorham Press, 1918. Available online at: http://www.archive.org/stream/mulattoinamerica00reutrich/mulattoinamerica00reutrich_djvu.txt. Access date: June 13, 2013. See also Tennessee Department of State. "Miscegenation." http://www.tn.gov/tsla/exhibits/blackhistory/pdfs/Miscegenation%20laws.pdf. Access date: June 29, 2013.

158. *State v. Treadaway et al.*, 126 La. 300, 52 So. 500 (1910). After an exhaustive review of the meaning of "negro" and "colored," the court held that black, not white, blood determined the ethnicity of an individual. *See also* Kein, Sybil. *Creole: The History and Legacy of Louisiana's Free People.* Baton Rouge: Louisiana State University Press, 2000. http://www.scribd.com/doc/118325700/Creole-The-History-and-Legacy-Of-Louisiana-s-Free-People. Access date: June 9, 2013.

159. An octoroon was anyone who was 1/16 "negro." A mulatto (one who was half black and half white) and a quadroon (one who was a quarter black) were considered negroes.

160. *Lee v. New Orleans and Great Northern Railroad Co.* 125 La. 236 (1910). See also "The Negro Defined." *Yale Law Journal* 20, no. 3 (January 1911): 224–225.

161. Louisiana Black Code, 1865, Senate Executive Document No. 2, 39th Congress, 1st Session. The code included

"Sec. 1 Be it ordained by the police jury of the parish of St. Landry, That no negro shall be allowed to pass within the limits of said parish without special permit in writing from his employer. Whoever shall violate this provision shall pay a fine of two dollars and fifty cents, or in default thereof shall be forced to work four days on the public road, or suffer corporal punishment as provided hereafter . . .

Sec. 5 . . . No public meeting or congregations of negroes shall be allowed within said parish after sunset; but such public meetings and congregations may be held between the hours of sunrise and sunset, by the special permission in writing of the captain of patrol, within whose beat such meetings shall take place . . .

Sec. 6 . . . No negro shall be permitted to preach, exhort, or otherwise declaim to congregations of colored people, without a special permission in writing form the president of the police jury . . .

Sec. 7 . . . No negro who is not in the military service shall be allowed to carry firearms, or any kind of weapons, within the parish, without the special written permission of his employers, approved and endorsed by the nearest and most convenient chief of patrol . . .

Sec. 8 . . . No negro shall sell, barter, or exchange any articles of merchandise or traffic within said parish without the special written permission of his employer, specifying the article of sale, barter or traffic . . .

Sec. 9 . . . Any negro found drunk within the said parish shall pay a fine of five dollars, or in default thereof work five days on the public road, or suffer corporal punishment as hereinafter provided.

Sec. 11 . . . It shall be the duty of every citizen to act as a police officer for the detection of offences and the apprehension of offenders, who shall be immediately handed over to the proper captain or chief of patrol."

162. *Pace v. Alabama*, 106 U.S. 583 (1883). Section 4189 of the Alabama code declared: "If any white person and any negro, or the descendant of any negro to the third generation, inclusive, though one ancestor of each generation was a white person, intermarry or live in adultery or fornication with each other, each of them must, on conviction, be imprisoned in the penitentiary or sentenced to hard labor for the county for not less than two nor more than seven years."

163. The storm is also referred to as the Cheniere Storm.

164. See La. Acts 1890, No. 111, p. 152. That statute required "that the officers of such passenger trains shall have power and are hereby required to assign each passenger to the coach or compartment used for the race to which such passenger belongs; any passenger insisting on going into a coach or compartment to which by race he does not belong, shall be liable to a fine of twenty-five dollars, or in lieu thereof to imprisonment for a period of not more than twenty days in the parish prison, and any officer of any railroad insisting on assigning a passenger to a coach or compartment other than the one set aside for the race to which said passenger belongs, shall be liable to a fine of twenty-five dollars, or in lieu thereof to imprisonment for a period of not more than twenty days in the parish prison; and should any passenger refuse to occupy the coach or compartment to which he or she is assigned by the officer of such railway, said officer shall have power to refuse to carry such passenger on his train, and for such refusal neither he nor the railway company which he represents shall be liable for damages in any of the courts of this state."

165. Homer Plessy would be considered an octoroon, according to Louisiana law at the time. However, logic (in applying the law at that time) would dictate that he was not legally a negro. It was by his own admission that he was a negro.

166. *Plessy v. Ferguson*. 163 U.S. 537, 539 (1896). Herinafter referred to as *Plessy*.

167. Id. at 543.

168. Id. at 544.

169. Id. at 544.

170. Id. at 560.

171. Id. at 558, 559.

172. Such prejudice was evident in the treatment of and government policies over more than 250 million people worldwide, including nonwhites in America, as can be seen in the caste systems of India, Sri Lanka, Bangladesh, Nepal, and

Japan; apartheid in Papau New Guinea and South Africa; the Nuremburg laws of Germany pre–World War II; and the genocides in Germany, Armenia, Yugoslavia, Rwanda, Cambodia, and Dafur.

173. *Buchanan v. Warley*, 245 U.S. 60, 75 (1917). Hereinafter referred to as *Buchanan*.

174. Id. at 82.

175. Louisiana No. 8037. Commission Council Series. September 16, 1924.

176. Louisiana Constitution 1913, Art. 248.

177. Louisiana Constitution 1921, Art. 19, Sec. 21. "No alien who is ineligible to citizenship of the United States shall be permitted or allowed or shall have any right whatsoever to acquire by purchase . . . lease . . . own or control, directly or indirectly any land or real property . . . whatsoever within the state of Louisiana."

178. It was derived from Acts 1921, Ex. Sess., No. 106, §§ 1 through 3 and amended by Acts 1952, No. 127, §4.

179. *Tyler v. Harmon*, 158 La. 439 (La. 1925).

180. *Land Development Co. of Louisiana v. City of New Orleans*, 13 F.2d 898 (1926). http://www.leagle.com/xmlResult.aspx?xmldoc=192691113F2d898_1583.xml&docbase=CSLWAR1-1950-1985. Access date: February 11, 2012.The dismissal was reversed the next year in the case *Land Development Co of Louisiana v. City of New Orleans*, 17 F.2d 1016 (1927).

181. *Land Development* at 901.

182. Risk Management Solutions. "The 1927 Great Mississippi Flood: 80-year retrospective, 2007. https://support.rms.com/publications/1927_MississippiFlood.pdf. Access date: July 7, 2013.

183. "Looking Back at the Blasting of the Mississippi River Levee at Caernarvon." *Times-Picayune*, April 7, 2012. http://www.nola.com/175years/index.ssf/2012/04/our_times_blasting_mississippi.html. Access date: July 7, 2013.

184. Id.

185. *Id.*

186. "1927: The Greatest Flood in American History Inundates 10 states." *Times-Picayune*, October 31, 2011. http://www.nola.com/175years/index.ssf/2011/10/1927_the_greatest_flood_in_ame.html. Access date: July 7, 2013.

187. "Jim Crow in the South." History of Jim Crow. http://ww.jimcrowhistory.org/geography/geography.htm. Access date: December 9, 2007.

188. *McCain v. Davis*, 217 F. Supp. 661, (1963).

189. Smith, Andrene. "A Different World: Financial Determinants of Well-Being in New Orleans in Black and White." *Geo. J. Poverty Law & Pol'y* 14 (2007): 179, 181.

190. Spain, Daphne. "Race Relations and Residential Segregation in New Orleans: Two Centuries of Paradox." *Annals of the American Academy of Political and Social Science* 441 (January 1979).

191. "New Orleans: An American Experience." PBS.org. http://www.pbs.org/wgvh/amex/neworleans/filmmore/pt.html. Access date: December 9, 2007.

According to historian Ari Kelman, "The 1940s are a period in which you see radical cultural changes happening in New Orleans, as . . . the old residential settlement patterns in the city disappear."

192. 36 USC §302.

193. *Brown v. Board of Education*, 347, U.S. 483 (1954).

194. Justice John Marshall Harlan II (1899–1971) was appointed to the Court upon the death of Justice Robert H. Jackson in 1955 and thus was not on the bench of the Supreme Court of the United States when the initial *Brown* case was presented to the Court. He served on the Court from 1955 until 1971.

Chapter 2

1. *Brown v. Board of Education*, 347 U.S. 483 (1954). Throughout this chapter, italics added for emphasis.

2. *Berea College v. Kentucky*. 211 U.S. 45 (1908).

3. The state legislature of Kentucky dictated in the act of March 22, 1904, Acts of Kentucky, 1904, c. 85, p. 181, SEC. 1.

> "That it shall be unlawful for any person, corporation, or association of persons to maintain or operate any college, school, or institution where persons of the white and negro races are both received as pupils for instruction, and any person or corporation who shall operate or maintain any such college, school, or institution shall be fined $1,000, and any person or corporation who may be convicted of violating the provisions of this act shall be fined $100 for each day they may operate said school, college, or institution after such conviction."

4. "Jim Crow Laws: Louisiana." History of Jim Crow. http://www.jimcrowhistory.org/scripts/jimcrow/insidesouth.cgi?state=Louisiana. Access date: October 27, 2007.

5. Library of Congress. "Timeline of African American History, 1901–1925." http://memory.loc.gov/ammem/aap/timelin3.html. Access date: February 13, 20072/13/07.

6. Notable performers who performed on the chitlin' circuit included Count Basie, Peg Leg Bates, James Brown & the Famous Flames, Cab Calloway, Ray Charles, Dorothy Dandridge, Sammy Davis Jr., Duke Ellington, Ella Fitzgerald, and Motown greats like Michael Jackson (the Jackson 5), Gladys Knight and the Pips, Marvin Gaye, Tammie Terrell, the Supremes, the Temptations, the Miracles, and the Four Tops. Comedians also performed on this circuit, including Moms Mabley, Redd Foxx, Richard Pryor, and Flip Wilson. Other great artists included Jimi Hendrix, Billie Holiday, John Lee Hooker, Lena Horne, Etta James, B. B. King, the Delfonics, Wilson Pickett, Otis Redding, Dr. Lonnie Smith, Little Richard, Ike and Tina Turner, Little Anthony and the Imperials, and Muddy Waters.

Chitlin' circuit veterans who still perform include: George Benson, Gladys Knight, Diana Ross, Smokey Robinson, Stevie Wonder, Aretha Franklin, Patti LaBelle, Tina Turner, the Isley Brothers, Jimmie Walker, and Bernie Mac.

7. Fensterstock, Allison. "Chitlin' Circuit Characters Live Again in Book Mapping the Birth of Rock and Roll." *Times-Picayune*, July 26, 2011. http://www.nola.com/music/index.ssf/2011/07/chitlin_circuit_characters_liv.html. Access date: July 8, 2013.

8. Brown, Nikki. "Jim Crow/Segregation." In *KnowLA Encyclopedia of Louisiana*, edited by David Johnson. Louisiana Endowment for the Humanities, May 20, 2010. http://www.knowla.org/entry/735/. Access date: June 23, 2013.

9. This phenomenon is currently referred to as colorism.

10. Chafe, William H., Raymond Gavins, et al. *Remembering Jim Crow: African Americans Tell about Life in the Segregated South*. Center for Documentary Studies for the Behind the Veil Project. New York: New Press, 2001.

11. See also *From Swastika to Jim Crow: Historically Black Colleges and Universities*. PBS.org. http://www.pbs.org/itvs/fromswastikatojimcrow/blackcolleges.html. Access date: June 22, 2013.

12. More than 100 institutions comprise HBCUs (instituted before 1964). Originally created in 1837, the system provided for only elementary and secondary education. Higher education through black colleges and universities was created after World War I in 1919 due the nonexistence of colleges for African Americans in the United States. HBCUs include Fisk University, Florida A & M University, Howard University, Southern University at New Orleans, Xavier University of Louisiana, and the now defunct Leland University of New Orleans. Leland University, originally a grade school, operated for over 100 years until it was closed in the 1970s. In 1982, Leland was placed on the National Register of Historic Places. Always open to all races, according to a 2004 study by the U.S. Department of Education, HBCUs provide education to only 13 percent of all African-American students. In the new millennium, according to U. S. News and World Report:

> Societal desegregation and improvements to financial aid packages by wealthy and historically white schools are luring many top African-American students away from HBCUs to elite private colleges and increasingly diverse state universities. While the number of African-Americans in college has risen by about 1 million in the past 30 years, almost all of the students in that increase have gone to low-cost community colleges or wealthier, majority-white schools.

See Clark, Kim. "Why Black Colleges Might Be the Best Bargains." *U.S. News & World Report,* February 9, 2009. http://www.usnews.com/education/articles/2009/02/09/why-black-colleges-might-be-the-best-bargains. Access date: December 6, 2013.

13. Booker T. Washington (1856–1915) founded the Tuskegee Institute. He was born a slave. In his 1895 Atlanta Compromise address given at the Cotton States and International Exposition in Atlanta, he conceded that "[o]ne-third of the population of the South is of the Negro race." However, he espoused a controversial position:

> Our greatest danger is that in the great leap from slavery to freedom we may overlook the fact that the masses of us are to live by the productions of our hands, and fail to keep in mind that we shall prosper in proportion as we learn to dignify and glorify common labor . . . It is at the bottom of life we must begin, and not at the top . . . The wisest among my race understand that the agitation of questions of social equality is the extremist folly, and that progress in the enjoyment of all the privileges that will come to us must be the result of severe and constant struggle rather than of artificial forcing. No race that has anything to contribute to the markets of the world is long in any degree ostracized. It is important and right that all privileges of the law be ours, but it is vastly more important that we be prepared for the exercise of these privileges.

Washington's address made him nationally famous. In this vein, he was viewed as tolerant of second-class citizenship and not challenging the system of segregation. His views have sometimes been referred to as accommodationism.

14. W. E. B. Du Bois (1868–1963) was a Harvard-educated scholar and the first African American to graduate from that prestigious institution. He was critical of Booker T. Washington's position, which downplayed intellectual ambition for African Americans. Du Bois was the first African American to earn a doctorate, and he co-founded the NAACP. The Niagara movement led by Du Bois was in direct opposition to Washington's 1895 Atlanta Compromise address. Du Bois advocated for nothing less than full social equality for all nonwhites and for increased representation in politics, which he believed would occur as a result of African-American elite, according to his essay entitled "The Talented Tenth" that was published in *The Negro Problem* (1903). The Civil Rights Act of 1964, which included many of the reforms suggested by Du Bois, was signed into law one year after his death. Du Bois's views have sometimes been referred to as socialistic. See also Lewis, David Levering. *W. E. B. Du Bois: The Fight for Equality and the American Century, 1919–1963*. New York: Henry Holt and Co., 2000.

15. The NAACP is the United States' oldest and largest civil rights organization and was formed partly in response to the practice of lynching and the 1908 race riot that occurred in Springfield, Illinois. Original members included W. E. B. Du Bois, Ida B. Wells-Barnett, and Mary Church Terrell. Early members included Joel and Arthur Spingarn, Josephine Ruffin, Mary Talbert, Inez Mulholland (labor attorney and female suffragist), Jane Addams, Florence Kelley, Sophonisba

Breckinridge, John Haynes Holmes, Mary McLeod Bethune, George Henry White, Charles Edward Russell, John Dewey, William Dean Howells, Lillian Wald, Charles Darrow, Lincoln Steffens, Ray Stannard Baker, Fanny Garrison Villard, and Walter Sachs. Only seven of the original 60 members were African American. The objective of the NAACP is "to ensure the political, educational, social and economic equality of minority group citizens of United States and eliminate race prejudice. The NAACP seeks to remove all barriers of racial discrimination through the democratic processes." See the organization's website at http://www.naacp.org/. Access date: June 22, 2013.

16. A more comprehensive list of civil rights organizations and activists is found in the appendix of this book.

17. *Missouri ex rel, Gaines v. Canada*. 305 U.S. 337, 344 (1938). Hereinafter referred to as *Gaines*.

18. Alexander Pierre Tureaud was born just three years after the *Plessy* decision and died in 1972.

19. Minden is the parish seat of Webster Parish and is approximately 28 miles east of Shreveport.

20. Watson, Bret D. "The Lynching of John C. Jones and the Ordeal of Albert Harris, Jr." *Civil Rights and Restorative Justice*, May 2012. http://nuweb9.neu.edu/civilrights/wp-content/uploads/Jones-essay-final.pdf. Access date: June 29, 2013.

21. Anderson, Annie. "NAACP Asking for Apology for 1946 Lynching." KMSS-TV Fox 33, Shreveport, Louisiana, May 7, 2013. http://www.kmsstv.com/news/naacp-asking-apology-1946-lynching. Access date: June 29, 2013. On May 7, 2013, the Webster Parish branch of the NAACP sought an apology from local officials for the lynching.

22. *Shelley v. Kraemer*. 334 U.S. 1 (1948). Hereinafter referred to as *Shelley*. The Missouri agreements stated in part: "the said property is hereby restricted to the use and occupancy for the term of Fifty (50) years from this date, so that it shall be a condition all the time and whether recited and referred to as [sic] not in subsequent conveyances and shall attach to the land, as a condition precedent to the sale of the same, that hereafter no part of said property or any portion thereof shall be, for said term of Fifty-years, occupied by any person not of the Caucasian race, it being intended hereby to restrict the use of said property for said period of time against the occupancy as owners or tenants of any portion of said property for resident or other purpose by people of the Negro or Mongolian Race." The Michigan contracts provided in part: "This property shall not be used or occupied by any person or persons except those of the Caucasian race. It is further agreed that this restriction shall not be effective unless at least eighty percent of the property fronting on both sides of the street in the block where our land is located is subjected to this or a similar restriction."

23. *Shelley* at 10.

24. *Shelley* at 21.

25. For example, see 70 Okla. Stat. (1941) 455, 456, and 457.

26. Hereinafter referred to as *McLaurin.*

27. Hereinafter referred to as *Sweatt.*

28. Oklahoma state law required segregated educational facilities. 70 Okla.Stat. (1941) §§ 455, 456, 457, "made it a misdemeanor to maintain or operate, teach or attend a school at which both whites and Negroes are enrolled or taught."

29. *Sweatt v. Painter.* 339 U.S. 629, 634 (1950).

30. Supra. Brown, "Jim Crow/Segregation."

31. *Brown v. Board of Education.* 347 U.S. 483 (1954).

32. *Brown* at 495.

33. Stephens, Nicole M. "*Brown v. Board of Education*, 347, U.S. 483 (1954)." *Affirmative Action: An Encyclopedia*, edited by James Beckman. Westport, CT: Greenwood, 2004, Vol. 1, 123.

34. *Brown* at 497.

35. Thurgood Marshall succeeded Charles H. Houston (his mentor) as chief legal counsel for the NAACP. He was later appointed by President John F. Kennedy to the U.S. Court of Appeals for the Second Circuit. Subsequently, he was appointed as the first African-American solicitor general by President Lyndon Johnson in 1965. Within two years (1967), President Johnson appointed Marshall to the Supreme Court as the first African-American justice.

36. Kenneth Clark wrote "Effect of Prejudice and Discrimination on Personality Development" in 1950 for the White House Mid-Century Conference on Children and Youth, thus gaining the attention of the NAACP. Clark's report and testimony was used during the court hearings. See also Library of Congress. "*Brown v. Board* at Fifty: 'With an Even Hand.'" http://www.loc.gov/exhibits/brown/brown-brown.html. Access date: June 22, 2013.

37. *Brown*, Footnote 11. The Court considered the following "modern" authorities in its *Brown* ruling: K. B. Clark, "Effect of Prejudice and Discrimination on Personality Development" (Mid-Century White House Conference on Children and Youth, 1950); Witmer and Kotinsky, *Personality in the Making* (1952), c. 6; Deutscher and Chein, "The Psychological Effects of Enforced Segregation: A Survey of Social Science Opinion." 26 *J. Psychol.* 259 (1948); Chein, "What Are the Psychological Effects of Segregation under Conditions of Equal Facilities?" 3 *Int. J. Opinion and Attitude Res.* 229 (1949); Brameld, *Educational Costs, in Discrimination and National Welfare* (MacIver, ed., 1949), 44-48; Frazier, *The Negro in the United States* (1949), 674-681. And see generally Myrdal, Gunnar. *An American Dilemma: The Negro Problem and Modern Democracy* (1944), Harper and Brothers Publishers. New York; London. Found online at: http://archive.org/stream/AmericanDilemmaTheNegroProblemAndModernDemocracy/AmericanDelemmaVersion2_djvu.txt. Access date: December 6, 2013.

38. *Brown* at 494.

39. *Brown* at 495. Chief Justice Earl Warren (1891–1974) was five years old at the time of the *Plessy* decision.

40. *Brown v. Board of Education II*. 349 U.S. 294 (1955). See also Library of Congress. "With All Deliberate Speed." *Reason Expedition*. American Treasures of the Library of Congress. http://www.loc.gov/exhibits/treasures/trr007.html. Access date: June 22, 2013.

41. Smithsonian National Museum of American History. "With All Deliberate Speed." *Separate Is Not Equal: Brown v. Board of Education*. http://americanhistory.si.edu/brown/history/6-legacy/deliberate-speed.html. Access date: June 22, 2013.

42. "The History of Jim Crow." n.d. http://jimcrowhistory.org. November 25, 2009 See also Littlejohn, Jeffrey F. "Study the Past." "Jim Crow Laws: Louisiana." Sam Houston State University. Available online at: http://www.studythepast.com/weekly/LouisianaCrow.html. Access date: August 7, 2013.

43. Louisiana State University. "The Baton Rouge Boycott of 1953: A Recaptured Past." Special Collections of Hill Memorial Library. http://www.lib.lsu.edu/special/exhibits/e-exhibits/boycott/. Access date: February 11, 2012.

44. Id.

45. La. Act No. 630 of 1960, to amend Article 10 of the Louisiana Constitution.

46. *Garner v. State of La*. 368 U.S. 157, 174 (1961). Justice Warren wrote the Court's majority opinion in this case involving a restaurant's refusal to serve two "Negro" university students at a lunch counter. The patrons were arrested by police officers and convicted for "disturbing the peace." The Supreme Court of the United States held that "[t]he convictions were so totally devoid of evidentiary support as to violate the Due Process Clause of the Fourteenth Amendment . . . In the circumstances of these cases, merely sitting peacefully in places where custom decreed that petitioners should not sit was not evidence of any crime, and it cannot be so considered either by the police or by the courts."

47. *Brown v. Bd. of Educ*. 347 U.S. 483, 495 (1954). The class action lawsuit, comprised of five cases involving four states, is actually a set of three decisions: *Brown* I (1954), *Brown* II (1955), and *Brown* III (1978). *Brown* II ordered an implementation of *Brown* I "with all deliberate speed." The set of decisions is collectively referred to as *Brown*.

48. McMillen, Neil. *The Citizen's Council: Organized Resistance to the Second Reconstruction, 1954–1964*. Illini Books, 1994, 59. Board of Trustees of the University of Illinois.

49. Declaration of Constitutional Principles (1956). http://americanradioworks.publicradio.org/features/marshall/manifesto.html. Access date: June 23, 2013. The declaration was not a provision of legal authority; however, it is significantly valuable as evidence of the extent of the indoctrination of white supremacist values in America. It was signed by 19 senators representing the Deep South states of Georgia, Mississippi, North Carolina, South Carolina, Virginia, Arkansas, Louisiana, Alabama, Texas, and Florida. All were white males. Not surprisingly, all of these senators were born between 1878 and 1918, the time of *Plessy* and the reverberation of the separate but equal doctrine. The average

length of the senators' terms was 28 years. Eleven of the 19 senators would remain in office for at least another 15 years following the signing of the manifesto. One of the most famous signers Strom Thurmond (R-SC) (in office from 1956 to 2003) remained in the Senate for nearly *half a century*. Thurmond lived to see his own centennial. Sixty-three members of the House of Representatives also signed the document representing Alabama, Arkansas, Georgia, Louisiana, Florida, Mississippi, North Carolina, South Carolina, and Tennessee. All were white males with the exception of one white female, Iris F. Blitch (D-GA). The youngest representatives were born in 1918. The oldest, George Huddleston Jr. (D-AL), was born barely three years after the end of the Civil War. Needless to say, they were also born within the *Plessy* time frame. The last survivor of these representatives was Charles E. Bennett (D-FL), who died in 2003. See the transcript of the Declaration of Constitutional Principles (Southern Manifesto) in the appendix of this book.

50. The 26 states comprised 54 percent of the nation. The 48 states of the continental United States had all achieved statehood prior to this time. Hawaii and Alaska would join the Union in 1959, three years after the manifesto was drafted.

51. Theoretically, the federal government could have pursued the case as a capital crime without violating the double jeopardy principle; however, such a trial was never pursued.

52. "Former Klansman Found Guilty of Manslaughter: Conviction coincides with the 41st Anniversary of Civil Rights Killings." CNN.com. http://www.cnn.com/2005/LAW/06/21/mississippi.killings/. Access date: June 26, 2013. Accordingly,

> On June 21, 1964, Chaney, Goodman , and Schwerner were on their way to investigate the burning of a black church when they were briefly taken into custody for speeding. According to testimony, the Klan had burned the church to lure the three men back to Neshoba County. After they were released from the county jail in Philadelphia, a KKK mob tailed their car, forced if off the road, and shot them to death. Their bodies were found 44 days later buried in an earthen dam—in a trench dug in anticipation of the killings, according to testimony."

53. Two previous trials resulted in deadlocked juries. Both juries were all white. Thirty years later, De La Beckwith was brought to trial based on new evidence. Evers' body was exhumed for an autopsy. De La Beckwith was convicted of the murder of February 5, 1994. He appealed but was unsuccessful and died in prison in 2001.

54. Slave catchers hired to capture runaway slaves used dogs to "hunt them (slaves) down." Whips were also used during slavery to control and punish slaves, making an example of those who violated the slave code.

55. James Meredith was the first African-American student admitted to the University of Mississippi.

56. George C. Wallace served three terms as governor of Alabama (1963–1967, 1971–1979, and 1983–1987). He survived an assassination attempt in 1972 that left him wheelchair bound. Later in life, he recanted his position on segregation. Wallace died in 1998.

57. Wallace, George C. "The Inaugural Address of Governor George C. Wallace." January 14, 1963. http://digital.archives.alabama.gov/cdm/ref/collection/voices/id/2952. Access date: June 27, 2013.

58. Brasted, Chelsea. "Unsolved Murders." WAFB News, January 16, 2012. http://wafb.ddev4.worldnow.com/story/16527813/unsolved-murders. Access date: June 27, 2013.

59. Ferriday is located in Concordia Parish in northeastern Louisiana. Today, African Americans comprise 75 percent of the town's population.

60. Franklinton is located in Washington Parish approximately 60 miles north of New Orleans. The small town was originally named Franklin but was changed to Franklinton in 1826 some six years after its founding.

61. Varnado, a village, is located in Washington Parish.

62. Supra. Brasted. "Unsolved Murders."

63. Thibodeaux, Kevin. "5 Louisiana Civil Rights-Era Murder Cases Remain Open, Justice Department Reports to Congress." *Times-Picayune*, November 14, 2012. http://www.nola.com/politics/index.ssf/2012/11/5_louisiana_civil_rights_era_m.html. Access date: June 27, 2013.

64. King, Martin Luther, Jr. "Letter from Birmingham Jail," April 16, 1963. http://www.africa.upenn.edu/Articles_Gen/Letter_Birmingham.html. Access date: February 17, 2012. Grammatical alterations have been made by this author.

65. U.S. Const. amend. XXIV. Section 1 of the amendment provides:

> The right of citizens of the United States to vote in any primary or other election for President or Vice President, for electors for President or Vice President, or for Senator or Representative in Congress, shall not be denied or abridged by the United States or any State by reason of failure to pay any poll tax or other tax."

Proposed by Congress to the states on August 27, 1962, it was ratified by the states on January 23, 1964. It was necessary to pass this particular amendment because most states denied African Americans the right to vote and as a means to that end, states instituted numerous procedures to discourage African Americans from voting, including voting taxes, literacy tests, and violent intimidation. Voter suppression continues today in numerous ways: photo ID laws, purging voter rolls, felon disenfranchisement, inequality in voter resources, and deliberate misinformation about voting procedures.

66. The Nation of Islam was founded by Wallace D. Fard Mohammed in 1930. In 1931, he included Elijah Mohammed, who led the Nation beginning in 1934.

Elijah continued to lead the Nation until his death in 1975. Today, Louis Farrakhan is one of the major leaders of the Nation of Islam.

67. The term "field negroes" referred to the darker-skinned slaves who worked plantation fields and were considered to be of "stronger physical stock" of the "Negro race." Malcolm X used the term to describe African Americans who were radically opposed to dehumanization.

68. The term "house negroes" referred to the usually lighter-skinned slaves who worked in a domestic capacity in the slaveholder's home on the plantation. House negroes were sometimes granted special favors by their masters. Malcolm X used the term to describe African Americans who were more reserved in their opposition to dehumanization.

69. "Uncle Toms" was a reference to the character in the novel *Uncle Tom's Cabin* by Harriet Beecher Stowe. Malcom X used the term to describe African Americans who, in his opinion, sided with white ideals and values and were willing to wait for the government to bestow human rights upon the African-American community.

70. Malcolm X. "Message to the Grass Roots." Northern Negro Grass Roots Leadership Conference. November 10, 1963. Malcolm X (1925–1965), born Malcolm Little, was a member and leader of the Nation of Islam. When his views conflicted with those of the organization, he was asked to leave. He went on to establish the Muslim Mosque, Inc., and the Organization of Afro-American Unity. His views changed substantially over time. He once advocated black supremacy and the separation of black and white Americans. After making a pilgrimage to Mecca, Malcolm X stated: "I did many things as a [Black] Muslim that I'm sorry for now. I was a zombie then . . . pointed in a certain direction and told to march." See Parks, Gordon. "Malcolm X: The Minutes of Our Last Meeting." *Malcolm X: The Man and His Times*. Edited by John H. Clarke. Africa World Press. 1990. Trenton, NJ. 122.

Malcolm X was gunned down on February 21, 1965. There was, and remains, much suspicion regarding the assassination. Numerous theories exist regarding who was responsible including: drug dealers, the New York Police Department, the FBI, the Central Intelligence Agency (CIA), and the Nation of Islam. Three African-American men, all members of the Nation of Islam, were arrested, tried, and convicted for the murder. The men, now paroled, continue to maintain their innocence.

71. Malcolm X. *By Any Means Necessary (Malcolm X Speeches & Writings)*. New York: Pathfinder. 1992.

72. Hereinafter referred to as 1982.

73. *Jones v. Mayer Co.* 392 U.S. 409, 412 (1968). Hereinafter referred to as *Jones*.

74. Library of Congress. Civil Rights History Project: Survey of Collections and Repositories A. P. Tureaud Collection. http://www.loc.gov/folklife/civilrights/survey/view_collection.php?coll_id=784. Access date: June 26, 2013.

75. Foley, Melissa. "LSU Civil Rights Symposium Celebrates the Life of Legendary Civil Rights Leader A. P. Tureaud." Nobel Cause. http://www.lsu.edu/departments/gold/2011/04/tureaud.shtml. Access date: June 27, 2013.

76. Bridges-Hall, Ruby. "The Education of Ruby Nell." *Guideposts*, March 2000. http://www.rubybridges.com/story.html. Access date: June 27, 2013.

Only black girls were integrated into the New Orleans, all-white schools. Black boys were considered threatening at the time of integration.

77. Thevenot, Brian. "The McDonogh 3." *Times Picayune*, May 16, 2004. http://www.nola.com/education/content/stories/three.html. Access date: July 11, 2003.

78. Id.

79. Bankston, Carl L., III, Stephen J. Caldas, and Roslin Growe. "The African-American Reaction to School Desegregation in Lafayette Parish." *J. Negro Education*. Vol 71, Nos. 1/2 (Winter-Spring 2002). http://www.academia.edu/1010245/The_African_American_Reaction_to_School_Desegregation_in_Lafayette_Parish. Access date: June 23, 2013.

80. Supra. Thevenot.

81. Id.

82. Reckendahl, Katy. "Fifty years later, students recall integrating New Orleans public schools." *Times Picayune*, November 13, 2010. http://www.nola.com/politics/index.ssf/2010/11/fifty_years_later_students_rec.html. Access date: July 7, 2013.

83. "The Experiment." Fleurish Production. 2011. Ken J. Saltman is a professor of educational policy studies and research at DePaul University.

84. Mahoney, Martha. "Law and Racial Geography: Public Housing and the Economy in New Orleans." *42 Stan. L. Rev.* 1251, 1283. May 1990.

85. "Integration North and South." *Time*, September 15, 1961. http://www.time.com/time/magazine/article/0,9171,938753,00.html. Access date: November 4, 2007.

86. Id. "Congolese" referred to those with African blood and is used as a negative racial epithet.

87. Id. "Burrhead" is a negative racial epithet used to insult those of African descent, specifically by comparing African-American hair to a steel wool scouring pad.

88. Id.

89. "Civil Rights: The Continuing Confrontation." *Time*, April 9, 1965. http://www.time.com/time/magazine/article/0,9171,898580,00.html#paid-wall. Access date: June 27, 2013.

90. For a complete history on Leander Perez, see Jeansonne, Glen. *Leander Perez: Boss of the Delta*. University of Southwestern Louisiana, 1995.

91. Chatelain, Kim. "St. Bernard Needs to End Losing Battle." *Times-Picayune*, July 17, 2011. http://www.nola.com/opinions/index.ssf/2011/07/st_bernard_needs_to_end_losing.html. Access date: July 2, 2013.

92. Supra. Brown. "Jim Crow/Segregation."

93. Supra. Bankston.

94. Supra. Brown. "Jim Crow/Segregation."

95. Id..

96. Id..

97. Landphair, Juliette. "The Forgotten People of New Orleans: Community, Vulnerability, and the Lower Ninth Ward." *J. of Amer. History*, 94, Dec. 2007, 837-845. http://www.journalofamericanhistory.org/projects/katrina/Landphair.html. Access date: June 26, 2013.

98. "1965: Hurricane Betsy smashes ashore near New Orleans." *Times-Picayune*, December 8, 2011. http://www.nola.com/175years/index.ssf/2011/12/1965_hurricane_betsy_smashes_a.html. Access date: July 18, 2005.

99. "Our Brother's Keeper." *Louisiana Weekly*, September 10, 1965.

100. *State of Louisiana, ex rel. Frank Plaia v. Louisiana State Board of Health.* 275 So.2d 201 (1973), footnote 4.

101. *Jane Doe v. State of Louisiana, Through the Department of Health and Human Resources, Office of Vital Statistics and Registrar of Vital Statistics.* 479 So. 2d 369 (1985). Hereinafter referred to as *Doe v. La.*

102. Id., footnote 1.

103. Id..

104. Marcus, Frances Frank. "Louisiana Repeals Black Blood Law." *New York Times*, July 6, 1983. http://www.nytimes.com/1983/07/06/us/louisiana-repeals-black-blood-law.html. Access date: August 7, 2013.

105. Id.

106. Alexander-Bloch, Benjamin. "St. Bernard Parish Land Use's Past, Present and Possible Future Discussed." *Times-Picayune*. http://www.nola.com/politics/index.ssf/2012/12/st_bernard_parish_land_uses_pa.html. Access date: July 18, 2013.

107. Sixteen states (including all of those in the Deep South) continued their antimiscegenation laws until the Supreme Court of the United States decided *Loving v. Virginia* (1967), holding that such statutes were unconstitutional. The states were: Louisiana, Alabama, Florida, Georgia, Mississippi, North Carolina, South Carolina, Texas, Arkansas, Delaware, Kentucky, Missouri, Oklahoma, Tennessee, Virginia, and West Virginia. *See* "Miscegenation." Tennessee Department of State. http://www.tn.gov/tsla/exhibits/blackhistory/pdfs/Miscegenation%20laws.pdf. Access date: June 29, 2013.

The case of *Loving v. Virgina* (388 U.S. 1 [1967]) is hereinafter referred to as *Loving*.

108. Antimiscegenation laws in the United States clearly set out to keep the white race "pure" by forbidding whites to intermarry with other races. Members of other races were permitted to intermarry if such marriages were acknowledged by the state. In France during the 1700s, intermarriage between those of African

descent and whites was prohibited, and, these laws transferred to the French colonies in America (including Louisiana). See France's Order of the Council of State of April 5, 1778. Such laws were also pervasive in anti-Semitic Nazi Germany. See *Gesetz zum Schutze des deutschen Blutes und der deutschen Ehre* [Protection of German Blood and German Honor Act [1935]]. They also were present in apartheid in South Africa (1949) during the 20th century. See South Africa's Prohibition of Mixed Marriages Act.

109. The statute at issue before the Court in *Loving* was § 258 of the Virginia Code:

> *Leaving State to evade law.* —If any white person and colored person shall go out of this State, for the purpose of being married, and with the intention of returning, and be married out of it, and afterwards return to and reside in it, cohabiting as man and wife, they shall be punished as provided in § 20-59, and the marriage shall be governed by the same law as if it had been solemnized in this State. The fact of their cohabitation here as man and wife shall be evidence of their marriage.

Section 259, defined the penalty for miscegenation:

> *Punishment for marriage.* —If any white person intermarry with a colored person, or any colored person intermarry with a white person, he shall be guilty of a felony and shall be punished by confinement in the penitentiary for not less than one nor more than five years.

110. The *Loving* case involved "Mildred Jeter, a Negro woman and Richard Loving, a white man," who were married in Washington, DC, where such marriages were permitted. They moved to Virginia to "establish their marital abode." This establishment, within the state of Virginia, violated the antimiscegenation statute. Loving received a jail term of one year, which was suspended. The sentencing court stated:

> "Almighty God created the races white, black, yellow, malay and red, and he placed them on separate continents. And, but for the interference with his arrangement, there would be no cause for such marriage. The fact that he separated the races shows that he did not intend for the races to mix." *Loving* at 3

111. *Loving* at 12.

112. In Louisiana, marriage is currently defined under Art. 86 as ". . . a legal relationship between a man and a woman that is created by civil contract. The relationship and the contract are subject to special rules prescribed by law. Acts 1987, No. 886, §1, eff. Jan. 1, 1988."

113. Made popular by the 1991 film of the same name directed by Spike Lee.

114. "Civil Rights Struggle Lives on in La.'s Public Schools: Segregation Rising since the mid-1980s." *Times-Picayune*, July 29, 2007. Sunday Correction Appended.

115. Id.

116. See also Bankston, Caldas, and Growe. "African-American Reaction to School Desegregation."

117. For an in-depth explanation of the Housing and Urban Development Act of 1968, see Senediak, Mark. J. "Housing and Urban Development Act of 1968." *Affirmative Action: An Encyclopedia*, edited by James A. Beckman. Greenwood, 2004, Vol. 1, 493.

118. "HUD History." U.S. Department of Housing and Urban Development. http://portal.hud.gov/hudportal/HUD?src=/about/hud_history. Access date: June 26, 2013. Hereinafter referred to as HUD.

119. Souther, J. Mark. "The Disneyfication of New Orleans: The French Quarter as Façade in a Divided City." *J. of Amer. History*, 94 (Dec. 2007), 804-811. http://www.journalofamericanhistory.org/projects/katrina/Souther.html. Access date: June 26, 2013.

120. *Arlington Heights v. Metropolitan Housing Corp*. 429 U.S. 252 (1977). Hereinafter referred to as *Arlington Heights*.

121. *Arlington Heights* at 264-268.

122. *Arlington Heights* at 271.

123. For an in-depth explanation of housing segregation and federal law, see Lee, Michael K. "Housing." *Affirmative Action: An Encyclopedia*, edited by James A. Beckman. Greenwood, 2004, Vol. 1, 489.

124. "History." Greater New Orleans Fair Housing Action Center. http://www.gnofairhousing.org/the-center/history/. Access date: June 26, 2013. GNOFHAC is a private nonprofit civil rights organization. Its mission includes a dedication "to fighting housing discrimination not only because it is illegal, but also because it is a divisive force that perpetuates poverty, segregation, ignorance, fear and hatred."

125. Members of the National Black Farmers Association filed suit against the USDA in the case of *Pigford v. Glickman*. The parties agreed to settlements: $1.25 billion in 1999 and $1.15 billion in 2009.

126. As defined by the FBI, hate crimes include "destruction/damage/vandalism, intimidation, simple assault, aggravated assault, murder, rape, crimes against society, and crimes against persons and property." More information available online at: http://www.fbi.gov/about-us/investigate/civilrights/hate_crimes. Access date: December 6, 2013.

127. The FBI uses the terms "anti-white" and "anti-black." The passage of the 1990 Hate Crime Statistics Act directed law enforcement agencies to volunteer information to a national data collection system. The Church Arson Prevention

Act was passed in 1996. Therefore, no national statistical reports existed prior to 1990. According to the FBI, "The Hate Crime Statistics Program has been endorsed by the International Association of Chiefs of Police, the National Sheriffs' Association, the former UCR Data Providers' Advisory Policy Board . . . the International Association of Directors of Law Enforcement Standards and Training, and the Association of State Uniform Crime Reporting Programs." *See* U.S. Department of Justice, Federal Bureau of Investigation, Criminal Justice Information Services Division. *Hate Crime Statistics 1996: Uniform Crime Reports.* http://www.fbi.gov/about-us/cjis/ucr/hate-crime/1996/hatecrime96.pdf. Access date: July 8, 2013.

128. Data taken from the FBI's *Hate Crime Statistics* 1996, 1997, 1998, and 1999.

129. "Definition." DomesticViolence.org. http://www.domesticviolence.org/definition/. Access date: July 8, 2013. According to DomesticViolence.org, domestic violence includes name-calling or putdowns; keeping a partner from contacting family or friends; withholding money; stopping a partner from getting or keeping a job; actual or threatened physical harm; sexual assault; and, stalking and intimidation. Similarly, according to the National Coalition against Domestic Violence, examples of abuse include coercion and threats; intimidation; emotional abuse; isolation; minimizing, denying, and blaming; using children; economic abuse; and male privilege, that is, being the "master" of the house. See "Domestic Violence Fact Sheet." National Coalition against Domestic Violence. http://www.ncadv.org/files/DomesticViolenceFactSheet(National).pdf. Access date: July 8, 2013.

130. Jerome, Fred, and Rodger Taylor. *Einstein on Race and Racism.* New Brunswick, NJ: Rutgers University Press, 2006. According to the authors of this text, Einstein's view in 1946 was omitted from "more than one hundred biographies and monographs." Einstein was the recipient of the Nobel Prize in the area of physics, *Time* magazine's Person of the [Twentieth] Century for his formula $E = MC^2$, and famous for the general theory of relativity. Einstein participated in antilynching campaigns, was a member of the NAACP, and wrote for its magazine the *Crisis.*

131. The "nadir of American race relations" was a term first coined by notable historian Rayford Logan in 1954 in his book *The Negro in American Life and Thought: The nadir, 1877-1901.* This nadir covered the period from the late 1800s through the early 20th century. Today, the term is used to describe the period from the end of the Civil War through the 1960s.

132. Clarence Thomas, who is currently serving on the Court, was appointed by President George H. Bush in 1991 to become the second African-American Supreme Court justice nearly 25 years after Marshall's appointment. President Bush submitted Thomas's name for consideration once Justice Marshall announced his retirement. Three females are currently serving on the Court

together: Ruth Bader Ginsburg (appointed in 1993), Sonia M. Sotomayor (appointed in 2009), and Elena Kagan (appointed in 2010). Sotomayor and Kagan were appointed by President Barack H. Obama, the nation's first African-American president.

133. Nyangoni, Betty. "Du Bois, William Edward Burghardt." *Affirmative Action: An Encyclopedia*, edited by James Beckman. Westport, CT: Greenwood, 2004, Vol. 1, 298. See also Du Bois, W. E. B. *The Souls of Black Folk*. 1903.

134. Lugo, Liza. "Affirmative Action: Is It Really Necessary in the Twenty-First Century?" *Affirmative Action: Contemporary Perspectives*, edited by James Beckman. Westport, CT: Greenwood Press, forthcoming, Chapter 28. See also Lugo, Liza. "Liza Lugo: Reaction to Zimmerman Verdict." *Gainesville Sun*, July 17, 2013. http://www.gainesville.com/article/20130716/OPINION/130719745/1109/sports?p=1&tc=pg. Access date: July 17, 2013.

Chapter 3

1. "This" references the shelters that provided cots, food, and donated clothing.

2. The Bush family lives in Texas. The "arenas" were makeshift shelters for Katrina's diaspora like the Superdome in New Orleans and the Astrodome in Houston.

3. "The Axe in the Attic." [Film]. Ed Pincus and Lucia Small. Small Angst Films, 2007.

4. Id.

5. Gabe, Thomas, Gene Falk, and Maggie McCarty. "Hurricane Katrina: Social-Demographic Characteristics of Impacted Areas." *CRS Report for Congress*. Library of Congress. Domestic Social Policy Division. Congressional Cartography Program, November 4, 2005. http://gnocdc.s3.amazonaws.com/reports/crsrept.pdf. 7/27/2013.

6. "New Orleans Murder Rate on the Rise Again: Homicide Rate Nowhere Near '94 Peak but Still 10 Times National Average." NBC.com, August 18, 2005. http://www.nbcnews.com/id/8999837/ns/us_news-crime_and_courts/t/new-orleans-murder-rate-rise-again/#.UfL6cI3VCVo. Access date: July 26, 2013.

7. Id.

8. Id.

9. Id.

10. Nossiter, Adam. "New Orleans Crime Swept Away, with Most of the People." *New York Times*, November 10, 2005. http://www.nytimes.com/2005/11/10/national/nationalspecial/10crime.html?_r=0. Access date: July 26, 2013.

11. Landphair, Juliette. "The Forgotten People of New Orleans: Community, Vulnerability, and the Lower Ninth Ward." *J. Amer. History*, 94 (Dec. 2007), 837-845. http://www.journalofamericanhistory.org/projects/katrina/Landphair.html. Access date: July 26, 2013.

12. Id.

13. See The Leadership Conference on Civil and Human Rights/The Leadership Conference. "Matthew Shepard and James Byrd, Jr. Hate Crimes Prevention Act." http://www.civilrights.org/hatecrimes/llehcpa/. Access date: July 11, 2011. The Matthew Shepard and James Byrd, Jr. Hate Crimes Prevention Act (formerly the Local Law Enforcement Hate Crimes Prevention Act of 2009) was signed into law on October 28, 2009.

14. The offenders were charged with capital murder. Berry was sentenced to life in prison; and King and Brewer were sentenced to death. Brewer was executed in September 2011.

15. U.S. Department of Justice. "Church Arsons and Hate Crimes." *USA Bulletin* 46, no. 2 (February 1998). http://www.justice.gov/usao/eousa/foia_reading_room/usab4602.pdf. Access date: July 11, 2013.

16. Casillas, Ofelia. "Devastated Parish Feels "Neglected: St. Bernard Says It Has Played 2nd Fiddle to New Orleans in Storms' Aftermath." *Chicago Tribune*, September 29, 2005.

17. Ragsdale, Amy. "A Councilman's Ill-Chosen Words." *Times-Picayune*, September 20, 1997.

18. LaBella, Jerry. "Fishing Delacroix Island, Louisiana." http://www.landbigfish.com/articles/default.cfm?ID=2308. Access date: December 7, 2013.

The area can be found by traveling east down La. State Hwy 39 through St. Bernard Parish, to La. Hwy 46 at Reggio, and onto La. Hwy 300. Black Bay, historically popular for local commercial fishermen and trappers, opens into Breton Sound. This entire area, a mere three feet above sea level, was devastated by Hurricane Katrina and the majority of buildings were destroyed. According to the Times Picayune; "For more than 200 years, the wetlands along Bayou Terre aux Boeufs and the St. Bernard delta had supported a unique culture, provided livelihoods and buffered a community from the rapid societal changes sweeping the nation beyond their cypress trees. They lived lifestyles little changed from the subsistence culture established by their ancestors in the mid-1700s: fishing, trapping, hunting, speaking Spanish—and hardly traveling outside." See Marshall, Bob. "Delacroix residents 'never imagined how bad it would get.' " *Times-Picayune*. August 4, 2010. http://www.nola.com/news/gulf-oil-spill/index.ssf/2010/08/delacroix_residents_never_imag.html. Access date: December 8, 2013.

19. Id.

20. "The Rodriguez Apology." *Times-Picayune*, September 18, 1997. The local paper published the complete transcript of Rodriguez's comment made on September 16, 1997, at a parish council meeting. Rodriguez also said, "As long as you're [rap artists] making money by calling each other the nasty word, it's fine. But if a white politician makes a mistake and says the 'N' word, you want to crucify him. I don't consider myself a racist and I probably never will be . . . I'll also apologize when New Orleans is as safe as St. Bernard, even with racists like me in it.

I don't blame you all for coming down here and protesting. It's a lot safer in St. Bernard Parish. Nobody's going to get hurt."

21. Strachan, Sue. "Persona: Henry 'Junior' Rodriguez." *New Orleans Magazine*, March 6, 2006. http://www.myneworleans.com/New-Orleans-Magazine/June-2006/PERSONA-Henry-Junior-Rodriguez/. Access date: December 9, 2007. In 2005, approximately 70,000 residents lived in St. Bernard Parish within 26 square miles just a few feet above sea level.

22. Nolan, Bruce. "StoryCorps New Orleans: Junior Rodriguez Mourns Loss of His Boyhood Wilderness." *Times-Picayune*, June 3, 2010. http://www.nola.com/storycorps/index.ssf/2010/06/storycorps_new_orleans_junior.html. Access date: July 26, 2013.

23. Louisiana is unique not only because it is separated into parishes and follows Napoleonic Code but 41 of its 64 parishes operate under a police jury form of local government beginning in 1807. Originally, the Louisiana territory was divided into 12 counties, including Orleans, following its purchase by the United States in 1804. Counties, however, were too large for satisfactory administration; therefore, Louisiana was divided into parishes based on the boundaries that existed under Spanish rule in the 1700s. Parishes then became the local government district. Police juries consist of 5 to 15 elected members who serve with the judge and justice of the peace. Members are known as police jurors and are responsible for "execution of whatever concerns the interior and local police and for administration of the parish." A police jury has a similar function to the traditional county commission found in other states. St. Bernard Parish now functions as a local government under Louisiana's Home Rule Charter. "A home rule charter provides the structure and organization, powers and functions of the parish, which may include the exercise of any power and performance of any function necessary, requisite or proper for the management of its affairs, not denied by general law or inconsistent with the constitution." For further information see the Police Jury Association of Louisiana website. "Parish Government Structure - The Forms of Parish Government." http://www.lpgov.org/PageDisplay.asp?p1=3010. Access date: December 7, 2013.

24. "The Rodriguez Apology." *Times-Picayune*, September 18, 1997.

The local paper published the complete transcript of Rodriguez's comment made on September 16 at a Parish Council Meeting. Rodriguez also said, "There may be racists here, but they're not violent."

25. Gueydan is located in Vermillion Parish, 176 miles west of New Orleans, with a population of just 1,598 people, according to the 2000 census.

26. Mermentau is located in Acadia Parish 15 miles west of Gueydan. According to the 2010 census, 661 people make up the tiny town.

27. U.S. Department of Justice. *U.S. v. Byron*, Civil Action No. 99-1594. Consent Decree. http://www.justice.gov/crt/about/hce/documents/hylitessettle.php. Access date: July 10, 2013.

28. Longville is located in Beauregarde Parish and is approximately 193 miles from New Orleans.

29. "Appeals Court Affirms Thirteen-Year Sentence for Klan Leader in Louisiana Cross-Burning." U.S. Department of Justice, April 21, 2004. http://www.justice.gov/opa/pr/2004/April/04_crt_259.htm. Access date: July 10, 2013.

30. Anti-Defamation League. "Ku Klux Klan Criminal Activity and Violence." Extremism in America. http://archive.adl.org/learn/ext_us/kkk/crime.asp?xpicked=4&item=kkk. Access date: July 7, 2013.

31. Id.

32. See the assistant attorney general's opposing brief to Fuselier's appeal at http://www.justice.gov/crt/about/app/briefs/fuselier.pdf. Access date: July 10, 2013.

33. "Justice Department Reaches Settlement Regarding Unconstitutional Conditions at Two Louisiana Developmental Centers." U.S. Department of Justice, January 12, 2004. http://www.justice.gov/opa/pr/2004/January/04_crt_011.htm. Access date: July 10, 2013.

34. "Justice Department Sues Louisiana Apartment Owners for Engaging in Race Discrimination." U.S. Department of Justice, April 15, 2004. http://www.usdoj.gov/opa/pr/2004/April/04_crt_240.htm. Access date: October 29, 2007.

35. "Chalmette-Based Property Owners and Managers to Pay $100,000 in Civil Penalties as Part of Settlement of Justice Department Housing Discrimination Lawsuit." U.S. Department of Justice, March 31, 2005. The suit was filed nearly a year before, in April 2004.

36. Hancock, Lee. "Is It Black and White? In a City Split and Sinking before Storm, Racial Issues Boil." *Dallas Morning News*, December 4, 2005.

37. U.S. Department of Justice, Federal Bureau of Investigation, Criminal Justice Information Services Division. *Hate Crime Statistics: Uniform Crime Reports; Years 2000, 2002, 2003, and 2004.* At the time of this writing, the FBI statistics did not include 2001 because of the events associated with 9/11. The FBI uses the terms "anti-white," "anti-black," "white," and "black."

38. For an in-depth perspective on the catastrophe, see Brinkley, Douglas. *The Great Deluge: Hurricane Katrina, New Orleans, and the Mississippi Gulf Coast.* Harper Perennial, 2007.

39. "Hurricane Katrina: Most Destructive Hurricane Ever to Strike the U.S." National Oceanic and Atmospheric Administration, February 12, 2007. http://www.katrina.noaa.gov. Access date: September 29, 2007.

40. Id.

41. Id. See also "Preliminary Report: Hurricane Andrew 16–28 August, 1992." National Oceanic and Atmospheric Administration, http://www.nhc.noaa.gov/1992andrew.html. Access date: July 16, 2013. Hurricane Andrew, originally a category 4 and then upgraded to a category 5, struck south of Miami in 1992 and caused nearly $21 billion (in today's dollars) in insured losses. More recent

estimates on the economic damage of Katrina are five times greater than that of Andrew, approximately $100 billion.

42. Id. "Sen. David Vitter (R-La.) gave a chilling preview of Katrina's rampage. 'This isn't a simulation of World War III or "The Day After Tomorrow," or Atlantis—but one day, it may be Atlantis," Vitter warned at a hearing. Then he displayed a computer model of a Category 4 hurricane smashing New Orleans and flooding the city under 18 feet of water." This testimony was given two months before Katrina.

43. Warrick, Joby. "White House Got Early Warning on Katrina." *Washington Post*, January 23, 2006. http://www.washingtonpost.com/wp-dyn/content/article/2006/01/23/AR2006012301711.html. Access date: September 29, 2007.

44. "In-Depth: Hurricane Katrina." BBC News. http://news.bbc.co.uk/1/shared/spl/hi/americas/05/katrina/html/landfall.stm. Access date: September 29, 2007.

45. Id.

46. "Weather." CNN, August 30, 2005. http://www.cnn.com/2005/WEATHER/08/29/hurricane.katrina/index.html. Access date: September 29, 2007.

47. Gabe, Thomas, Gene Falk, et al. "Hurricane Katrina: Social-Demographic Characteristics of Impacted Areas." Congressional Research Service, Library of Congress. CRS Report for Congress Order Code RL33141, November 4, 2005. http://www.gnocdc.org/reports/crsrept.pdf. September 29, 2007.

48. Id. The eye of Katrina passed directly over St. Bernard Parish, which borders the Lower Ninth Ward, at 8 a.m. CDT on August 29, 2005, as a category 4 hurricane.

49. Griffin, Candace. "Arabi resident 'paints' tribute to Carolyn Park." *St. Bernard Voice*. August 5, 2013. "Pre-Hurricane Katrina almost every major neighborhood [in St. Bernard Parish] had its own recreation facility, but now the Parish has only one main park [Carolyn Park]." http://thestbernardvoice.com/arabi-resident-paints-tribute-to-carolyn-park/. Access date: December 15, 2013.

Carolyn Park is located in the New Orleans suburb of Arabi, which is between the Lower Ninth Ward and Chalmette. The racial make-up of this community is over 95 percent white and .3 percent African American.

50. "St. Bernard Parish Officials Detail Devastation." *Times-Picayune*, September 13, 2005. http://www.nola.com/katrina/index.ssf/2005/09/st_bernard_parish_officials_detail_devastation.html. Access date: July 26, 2013.

51. *St. Bernard Citizens for Better Government v. St. Bernard Parish School Board*. 202 WL 2022589 (E.D.La.).

52. Logan, John R. "The Impact of Katrina: Race and Class in Storm-Damaged Neighborhoods." http://www.s4.brown.edu/katrina/report.pdf. Access date: September 29, 2007. Professor Logan is a professor of sociology at Brown University and director of spatial structures in the social sciences. The total population of St. Bernard (predominantly white residents) was 67,229. But 53,029 lived in heavily damaged areas (78 percent).

53. Id., 14.

54. Supra. Gabe.

55. Supra. Casillas. "Devastated Parish Feels 'Neglected.'" Parish president Henry J. Rodriguez Jr. was quoted as saying that "the parish is 99.9 percent destroyed."

56. Congressional testimony of James Perry, executive director of the Greater New Orleans Fair Housing Action Center, February 6, 2007.

57. Torres, Manuel. "Parishes Hope to Get Insurance Firms Moving: Delays on Claims May Soon Be Over." *Times-Picayune*, September 30, 2005. http://www.nola.com/newslogs/tporleans/index.ssf?/mtlogs/nola_toirkeabs/archives/2005_09_30.html. Access date: September 29, 2007.

58. Supra. Gabe, Falk, et al. "Hurricane Katrina."

59. Id.

60. Id.

61. Id.

62. "When the Levees Broke: A Requiem in Four Acts." HBO Documentary Films, 2006. Garland Robinette has been a news anchor for 20 years and hosts a radio program entitled "The Think Tank." Robinette was comparing the destruction of New Orleans to the civil war in Beirut, Lebanon; Calcutta, India; and the 2004 Indonesian tsunami that killed over 250,000 people.

63. "Axe in the Attic."

64. Id.

65. Id.

66. Id.

67. The New Orleans diaspora was consistently referred to as "refugees" by numerous media outlets, including the *Washington Post*, the *Boston Globe*, the Associated Press, the *New York Times*, the *Texas Tribune*, and numerous television news reporters. Leaders of the African-American community—including Rev. Jesse Jackson and members of the Congressional Black Caucus—called the term racist. President Bush made a statement on Tuesday immediately following the storm, saying, "The people we're talking about are not refugees. They are Americans, and they need the help and love and compassion of our fellow citizens." See also "Calling Katrina Survivors 'Refugees' Stirs Debate." NBCNews.com, September 7, 2005. http://www.nbcnews.com/id/9232071/ns/us_news-katrina_the_long_road_back/t/calling-katrina-survivors-refugees-stirs-debate/#.Ue0t9Y3VCVo. Access date: July 22, 2013.

68. White House, George W. Bush, President. "The Federal Response to Hurricane Katrina: Lessons Learned." Chapter 4, 2006. http://georgewbush-whitehouse.archives.gov/reports/katrina-lessons-learned/chapter4.html. Access date: July 20, 2013.

69. "New Orleans Man Charged with Shooting African-Americans in the Aftermath of Hurricane Katrina." U.S. Department of Justice, July 15, 2010. http://www.justice.gov/opa/pr/2010/July/10-crt-816.html. Access date: July 11, 2013. The

comment "brown paper bag" refers to the "brown paper bag test," which is rooted in slavery. This form of colorism or color complex is the belief in the superiority of light skin and European-like hair and facial features. Slaves were separated according to the shade of their skin. Those who were lighter-skinned generally worked in the plantation house and may have had certain privileges whereas those with darker skin worked in the fields and were punished more severely. Such colorism continues to exist, most prevalent in the African-American community. Marita Golden, author of *Don't Play in the Sun: One Woman's Journey Through the Color Complex*, described her own mother's comment to her: "Come on inside out of that sun — you're already gonna have to get a light-skinned husband for the sake of your children." See also Golden, Marita. "The color complex in black communities: It's time for all shades to unite." *Washington Post*. October 12, 2012. http://www.washingtonpost.com/blogs/therootdc/post/the-color-complex-in-black-communities-its-time-for-all-shades-to-unite/2012/10/11/ab9ebabe-d1b9-11e1-adf2-d56eb210cdcd_blog.html. Access date: December 9, 2013.

70. Id.

71. Thompson, A. C., and Brendan McCarthy. "Feds Exploring Claims of Racial Vigilantism in Algiers Point in Days after Hurricane Katrina." *Times-Picayune*, April 12, 2010. http://www.nola.com/crime/index.ssf/2010/04/algiers_point_vigilantes_terro.html. Access date: July 11, 2012.

72. See also Maggi, Laura. "Post-Katrina Algiers Shooting Suspect Asks for Trial Delay." *Times-Picayune*, February 24, 2012. http://www.nola.com/crime/index.ssf/2012/02/post-katrina_shooting_suspect.html. Access date: July 22, 2013.

73. "Former Police Officer David Warren Sentenced to 25 Years in Henry Glover Shooting." *Times-Picayune*, March 31, 2011. http://www.nola.com/crime/index.ssf/2011/03/former_police_officer_david_wa.html. Access date: July 11, 2013.

74. "Three New Orleans Police Officers Found Guilty in the Post-Katrina Shooting and Burning of Henry Glover." U.S. Department of Justice, December 9, 2010. http://www.justice.gov/opa/pr/2010/December/10-crt-1420.html. Access date: July 11, 2013.

75. Id. See also "NOPD Cop Convicted in Henry Glover Case Getting New Trial, Appeals Court Decides." *Times-Picayune*, December 13, 2012. http://www.nola.com/crime/index.ssf/2012/12/nopd_cop_convicted_in_henry_gl.html. Access date: July 11, 2013.

76. "Three New Orleans Police Officers Found Guilty." U.S. Department of Justice.

77. The entire transcript of the interview is available at CNN: "Mayor to Feds: 'Get off Your Asses.' Transcript of Radio Interview with New Orleans' Nagin." September 2, 2005. http://www.cnn.com/2005/US/09/02/nagin.transcript/index.html. Access date: July 18, 2013.

78. "Assistant Attorney General for the Civil Rights Division Thomas E. Perez Testifies Before the Senate Judiciary Committee, Washington, D.C." U.S. Department of Justice, April 20, 2010. http://www.justice.gov/crt/speeches/2010/crt-speech-100420.html. Access date: July 11, 2013.

79. "Ex–New Orleans Cops Get Prison Time in Danziger Bridge Shootings." CNN, April 4, 2012. http://www.cnn.com/2012/04/04/justice/louisiana-danziger-bridge-case/index.html. Access date: July 11, 2013.

80. Id. On September 13, 2013, federal judge Kurt Engelhardt granted a new trial for former NOPD officers Kenneth Bowen, Robert Gisevius, Robert Faulcon, Anthony Villavaso, and Arthur Kaufman, who were convicted. See "Judge Orders NOPD Officers Tried in Danzinger Bridge Shooting to Get a New Trial." WGNO. http://wgno.com/2013/09/17/judge-orders-nopd-officers-tried-in-danziger-bridge-shooting-to-get-a-new-trial/#ixzz2g1NAw2Tb. Access date: September 26, 2013.

81. Hancock. "Is It Black and White?"

82. Sulny, Susan, and Gary Rivlin. "Renewal Money for New Orleans Bypasses Renters." *New York Times*, September 17, 2006. http://www.nytimes.com/2006/09/17/us/nationalspecial/17rent.html?pagewanted=all. Access date: December 9, 2013.

83. Hispanic populations for census purposes are made up of those individuals whose ancestry is linked to Spanish-speaking nations in the Americas (also referred to as Latin America), *not* European nations, for example, Spain.

84. *Greater New Orleans Fair Housing Action Center, Inc. v. St. Bernard Parish and St. Bernard Parish Council.* "Amended complaint for Injunctive Relief, Declaratory Judgment, and Remedial Relief." Filed November 2, 2006.

The amended complaint describes the damage following Katrina affecting "97% of all rental units."

85. Supra. Logan. The most segregated areas in the New Orleans area with the highest poverty rates were predominantly African American (90 percent), and five combined areas had a population of 15,000 (Calliope, Iberville, St. Bernard, Desire, and Florida).

86. St. Bernard Parish Government. "FOR IMMEDIATE RELEASE: CONTACT: steve cannizaro." Press Release. October 2, 2005; 4:00 PM CST. http://votegarofalo.com/spg/PressReleases.htm. Access date: July 27, 2013.

87. Bennet, James. "From Oil Refinery, Directing Parish's Efforts to Recover." *New York Times*, September 20, 2005. http://www.nytimes.com/2005/09/20/national/20parish.html?pagewanted=all&_r=0. 7/27/2013.

88. Id.

89. See "Axe in the Attic."

90. Id.

91. Id.

92. Snyder, Mary Gail. "It Didn't Begin with Katrina." *Shelterforce Online* 143, September/October 2005. http://www.nhi.org/online/issues/143/beforekatrina.html. 6/27/2013.

93. Sills, G. L., N. D. Vroman, et al. "Overview of New Orleans Levee Failures: Lessons Learned and Their Impact on National Levee Design and Assessment." *J. Geotechnical and Geoenvironmental Engineering.* May 2008, 558.

94. See van Heerden, Ivor. "How New Orleans Flooded." NOVA. PBS.org, November 22, 2005. http://www.pbs.org/wgbh/nova/earth/how-new-orleans-flooded.html. Access date: July 19, 2013.

95. See Brown, David. "Floodwater Not as Toxic as Feared, Experts Say." *Washington Post,* October 12, 2005. http://www.washingtonpost.com/wp-dyn/content/article/2005/10/11/AR2005101101909_2.html . Access date: July 19, 2013. "The floodwater averaged about 100,000 coliform bacteria per 100 milliliters of water, far above the government standard of 200 for swimming and other 'primary contact.' For drinking, the standard is zero."

96. Presley, S. M., T. R. Rainwater, et al. "Assessment of Pathogens and Toxicants in New Orleans, LA following Hurricane Katrina." *Environ. Sci. Technol.* 40, no. 2 (January 15, 2006): 468-474. http://www.ncbi.nlm.nih.gov/pubmed/16468391. Access date: July 19, 2013.

97. Bush. "Federal Response to Hurricane Katrina."

98. Goldman, Lynn, and Christine Coussens. "Environmental Public Health Impacts of Disasters: Hurricane Katrina Workshop Summary." Presented in 2007 at the Roundtable on Environmental Health Sciences, Research, and Medicine Board on Population Health and Public Health Practice. Institute of Medicine of the National Academies. National Academies Press. Washington, DC. http://www.nap.edu/openbook.php?record_id=11840&page=14. Access date: July 20, 2013.

99. Dwyer, Timothy, Jacqueline L. Salmon, and Dan Eggen. "Katrina Takes Environmental Toll." *Washington Post,* September 7, 2005. http://www.washingtonpost.com/wp-dyn/content/article/2005/09/06/AR2005090600498.html. Access date: July 20, 2013.

100. "Hurricane Katrina Floods New Orleans." National Aeronautics and Space Administration. http://visibleearth.nasa.gov/view.php?id=15445. Access date: July 18, 2013."As much as 380 cubic meters (380,975 liters or 11,300 cubic inches) of water were being pumped out of New Orleans every second."

101. Bush. "Federal Response to Hurricane Katrina," Chapter 1.

102. Id. The federal government estimated the total number of damaged and destroyed homes in the affected region to be 300,000.

103. Dwyer et al. "Katrina Takes Environmental Toll."

104. Hurricane Rita, like Katrina, also reached category 5 status while in the Gulf of Mexico. Rita made landfall on the Texas/Louisiana border on September 24, 2005. Loss of life was less severe with Hurricane Rita because Katrina caused the permanent evacuation of many residents in the area. Furthermore, since Katrina wreaked havoc just weeks before Rita, remaining residents followed evacuation orders. See National Climatic Data Center. "Hurricane Rita."

September 22, 2005. http://www.ncdc.noaa.gov/extremeevents/specialreports/Hurricane-Rita2005.pdf. Access date: December 9, 2013.

105. U.S. Energy Information Administration. Report dated December 27, 2005. http://www.eia.gov/oog/special/eia1_katrina.html. Access date: June 7, 2012.

106. Bush. "Federal Response to Hurricane Katrina," Chapter 4.

107. Weaver, Jane. "Katrina Health Risks Rise with Flooding: Residents Should Be Wary of Contaminated Water And Food." NBCNews.com. http://www.nbcnews.com/id/9109689/ns/health-health_care/t/katrina-health-risks-rise-flooding/. Access date: July 18, 2013.

108. Bush. "Federal Response to Hurricane Katrina," Chapter 4.

109. Id.

110. Ray Nagin, Mayor of New Orleans, testimony before a hearing on Hurricane Katrina: Preparedness and Response by the State of Louisiana, on December 14, 2005, House Select Committee to Investigate the Preparation for and Response to Hurricane Katrina, 109th Congress, 1st session, 3.

111. The Select Bipartisan Committee to Investigate the Preparation for and Response to Hurricane Katrina. "A Failure of Initiative: Final Report of the Select Bipartisan Committee to Investigate the Preparation for and Response to Hurricane Katrina." February 15, 2006. U. S. Government Printing Office. http://www.uscg.mil/history/katrina/docs/USHouseOfRepKatrina2006MainR1eport.pdf. Access date: July 20, 2013.

112. Id.

113. Throughout the chapter, italics are added for emphasis.

114. Thompson, Patricia. New Orleans Resident and Evacuee. Select Committee Hearing, December 6, 2005. See also Alperen, Martin J. *Foundations of Homeland Security*. John Wiley & Sons, 2011, 97.

115. Tally is as of August 2, 2006.

116. See also Brunkard, Joan, Gonza Namulanda, and Raoult Ratard. "Research: Hurricane Katrina Deaths, Louisiana, 2005." August 28, 2008. http://dhh.louisiana.gov/assets/oph/Center-PHCH/Center-CH/stepi/specialstudies/DisasterMedPHPrep2008No1KatrinaDeaths.pdf. Access date: July 27, 2013.

117. Jonkman, Sebastiaan Nicolaas. "Loss of Life Estimation in Flood Risk Assessment: Theory and Applications." Risk Assessment, May 2009. Delft Cluster. http://www.citg.tudelft.nl/fileadmin/Faculteit/CiTG/Over_de_faculteit/Afdelingen/Afdeling_Waterbouwkunde/sectie_waterbouwkunde/people/personal/jonkman/doc/SNJonkman_dissertation_smallest.pdf. Access date: July 18, 2013.

118. Id.

119. Id.

120. Supra. Brunkard.

121. Bush. "Federal Response to Hurricane Katrina," Chapter 4. According to the federal government, 34 residents died.

122. See Jonkman," Loss of Life Estimation in Flood Risk Assessment." Some studies show that African Americans represented 55 percent of deaths, while whites comprised 40 percent.

123. Supra. Brunkard.

124. Schleifstein, Mark. "Study of Hurricane Katrina's Dead Show Most Were Old, Lived near Levee Breaches." *Times-Picayune*, August 27, 2009. http://www.nola.com/hurricane/index.ssf/2009/08/answers_are_scarce_in_study_of.html. Access date: July 19, 2013.

125. The poverty rate for the entire New Orleans area was 30 percent at the time of the storm.

Chapter 4

1. Cho, Alina, and Susan Roesgen. "Katrina Victims: 'Living in Barns'; Parish President Blasts FEMA over Temporary Homes." CNN.com, December 13, 2005. http://www.cnn.com/2005/US/12/13/katrina.trailers/. Access date: July 27, 2013.

2. Letter from Henry "Junior" Rodriguez to President George W. Bush dated August 29, 2005. The letter was posted on Nola.com on August 29, 2005, by Ray Garofalo. The letter is now available at http://stbernardafterkatrina.blogspot.com/2005/08/juniors-letter.html. Access date: July 27, 2013.

3. St. Bernard Parish and New Orleans had standing water of four to 25 feet for up to four weeks following Katrina. St. Bernard Parish allowed residents to return in increments for viewing only. Hurricane Rita landed on Sabine Pass, Texas, less than one month after Katrina, on September 24, 2005. Rita's storm surge worsened Katrina's effects. St. Bernard was so severely damaged (98-99 percent from Katrina and the balance from Rita) residents could not return to the Parish until the day after Rita passed. The parish government communicated information on Rita and its resident return policy through the same weblink provided for official information on Katrina. The proximity and timing between the two storms delayed reentry to the New Orleans metropolitan area. See also St. Bernard Project. "Community and Storm." 2010. http://www.stbernardproject.org/get-involved/community-and-storm-story/. Access date: December 15, 2013.

4. "Official Hurricane Information." St. Bernard Parish Government, September 25, 2005. http://votegarofalo.com/spg/. Access date: August 8, 2013.

5. Throughout the chapter, italics added for emphasis.

6. Gabe, Thomas, Gene Falk, and Maggie McCarty. "Hurricane Katrina: Social-Demographic Characteristics of Impacted Areas." *CRS Report for Congress*. November 4, 2005. Library of Congress. Domestic Social Policy Division. Congressional Cartography Program. http://gnocdc.s3.amazonaws.com/reports/crsrept.pdf. Access date: July 27, 2013.

7. Hancock, Lee. "Is It Black and White? In a City Split and Sinking Before Storm, Racial Issues Boil." *Dallas Morning News*, December 4, 2005.

8. Id.

9. Id.

10. Supra. Gabe.

11. *Greater New Orleans Fair Housing Action Center and Wallace Rodrigue v. St. Bernard Parish and St. Bernard Parish Council.* Civil Action No. 2:06-CV-07185. "Plaintiffs' Proposed Findings of Fact and Conclusions of Law." Filed March 18, 2009. http://www.lawyerscommittee.org/admin/fair_housing/documents/files/0040.pdf. Access date: July 27, 2013.

12. St. Bernard Parish Council. "Minutes of the St. Bernard Parish Council Meeting of March 7, 2006." #47. Provided by the Fair Housing Center of New Orleans. Submitted to a vote, the result was Yeas: Chairman Lynn B. Dean, Kenneth Henderson, Joseph DiFatta, Craig Taffaro, and Tony Melerine. Nays: Mark Madary and Judy Darby Hoffmeister. None of these individuals serve on the council today. See also *Greater New Orleans Fair Housing Action Center, Inc. v. St. Bernard Parish and St. Bernard Parish Council.* "Complaint for Injunctive Relief, Declaratory Judgment, and Remedial Relief." Filed in U.S. District Court for the Middle District. All capital letters are used in the original meeting minutes regarding this statement.

13. Id.

14. St. Bernard Parish Council. "Minutes of the St. Bernard Parish Council Meeting of March 7, 2006." #47, p. 3. Provided by the Fair Housing Center New Orleans. The statement is capitalized as such in the meeting minutes.

15. *Greater New Orleans Fair Housing Action Center and Wallace Rodrigue v. St. Bernard Parish and St. Bernard Parish Council.* Civil Action No. 2:06-CV-07185. "Plaintiffs' Proposed Findings of Fact and Conclusions of Law." Filed March 18, 2009. http://www.lawyerscommittee.org/admin/fair_housing/documents/files/0040.pdf. Access date: July 27, 2013.

16. Stone, Geoffrey R., Louis Michael Seidman, et al. *Constitutional Law*, 5th ed. Aspen, 2005, 1146.

17. *Los Angeles City Council v. Taxpayers for Vincent*, 466 U.S. 789 (1984).

18. *Virginia v. Hicks*, 539 U.S. 113 (2003).

19. *Grayned v. City of Rockford*, 408 U.S. 104, 108-09 (1972). Quoted in *Village of Hoffman Estates v. The Flipside*, 455 U.S. 489, 498 (1982).

20. See Alexander-Bloch, Benjamin. "St. Bernard Parish President Craig Taffaro Will Resign Parish Post on Thursday." *Times-Picayune*, December 14, 2011. http://www.nola.com/politics/index.ssf/2011/12/st_bernard_parish_president_cr_2.html. Access date: July 11, 2013. Craig Taffaro served as St. Bernard Parish president for one term beginning in 2008 following the departure of Junior Rodriguez. Taffaro stepped down and accepted a position as Louisiana's new director of hazard mitigation and recovery under Governor Bobby Jindal.

21. St. Bernard Parish Government. Ordinance SBPC #370-09-06, Summary No. 1911. September 19, 2006.

22. The ordinance was approved by Judy Darby Hoffmeister, Kenneth Henderson, Joseph Di Fatta, Craig Taffaro, and Tony Melerine. Mark Madary and Council Chairman Lynn B. Dean voted against it.

23. St. Bernard Project. "Community and Storm." 2010. http://www.stbernard project.org/get-involved/community-and-storm-story/. Access date: December 15, 2013.

The St. Bernard Project, according to its website, "is an award-winning rebuilding, nonprofit organization whose mission is to ensure that disaster-impacted communities recover in a prompt, efficient, and predictable way."

24. St. Bernard Parish Government. Ordinance SBPC #370-09-06, Summary No. 1911 (f) and (h). September 19, 2006.

25. Alexander-Bloch, Benjamin. "St. Bernard Housing Trial Would Have Included Allegation against Peralta." *Times-Picayune*. http://www.nola.com/politics/index.ssf/2013/05/st_bernard_housing_trial_would.html. Access date: July 27, 2013.

26. "Jim Crow in the South." History of Jim Crow. http://ww.jimcrowhistory.org/geography/geography.htm. Access date: December 9, 2007.

27. Louisiana Act 118 of 1924.

28. Louisiana Constitution 1921, Art. 19, Sec. 2. "[N]o alien who is ineligible to citizenship of the United States shall be permitted or allowed or shall have any right whatsoever to acquire by purchase . . . lease . . . own or control, directly or indirectly any land or real property . . . whatsoever within the state of Louisiana."

29. This was derived from Acts 1921, Ex. Sess., No. 106, §§ 1 through 3 and amended by Acts 1952, No. 127, §4.

30. *Tyler v. Harmon*, 158 La. 439 (1925).

31. Warren, Bob. "St. Bernard Parish Won't Enforce Controversial Housing Ordinance until It Goes before Judge." *Times-Picayune*, November 13, 2006. http:://www.nola.com/newslogs/tpupdates/index.ssf? /mtlogs/nola_tpupdates/archives/2006_11_13.html. Access date: September 2, 2007.

32. Steve Cannizaro. "Council Alters Rental Law by Dropping Reference to Blood Relative." St. Bernard Parish Government, December 20, 2006. http://www.sbpg.net/newsdec2006c.html. Access date: September 13, 2007.

33. Lynn Dean was the parish president from 1992 to 1996 and served on the Louisiana State Legislature from 1996 through 2004. He became a council member in 2004 but did not seek re-election in 2007.

34. Turni Bazile, Karen. "Bias Lawsuit Puts Council on Defensive: Lawyer Hired to Fight Allegation of Discrimination in St. Bernard." *Times-Picayune*, November 8, 2006.

35. Id.

36. "St. Bernard Parish Agrees to Halt Discriminatory Zoning Rule, Fair Housing Groups Call 'Blood Relative Ordinance' Illegal." U.S. Newswire, November 13, 2006.

37. Chen, Michelle. "Housing Watchdogs Call Post-Katrina Ordinance 'Racist.'" *New Standard*. http://newstandardnews.net/content/index.cfm/items/3731. Access date: October 7, 2006.The *New Standard* was a nonprofit online publication that has since ceased publication. At the time of his comment, Chairman Dean had been a resident of St. Bernard Parish for 70 years.

38. *Keyes v. School Dist. No.* 1, 413 U. S. 189, 413 U. S. 205 (1973).

39. *Id.* at 413 U. S. 208. *See also id.* at 413 U. S. 199, 413 U. S. 211, 413 U. S. 213.

40. Rauch, Jonathan. "Struggling to Survive after Katrina: A Hard Year for the Big Easy." *Reason*, August 14, 2006. http;//www.reason.com/news/show/36970.html. Access date: November 3, 2007.

41. *Yick Wo v. Hopkins*, 118 U. S. 356 (1886).

42. *Washington v. Davis*, 426 U.S. 229, 242 (1976).

43. Turni Bazile. "Bias Lawsuit Puts Council on Defensive."

44. DeBerry, Jarvis. "Despite St. Bernard Parish President Craig Taffaro's Claim, the Feds Are Not the Enemy." *Times-Picayune*. http://www.nola.com/opinions/index.ssf/2011/03/despite_st_bernard_parish_pres.html. Access date: July 29, 2013.

45. Id.

46. Id.

47. Quigley, Bill. "Eighteen Months after Katrina." Truthout.org, February 27, 2007. http://www.truth-out.org/archive/item/68978:bill-quigley—eighteen-months-after-katrina. Access date: July 27, 2013.

48. Id.

49. Torres, Manuel. "Lawsuit by Former Jefferson Parish Housing Authority Commissioners Escalates War with Parish." *Times-Picayune*, December 20, 2012. http://www.nola.com/politics/index.ssf/2012/12/lawsuit_by_former_jefferson_pa.html. Access date: August 8, 2013.

50. Id.

51. American Civil Liberties Union. "7.5.2006: ACLU Issues Open Letter to Sheriff Strain for Comments Made." Letter to Sheriff Strain from Katie Schwartzmann, Staff Attorney. https://www.laaclu.org/press/2006/070506.htm. Access date: July 27, 2013.

52. Kessler, Ronad C., Sandro Galea, et al. "Research: Mental Illness and Suicidality after Hurricane Katrina." *Bulletin of the World Health Organization* 84, no. 12 (December 2006). http://www.who.int/bulletin/volumes/84/12/06-033019.pdf. Access date: July 2, 2013.

53. Saulny, Susan. "A Legacy of the Storm: Depression and Suicide." *New York Times*. http://www.nytimes.com/2006/06/21/us/21depress.html?pagewanted=all. Access date: 7/27/2013.

54. Id.

Chapter 5

1. Lugo, Liza. "Is Affirmative Action Really Necessary in the 21st Century?" In *Affirmative Action: Contemporary Perspectives*, edited by James A. Beckman. ABC-CLIO, 2014.

2. Greater New Orleans Fair Housing Action Center. News Release: "Fair Housing Center Files Suit against St. Bernard Parish, Announces News Conference Regarding Lawsuit." October 3, 2006. http://www.gnofairhousing.org/pdfs/10-03-06%20-%20press%20release%20lawsuit%20-%20ST%20Bernard.pdf. Access date: October 6, 2007. The "ordinances" refer to the evolution of ordinances to restrict housing post-Katrina, not just the "blood-relative" ordinance.

3. Id..

4. "White resident joins housing bias lawsuit in St. Bernard." *Louisiana Weekly*, November 6, 2006. http://www.louisianaweekly.com/weekly/news/articlegate.pl?20061106c. Access date: October 27, 2007.

5. *The Slaughter-House Cases*, 83 U.S. 36 (1873).

6. *Strauder v. West Virginia*, 100 U.S. 303 (1879).

7. *United States v. Cruikshank*, 92 U.S. 542 (1875).

8. *Plessy v. Ferguson*, 163 U.S. 537 (1896).

9. *Washington v. Davis*, 426 U.S. 229, 239 (1976).

10. U.S. Const. Amend. 14, Sec. 1.

11. Id. at 242.

12. *Village of Arlington Heights v. Metropolitan Housing Dev. Corp.*, 429 U.S. 252, 267 (1977).

13. Id. at 168.

14. *Washington v. Davis*, 424 U.S. 229, 242 (1976). Throughout the chapter, italics added for emphasis.

15. *Rice v. Cayetano*, 528 US 495, 517 (2000).

16. U.S. Const. Amend. 14, Sec. 1.

17. *Ex parte Va.*, 100 U.S. 339, 347 (U.S. 1879). "Whoever, by virtue of public position under a State government, deprives another of property, life, or liberty, without due process of law, or denies or takes away the equal protection of the laws, violates the constitutional inhibition; and he acts in the name and for the State, and is clothed with the State's power, his act is that of the State."

18. *Buchanan v. Wharley*, 245 U.S. 412, 415 (1920).

19. The intent of the legislators was clear in the title of the Louisville ordinance: "An ordinance to prevent conflict and ill feeling between the white and colored races in the City of Louisville, and to preserve the public peace and promote the general welfare by making reasonable provisions requiring, as far as practicable, the use of separate blocks for residences, places of abode and places of assembly by white and colored people respectively."

20. *Buchanan v. Wharley*, 245 U.S. 412, 415 (1920).

21. Id. at 245.

22. *F. S. Royster Guano Co. v. Virginia*, 253 U.S. 412, 415 (1920).

23. Stone, Geoffrey R, Louis M. Seidman, et al. *Constitutional Law*. Aspen, 2005, 501.

24. *Cleburne v. Cleburne Living Center, Inc.*, 473 U.S. 432 (1985).

25. Manheim, Karl M. "Text Assist for Suspect Classes Flowchart." Los Angeles: Loyola Law School, Fall 1997. http://classes.lls.edu/archive/manheimk/114d3/echarts/suspect.htm. Access date: October 10, 2007.

26. *Califano v. Webster*, supra at 317, quoting *Craig v. Boren*, 429 U.S. 190, 197 (1976).

27. *City of Cleburne v. Cleburne Living Ctr.*, 473 U.S. 432 (1985).

28. Id. at 440.

29. Fundamental interests include those granted by the Constitution.

30. According to *Black's Law Dictionary*, 6th Ed., the term "alienage" is the condition or state of an alien.

31. *Wygant v. Jackson Board of Education*, 476 U.S. 267, 274 (1986). First articulated in *McLaughlin v. Florida*, 379 U.S. 184 (1964). See also *Korematsu v. United States*, 323 U.S. 214 (1944) upholding a race-specific statute providing for "relocation camps" for Japanese Americans and holding racial classifications should be reviewed under "rigid scrutiny." Additionally, in *Loving v. Va*, 388 U.S. 1, 8 (1967), a case involving antimiscegenation statutes, the court rejected "the notion that the mere 'equal application' of a statute containing racial classifications is enough to remove the classifications from the Fourteenth Amendment's proscription of all invidious racial discriminations."

32. *Bankers Life and Casualty Co. v. Crenshaw*, 486 U.S. 71 (1988).

33. *Metropolitan Hous. Dev. Corp. v. Village of Arlington Heights*, 558 F. 2d 1283, 1285 (1977).

34. Id. at 1287.

35. Id.. Summary No. 1911; Ch. 14, Art. 1, Section 14-3(a). The ordinance does not apply to properties used as rentals before adoption.

36. 1866 Civil Rights Act, 14 Stat. 27-30, Ch. 31. April 9, 1866.

37. 42 USCS §3601, Sec. 2.

38. *Secretary on behalf of Steve Ellis Times and Betty A. Brinson v. Annete Banai, et al.* HUDALJ 04-93-2060-8 (2/3/95).

39. 42 U.S.C.A. §3615.

40. 42 U.S.C.A. §3604(b).

41. 42 U.S.C.A. §3613.

42. *Williamson v. Hampton Management Co.*, 339 F. Supp. 1146 (1972) referencing *Walker v. Pointer*, 304 F. Supp. 56 (1969).

43. 42 U.S.C. 3602, Sec. 802(i).

44. 42 U.S.C. 3604, Sec. 804. "Discrimination in sale or rental of housing and other prohibited practices." It is also unlawful to do the same against persons based on religion, sex, handicap, and familial status.

45. *Oliver v. Shelly*, 538 F. Supp. 600, (1982). Landlord denied tenants housing because the applicants were an interracial couple.

46. See the actual order at: http://www.relmanlaw.com/docs/September_11_order.pdf. See also Lugo, "Is Affirmative Action Really Necessary in the 21st Century?"

47. Kirkham, Chris. "Drive to Demolish Blighted Houses Stirs Controversy in St. Bernard." *Times-Picayune*. http://www.nola.com/news/index.ssf/2009/03/drive_to_demolish_blighted_hou.html. Access date: July 27, 2013.

48. Id.

49. Grunfeld, David. "New Orleans City Council Delays Vote on Housing Code Reforms." *Times-Picayune*, July 16, 2013. http://www.nola.com/politics/index.ssf/2013/07/new_orleans_city_council_delay_2.html. Access date: July 27, 2013.

50. Supra. Lugo, "Is Affirmative Action Really Necessary in the 21st Century?"

51. *Shelby County Alabama v. Holder, Attorney General*, 570 U.S. (2013) (Slip op.).

52. Id.

53. *Northwest Austin*, 557 U. S., at 203.

Chapter 6

1. Chen, Michelle. "Housing Watchdogs Call Post-Katrina Ordinance Racist." *New Standard*, October 6, 2006. http://newstandardnews.net/content/index.cfm/items/3731. Access date: July 29, 2013.

2. Greater New Orleans Fair Housing Action Center. News Release: "Fair Housing Center Files Suit against St. Bernard Parish, Announces News conference Regarding Lawsuit." October 3, 2006. http://www.gnofairhousing.org/pdfs/10-03-06%20-%20press%20release%20lawsuit%20-%20St%20Bernard.pdf. Access date: October 6, 2007.

3. *Greater New Orleans Fair Housing Action Center, Inc. v. St. Bernard Parish and St. Bernard Parish Council*. "Complaint for Injunctive Relief, Declaratory Judgment, and Remedial Relief."

4. Cannizaro, Steve. "St. Bernard Parish Government Latest News." September 20, 2006. "Council won't allow homeowners to rent out single-family residences except to blood relatives, without a special permit; council members say they want to restore parish to mostly owner-occupied neighborhoods like in past Council member Kenny Henderson said, "If someone is going to stop us (in court), fine. Let's do it until then."

5. Sisco, Annette. "The Cost of Stubbornness." *Times-Picayune*, July 7, 2008. http://blog.nola.com/editorials/2008/07/editorial_the_cost_of_stubborn.html. Access date: July 29, 2013.

6. Torres, Manuel. "St. Bernard Parish's Housing Restrictions Are Legally and Morally Wrong." *Times-Picayune*, September 12, 2009. http://blog.nola.com/editorials/2009/09/st_bernard_parishs_housing_res.html. Access date: July 29, 2013.

7. Alexander-Bloch, Benjamin. "Federal Judge Again Finds St. Bernard Parish in Contempt for Racial Discrimination." *Times-Picayune*, October 19, 2011. http://www.nola.com/crime/index.ssf/2011/10/federal_judge_again_finds_st_b.html. Access date: July 29, 2013.

8. DeBerry, Jarvis. "Housing Fight Prompts Racists to Speak: Jarvis DeBerry." *Times-Picayune*, June 12, 2011. http://www.nola.com/opinions/index.ssf/2011/06/housing_fight_prompts_racists.html. Access date: July 11, 2013.

9. Alexander-Bloch, Benjamin. "Department of Justice and St. Bernard Settle in Post-Katrina Housing Discrimination Case." *Times Picayune*, May 10, 2013. http://www.nola.com/crime/index.ssf/2013/05/department_of_justice_and_st_b.html. Access date: May 11, 2013.

10. DeBerry, Jarvis. "Don't Give the Bigots a Reason to Gloat." *Times-Picayune*, February 13, 2011. http://www.nola.com/opinions/index.ssf/2011/02/dont_give_the_bigots_a_reason.html. Access date: July 29, 2013.

11. Alexander-Bloch, Benjamin. "St. Bernard Authority Usurped in Battle over Mixed-Income Apartments, Parish President Says." *Times-Picayune*, March 2, 2011. http://www.nola.com/politics/index.ssf/2011/03/st_bernard_authority_usurped_i.html. Access date: July 29, 2013.

12. Rosen, Sophie. "Federal Judge Grants Motion for Summary Judgment in Housing Discrimination Case against St. Bernard Parish." Greater New Orleans Fair Housing Action Center, October 19, 2013. http://www.gnofairhousing.org/2012/10/19/federal-judge-grants-motion-for-summary-judgement-in-housing-discrimination-case-against-st-bernard-parish/. Access date: July 29, 2013. See also Gonzalez, Jessica. "Judge Rules in Favor of Provident and GNOFHAC." *St. Bernard Voice*, November 9, 2012. http://thestbernardvoice.com/judge-rules-in-favor-of-provident-and-gnofhac/. Access date: July 29, 2013.

13. Alexander-Bloch, Benjamin. "St. Bernard Parish President Craig Taffaro's Storage Unit Searched, Documents Seized." *Times-Picayune*, October 25, 2012. http://www.nola.com/crime/index.ssf/2012/10/st_bernard_parish_craig_taffar.html. Access date: July 29, 2013.

14. St. Bernard Parish Government. "Early Voting for the November 6th Election October 23rd[d] through October 30th." http://www.sbpg.net/index.php?option=com_content&view=article&id=3488&catid=2&Itemid=440. Access date: August 14, 2013.

15. Alexander-Bloch, Benjamin. "St. Bernard Parish Council Approves Ethics Board Members." *Times-Picayune*, June 4, 2013. http://blog.nola.com/politics/print.html?entry=/2013/06/st_bernard_parish_council_appr.html. Access date: August 14, 2013.

16. Alexander-Bloch, Benjamin. "St. Bernard Parish Undergoes Sweeping Political Change." *Times-Picayune*, November 19, 2011. http://www.nola.com/

politics/index.ssf/2011/11/political_change_sweeps_st_ber.html. Access date: August 8, 2013.

17. DeBerry, Jarvis. "St. Bernard Parish Loses Housing Battle Two Different Ways." *Times-Picayune*, October 25, 2012. http://www.nola.com/opinions/index.ssf/2012/10/st_bernard_parish_loses_housin.html. Access date: July 29, 2013.

18. Alexander-Bloch, Benjamin. "Department of Justice and St. Bernard Settle in Post-Katrina Housing Discrimination Case." *Times Picayune*, May 10, 2013. http://www.nola.com/crime/index.ssf/2013/05/department_of_justice_and_st_b.html. Access date: May 11, 2013.

19. *U.S. v. St. Bernard Parish*. Case 2:12-cv-00321-HGB-SS Document 334-1. Filed May 10, 2013, page 2 of 27. http://www.nola.com/crime/index.ssf/2013/05/department_of_justice_and_st_b.html. Access date: July 11, 2013. See also Alexander-Bloch, "Department of Justice and St. Bernard Settle."

20. Gonzalez, Jessica. "Parish to Pay over $2 Million in Damages." *St. Bernard Voice*, May 20, 2013. http://thestbernardvoice.com/parish-to-pay-over-2-million-in-damages/. Access date: July 29, 2013.

21. Id.

22. Alexander-Bloch, Benjamin. "St. Bernard Fair Housing Coordinator Begins Work, as Required under Federal Settlement." *Times-Picayune*, August 7, 2013. http://www.nola.com/politics/index.ssf/2013/08/st_bernard_fair_housing_coordi.html. Access date: August 8, 2013.

23. Id.

Chapter 7

1. Roth, David. "Louisiana Hurricane History." National Weather Service. http://www.srh.noaa.gov/images/lch/tropical/lahurricanehistory.pdf. Access date: August 6, 2013.

2. "Former U.S. Army Corps of Engineers Contract Employee Charged with Bribery on a New Orleans Levee Reconstruction Project." U.S. Department of Justice, August 23, 2007. http://www.justice.gov/opa/pr/2007/August/07_at_647.html. Access date: July 10, 2013.

3. According to 18 U.S.C. § 1346, the federal mail and wire fraud statute adopted in 1988, honest service wire fraud is a scheme or artifice to deprive another of the intangible right of honest services.

4. "C. Ray Nagin, Former New Orleans Mayor, Indicted on Federal Bribery, Honest Services Wire Fraud, Money Laundering, Conspiracy, and Tax Charges." U.S. Department of Justice, January 18, 2013. http://www.justice.gov/usao/lae/news/2013/2013_01_18_c_ray_nagin_ind.html. Access date: August 17, 2013.

5. Finn, Kathy. "Ex-New Orleans Mayor Seeks Delay in Corruption Trial." Reuters.com. http://www.reuters.com/article/2013/09/19/us-usa-crime-neworleans-idUSBRE98I15I20130919?feedType=RSS. Access date: September 26, 2013.

6. Hammer, David. "Ex-N.O. Mayor Ray Nagin's corruption trial pushed back to 2014." WWLTV.com. October 24, 2013. http://www.wwltv.com/news/nagin-indictment/Nagin-trial-delayed-until-Jan-27-229111321.html. Access date: December 16, 2013.

7. "Louisiana Man Pleads Guilty to Conspiring to Violate Civil Rights of Homeowner." U.S. Department of Justice, December 18, 2008. http://www.justice.gov/opa/pr/2008/December/08-crt-1128.html. Access date: July 10, 2013.

8. "Louisiana Man Indicted for Federal Civil Rights Violations for Nooses Targeting 'Jena Six' Marchers." U.S. Department of Justice, January 24, 2008. http://www.justice.gov/opa/pr/2008/January/08_crt_054.html. Access date: July 11, 2013.

9. "Louisiana Man Pleads Guilty to Federal Civil Rights Violations." U.S. Department of Justice, April 28, 2011. Press Release. http://www.justice.gov/opa/pr/2011/April/11-crt-539.html. Access date: July 23, 2013.

10. At the time of the "crime," the couple lived together but were not married.

11. "Louisiana Man Sentenced for Civil Rights Violation in Connection with Cross-Burning." U.S. Department of Justice, May 27, 2010. http://www.justice.gov/opa/pr/2010/May/10-crt-624.html. Access date: July 23, 2013.

12. Piyush "Bobby" Jindal was born in Louisiana to parents who immigrated from India. He was elected governor, began his term in 2008, and was reelected in 2011. He served in the House of Representatives from 2005 to 2008. Jindal is the first nonwhite to serve as governor since P. B. S. Pinchback; and he is the first nonwhite to be elected to the office since Pinchback as lieutenant governor assumed the office after the death of Oscar Dunn.

13. Dilella, William. "Taffaro's Appointment Makes Farewell Official." *St. Bernard Voice*, December 13, 2011. http://thestbernardvoice.com/taffaro%E2%80%99s-appointment-makes-farewell-official/. Access date: July 29, 2013.

14. Alexander, Michelle. *The New Jim Crow: Mass Incarceration in the Age of Colorblindness*. New York: New Press, 2 010.

15. Banks, Ralph Richard. *Is Marriage for White People? How the African American Marriage Decline Affects Everyone*. Dutton. 2011.

16. Id.

17. Id. The reality is that this number does not represent the number of convictions. A significant percentage of these individuals are incarcerated pending trial.

18. Carson, E. Ann, and Daniela Golinell. "Prisoners in 2012: Advance Counts." NCJ 242467. U.S. Department of Justice, Office of Justice Programs, Bureau of Justice Statistics, July 2013. http://www.bjs.gov/content/pub/pdf/p12ac.pdf. Access date: August 9, 2013.

19. Id.

20. See Kuebler, Meghan. "Closing the Wealth Gap: A Review of Racial and Ethnic Inequalities in Homeownership." *Sociology Compass* 7, no. 8 (August 2013): 670–685.

21. Id.

22. Id.

23. Id.

24. Lugo, Liza. "Is Affirmative Action Really Necessary in the 21st Century?" *Affirmative Action: Contemporary Perspectives*, edited by James A. Beckman. ABC-CLIO, 2014. See also U.S. Department of Labor, Bureau of Labor Statistics, April 22, 2003.

25. Censky, Annalyn. "Black Unemployment: Highest in 27 Years." CNN.com, September 2, 2011. http://money.cnn.com/2011/09/02/news/economy/black_unemployment_rate/index.htm. Access date: September 26, 2013.

26. Id. See also U.S. Census Bureau. "Number of Poor and Poverty Rate by Race and Hispanic Origin, 1999–2001."

27. Id. Throughout the chapter, italics are added for emphasis.

28. Id.

29. Ryan, Jason. "FBI: Reported Hate Crimes up in 2006." ABC News, November 19, 2007. http://abcnews.go.com/TheLaw/story?id=3887681&page=1. Access date: July 23, 2013.

30. Id. The study analyzed data from June 2000 to December 2003 based on interviews with more than 77,000 people per year.

31. Id.

32. "Assistant Attorney General Thomas E. Perez Speaks at the UT Diversity and Civility Conference." U.S. Department of Justice, November 15, 2012. http://www.justice.gov/crt/opa/pr/speeches/2012/crt-speech-1211151.html. Access date: July 23, 2013.

33. Statistics compiled from the FBI's "Uniform Crime Reports: Hate Crime Statistics" in 2006, 2007, 2008, 2009, 2010, and 2011.

34. Other hate crimes assessed by the FBI include those based on biases toward sexual orientation, religion, ethnicity/nation of origin, and disability. In 2011, more than 20 percent of hate crimes were based on sexual orientation bias.

35. Hamilton, Reeve. "Five Years Later Houstonians Conflicted about Katrina." *Texas Tribune*. http://www.texastribune.org/texas-politics/texas-political-news/five-years-houstonians-conflicted-about-katrina/. Access date: July 22, 2013.

36. "Federal Protections against National Origin Discrimination." U.S. Depatment of Justice, October 2000. http://www.justice.gov/crt/legalinfo/natorigin.php. Access date: December 16, 2013.

37. According to AIG's website: "American International Group, Inc., (AIG), is a leading international insurance organization serving customers in more than 130 countries. AIG companies serve commercial, institutional, and individual customers through one of the most extensive worldwide property-casualty networks of any insurer. In addition, AIG companies are leading providers of life insurance and retirement services in the United States." http://www.aig.com/about-us_3171_437773.html. Access date: August 3, 2013.

38. "Assistant Attorney General for the Civil Rights Division Thomas E. Perez Testifies Before the Senate Judiciary Committee, Washington, D.C." U.S. Department of Justice, April 20, 2010. http://www.justice.gov/crt/speeches/2010/crt-speech-100420.html. Access date: July 11, 2013.

39. Mitch Landrieu is currently the lieutenant governor of Louisiana, serving with Governor Bobby Jindal.

40. Id.

41. "Assistant Attorney General Thomas E. Perez Speaks at the UT Diversity and Civility Conference." U.S. Department of Justice,November 15, 2012. http://www.justice.gov/crt/opa/pr/speeches/2012/crt-speech-1211151.html. Access date: July 23, 2013.

42. Id.

43. "Assistant Attorney General Thomas E. Perez Speaks at the City of New Orleans Consent Decree Press Conference." U.S. Department of Justice, July 24, 2012. http://www.justice.gov/crt/opa/pr/speeches/2012/crt-speech-120724.html. Access date: July 23, 2013.

44. The Cabinet of President Obama is currently comprised of Vice President Joseph R. Biden, Secretary of State John Kerry, Treasury Secretary Jack Lew, Defense Secretary, Chuck Hagel, Attorney General Eric H. Holder Jr., Interior Secretary Sally Jewell, Agriculture Secretary, Thomas J. Vilsack, Commerce Secretary Penny Pritzker, Labor Secretary Thomas E. Perez, Health and Human Services Secretary Kathleen Sebelius, Housing and Urban Development Secretary Shaun L. S. Donovan, Transportation Secretary Anthony Foxx; Energy Secretary Ernest Moniz, Education Secretary Arne Duncan, Veterans Affairs Secretary Eric K. Shinseki, and Homeland Security Secretary Janet A. Napolitano.

45. Haslam, Nick. "Dehumanization: An Intergrative Review." *Pers. Soc. Psychol. Rev.* 10, no. 3 (August 2006): 252-264. Haslam is with the Department of Psychology of the University of Melbourne.

46. Costello, Kimberly, and Gordon Hodson. "Exploring the Roots of Dehumanization: The Role of Animal–Human Similarity in Promoting Immigrant Humanization." *Group Processes Intergroup Relations* 13, no. 1 (January 2010): 3–22.

47. Merriam-Webster Dictionary. http://www.merriam-webster.com/dictionary/dehumanization. Access date: August 3, 2013.

48. Dictionary.com. http://dictionary.reference.com/browse/Dehumanization. Access date: August 3, 2013.

49. Medical Dictionary of FreeDictionary.com. http://medical-dictionary.thefreedictionary.com/dehumanization. Access date: August 3, 2013.

50. Id.

51. National Coalition against Domestic Violence. http://www.ncadv.org/. Access date: August 3, 2013.

52. Centers for Disease Control and Prevention (CDC). "Intimate Partner Violence." http://www.cdc.gov/violenceprevention/intimatepartnerviolence/index.html. Access date: August 3, 2013.

53. World Health Organization. *Violence by Intimate Partners*. Chapter 4. http://www.who.int/violence_injury_prevention/violence/global_campaign/en/chap4.pdf. Access date: August 3, 2013.

54. CDC. "Intimate Partner Violence: Risk Protective Factors." http://www.cdc.gov/violenceprevention/intimatepartnerviolence/riskprotectivefactors.html. Access date: August 3, 2013.

55. Id.

56. National Coalition against Domestic Violence. "The Problem." http://www.ncadv.org/learn/TheProblem.php. Access date: August 3, 2013. Socially oppressed groups include women, children, people of color, people with disabilities, LGBTs, the elderly, Jews, and other marginalized groups.

57. Hale, Sir Matthew. *The History of the Pleas of the Crown*. 1736. See also Bennice, Jennifer A., and Patricia A. Resick. "Marital Rape History, Research, and Practice." July 2003. http://www.sagepub.com/lippmanstudy/articles/Bennice.pdf. Access date: August 4, 2013.

58. This is true in many areas of the world today.

59. Greenson, Thadeus. "An Evolution of Law: Spousal Rape Recently Prosecutable." *Times Standard*, March 3, 2008. http://www.times-standard.com/ci_8668539. Access date: August 4, 2013. Statutes like these were pervasive in America. Currently, all 50 states have laws making marital rape a crime, although the degrees vary, and they are prosecuted differently. Virginia, Arizona, South Carolina, and Tennessee have lesser penalties than other states.

60. National Coalition against Domestic Violence. "The Impact of Disaster." http://www.ncadv.org/learn/TheImpactofDisaster.php. Access date: August 4, 2013.

61. National Coalition against Domestic Violence. "The Problem." http://www.ncadv.org/learn/TheProblem.php. Access date: August 4, 2013.

62. CDC. "Intimate Partner Violence: Consequences." http://www.cdc.gov/violenceprevention/intimatepartnerviolence/consequences.html. Access date: August 4, 2013.

63. Id.

64. Id.

65. Global Conference on the Prevention of Genocide. "Background: What Is Genocide?" http://efchr.mcgill.ca/WhatIsGenocide_en.php?menu=2. Access date: August 5, 2013.

66. Stanton, Gregory H. "The 8 Stages of Genocide." Genocide Watch, 1998. Originally presented as a briefing paper at the U.S. State Department in 1996. http://www.genocidewatch.org/aboutgenocide/8stagesofgenocide.html. Access date: August 5, 2013.

67. Id.

68. Id.

69. Id.

70. See Prichard, J. C. *A Treatise on Diseases of the Nervous System: Comprising Compulsive and Maniacal Affections*. London: Thomas and George Underwood, Fleet Street, 1822. http://www.archive.org/stream/treatiseondiseas00pric#page/n9/mode/2up. Access date: August 9, 2013.

71. Schwartz, Steven. *Abnormal Psychology: A Discovery Approach*. Mayfield, 2000, 426.

72. "Antisocial Personality Disorder." Mayo Foundation for Medical Education and Research (MFMER), April 12, 2013. http://www.mayoclinic.com/health/antisocial-personality-disorder/DS00829/METHOD=print. Access date: August 6, 2013.

73. The DSM V was published in May 2013 and, therefore, is only recently being used. In the context of the recent study of disorders such as antisocial personality disorder, the DSM IV is the more appropriate on which to rely. The DSM IV was published in 1994 with a text revision published in 2000.

74. *Psychiatric News* 39, no. 1 (2004): 25.

75. "Antisocial Personality Disorder." National Center for Biotechnology Information, U.S. National Library of Medicine, 2010, Sec. 2.1. http://www.ncbi.nlm.nih.gov/pubmedhealth/PMH0015230/. Access date: August 6, 2013.

76. Brain injury differs from brain damage in that injury does not necessarily result in long-term impairment.

77. Schwartz, *Abnormal Psychology*, 426.

78. Garbarino, James. "Violent Children: Where Do We Point the Finger of Blame?" *Pediatrics and Adolescent Medicine* 155, no. 1 (January 2001).

79. The "pervasive pattern of disregard for, and violation of, the rights of others" is a focus on behavior and not a personality trait.

80. See Levene, Mark. "Why Is the Twentieth Century the Century of Genocide?" *Journal of World History*, Vol. 11, No. 2 (Fall, 2000), pp. 305-336. Available online at: http://www.yadvashem.org/yv/en/education/international_projects/chairmanship/mark_levene1.pdf. Access date: December 16, 2013.

81. See "Violence Against Women, A Majority Staff Report," Committee on the Judiciary, United States Senate, 102nd Congress, October 1992, p.3.

82. Domestic Violence Statistics. "Domestic Violence Statistics." 2013. http://domesticviolencestatistics.org/domestic-violence-statistics/. Access date: August 6, 2013.

83. Id.

84. United States Department of Justice. Uniform Crime Reporting Statistics. Federal Bureau of Investigations. See "Estimated Violent Crime in United States 1960 – 2011" in Appendix.

85. Locke, John. *Second Treatise of Government*. 1689, Chapter 2.

86. Such political philosophy was practiced throughout human history and the present date around the world and is the basis for justifying notable rebellions including the American Revolution and the French Revolution.

87. Much evolutionary theory suggests that humans are descended from primitive animals, most notably members of the primate species. The major fault with evolutionary theory is that it underscores the dehumanization principle by planting the seed that humans are instead animals. The theory morphed into designating some humans, particularly Africans, as more closely related to primates and thus "less human."

88. Lee-St. John, Jeninne. "Should States Apologize for Slavery?" *Time*, March 27, 2007. http://www.time.com/time/nation/article/0,8599,1603581,00.html. Access date: July 26, 2013.

89. See *Meritor Savings Bank, FSB v. Vinson, et al*, 477 U.S. 57 (1986); *Rogers v EEOC*, 454 F. 2d 234 (CA5 1971), cert. denied, 406 U. S. 957 (1972); *Firefighters Institute for Racial Equality* v. *St. Louis*, 549 F. 2d 506, 514-515 (CA8), cert. denied *sub nom; Banta* v. *United States*, 434 U. S. 819 (1977); *Gray* v. *Greyhound Lines, East*, 178 U. S. App. D. C. 91, 98, 545 F. 2d 169, 176 (1976), religion, *e.g.; Compston* v. *Borden, Inc.*, 424 F. Supp. 157 (SD Ohio 1976); and national origin, *e.g., Cariddi* v. *Kansas City Chiefs Football Club*, 568 F. 2d 87, 88 (CA8 1977). *Katz* v. *Dole*, 709 F. 2d 251, 254-255 (CA4 1983); *Bundy* v. *Jackson*, 205 U. S. App. D. C., at 444-454, 641 F. 2d, at 934-944; *Zabkowicz* v. *West Bend Co.* 589 F. Supp. 780 (ED Wis. 1984).

90. "Assistant Attorney General Thomas E. Perez at a Press Conference to Announce NOPD Investigation Findings ." U.S. Department of Justice. March 17, 2011. http://www.justice.gov/crt/opa/pr/speeches/2011/crt-speech-110317.html. Access date: December 16, 2013.

Requirements for the NOPD overhaul stemmed from a lawsuit filed by the United States against the City of New Orleans. See the complaint online at: http://media.nola.com/crime_impact/other/nopd-consent-decree.pdf. Access date: December 16, 2013.

The U.S. Department of Justice's Civil Rights Division conducted an investigation on the NOPD and compiled a report in March 2011. The report can be found online at: http://www.propublica.org/documents/item/justice-department-report-on-the-new-orleans-police-department. Access date: December 16, 2013.

91. Id.

92. Lugo. "Is Affirmative Action Really Necessary in the 21st Century?"

93. "Senate Approves Resolution Apologizing for Slavery." CNN.com, June 18, 2009. http://www.cnn.com/2009/POLITICS/06/18/senate.slavery/. Access date: July 25, 2013.

94. Koch, Wendy. "Lawmakers to Push for U.S. Apology for Slavery." *USA Today*, February 28, 2008. http://usatoday30.usatoday.com/news/nation/2008-02-27-slavery_N.htm. Access date: July 25, 2013.

95. The summary of H.R. 40 states: "Commission to Study Reparation Proposals for African Americans Act Establishes the Commission to Study Reparation

Proposals for African Americans to examine slavery and discrimination in the colonies and the United States from 1619 to the present and recommend appropriate remedies."

96. "C. Ray Nagin, Former New Orleans Mayor, Indicted on Federal Bribery. . . Charges." U.S. Departement of Justice. See the official indictment at *United States of Amerca v. C. Ray Nagin "aka Mayor Nagin."* Criminal No. 13-011 http://www.justice.gov/usao/lae/news/2013/downloads/indictment_C_Ray_Nagin.pdf.

97. Peralta, David. Email from St. Bernard Parish president David Peralta to Liza Lugo, August 17, 2013.

98. Nakamura, David. "Obamas Visit Door of No Return, Where Slaves Once Left Africa." *Washington Post*, June 27, 2013. http://www.washingtonpost.com/blogs/post-politics/wp/2013/06/27/obamas-visit-door-of-no-return-where-slaves-once-left-africa/. Access date: June 29, 2013.

99. Obama, Michelle. "FLOTUS Travel Journal: Visiting Goree Island." June 27, 2013. http://www.whitehouse.gov/blog/2013/06/27/flotus-travel-journal-visiting-goree-island. Access date: June 29, 2013.

100. Id.

101. Lugo. "Is Affirmative Action Really Necessary in the 21st Century?"

102. Id.

103. *Brown* at 494.

Author's Note

1. "Caucasian" was first defined by the German philosopher Christoph Meiners in his work *The Outline of History of Mankind* (1785), long after the Transatlantic Slave Trade began. It was further developed in the 1790s by German professor of medicine Johann Friedrich Blumenbach as researched according to craniotomy and the theory of facial angle. In 1962, Harvard-educated American anthropologist Carlton S. Coon theorized the construct of race in accordance with Darwinian theory in his book *The Origin of Race*. Undoubtedly, this affected the curriculum of American education. His last book, *Racial Adaptations: A Study of the Origins, Nature, and Significance of Racial Variations in Humans* (1982), summarized his theories, which remained the same.

Appendix A

1. Barack Obama resigned on November 16, 2008, having been elected as the forty-fourth president of the United States on November 4, 2008.

2. Roland Burris was appointed to the U.S. Senate on December 31, 2008, to fill the vacancy caused by the resignation of Barack Obama. However, Burris's credentials were not in order until January 12, 2009. He took the oath of office on

January 15, 2009, and served until November 29, 2010, when he was succeeded in a special election by Mark Kirk.

3. "Mo" Cowan was appointed as a Democrat to the U.S. Senate on February 1, 2013, to fill the vacancy caused by the resignation of Senator John F. Kerry when Kerry was appointed to the position of secretary of state by President Obama.

4. Adam Clayton Powell, Jr. was elected to the 90th Congress, but the House refused to seat him. He was subsequently elected to that Congress in a special election to fill his own vacancy, although he chose not to occupy the seat for the duration of the term.

5. Charles Coles Diggs, Jr. resigned on June 3, 1980, and was succeeded by George Crockett on November 4, 1980.

6. Katie Beatrice Hall was elected to the 97th Congress in a special election to succeed Adam Benjamin on November 2, 1982.

7. Eva Clayton was elected by special election on November 3, 1992, to succeed Walter B. Jones.

8. William Herbert Gray III resigned on September 11, 1991, and was succeeded by Lucien Edward Blackwell on November 5, 1991.

9. Michael Alphonso (Mike) Espy resigned on January 22, 1993, and was succeeded by Bennie Thompson on April 13, 1993.

10. Kweisi Mfume resigned on February 15, 1996, and was succeeded by Elijah Eugene Cummings on April 16, 1996.

11. Juanita Millender-McDonald was elected by special election on March 26, 1996, to succeed Walter R. Tucker III.

12. Mel Reynolds resigned on October 1, 1995, and was succeeded by Jesse L. Jackson, Jr., on December 12, 1995.

13. Walter R. Tucker III resigned on December 15, 1995, and was succeeded by Juanita Millender-McDonald on March 26, 1996.

14. Donna Christensen served under the name Donna Christian-Green in the 105th Congress.

15. Ronald V. Dellums resigned on February 6, 1998, and was succeeded by Barbara Lee on April 7, 1998.

16. Floyd Harold Flake resigned on November 17, 1997, and was succeeded by Gregory Meeks on February 3, 1998.

17. Barbara Lee was elected by special election on April 7, 1998, to succeed Ronald V. Dellums.

18. Diane Edith Watson was elected by special election on June 5, 2001, to succeed Julian Dixon.

19. Frank W. Ballance Jr., resigned on June 11, 2004, and was succeeded by George Kenneth ("G. K.") Butterfield Jr., on July 20, 2004.

20. Julia May Carson died on December 15, 2007, and was succeeded in a special election by her grandson André Carson on March 11, 2008.

21. Marsha Fudge was elected by special election on November 18, 2008, to succeed Stephanie Tubbs Jones.

22. Stephanie Tubbs Jones died on August 20, 2008, and was succeeded in a special election by Marcia Fudge on November 18, 2008.

23. Juanita Millender-McDonald died on April 22, 2007, and was succeeded in a special election by Laura Richardson on August 21, 2007.

24. Laura Richardson was elected by special election on August 21, 2007, to succeed Juanita Millender-McDonald.

25. Albert Russell Wynn resigned on May 31, 2008, and was succeeded by Donna F. Edwards on June 17, 2008.

26. Donald Milford Payne died on March 6, 2012, and was succeeded in a special election by his son Donald Payne Jr., on November 6, 2012.

27. Robin Kelly was elected by special election on April 9, 2013, to succeed Jesse Jackson, Jr.

Bibliography

18 U.S.C. § 245(b)(2).

36 USC §302.

42 U.S.C. 1982.

42 U.S.C. 3602, Sec. 802(i).

42 U.S.C. 3604, Sec. 804.

42 U.S.C.A. §3604(b).

42 U.S.C.A. §3613.

42 U.S.C.A. §3615.

42 USCS §3601, Sec. 2.

70 Okla. Stat. (1941) 455, 456, and 457.

Adams, John Quincy. Argument before the Supreme Court of the United States in the case of *United States v. Cinque and others, Africans captured on the schooner Amistad by Lieut. Gedney*. February 24 and March 1, 1841.

Alexander, Michelle. *The New Jim Crow: Mass incarceration in the age of colorblindness*. New York: New Press, 2010.

Alexander-Bloch, Benjamin. "Department of Justice and St. Bernard Settle in post-Katrina Housing Discrimination Case." *Times Picayune*, May 10, 2013.

Alexander-Bloch, Benjamin. "Federal Judge again finds St. Bernard Parish in Contempt for Racial Discrimination." *Times-Picayune*, October 19, 2011.

Alexander-Bloch, Benjamin. "St. Bernard Authority Usurped in Battle over Mixed-Income Apartments, Parish President Says." *Times-Picayune*, March 2, 2011.

Alexander-Bloch, Benjamin. "St. Bernard Fair Housing Coordinator Begins Work, as Required under Federal Settlement." *Times-Picayune*, August 7, 2013.

Alexander-Bloch, Benjamin. "St. Bernard Housing Trial Would Have Included Allegation against Peralta." *Times-Picayune*, May 16, 2013.

Alexander-Bloch, Benjamin. "St. Bernard Parish Council Approves Ethics Board Members." *Times-Picayune*, June 4, 2013.

Alexander-Bloch, Benjamin. "St. Bernard Parish Land Use's Past, Present and Possible Future Discussed." *Times-Picayune*, December 12, 2012.

Alexander-Bloch, Benjamin. "St. Bernard Parish President Craig Taffaro Will Resign Parish Post on Thursday." *Times-Picayune*, December 14, 2011.

Alexander-Bloch, Benjamin. "St. Bernard Parish President Craig Taffaro's storage Unit Searched, Documents Seized." *Times-Picayune*, October 25, 2012.

Alexander-Bloch, Benjamin. "St. Bernard Parish Undergoes Sweeping Political Change." *Times-Picayune*, November 19, 2011.

Allen, James. *Without Sanctuary: Lynching Photography in America*. Santa Fe, NM: Twin Palms. 2000.

American Civil Liberties Union. "7.5.2006: ACLU Issues Open Letter to Sheriff Strain for Comments Made." Letter to Sheriff Strain from Katie Schwartzmann, Staff Attorney. https://www.laaclu.org/press/2006/070506.htm.

The American Heritage Dictionary of the English Language, 4th ed. Boston: Houghton Mifflin, 2000.

Anderson, Annie. "NAACP Asking for Apology for 1946 Lynching." KMSS-TV Fox 33, Shreveport, Louisiana, May 7, 2013.

Anti-Defamation League. "Ku Klux Klan Criminal Activity and Violence." Extremism in America. http://archive.adl.org/learn/ext_us/kkk/crime.asp?xpicked=4&item=kkk.

Anti-Slavery.org. "Breaking the Silence: Learning about the Transatlantic Slave Routes; Spain." http://www.antislavery.org/breakingthesilence/slave_routes/slave_routes_spain.shtml.

Arlington Heights v. Metropolitan Housing Corp., 429 U.S. 252 (1977).

Associated Press. "Lynching Postcard Sold for $240." KARE11 News, October 8, 2008.

Bacon-Blood, Littice. "The Largest Slave Revolt in U.S. History Is Commemorated." *Times-Picayune*, Jan. 3, 2011.

Badger, Richard G. *The Mulatto in the United States, Including a Study of the Role of Mixed-Blood Races throughout the World*. Boston: Gorham, 1918.

Bankers Life and Casualty Co. v. Crenshaw, 486 U.S. 71 (1988).

Banks, Ralph Richard. *Is Marriage for White People? How the African American Marriage Decline Affects Everyone*. New York: Dutton. 2011.

Bankston, Carl L., III, Stephen J. Caldas, and Roslin Growe. "The African-American Reaction to School Desegregation in Lafayette Parish." *J. Negro Education* 71, nos. 1/2 (Winter-Spring 2002, 43-59).

BBC News. "In-Depth: Hurricane Katrina." http://news.bbc.co.uk/1/shared/spl/hi/americas/05/katrina/html/landfall.stm.

Bennet, James. "From Oil Refinery, Directing Parish's Efforts to Recover." *New York Times*, September 20, 2005.

Bennice, Jennifer A., and Patricia A. Resick. "Marital Rape History, Research, and Practice." *Trauma, Violence, & Abuse* 4, no. 3 (July 2003): 228-246.

Berea College v. Kentucky, 211 U.S. 45 (1908).

Branley, Edward. "NOLA History: Congo Square and the Roots of New Orleans Music." GoNOLA.com, July 2, 2012.

Brasted, Chelsea. "Unsolved Murders." WAFB News, January 16, 2012. http://wafb.ddev4.worldnow.com/story/16527813/unsolved-murders.

Bridges-Hall, Ruby. "The Education of Ruby Nell." Guideposts, March 2000. http://www.rubybridges.com/story.html.

Brinkley, Douglas. *The Great Deluge: Hurricane Katrina, New Orleans, and the Mississippi Gulf Coast.* New York: Harper Perennial. 2007.

Brown, David. "Floodwater Not as Toxic as Feared, Experts Say." *Washington Post,* October 12, 2005.

Brown, Nikki. "Jim Crow/Segregation." In *KnowLA Encyclopedia of Louisiana,* edited by David Johnson. New Orleans, Louisiana Endowment for the Humanities, May 20, 2010. http://www.knowla.org/entry/735/.

Brown v. Bd. of Educ., 347 U.S. 483 (1954).

Brown v. Bd. of Educ. II, 349 U.S. 294 (1955).

Brunkard, Joan, Gonza Namulanda, and Raoult Ratard. "Research: Hurricane Katrina Deaths, Louisiana, 2005." Baton Rouge, Department of Health and Hospitals Louisiana. August 28, 2008.

Buchanan v. Warley, 245 U.S. 60, 75 (1917).

Buckser, Andre S. "Lynching as Ritual in the American South." *Berkeley Journal of Sociology* 37 (1992). 11-28.

Bureau of Refugees, Freedmen, and Abandoned Lands. *Miscellaneous Reports and Lists Relating to Murders and Outrages, Mar. 1867–Nov. 1868.* The Freedmen's Bureau Online. http://freedmensbureau.com/louisiana/outrages/outrages1.htm.

Cable News Network. "Ex-New Orleans Cops Get Prison Time in Danziger Bridge Shootings." CNN.com, April 4, 2012. http://www.cnn.com/2012/04/04/justice/louisiana-danziger-bridge-case/index.html.

Cable News Network. "Former Klansman Found Guilty of Manslaughter: Conviction coincides with the 41st Anniversary of Civil Rights Killings." CNN.com. June 22, 2005. http://www.cnn.com/2005/LAW/06/21/mississippi.killings/.

Cable News Network. "Mayor to Feds: 'Get off Your Asses.' Transcript of radio interview with New Orleans' Nagin." CNN.com, September 2, 2005.

Calhoun, John C. Address to the U.S. Senate, February 6, 1837, "Slavery Is a Positive Good." *Opposing Viewpoints in World History: Slavery,* edited by James D. Torr. Farmington Hills, MI: Greenhaven, 2004.

Califano v. Webster, 430 U.S. 313 (1977).

Campanella, Richard, and Marina Campanella. *New Orleans Then and Now.* Gretna, LA: Pelican, 1999.

Cannizaro, Steve. "Council Alters Rental Law by Dropping Reference to Blood Relative." St. Bernard Parish Government. December 20, 2006. http://www.sbpg.net/newsdec2006c.html.

Carson, E. Ann, and Daniela Golinell. "Prisoners in 2012: Advance Counts." NCJ 242467. Washington: U.S. Department of Justice, Office of Justice Programs, Bureau of Justice Statistics, July 2013.

Cartwright, Samuel. "Diseases and Peculiarities of the Negro Race." *De Bow's Review: Southern and Western States: Vol. 11. New Orleans, 1851.* New York: AMS Press, 1967.

Casillas, Ofelia. "Devastated Parish Feels "Neglected": St. Bernard Says It Has Played 2nd Fiddle to New Orleans in Storms' Aftermath." *Chicago Tribune*, September 29, 2005.

Censky, Annalyn. "Black Unemployment: Highest in 27 Years." CNN.com, September 2, 2011. http://money.cnn.com/2011/09/02/news/economy/black_unemployment_rate/index.htm.

Centers for Disease Control and Prevention. "Intimate Partner Violence." http://www.cdc.gov/violenceprevention/intimatepartnerviolence/index.html.

Centers for Disease Control and Prevention. "Intimate Partner Violence: Consequences." http://www.cdc.gov/violenceprevention/intimatepartnerviolence/consequences.html.

Centers for Disease Control and Prevention. "Intimate Partner Violence: Risk Protective Factors." http://www.cdc.gov/violenceprevention/intimatepartnerviolence/riskprotectivefactors.html.

Chafe, William H. Chafe, Raymond Gavins, et al. *Remembering Jim Crow: African Americans Tell about Life in the Segregated South.* New York: Center for Documentary Studies for the Behind the Veil Project, New Press, 2001.

Chatelain, Kim. "St. Bernard Needs to End Losing Battle." *Times-Picayune*, July 17, 2011.

Chen, Michelle. "Housing Watchdogs Call Post-Katrina Ordinance Racist." *New Standard*, October 6, 2006. http://newstandardnews.net/content/index.cfm/items/3731.

Cho, Alina, and Susan Roesgen. "Katrina Victims: 'Living in Barns': Parish President Blasts FEMA over Temporary Homes." CNN.com, December 13, 2005. http://www.cnn.com/2005/US/12/13/katrina.trailers/.

Church Arson Prevention Act (1996).

Civil Rights Act 1866, 14 Stat. 27-30, Ch. 31. April 9, 1866.

Civil Rights Cases, 109 U.S. 3 (1883).

Clark, Kenneth. "Effect of Prejudice and Discrimination on Personality Development." White House Mid-Century Conference on Children and Youth, 1950. Appendix to the appellants' briefs in Brown v. Board of Education of Topeka, Kansas, Briggs v. Elliott, and Davis v. Prince Edward County, Virginia, cases. "The Effects of Segregation and the Consequences of Desegregation A (September 1952) Social Science Statement in the Brown v. Board of Education of Topeka Supreme Court Case." *American Psychologist*, Vol. 59 (6), Sept. 2004, 495-501.

Cleburne v. Cleburne Living Center, Inc., 473 U.S. 432 (1985).

CNN.com. "Senate Approves Resolution Apologizing for Slavery." June 18, 2009. http://www.cnn.com/2009/POLITICS/06/18/senate.slavery/.

CNN.com. "Weather." August 30, 2005. http://www.cnn.com/2005/WEATHER/08/29/hurricane.katrina/index.html.

Colten, Craig E. *An Unnatural Metropolis: Wresting New Orleans from Nature.* Baton Rouge: Louisiana State University Press, 2005.

Constitution of the United States. http://www.archives.gov/exhibits/charters/constitution_transcript.html.

Cornell University Law School. Legal Information Institute. "Conspiracy: Definition from Nolo's Plain-English Law Dictionary." August 19, 2010. http://www.law.cornell.edu/wex/conspiracy.

Costello, Kimberly, and Gordon Hodson. "Exploring the Roots of Dehumanization: The Role of Animal–Human Similarity in Promoting Immigrant Humanization." *Group Processes & Intergroup Relations.* Vol. 13, No. 1 (January 2010) 3–22.

Cowan, Tadlock, and Jody Feder. "The Pigford Cases: USDA Settlement of Discrimination Suits by Black Farmers." Congressional Research Service. March 12, 2013. http://www.nationalaglawcenter.org/assets/crs/RS20430.pdf.

Craig v. Boren, 429 U.S. 190, 197 (1976).

Davis, Ronald L. F. "Creating Jim Crow: In-Depth Essay." http://www.jimcrowhistory.org/history/creating2.htm.

DeBerry, Jarvis. "Despite St. Bernard Parish President Craig Taffaro's Claim, the Feds Are Not the Enemy." *Times-Picayune*, March 11, 2011.

DeBerry, Jarvis. "Don't Give the Bigots a Reason to Gloat." *Times-Picayune*, February 13, 2011.

DeBerry, Jarvis. "Housing Fight Prompts Racists to Speak: Jarvis DeBerry." *Times-Picayune*, June 12, 2011.

DeBerry, Jarvis. "St. Bernard Parish Loses Housing Battle Two Different Ways." *Times-Picayune*, October 25, 2012.

Declaration of Constitutional Principles (1956).

De Jong, Greta. *A Different Day: African-American Struggles for Justice in Rural Louisiana, 1900–1970.* Chapel Hill: University of North Carolina Press. 2002.

Deyle, Steven. *Carry Me Back: The Domestic Slave Trade in American Life.* New York: Oxford University Press, 2005.

Dilella, William. "Taffaro's Appointment Makes Farewell Official." *St. Bernard Voice.* December 13, 2011. http://thestbernardvoice.com/taffaro%E2%80%99s-appointment-makes-farewell-official/.

"Domestic Violence Statistics." 2013. http://domesticviolencestatistics.org/domestic-violence-statistics/.

DomesticViolence.org. "Definition." http://www.domesticviolence.org/definition/.

Douglass, Frederick. *The Narrative of the Life of Frederick Douglass.* Boston: Anti-Slavery Office,1845.

Dred Scott v. Sandford, 60 U.S. 393 (1856).

Du Bois, W. E. B. *The Souls of Black Folk*. 1903. Electronic Text. Electronic Text Center, University of Virginia Library. Charlottesville: Electronic Text Center, University of Virginia Library. http://web.archive.org/web/20110116163046/http://etext.lib.virginia.edu/etcbin/toccer-new2?id=DubSoul.sgm&images=images/modeng&data=/texts/english/modeng/parsed&tag=public&part=all.

Du Bois, W. E. B. "The Talented Tenth." *The Negro Problem*. A Series of Articles by Representative Negroes of To-day (New York, 1903). Excerpts available online at http://www.yale.edu/glc/archive/1148.htm.

Dwyer, Timothy, Jacqueline L. Salmon, and Dan Eggen. "Katrina Takes Environmental Toll." *Washington Post*, September 7, 2005.

Eltis, David. "A Brief Overview of the Trans-Atlantic Slave Trade." Transatlantic Slave Trade Database, Emory University, 2007. http://slavevoyages.org/tast/index.faces. 5/14/2013.

Ex parte Va., 100 U.S. 339 (1879).

The Experiment. Covington, LA: Fleurish Productions, 2012.

F. S. Royster Guano Co. v. Virginia, 253 U.S. 412 (1920).

Falconbridge, Alexander. *An Account of the Slave Trade on the Coast of Africa*. London: J. Phillips, 1788.

Fensterstock, Allison. "Chitlin' Circuit Characters Live again in Book Mapping the Birth of Rock and Roll." *Times-Picayune*, July 26, 2011.

Finn, Kathy. "Ex-New Orleans Mayor Seeks Delay in Corruption Trial." Reuters.com. September 19, 2013. http://www.reuters.com/article/2013/09/19/us-usa-crime-neworleans-idUSBRE98I15I20130919?feedType=RSS. 9/26/2013.

Foley, Melissa. "LSU Civil Rights Symposium Celebrates the Life of Legendary Civil Rights Leader A. P. Tureaud." Nobel Cause. Baton Rouge: Louisiana State University. 2011. http://www.lsu.edu/departments/gold/2011/04/tureaud.shtml.

Foner, Phillip S. *The Life and Writings of Frederick Douglass: Vol. 2. Pre-Civil War Decade, 1850–1860*. New York: International Publishers, 1950.

Fort Ward Museum & Historic Site. "Fighting for Freedom: Black Union Soldiers of the Civil War." April 12, 2012. http://alexandriava.gov/historic/fortward/default.aspx?id=40018.

Fussel, Elizabeth. "Constructing New Orleans, Constructing Race: A Population History of New Orleans." *Journal of American History* 94, no. 3 (2007): 846-855.

Gabe, Thomas, Gene Falk, and Maggie McCarty. "Hurricane Katrina: Social-Demographic Characteristics of Impacted Areas." *CRS Report for Congress*. Library of Congress, Domestic Social Policy Division, Congressional Cartography Program, November 4, 2005. http://gnocdc.s3.amazonaws.com/reports/crsrept.pdf.

Garbarino, James. "Violent Children: Where Do We Point the Finger of Blame?" *Pediatrics and Adolescent Medicine* 155, no. 1 (January 2001). 13-14.

Garner v. State of La., 368 U.S. 157 (1961).

Genealogical Information for the State of Louisiana. "St. Bernard Parish History and Information." http://mylouisianagenealogy.com/la_county/sb.htm.

Gesetz zum Schutze des deutschen Blutes und der deutschen Ehre [Law for the Protection of German Blood and German Honor]. September 15, 1935. Jewish Virtual Library. http://www.jewishvirtuallibrary.org/jsource/Holocaust/nurmlaw2.html.

Global Conference on the Prevention of Genocide. "Background: What Is Genocide?" http://efchr.mcgill.ca/WhatIsGenocide_en.php?menu=2.

Goldman, Lynn and Christine Coussens. "Environmental Public Health Impacts of Disasters: Hurricane Katrina Workshop Summary." Washington, DC: Institute of Medicine of the National Academies, National Academies Press, 2007.

Gonzalez, Jessica. "Judge Rules in Favor of Provident and GNOFHAC." *The St. Bernard Voice*, November 9, 2012.

Gonzalez, Jessica. "Parish to Pay over $2 Million in Damages." *The St. Bernard Voice*, May 20, 2013.

Gratz v. Bollinger, 539 U.S. 244 (2003).

Greater New Orleans Fair Housing Action Center and Wallace Rodrigue v. St. Bernard Parish and St. Bernard Parish Council. Civil Action No. 2:06-CV-07185. "Plaintiffs' Proposed Findings of Fact and Conclusions of Law." Filed March 18, 2009. http://www.lawyerscommittee.org/admin/fair_housing/documents/files/0040.pdf.

Greater New Orleans Fair Housing Action Center, Inc. v. St. Bernard Parish and St. Bernard Parish Council. "Amended Complaint for Injunctive Relief, Declaratory Judgment, and Remedial Relief." Filed November 2, 2006.

Greater New Orleans Fair Housing Action Center, Inc. v. St. Bernard Parish and St. Bernard Parish Council. "Complaint for Injunctive Relief, Declaratory Judgment, and Remedial Relief." Filed in U.S. District Court for the Middle District. November 2, 2006. http://www.lawyerscommittee.org/admin/fair_housing/documents/files/0023.pdf.

Greater New Orleans Fair Housing Action Center. "Fair Housing Center Files Suit against St. Bernard Parish, Announces News Conference Regarding Lawsuit." News Release, October 3, 2006. http://www.gnofairhousing.org/pdfs/10-03-06%20-%20press%20release%20lawsuit%20-%20ST%20Bernard.pdf.

Greenson, Thadeus. "An Evolution of Law: Spousal Rape Recently Prosecutable." *Times Standard*, March 3, 2008.

Grolier Online Atlas. "U.S. African-American Population, 1860." http://go.grolier.com/atlas?id=mh00117.

Grunfeld, David. "New Orleans City Council Delays Vote on Housing Code Reforms." *Times-Picayune*, July 16, 2013.

Grutter v. Bollinger, 539 U.S. 306 (2003)

Hair, William I. "Henry J. Hearsey and the Politics of Race." *Louisiana History: The Journal of the Louisiana Historical Association* 17, no. 4 (Autumn 1976). 393-400.

Hair, William I. *Carnival of Fury: Robert Charles and the New Orleans Race Riot of 1900*. Baton Rouge: Louisiana State University Press, 2008.

Hale, Sir Matthew. *The History of the Pleas of the Crown*. 1736. E. Rider, Little-Britain. 1800. http://books.google.com/books?id=u1FDAAAAcAAJ&printsec=frontcover&source=gbs_ge_summary_r&cad=0#v=onepage&q&f=false.

Hamilton, Reeve. "Five Years Later Houstonians Conflicted about Katrina." *Texas Tribune*, August 30, 2010.

Hammer, David. "Prosecutors Gear Up for Ray Nagin Corruption Trial." WWLTV. August 12, 2013. http://www.wwltv.com/news/Prosecutors-ready-for-corruption-trial-against-former-Mayor-Ray-Nagin-219326031.html.

Hancock, Lee. "Is It Black and White? In a City Split and Sinking before Storm, Racial Issues Boil." *Dallas Morning News*, December 4, 2005.

Haslam, Nick. "Dehumanization: An Integrative Review." *Pers. Soc. Psychol. Rev.* 10, no. 3 (August 2006): 252-264.

Hate Crime Statistics Act (1990).

Hausman, Ken. "Psychiatrists Link Racism, Poor Mental Health." Psychiatric News. October 15, 2004. http://psychnews.psychiatryonline.org/newsarticle.aspx?articleid=107989.

H.R. 40 (111th): Commission to Study Reparation Proposals for African-Americans Act. 111th Congress. 2009-2010. Government Printing Office. https://www.govtrack.us/congress/bills/111/hr40/text

Huffington Post. "America's Poorest States." September 15, 2011.

Jane Doe v. State of Louisiana, Through the Department of Health and Human Resources, Office of Vital Statistics and Registrar of Vital Statistics. 479 So.2d 369 (1985).

Jeansonne, Glen. *Leander Perez: Boss of the Delta*. Lafayette: University of Southwestern Louisiana, 1995.

Jefferson, Thomas. Legal Argument, 1770. FE 1:376. April 1770. "Quotations on Slavery and Emancipation." Th. Jefferson Encyclopedia. Charlotesville: University of Virginia. http://www.monticello.org/site/jefferson/quotations-slavery-and-emancipation.

Jefferson, Thomas. "Rough Draught of the Declaration of Independence." Princeton, NJ: Princeton University Press. 1776/1950.

Jefferson, Thomas. Declaration of Independence. July 4, 1776. http://www.archives.gov/exhibits/charters/declaration_transcript.html.

Jerome, Fred, and Rodger Taylor. *Einstein on Race and Racism*. New Brunswick, NJ: Rutgers University Press, 2006.

JimCrowHistory.org. "The History of Jim Crow." November 25, 2009.

Jones v. Mayer Co., 392 U.S. 409 (1968).

Jonkman, Sebastiaan Nicolaas. "Loss of Life Estimation in Flood Risk Assessment: Theory and Applications." *Risk Assessment*, May 2009.

Karst, James. "Our Times: New Orleans and The Emancipation Proclamation." *Times-Picayune*, September 15, 2012.

Kein, Sybil. *Creole: The History and Legacy of Louisiana's Free People*. Baton Rouge: Louisiana State University Press, 2000.

Kessler, Ronad C., Sandro Galea, et al. "Research: Mental Illness and Suicidality after Hurricane Katrina." *Bulletin of the World Health Organization* 84, no. 12 (December 2006). 930-939. http://www.ncbi.nlm.nih.gov/pmc/articles/PMC1852424/pdf/17242828.pdf.

King, Martin Luther, Jr. "Letter from Birmingham Jail." April 16, 1963. http://www.africa.upenn.edu/Articles_Gen/Letter_Birmingham.html.

Kingery, Don. "Louisiana's Hurricanes State Has Centuries-Old History of Damaging Storms." American Press. www.louisiana101.com/Louisiana-hurricanes.doc.

Kirkham, Chris. "Drive to Demolish Blighted Houses Stirs Controversy in St. Bernard." *Times-Picayune*. March 7, 2009. http://www.nola.com/news/index.ssf/2009/03/drive_to_demolish_blighted_hou.html.

Koch, Wendy. "Lawmakers to Push for U.S. Apology for Slavery." *USA Today*, February 28, 2008.

Korematsu v. United States, 323 U.S. 214 (1944).

Kuebler, Meghan. "Closing the Wealth Gap: A Review of Racial and Ethnic Inequalities in Homeownership." *Sociology Compass* 7, no. 8 (August 2013): 670-685.

La. Act 1987, No. 886, §1, Art. 86. Effective January 1, 1988.

La. Act No. 630 of 1960.

La. Acts 1890, No. 111, p. 152.

La. Acts 1921, Ex. Sess., No. 106, §§ 1 through 3 and amended by Acts 1952, No. 127, §4.

Lake Pontchartrain Basin Foundation. "History of the Pontchartrain Basin." http://www.saveourlake.org/basin-history.php.

La-Legal.com. "How the Code Napoleon Makes Louisiana Law Different: Louisiana Law, a Short History Lesson." http://la-legal.com/history_louisiana_law.htm.

Land Development Co of Louisiana v. City of New Orleans, 17 F.2d 1016 (1927).

Land Development Co. of Louisiana v. City of New Orleans, 13 F.2d 898 (1926).

Landphair, Juliette. "The Forgotten People of New Orleans: Community, Vulnerability, and the Lower Ninth Ward." *J. Amer. History* 94 (December 2007). 837-845.

Law of Slavery in the State of Louisiana, 1847, Art. 35.

Law of Slavery in the State of Louisiana, 1847, Art. 95.

Law of Slavery in the State of Louisiana, 1847, Art. 173.
Law of Slavery in the State of Louisiana, 1847, Art. 174.
Law of Slavery in the State of Louisiana, 1847, Art. 175.
Law of Slavery in the State of Louisiana, 1847, Art. 176.
Law of Slavery in the State of Louisiana, 1847, Art. 177.
Law of Slavery in the State of Louisiana, 1847, Art. 182.
Law of Slavery in the State of Louisiana, 1847, Art. 183.
Law of Slavery in the State of Louisiana, 1847, Art. 631.
Law of Slavery in the State of Louisiana, 1847, Art. 1584.
Lawrence v. Texas, 539 U.S. 558 (2003).
Lee v. New Orleans and Great Northern Railroad Co., 125 La. 236 (1910).
Lee, Michael K. "Housing." *Affirmative Action: An Encyclopedia, Vol. 1*, edited by James A. Beckman. Westport, CT: Greenwood, 2004, 489.
Lee, Spike. "When the Levees Broke: A Requiem in Four Acts." Home Box Office, HBO Documentary Films, 2006.
Lee-St. John, Jeninne. "Should States Apologize for Slavery?" *Time Magazine*. March 27, 2007.
Lewis, David Levering. *W. E. B. Du Bois: The Fight for Equality and the American Century, 1919–1963*. New York: Owl, 2001.
Library of Congress. "Brown v. Board at Fifty: 'With an Even Hand.' " http://www.loc.gov/exhibits/brown/brown-brown.html.
Library of Congress. "Timeline of African American History, 1901–1925." http://memory.loc.gov/ammem/aap/timelin3.html.
Library of Congress. "With All Deliberate Speed." Reason Expedition, American Treasures of the Library of Congress. http://www.loc.gov/exhibits/treasures/trr007.html.
Library of Congress. *The Civil Rights History Project: Survey of Collections and Repositories; A. P. Tureaud Collection*. http://www.loc.gov/folklife/civilrights/survey/view_collection.php?coll_id=784.
Lincoln, Abraham. "The Emancipation Proclamation." January 1, 1863.
Littlejohn, Jeffrey F. "Jim Crow Laws: Louisiana." Study the Past–a co-curricular project. Huntsville, TX: Sam Houston State University. http://www.studythepast.com/weekly/LouisianaCrow.html.
Logan, John R. "The Impact of Katrina: Race and Class in Storm-Damaged Neighborhoods." http://www.s4.brown.edu/katrina/report.pdf.
Los Isleños Heritage and Cultural Society. *A Louisiana Local Legacy: Los Isleños*. St. Bernard, LA: The Los Isleños Heritage and Cultural Society Museum. 2000.
LosIsleños.org. "St. Bernard Parish's History: How We Began; Louisiana's Spanish Treasure." http://www.losisleños.org/history.htm.
Louisiana Black Code, 1865, Senate Executive Document No. 2, 39th Congress, 1st Session. Sec's. 1, 5-9, and 11.
Louisiana Constitution 1913, Art. 248.

Louisiana Constitution 1921, Art. 19, Sec. 2.

Louisiana Constitution 1921, Art. 19, Sec. 21.

Louisiana No. 8037. Commission Council Series. September 16, 1924.

Louisiana State Museum. "The Cabildo: Antebellum Louisiana; Immigration." http://lsm.crt.state.la.us/cabildo/cab8.htm.

Louisiana State Museum. "The Cabildo: Reconstruction; A State Divided." http://www.crt.state.la.us/museum/online_exhibits/Cabildo/11.aspx.

Louisiana State University. "The Baton Rouge Boycott of 1953: A Recaptured Past." Special Collections of Hill Memorial Library. http://www.lib.lsu.edu/special/exhibits/e-exhibits/boycott/.

Loving v. Virgina, 388 U.S. 1 (1967).

Lugo, Liza. "Is Affirmative Action Really Necessary in the 21st Century?" *Affirmative Action: Contemporary Perspectives*, edited by James A. Beckman. Santa Barbara, CA: ABC-CLIO, 2014.

Lugo, Liza. "Liza Lugo: Reaction to Zimmerman Verdict." *Gainesville Sun*, July 17, 2013.

Maggi, Laura. "Post-Katrina Algiers Shooting Suspect Asks for Trial Delay." *Times-Picayune*, February 24, 2012.

Mahoney, Martha. "Law and Racial Geography: Public Housing and the Economy in New Orleans." Stanford Law Review. Vol. 42, No. 5 (May, 1990), 1251-1290.

Malcolm X. "Message to the Grass Roots." Northern Negro Grass Roots Leadership Conference, Detroit. November 10, 1963.

Malcolm X. "By Any Means Necessary." *Malcolm X Speeches & Writings*. New York: Pathfinder, 1992.

Malpica, William, and Mauricio A. Espana. "Expanding Latino Participation in the Legal Profession: Strategies for Latino Law School Enrollments." Fordham Urban Law Journal. Vol. 30, Iss. 4 (2002). 1393-1427.

Manheim, Karl M. "Text Assist for Suspect Classes Flowchart." Los Angeles: Loyola Law School, Fall 1997. http://classes.lls.edu/archive/manheimk/114d3/echarts/suspect.htm.

Marcus, Frances Frank. "Louisiana Repeals Black Blood Law." *New York Times*, July 6, 1983.

Mayo Foundation for Medical Education and Research (MFMER). "Antisocial Personality Disorder." April 12, 2013. http://www.mayoclinic.com/health/antisocial-personality-disorder/DS00829/METHOD=print.

McCain v. Davis, 217 F. Supp. 661 (1963).

McLaughlin v. Florida, 379 U.S. 184 (1964).

McLaurin v. Oklahoma State Board of Regents, 339 U.S. 637 (1950).

McMillen, Neil. *The Citizen's Council: Organized Resistance to the Second Reconstruction, 1954–1964*. Champaign, IL: University of Illinois-Illini, 1994.

Metropolitan Hous. Dev. Corp. v. Village of Arlington Heights, 558 F. 2d 1283 (1977).

Midlo Hall, Gwendolyn. *The African Diaspora in the Americas: Regions, Ethnicities, and Cultures*. Chapel Hill: University of North Carolina Press, 2000.

Midlo Hall, Gwendolyn. *The Louisiana Slave Database and the Louisiana Free Database: 1719–1820*. http://www.afrigeneas.com/library/louisiana/.

Missouri ex rel. Gaines v. Canada, 305 U.S. 337 (1938).

Nagin, Ray. "Testimony before a Hearing on Hurricane Katrina: Preparedness and Response by the State of Louisiana." House Select Committee to Investigate the Preparation for and Response to Hurricane Katrina, 109th Congress, 1st session December 14, 2005.

Nakamura, David. "Obamas Visit Door of No Return, Where Slaves Once Left Africa." *Washington Post*, June 27, 2013.

National Aeronautics and Space Administration. "Hurricane Katrina Floods New Orleans." EOS Project Science Office, National Aeronautics and Space Administration. September 15, 2005. http://visibleearth.nasa.gov/view.php?id=15445.

National Archives and Records Administration. *Bureau of Refugees, Freedmen, and Abandoned Lands (Freedmen's Bureau) for Louisiana, 1865–1872*. Document RR#108. December 10, 2010. http://www.archives.gov/research/african-americans/freedmens-bureau/louisiana.pdf.

National Association for the Advancement of Colored People. http://www.naacp.org/.

National Center for Biotechnology Information, U.S. National Library of Medicine. "Antisocial Personality Disorder." Sec. 2.1. 2010. http://www.ncbi.nlm.nih.gov/pubmedhealth/PMH0015230/.

National Coalition against Domestic Violence. "Domestic Violence Fact Sheet." http://www.ncadv.org/files/DomesticViolenceFactSheet(National).pdf.

National Coalition against Domestic Violence. "The Impact of Disaster." http://www.ncadv.org/learn/TheImpactofDisaster.php.

National Coalition against Domestic Violence. "The Problem." http://www.ncadv.org/learn/TheProblem.php.

National Oceanic & Atmospheric Administration. "Preliminary Report: Hurricane Andrew, 16–28, August 1992." http://www.nhc.noaa.gov/1992andrew.html.

National Oceanic & Atmospheric Administration. "The Deadliest, Costliest, and Most Intense United States Tropical Cyclones from 1851–2006 (And Other Frequently Requested Hurricane Facts)." NOAA Technical Memorandum NWS TPC-5. April 15, 2007.

National Oceanic & Atmospheric Administration. "Top 10 Deadliest Hurricanes in U.S. History, 1900–1996." http://www.nhc.noaa.gov/pastdead.html.

NBC News Digital. "Louisiana's Great Hurricane of 1812 Reconstructed." February 8, 2011. http://www.nbcnews.com/id/41473917/ns/technology_and_science-science/t/louisianas-great-hurricane-reconstructed/.

NBCNews.com. "New Orleans Murder Rate on the Rise Again: Homicide Rate Nowhere Near '94 Peak but Still 10 Times National Average." August 18, 2005. http://www.nbcnews.com/id/8999837/.

NBCNews.com. "Calling Katrina Survivors 'Refugees' Stirs Debate." September 7, 2005. http://www.nbcnews.com/id/9232071/ns/us_news-katrina_the_long_road_back/t/calling-katrina-survivors-refugees-stirs-debate/#.Ue0t9Y3VCVo.

"The Negro Defined." *Yale Law Journal* 20, no. 3 (January 1911). 224-225.

New York Times. "The Domestic Slave Trade." July 26, 1852. http://query.nytimes.com/mem/archive-free/pdf?res=FA0713F63E55147B93C4AB178CD85F468584F9.

Njemanze, Paul Obiyo Mbanaso. "Jim Crow Laws." *Affirmative Action: An Encyclopedia, Vol. 2,* edited by James A. Beckman. Westport, CT: Greenwood, 2004, 524-526.

Nolan, Bruce. "Story Corps New Orleans: Junior Rodriguez Mourns Loss of His Boyhood Wilderness." *Times-Picayune,* June 3, 2010.

Nossiter, Adam. "New Orleans Crime Swept Away, with Most of the People." *New York Times,* November 10, 2005.

Notte, Jason. "U.S. Is still paying Civil War benefits." *MSN Money. MSN.com.* March 20, 2013. http://money.msn.com/now/post.aspx?post=dcac55b0-93d0-4fb1-9fde-26bee1aa7081.

Nyangoni, Betty. "Du Bois, William Edward Burghardt." *Affirmative Action: An Encyclopedia, Vol. 1,* edited by James A. Beckman. Westport, CT: Greenwood, 2004, 298.

Obama, Michelle. "FLOTUS Travel Journal: Visiting Goree Island." The White House Blog. June 27, 2013. http://www.whitehouse.gov/blog/2013/06/27/flotus-travel-journal-visiting-goree-island.

Oliver v. Shelly, 538 F. Supp. 600 (1982).

Owens, Maida. "Louisiana's Traditional Cultures: An Overview." Louisiana's Living Traditions. http://www.louisianafolklife.org/LT/Maidas_Essay/main_introduction_onepage.htm.

Pace v. Alabama, 106 U.S. 583 (1883).

Parks, Gordon. "Malcolm X Interview with Gordon Parks." February 19, 1965. http://www.malcolm-x.org/docs/int_parks.htm. 8/23/2013.

PBS.org "The Terrible Transformation Part 1: The African Slave Trade and the Middle Passage." http://www.pbs.org/wgbh/aia/part1/1narr4_txt.html.

PBS.org. "From Swastika to Jim Crow: Historically Black Colleges and Universities." http://www.pbs.org/itvs/fromswastikatojimcrow/blackcolleges.html.

PBS.org. "Rise of the Ku Klux Klan." http://www.pbs.org/wgbh/americanexperience/features/general-article/grant-kkk/.

PBS.org. "The Meaning of July Fourth for the Negro." Africans in America. http://www.pbs.org/wgbh/aia/part4/4h2927t.html.

PBS.org. "New Orleans: An American Experience." http://www.pbs.org/wgvh/amex/neworleans/filmmore/pt.html.

Peralta, David. Email from St. Bernard Parish President David Peralta to Liza Lugo, J. D. August 17, 2013.

Perez, Lizette. "Manumission and Gender in 18th-Century Spanish Louisiana: The Role of Women in the Establishment of a Free Black Society." *San Diego State University McNair Journal.* http://www.sci.sdsu.edu/mcnair/ejournal/Volume%20XI/perez.pdf.

Perry, James. "Congressional Testimony of James Perry, Executive Director of the Greater New Orleans Fair Housing Action Center Hearing before the Committee on Financial Services." 110th Congress, 1st Session. February 6, 2007. http://www.gpo.gov/fdsys/pkg/CHRG-110hhrg34671/html/CHRG-110hhrg34671.htm

Plessy v. Ferguson, 163 U.S. 537 (1896).

Pope, John. "Slave Trade in New Orleans Was a Thriving Business." *Times-Picayune*, April 13, 2010.

Presley, S. M., T. R. Rainwater, et al. "Assessment of Pathogens and Toxicants in New Orleans, LA following Hurricane Katrina."*Environ. Sci. Technol.* 40, no. 2 (January 15, 2006): 468-474.

Prichard, J. C. *A Treatise on Diseases of the Nervous System: Comprising Compulsive and Maniacal Affections.* London: Thomas and George Underwood, 1822.

Public Broadcasting Service. "The Slave Experience: Living Conditions." Slavery and the Making of America, Thirteen/WNET New York, Educational Broadcasting Corp., 2004.

Public Law 111-84 (2009).

Quigley, Bill. "Eighteen Months after Katrina." Truthout.org, February 27, 2007. http://www.truth-out.org/archive/item/68978:bill-quigley—eighteen-months-after-katrina.

Quigley, Bill, and Maha Zaki. "The Significance of Race: Legislative Racial Discrimination in Louisiana 1803-1865." Southern University Law Review 24 (Spring 1997). 145—205. http://billquigley.files.wordpress.com/2013/01/racialdiscriminationlouisianalegislative1803to1865.pdf.

Ragsdale, Amy. "A Councilman's Ill-Chosen Words." *Times-Picayune*, September 20, 1997.

Rasmussen, Daniel. "1811 Slave Revolt Can't Be Forgotten." *Times-Picayune*, January 4, 2011.

Rastogi, Sonya, Tallese D. Johnson, et al. "The Black Population: 2010, 2010 Census Briefs." U.S. Census Bureau, September 2011. Washington: U.S. Department of Commerce, Economics and Statistics Administration, U.S. Census Bureau. http://www.census.gov/prod/cen2010/briefs/c2010br-06.pdf.

Rauch, Jonathan. "Struggling to Survive after Katrina: A Hard Year for the Big Easy." *Reason*, August 14, 2006.

Reckendahl, Katy. "Fifty Years Later, Students Recall Integrating New Orleans Public Schools." *Times-Picayune*, November 13, 2010.

Reynolds, Donald. "The New Orleans Riot of 1866: Reconsidered." *Louisiana History: The Journal of the Louisiana Historical Association*. Vol. 5, No. 1 (Winter, 1964). 5-27.

Risk Management Solutions. "The 1927 Great Mississippi Flood: 80-Year Retrospective." 2007. https://support.rms.com/publications/1927_MississippiFlood.pdf.

Rodriguez. Henry "Junior." Letter to President George W. Bush. Nola.com, August 29, 2005. http://stbernardafterkatrina.blogspot.com/2005/08/juniors-letter.html.

Roe v. Wade, 410 U.S. 113 (1973).

Rosen, Sophie. "Federal Judge Grants Motion for Summary Judgment in Housing Discrimination Case against St. Bernard Parish." Greater New Orleans Fair Housing Action Center, October 19, 2013. http://www.gnofairhousing.org/2012/10/19/federal-judge-grants-motion-for-summary-judgement-in-housing-discrimination-case-against-st-bernard-parish/.

Roth, David. "Louisiana Hurricane History." National Weather Service. http://www.srh.noaa.gov/images/lch/tropical/lahurricanehistory.pdf.

Ryan, Jason. "FBI: Reported Hate Crimes Up in 2006." ABC News, November 19, 2007. http://abcnews.go.com/TheLaw/story?id=3887681.

Saulny, Susan. "A Legacy of the Storm: Depression and Suicide." *New York Times*, June 12, 2006.

Schleifstein, Mark. "Study of Hurricane Katrina's Dead Show Most Were Old, Lived near Levee Breaches." *Times-Picayune*, August 27, 2009.

Schomburg Center for Research in Black Culture. "The Black Republic and Louisiana." *In Motion: The African-American Migration Experience*. New York Public Library, 2005. http://www.inmotionaame.org/migrations/topic.cfm;jsessionid=f8305713913872572O7838?migration=5&topic=3&bhcp=1.

Schomburg Center for Research in Black Culture. "The Consequences of the Haitian Immigration." *In Motion: The African-American Migration Experience*. New York Public Library, 2005. http://www.inmotionaame.org/migrations/topic.cfm?migration=5&topic=9.

Schwartz, Steven *Abnormal Psychology: A Discovery Approach*. Houston, TX: Mayfield Publishing, 2000.

Secretary on behalf of Steve Ellis Times and Betty A. Brinson v. Annete Banai, et al. HUDALJ 04-93-2060-8 (2/3/95).

Senediak, Mark. J. "Housing and Urban Development Act of 1968." *Affirmative Action: An Encyclopedia, Vol. 1*, edited by James A. Beckman. Westport, CT: Greenwood Publishing, 2004, 493.

Shelby County Alabama v. Holder, Attorney General, 570 U.S. TBD (2013). Opinion available online at: http://www.supremecourt.gov/opinions/12pdf/12-96_6k47.pdf.

Shelley v. Kraemer, 334 U.S. 1 (1948).

Sills, G. L., N. D. Vroman, et al. "Overview of New Orleans Levee Failures: Lessons Learned and Their Impact on National Levee Design and Assessment." *J. Geotechnical and Geoenvironmental Engineering*, Vol. 135, Iss. 12. 1994-1995. December 2009.

Sisco, Annette. "The Cost of Stubbornness." *Times-Picayune*, July 7, 2008.

Smith, Andrene. "A Different World: Financial Determinants of Well-Being in New Orleans in Black and White." *Georgetown Journal on Poverty Law & Policy*. Vol. 14, Iss. 1. Winter 2007. 179.

Small Angst Films. "The Axe in the Attic: A Film by Ed Pincus and Lucia Small." 2007.

Smithsonian National Museum of American History. "With All Deliberate Speed." *Separate is not Equal: Brown v. Board of Education*. National Museum of American History, Behring Center. 2004. http://americanhistory.si.edu/brown/history/6-legacy/deliberate-speed.html.

Snyder, Mary Gail. "It Didn't begin with Katrina." *Shelterforce Online* 43 (September/October 2005). http://www.nhi.org/online/issues/143/beforekatrina.html.

Souther, J. Mark. "The Disneyfication of New Orleans: The French Quarter as Façade in a Divided City." *Journal of American History*, Vol. 94, No. 3 (Dec. 2007). 804–811.

Spain, Daphne. "Race Relations and Residential Segregation in New Orleans: Two Centuries of Paradox." *Annals of the American Academy of Political and Social Science*. Vol. 441 (January 1979). 82-96.

Stanton, Gregory H. "The 8 Stages of Genocide." Genocide Watch, 1998. http://www.genocidewatch.org/aboutgenocide/8stagesofgenocide.html.

State of Louisiana, ex rel. Frank Plaia v. Louisiana State Board of Health. 275 So.2d 201 (1973).

State v. Treadaway et al., 126 La. 300, 52 So. 500 (1910).

St. Bernard Citizens for Better Government v. St. Bernard Parish School Board. 202 WL 2022589 (E.D.La.) (2002).

St. Bernard Parish Council. "Minutes of the St. Bernard Parish Council Meeting of March 7, 2006." #47. Provided by the Fair Housing Center of New Orleans.

St. Bernard Parish Government. Ordinance SBPC #370-09-06, Summary No. 1911. September 19, 2006.

St. Bernard Parish Government. "Early Voting for the November 6th Election October 23rd through October 30th." October 23, 2013. http://www.sbpg.net/index.php?option=com_content&view=article&id=3488:early-voting-for-the-november-6th-election-october-23rd-thru-october-30th-&catid=2:local-news&Itemid=2.

St. Bernard Parish Government. "For Immediate Release: Contact: Steve Cannizaro." Press Release. October 2, 2005.

St. Bernard Parish Government. "Official Hurricane Information." September 25, 2005. http://votegarofalo.com/spg/.

St. Bernard Parish Government. Ordinance SBPC #370-09-06, Summary No. 1911. September 19, 2006.

Stephens, Nicole M. "Brown v. Board of Education, 347, U.S. 483 (1954)." *Affirmative Action: An Encyclopedia, Vol. 1*, edited by James A. Beckman. Westport, CT: Greenwood, 2004, 123.

Stone, Geoffrey R., Louis Michael Seidman, et al. *Constitutional Law*, 5th ed. New York: Aspen, 2005.

Strachan, Sue. "Persona: Henry 'Junior' Rodriguez." *New Orleans Magazine*, March 6, 2006.

Strauder v. West Virginia, 100 U.S. 303 (1879).

Sulny, Susan, and Gary Rivlin. "Renewal Money for New Orleans Bypasses Renters." *New York Times*, September 17, 2006.

Sweatt v. Painter, 339 U.S. 629, 634 (1950).

Tennessee Department of State. "Miscegenation." http://www.tn.gov/tsla/exhibits/blackhistory/pdfs/Miscegenation%20laws.pdf

The Associated Press. "New Orleans Fall in 1862 Created Emancipation Beachhead." *Times-Picayune*, May 28, 2012.

The Civil Rights Act of 1866.

The Civil Rights Act of 1964.

The Civil War Trust. "Civil War Casualties." http://www.civilwar.org/education/civil-war-casualties.html.

The Freedmen's Bureau Online. "Miscellaneous Reports and Lists Relating to Murders and Outrages." *Synopsis of Murder & c. (crimes) Committed in Parishes of Caddo and Bossier September and October 1868*. March 1867–November 1867. New Orleans: Records of the Bureau of Refugees, Freedmen, and Abandoned Lands http://freedmensbureau.com/louisiana/outrages/outrages4.htm.

The Greater New Orleans Fair Housing Action Center. "History." http://www.gnofairhousing.org/the-center/history.

The History Channel. "Ku Klux Klan." http://www.history.com/topics/ku-klux-klan.

The History of Jim Crow. "Jim Crow Laws: Louisiana." http://www.jimcrowhistory.org/scripts/jimcrow/insidesouth.cgi?state=Louisiana.

The History of Jim Crow. "Jim Crow in the South." http://ww.jimcrowhistory.org/geography/geography.htm.

The Leadership Conference on Civil and Human Rights/The Leadership Conference. "Matthew Shepard and James Byrd, Jr. Hate Crimes Prevention Act." http://www.civilrights.org/hatecrimes/llehcpa/.

The Louisiana Weekly. "Our Brother's Keeper." September 1965.

The Louisiana Weekly. "White Resident Joins Housing Bias Lawsuit in St. Bernard." November 6, 2006. http://www.louisianaweekly.com/weekly/news/articlegate.pl?20061106c.

The Prohibition of Mixed Marriages Act, Act No 55 (1949). South Africa.

The Select Bipartisan Committee to Investigate the Preparation for and Response to Hurricane Katrina. "A Failure of Initiative: Final Report of the Select Bipartisan Committee to Investigate the Preparation for and Response to Hurricane Katrina." Washington: U.S. Government Printing Office, February 15, 2006.

The Slaughter-House Cases, 83 U.S. 36 (1873).

Times-Picayune. "Civil Rights Struggle Lives on in La.'s Public Schools: Segregation Rising since the Mid-1980s." Sunday Correction Appended, July 29, 2007.

Times-Picayune. "NOPD Cop Convicted in Henry Glover Case Getting New Trial, Appeals Court Decides." December 13, 2012.

Times-Picayune. "1927: The Greatest Flood in American History Inundates 10 States." October 31, 2011.

Times-Picayune. "1965: Hurricane Betsy Smashes Ashore near New Orleans." December 8, 2011.

Times-Picayune. "Former Police Officer David Warren Sentenced to 25 Years in Henry Glover Shooting." March 31, 2011.

Times-Picayune. "Looking Back at the Blasting of the Mississippi River Levee at Caernarvon." April 7, 2012.

Times-Picayune. "St. Bernard Parish Officials Detail Devastation." September 13, 2005.

Times-Picayune. "Slavery in New Orleans." 1845. http://photos.nola.com/4500/gallery/1845_slavery_in_new_orleans/index.html#/3.

Times-Picayune. "The Rodriguez Apology." September 18, 1997.

The United Nations Organization for Education, Science and Culture (UNESCO). "Virtual Visit of Goree Island, Dakar, Senegal: The House of Slaves." http://webworld.unesco.org/goree/en/screens/0.shtml.

The United States v. The Libellants and Claimants of the Schooner Amistad, Her Tackle, Apparel, and Furniture, Together with Her Cargo, and the Africans Mentioned and Described in the Several Libels and Claims, 40 U.S. 518; 10 L. Ed. 826 (1841).

The White House, George W. Bush, President. "The Federal Response to Hurricane Katrina: Lessons Learned." 2006. Washington: The White House. http://library.stmarytx.edu/acadlib/edocs/katrinawh.pdf.

Thevenot, Brian. "The McDonogh 3." *Times-Picayune*, May 16, 2004.

Thibodeaux, Kevin. "5 Louisiana Civil Rights–Era Murder Cases Remain Open, Justice Department Reports to Congress." *Times-Picayune*, November 14, 2012.

Thompson, A. C., and Brendan McCarthy. "Feds Exploring Claims of Racial Vigilantism in Algiers Point in Days after Hurricane Katrina." *Times-Picayune*, April 12, 2010.

Time. "Civil Rights: The Continuing Confrontation." April 9, 1965.

Time. "Integration North and South." September 15, 1961.

Torres, Manuel. "Lawsuit by Former Jefferson Parish Housing Authority Commissioners Escalates War with Parish." *Times-Picayune*, December 20, 2012.

Torres, Manuel. "Parishes Hope to Get Insurance Firms Moving; Delays on Claims May Soon Be Over." *Times-Picayune*, September 30, 2005.

Torres, Manuel. "St. Bernard Parish's Housing Restrictions Are Legally and Morally Wrong." *Times-Picayune*, September 12, 2009.

Turni Bazile, Karen. "Bias Lawsuit Puts Council on Defensive, Lawyer Hired to Fight Allegation of Discrimination in St. Bernard." *Times-Picayune*, November 8, 2006.

Tyler v. Harmon, 158 La. 439 (1925).

United Nations. "Ending Violence against Women: From Words to Action." *Study of the Secretary-General*. October 9, 2006. http://www.un.org/womenwatch/daw/vaw/launch/english/v.a.w-exeE-use.pdf.

U.S. Newswire. "St. Bernard Parish Agrees to Halt Discriminatory Zoning Rule, Fair Housing Groups Call 'Blood Relative Ordinance' Illegal." November 13, 2006. http://six.pairlist.net/pipermail/stbernard/20061113/010739.html.

U.S. v. Fuselier, Case No. 03-30438. U.S. Court of Appeals for the Fifth Circuit. "Brief for the United States as Appellee." January 20, 2004.

U.S. v. St. Bernard Parish, Case 2:12-cv-00321-HGB-SS. Document 334-1. Filed May 10, 2013. http://www.nola.com/crime/index.ssf/2013/05/department_of_justice_and_st_b.html.

U.S. Census Bureau. "Poverty in the United States: 2001." *Current Population Reports: Consumer income*. Series P-60, Issue 219. Washington: U.S. Department of Commerce. September 2002. 7.

U.S. Department of Housing and Urban Development. "HUD History." http://portal.hud.gov/hudportal/HUD?src=/about/hud_history.

U.S. Department of Justice. "Former U.S. Army Corps of Engineers Contract Employee Charged with Bribery on a New Orleans Levee Reconstruction Project." Press Release. August 23, 2007.

U.S. Department of Justice. "Assistant Attorney General for the Civil Rights Division Thomas E. Perez Testifies before the Senate Judiciary Committee, Washington, D.C." Press Release. April 20, 2010.

U.S. Department of Justice. "Assistant Attorney General Thomas E. Perez Speaks at the UT Diversity and Civility Conference." Press Release. November 15, 2012.

U.S. Department of Justice. "C. Ray Nagin Former New Orleans Mayor, Indicted on Federal Bribery, Honest Services Wire Fraud, Money Laundering, Conspiracy, and Tax Charges." Press Release. January 18, 2013.

U.S. Department of Justice. "Chalmette-Based Property Owners and Managers to Pay $100,000 in Civil Penalties as Part of Settlement of Justice Department Housing Discrimination Lawsuit." Press Release. March 31, 2005.

U.S. Department of Justice. "Church Arsons and Hate Crimes." *United States Attorney Bulletin* 46, no. 2 (February 1998). http://www.justice.gov/usao/eousa/foia_reading_room/usab4602.pdf.

U.S. Department of Justice. "Justice Department Reaches Settlement Regarding Unconstitutional Conditions at Two Louisiana Developmental Centers." Press Release. January 12, 2004.

U.S. Department of Justice. "Justice Department Sues Louisiana Apartment Owners for Engaging in Race Discrimination." Press Release. April 15, 2004.

U.S. Department of Justice. "Louisiana Man Indicted for Federal Civil Rights Violations for Nooses Targeting 'Jena Six' Marchers." Press Release. January 24, 2008.

U.S. Department of Justice. "Louisiana Man Pleads Guilty to Conspiring to Violate Civil Rights of Homeowner." Press Release. December 18, 2008.

U.S. Department of Justice. "Louisiana Man Pleads Guilty to Federal Civil Rights Violations." Press Release. April 28, 2011.

U.S. Department of Justice. "Louisiana Man Sentenced for Civil Rights Violation in Connection with Cross-Burning." Press Release. May 27, 2010.

U.S. Department of Justice. "New Orleans Man Charged with Shooting African-Americans in the Aftermath of Hurricane Katrina." Press Release. July 15, 2010.

U.S. Department of Justice. "Three New Orleans Police Officers Found Guilty in the Post-Katrina Shooting and Burning of Henry Glover." Press Release. December 9, 2010.

U.S. Department of Justice. "Appeals Court Affirms Thirteen-Year Sentence for Klan Leader in Louisiana Cross-Burning." Press Release. April 21, 2004.

U.S. Department of Justice. "Assistant Attorney General Thomas E. Perez Speaks at the City of New Orleans Consent Decree Press Conference." Press Release. July 24, 2012.

U.S. Department of Justice. *U.S. v. Byron*, Civil Action No. 99-1594. Consent Decree. 2000. http://www.justice.gov/crt/about/hce/documents/hylitessettle.php.

U.S. Department of Justice. *Hate Crime Statistics 1996: Uniform Crime Reports*. Washington: Federal Bureau of Investigation, Criminal Justice Information Services Division. http://www.fbi.gov/about-us/cjis/ucr/hate-crime/1996.

U.S. Department of Justice. *Hate Crime Statistics 1997: Uniform Crime Reports*. Washington: Federal Bureau of Investigation, Criminal Justice Information Services Division. http://www.fbi.gov/about-us/cjis/ucr/hate-crime/1997.

U.S. Department of Justice. *Hate Crime Statistics 1998: Uniform Crime Reports*. Washington: Federal Bureau of Investigation, Criminal Justice Information Services Division. http://www.fbi.gov/about-us/cjis/ucr/hate-crime/1998.

U.S. Department of Justice. *Hate Crime Statistics 1999: Uniform Crime Reports*. Washington: Federal Bureau of Investigation, Criminal Justice Information Services Division. http://www.fbi.gov/about-us/cjis/ucr/hate-crime/1999.

U.S. Department of Justice. *Hate Crime Statistics 2000: Uniform Crime Reports.* Washington: Federal Bureau of Investigation, Criminal Justice Information Services Division. http://www.fbi.gov/about-us/cjis/ucr/hate-crime/2000.

U.S. Department of Justice. *Hate Crime Statistics 2002: Uniform Crime Reports.* Washington: Federal Bureau of Investigation, Criminal Justice Information Services Division. http://www.fbi.gov/about-us/cjis/ucr/hate-crime/2002.

U.S. Department of Justice. *Hate Crime Statistics 2003: Uniform Crime Reports.* Washington: Federal Bureau of Investigation, Criminal Justice Information Services Division. http://www.fbi.gov/about-us/cjis/ucr/hate-crime/2003.

U.S. Department of Justice. *Hate Crime Statistics 2004: Uniform Crime Reports.* Washington: Federal Bureau of Investigation, Criminal Justice Information Services Divisionhttp://www.fbi.gov/about-us/cjis/ucr/hate-crime/2004.

U.S. Department of Justice. *Hate Crime Statistics 2006: Uniform Crime Report.*

Washington: Federal Bureau of Investigation, Criminal Justice Information Services Division. http://www.fbi.gov/about-us/cjis/ucr/hate-crime/2006.

U.S. Department of Justice. *Hate Crime Statistics 2007: Uniform Crime Report.* Washington: Federal Bureau of Investigation, Criminal Justice Information Services Division. http://www.fbi.gov/about-us/cjis/ucr/hate-crime/2007

U.S. Department of Justice. *Hate Crime Statistics: 2008: Uniform Crime Report.* Washington: Federal Bureau of Investigation, Criminal Justice Information services Division. http://www.fbi.gov/about-us/cjis/ucr/hate-crime/2008.

U.S. Department of Justice. *Hate Crime Statistics: 2009: Uniform Crime Report.*

Washington: Federal Bureau of Investigation, Criminal Justice Information Services Division. http://www2.fbi.gov/ucr/hc2009/.

U.S. Department of Justice. *Hate Crime Statistics 2010: Uniform Crime Report.* Washington: Federal Bureau of Investigation, Criminal Justice Information Services Division. http://www.fbi.gov/about-us/cjis/ucr/hate-crime/2010/index.

U.S. Department of Justice. *Hate Crime Statistics 2011: Uniform Crime Report.* Washington: Federal Bureau of Investigation, Criminal Justice Information Services Division. http://www.fbi.gov/about-us/cjis/ucr/hate-crime/2011.

U.S. Department of Justice, Uniform Crime Reporting Statistics, Federal Bureau of Investigations. "Estimated Violent Crime in United States, 1960–2011."

U.S. Energy Information Administration. "Hurricane Impacts on the U.S. Oil and Natural Gas Markets."December 27, 2005. Washington: U.S. Department of Energy. http://www.eia.gov/oog/special/eia1_katrina.html.

United States of America v. C. Ray Nagin "aka Mayor Nagin." Indictment for Conspiracy, Honest Services Wire Fraud, Bribery Concerning Programs Receiving Federal Funds, Money Laundering, and Filing False Tax Returns. Criminal No. 13-011 January 13, 2013. http://www.justice.gov/usao/lae/news/2013/downloads/indictment_C_Ray_Nagin.pdf.

United States v. Cruikshank, 92 U.S. 542 (1875).

United States v. Windsor, Executor of the Estate of Spyer, et al., 570 U.S. ____ (2013). http://www.supremecourt.gov/opinions/12pdf/12-307_6j37.pdf.

van Heerden, Ivor. "How New Orleans Flooded." NOVA, PBS.org, November 22, 2005. http://www.pbs.org/wgbh/nova/earth/how-new-orleans-flooded.html.

Village of Arlington Heights v. Metropolitan Housing Dev. Corp., 429 U.S. 252 (1977).

Warren, Bob. "St. Bernard Parish Won't Enforce Controversial Housing Ordinance Until It Goes Before Judge." *Times-Picayune*, November 13, 2006.

Warrick, Joby. "White House Got Early Warning on Katrina." *Washington Post*, January 23, 2006.

Washington v. Davis, 426 U.S. 229, 239 (1976).

Watson, Bret D. "The Lynching of John C. Jones and the Ordeal of Albert Harris, Jr." Civil Rights and Restorative Justice, Boston: Northeastern University, May 2012. http://nuweb9.neu.edu/civilrights/wp-content/uploads/Jones-essay-final.pdf.

Weaver, Jane. "Katrina Health Risks Rise with Flooding: Residents Should Be Wary of Contaminated Water and Food." NBCNews.com. September 1, 2005. http://www.nbcnews.com/id/9109689/ns/health-health_care/t/katrina-health-risks-rise-flooding/.

Williamson v. Hampton Management Co., 339 F. Supp. 1146 (1972).

World Health Organization. *Violence by Intimate Partners*, Chapter 4. http://www.who.int/violence_injury_prevention/violence/global_campaign/en/chap4.pdf.

WWL-TV. "Prosecutors Ready for Corruption Trial against Former Mayor Ray Nagin." August 12, 2013. http://www.wwltv.com/news/Prosecutors-ready-for-corruption-trial-against-former-Mayor-Ray-Nagin-219326031.html.

Wygant v. Jackson Board of Education, 476 U.S. 267 (1986).

Index

About the Author

Liza Lugo, JD, is a legal scholar with expertise in constitutional law, international human rights law, civil liberties, and criminal law. Her published works include "Is Affirmative Action Really Necessary in the 21st Century?" in ABC-CLIO's upcoming *Affirmative Action: Contemporary Perspectives* (James A. Beckman, Editor), and dozens of her articles appear online at HubPages.com under the pen name lawdoctorlee. She is the president of her own consulting firm, Monarch Consulting. Lugo holds a Juris Doctor from the University of Florida Levin College of Law and a Bachelor's degree in government and world affairs from the University of Tampa, where she graduated magna cum laude.